INSIGHT GUIDES

TURKISH COAST

Created and Directed by Hans Höfer
Edited by Metin Demirsar

APA
PUBLICATIONS

TURKISH COAST

First Edition
© 1990 APA PUBLICATIONS (HK) LTD
All Rights Reserved
Printed in Singapore by Höfer Press Pte. Ltd

ABOUT THIS BOOK

The authors of this book examine Aegean and Mediterranean Turkey from a contemporary angle rather than from a nostalgic-historical perspective that most travel books about Turkey are based on. The emphasis is on the modern-day Turkish Coast and its people.

Insight Guide: Turkish Coast is the fourth travel book on Turkey to be published by Apa Publications in two years. This indicates Apa's firm commitment to the country's development as an important international tourism destination in the 1990s. Apa, a Hong Kong and Singapore-based publishing house, is the creator of the innovative, award-winning Insight Guides series of travel books.

We would like to introduce you to the principal contributors of this book:

Alev Alatlı wrote many chapters in the history section and co-authored the feature about Turkish people. Alatlı was also one of the main contributors to *Insight City Guide: Istanbul*. Alatlı has won many literary journalistic awards.

Project editor **Metin Demirsar** is a Turkish journalist whose articles have appeared in many foreign newspapers and magazines, including *The Wall Street Journal*. Demirsar also contributed to, and later revised and updated, both *Insight Guide: Turkey* and *Insight City Guide: Istanbul*. He also wrote *Short Stay on the Turquoise Coast*. Demirsar has an M.A. from the Graduate School of Journalism of the University of Southern California. His wife, **Tülay Demirsar**, acted as his secretary during the project, completed the index, and helped put the text of this book on computer.

A husband-wife team, **William A. Edmonds** and **Anna G. Edmonds**, wrote several sections. The Edmonds are American missionaries who have lived in Turkey for 35 years. William Edmonds, director of the Redhouse Press, an English language publishing house in Istanbul which produces dictionaries and other special topic books, also penned an article on Turkish carpets. Anna Edmonds, a Redhouse Press writer and editor, wrote parts of the history section and contributed several key features. She is the co-author of *Biblical Sites in Turkey*.

Sevâ Ülman Erten, an Ankara-based correspondent for *United Press International*, contributed the features about holiday villages and Yaşar Kemal, Turkey's best known novelist. Erten is a Turkish national.

Hans Höfer, Apa's founder and publisher, has brought out more than 100 titles in the Insight Guides series in 20 years of publishing. Höfer, who has a keen interest in Turkey, has visited the Coast many times.

Jay Courtney Fikes, an American anthropologist who works in Washington D.C. as a political advocate for American Indians, wrote the chapter on Ionia with related features about Izmir and Ephesus. Fikes is author of *Step Inside the Sacred Circle*, a collection of American Indian allegorical animal stories. Fikes is married to a Turk and has taught at Marmara University in Istanbul.

Laura Le Cornu, an editor with the *Turkish Times*, teamed up with **Juliette Rossant**, a freelance journalist, to contribute several features. Le Cornu and Rossant, both Americans, also sub-edited *Short Stay on the Turquoise Coast*. Le Cornu has a B.A. in political science from Goucer College in Baltimore, Maryland. Rossant has a B.A. in classical archaeology from Dartmouth College and an M.A. in creative writing from Johns Hopkins University.

Demirsar

W. Edmonds

A. Edmonds

Erten

Fikes

British citizens **Robert Love** and **Brenda Wild**, a husband-wife team, joined project editor Demirsar to write the feature on the 1915 military Gallipoli campaign. Love and Wild teach physics at Istanbul's Marmara University.

Ara Güler, one of the world's great living photojournalists, provided many of the pictures in this book. Güler is correspondent of *Time-Life Books*, *Magnum Photos* and *Stern Magazine*. Güler's discovery and stunning photography of Aphrodisias in the 1950s has made the ancient Roman city an important destination for travelers and paved the way for important excavations at the site.

Şemsi Güner, the chief photographer of this book, is no newcomer to Apa. His superb photography has also appeared in all three previous Apa titles dealing with Turkey – *Insight Guide: Turkey*, *Insight City Guide: Istanbul*; and *Short Stay on the Turquoise Coast*. A former opera baritone and graphic artist, Güner has been taking pictures of Turkey and the world for the foreign as well as local media for 30 years.

The article on the Blue Voyage was written by **Galip Isen**, who spends his summers taking well-to-do tourists on cruises along the Greek islands and Turkish Aegean and Mediterranean coasts aboard his yacht.

Selma Manizade, a graphic artist, compiled the travel tips at the back of the book. Manizade, a Turk who has lived most of her life in the United States, works for Türkiye Emlak Bankası, a large state bank.

Aliza Marcus and **Yuri Feher** collaborated to write the section about Adana and the East. Marcus, an American freelance journalist who works for *Turquoise* magazine in New York, also penned the article on the late industrialist Hacı Ömer Sabancı. Marcus, who contributed to *The Book of World City Rankings*, is a graduate of Columbia University's School of Journalism. Hungarian-born Feher is getting a Ph.D. at New York University in Anthropology.

Enis Özbank, who contributed many pictures to this book, is a *Sipa Press* photojournalist who has had his photos featured in *Time Magazine*, *Newsweek*, *Paris Match* and *Epocha*.

Patricia Roberts, a freelance American journalist and writer who works at *Turquoise* magazine in Istanbul, wrote the section on Rough and Smooth Cilicia and the features on Turkey's olive oil industry and water sports.

Nergis Yazgan and **Gernant Magnin** teamed up to write about wildlife and environmental issues of the Turkish Coast. Yazgan is Turkey's leading wildlife conservationist. Magnin is a project officer with the International Council for Bird Preservation (ICBP), a Cambridge U.K.-based ornithological society. His publications for ICBP include: *Bird Killing in Malta*; *An Account of Illegal Bird Catching in Cyprus during 1987*; and *Falconry and Hunting in Turkey*.

The project editor also wants to thank Kuşadası-based **Demir Ünsal**, one of Turkey's leading travel guides, for giving him a personal tour of the ancient sites on the Menderes (Maeander) River Valley.

The project editor is also grateful to **Artun Altıparmak**, publisher of Istanbul's *ABC Kitabevi A.S.*, without whose constant encouragement and support this book could not have possibly been conceived, started and finished.

–Apa Publications

Le Cornu

Rossant

Güler

Güner

Roberts

CONTENTS

PLACES

TRAVEL TIPS

The Turkish Coast, consisting of Turkey's Aegean and Mediterranean shores, is developing into an important international travel destination. Looking beyond the usual haunts of Spain, Italy and Greece, foreign tourists have begun to discover the Turkish Coast, long neglected by the international travel industry. Inexpensive charter flights, low-priced package holidays from Europe and the United States, and new airports and highways on the coast have made the region easily accessible to foreign travel.

Stretching from the nation's border with Greece to its frontier with Syria, this coastal strip has thousands of miles of unspoiled sandy beaches and coves fringed by pine forests, hundreds of pristine fishing villages and market towns, and a wealth of ancient ruins found nowhere else in the world.

The ruins of fabled cities like Troy, Pergamum, Ephesus, Halicarnassus, Xanthus, Side and Karatepe are just a few of the sites of antiquity that dot the coast, waiting to be explored by travelers.

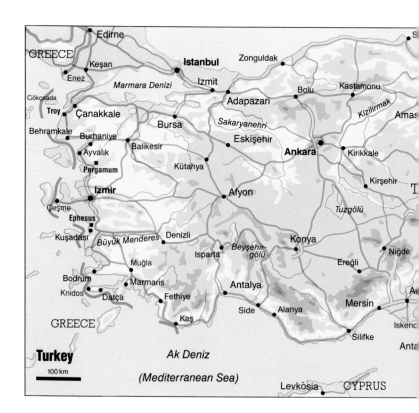

Fertile areas: The region includes modern cities like Izmir, Antalya and Adana, and bustling resorts like Kuşadası, Bodrum and Marmaris. The Turkish Coast, a cradle for many early civilizations, is one of the world's most fertile areas. Nurtured by a dozen rivers, it produces an abundance of sunflower seeds, grains, figs, cotton, olives, melons, citrus fruits and fresh vegetables for local consumption and export markets, making Turkey one of only seven countries in the world that are self-sufficient in food supplies.

Surrounded by mountains, the area is rich in wildlife and unusual bird species – a delight to nature lovers. More species of fauna and flora can be seen on the Turkish Coast than in most regions of Continental Europe. It is one of the few areas in the Mediterranean where giant marine turtles wade ashore to lay their eggs, or endangered monk seals frolic on offshore islands. Several Turkish travel agencies offer special wildlife observation tours.

The coast is also a hunter's paradise, rich in wild boar, game birds

Preceding pages: Columns of Perge; bejeweled Turkish women; strolling along the beach; the ruins of Aphrodisias; frieze from the Myra theater; windsurfing at Gümbet.

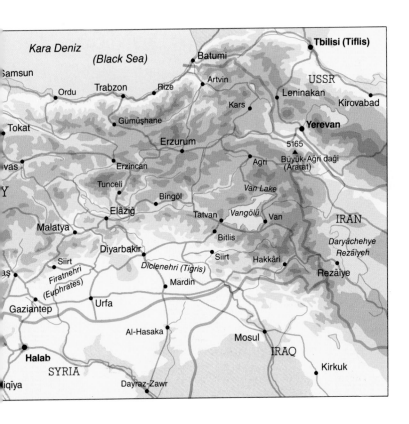

and mountain goats. Travelers come from as far as Japan to hunt for the ibex, a wild goat with long backward-curved horns which inhabits Turkey's southern mountains. Visitors also fish for *alabalık*, or trout, on the Manavgat River.

The hidden city: Travelers to the region can climb the Bey and Taurus mountains on the Mediterranean Coast and explore the Karain Caves, near Antalya, where people from the Stone Age once lived. In March and April, they can ski at Saklıkent (the Hidden Village), a resort near Antalya, and swim in the Mediterranean on the same day.

Many resorts along the Aegean and Mediterranean Turkey offer all forms of water sports, from windsurfing and waterskiing to parasailing and banana boat riding. Scuba diving is particularly popular around Çeşme and Bodrum, which are famous for its sponge fishers and underwater archaeologists. Turkey's main windsurfing center is at Gümbet, where world champion windsurfers often compete. Visitors to Ölüdeniz (the Dead Sea), a lagoon-like inlet on the Mediterranean near Fethiye, can paraglide from the 6,400-foot summit of rocky Babadağ, to the beach below.

Since the days of Antony and Cleopatra, the southwest corner of Turkey, known today as the Turquoise Coast, has been a playground for yachtsmen cruising to the deserted coves of the Gulf of Gökova, Hisarönü and Sömbeki bays and the Gulf of Fethiye. The so-called Blue Voyage into one of these bays is the ultimate form of relaxation that the harried westerner should experience.

The Coast: The Turkish Coast begins in Thracian (European) Turkey at the town of Enez, near the Greek border, and the wide Bay of Saros, which has some of the finest beaches of Turkey. It continues south to the desolate Gallipoli Peninsula, scene of a fierce World War I military campaign, and the Dardanelles, the strategic strait where the legendary Leander drowned while swimming to his lover, the Virgin Priestess Hero. Gökçeada, Turkey's largest island, and Bozcaada, an island known for its tasty wines, guard the Aegean mouth of the Dardanelles.

The Troad: The major part of the Turkish Coast lies in Asia across the Dardanelles. The Asian part of the Turkish Coast begins at the town of Çanakkale and covers a bulging peninsula that in ancient times was known as the Troad. The ruins of Troy, Assos and Alexandria Troas dominate this peninsula.

Further south is the Gulf of Edremit, one of Turkey's most picturesque bays. The Gulf is famed for its long stretches of beaches and resort towns of Edremit, Burhaniye and Ayvalık, facing the Greek island of Lesbos. Pergamum, one of the magnificent sites of antiquity, is just south of the area near the modern town of Bergama. The region from the Gulf of Edremit to Izmir, Turkey's third largest city and second biggest port, was known in the past as the Aeolian Coast. It also includes the resort town of Foça, where Club Méditerranée operates a holiday village.

The Izmir area was known as Ionia in the past. The ruins of more than 50 Ionian cities are within a two-hour-drive from Izmir. Ephesus, a Hellenistic city just south of Izmir, is one of the world's most frequented ancient sites. The region also has the popular resort towns of Çeşme with its fine silt sand beaches, and Kuşadası (the

Rakı-drinking fife players perform at a camel fight.

Bird's Island) with its Genoese fortress. The modern market towns of Aydın and Denizli are located along the fertile Menderes River Valley (the Maeander), which runs east of the Ionian Coast.

Yachting centers: Further south is the province of Muğla. In ancient times it was known as Caria and was inhabited by the Carians, a sea-going people. Peasants in the Anatolian town of Milas in this province produce handmade carpets famous for its pastel colors. The swinging resorts of Bodrum (ancient Halicarnassus), Marmaris and Fethiye, all important yachting centers, are in Muğla province. Marmaris lies at the confluence of the Aegean and Mediterranean.

The coast runs east and northeast through the ancient province of Lycia with its rugged coastline and monumental rock tombs. The coastal road also takes one to the eternal flames of the Chimera and the ruins of Olympus, an ancient hideout for pirates, before reaching the flashy resort town of Kemer, Antalya and Pamphylian plains.

Antalya is the commercial and agricultural hub and tourist center of southwest Turkey. Its 270,000 population doubles during the 10-month summer season. Further east are the ruins of Perge, Aspendos and Side.

Crenellated castle: Further east is the popular resort of Alanya with its crenellated castle dominating the shore and beaches. The next 156 miles (250 km) takes the traveler through the rugged coast, an area the ancients appropriately called "Rough Cilicia." Here jagged mountains plunge suddenly into the sea. The only coastal road winds along the vertebrae of the cliffs, stopping off at Anamur, the banana-growing center of Turkey. Anamur is also renowned for its miles of deserted beaches and its stupendous Armenian castle.

The mountainous region soon ends and the vast plain known as Çukurova, a flat breadbasket region that produces an abundance of cotton and other crops, begins.

The market towns of Silifke with its "Maiden's Fortress" and Tarsus, where St. Paul was born, dominate the western part of the plain. Further east is Mersin, a bustling port city. Adana, Turkey's fourth largest city, is the industrial and commercial hub of southern Turkey.

Commercial towns: It gets more commercial further east. Yumurtalık, southeast of Adana, has the gigantic terminal for the Iraq-Turkey crude oil pipeline. Iskenderun, founded by Alexander the Great, has a large population of Arabs.

Foreign tourists visiting Aegean and Mediterranean Turkey travel mainly to the Turquoise Coast, the southwest corner of Anatolia, or focus their attention on famous sites such as Ephesus, or resorts such as Çeşme and Kuşadası. Very few of these travelers have ventured east of Alanya, on the Mediterranean, or regions north of Izmir, on the Aegean, except for Troy and Pergamum, mainly because of the lack of information about these areas and the absence of sufficient hotels and pensions.

This book partly fills this gap with information about the lesser known sites as well as with insight to better known destinations such as Izmir, Bodrum and Marmaris.

A blond beauty suns in front of the Head of Medusa.

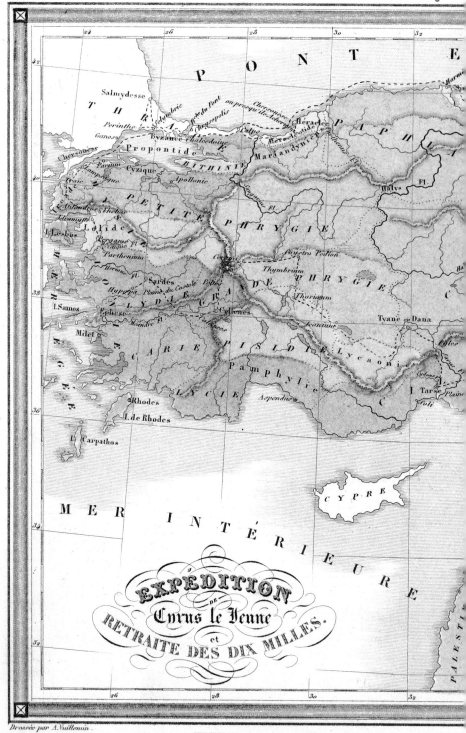

EXPÉDITION
DE
Cyrus le Jeune
et
RETRAITE DES DIX MILLES.

Dressée par A.Vuillemin.

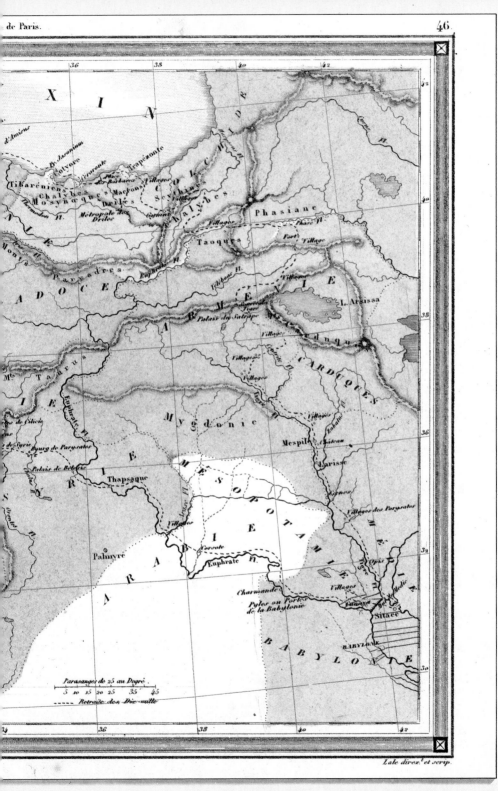

DECISIVE DATES

Old Stone Age 600,000-7000 B.C.: Cave-dwellings at Karain.

Neolithic Period 7000- 5500 B.C.: First settlement at Hacılar, earliest agriculture; Çatal Höyük, first cultural center.

Calcholithic Period 5500-3000 B.C.: Development of Hacılar and Çatal Höyük; new settlements at Canhasan, Beycesultan and Aphrodisias.

Bronze Age 3000-800 B.C.

3000-1900 B.C.: Troy I through Troy IV.

2000-1200 B.C.: Hittites establish their capital at Hattusa and extend rule over central and western Anatolia; first written history.

1900-1260 B.C.: Troy V through Troy VII.

circa 1260 B.C.: Fall of Troy.

circa 1100-1000 B.C.: Aeolian and Ionian Greek migrants establish settlements along the Aegean Coast.

circa 900 B.C.: Rise of the Carians, Lycians and Phrygians.

circa 800 B.C.: Foundation of the Panionic League; rise of Ionian/Aeolian Greek culture in Western Anatolia.

Dark Ages 700-480 B.C.

circa 700 B.C.: Birth of Homer in Smyrna (Izmir); rise of the Lydians.

667 B.C.: The city of Byzantium (now Istanbul) is founded.

561-546 B.C.: Reign of King Croesus of Lydia.

546 B.C.: King Cyrus of Persia defeats Croesus, beginning Persian domination of western Anatolia.

499 B.C.: Ionian cities revolt against Persian rule. The rebellion is crushed.

490 B.C.: First Persian invasion of Greece led by Darius defeated at the Plains of Marathon.

circa 484 B.C.: Herodotus is born in Halicarnassus.

480 B.C.: Second Persian invasion of Greece by Xerxes ends in defeat at Salamis (480) and Plataea (479).

Classical Period 479-323 B.C.

405 B.C.: Sparta destroys the Athenian Navy in the Battle of Aegospotami on the Dardanelles.

386 B.C.: Persia subjugates Ionia again.

334 B.C.: Alexander the Great invades western Anatolia in his campaign of empire building.

Hellenistic Period 323-131 B.C.

323-188 B.C.: Wars between Alexander's successors.

261-241 B.C.: Eumenes I reigns in Pergamum.

230 B.C.: Alliance between Rome and Pergamum; Attalus I defeats the Gauls invading Anatolia.

133 B.C.: Attalus III bequeaths his kingdom to Rome.

Roman Period 130 B.C.-A.D. 331

88 B.C.: Mithridates, king of the Pontus, revolts against Romans.

64 B.C.: Romans win war with Mithridates, securing most of Asia Minor.

41-40 B.C.: Antony summons Cleopatra to Tarsus and begins love affair.

31 B.C.: Antony is defeated at the battle of Actium. Antony and Cleopatra commit suicide in Egypt (30 B.C.).

A.D. 44-56: St. Paul journeys through southern and western Anatolia to spread teachings of Jesus; followers of Jesus are called Christians for the first time in Antioch.

A.D. 313: Christianity becomes state religion of the Roman Empire.

Byzantine Period A.D. 330-1453

A.D. 330: Constantine establishes Constantinople as new capital of Roman Empire.

A.D. 527-565: Reign of Justinian; period of greatest Byzantine power and influence.

A.D. 677-718: Arab armies sweep across southern and western Anatolia, but fail to conquer Constantinople.

A.D. 1071: Seljuk Turks defeat Byzantines at the Battle of Manzikert and overrun most of Anatolia.

A.D. 1071-1238: Seljuks rule Anatolia from Konya; the Sultanate of Rum.

A.D. 1096: First Crusade of Latin armies invade western and southern Anatolia on their way to Jerusalem.

A.D. 1204: Latin armies of the Fourth Crusade sack Constantinople.

A.D. 1240: Ottoman Turks descend on western Anatolia as vassals of the Seljuk Dynasty.

A.D. 1261: Michael VIII Pelaeologos recaptures Constantinople and restores the Byzantine Empire.

A.D. 1354: Ottoman armies, led by Ghazi Süleyman Pasha, cross the Dardanelles into Europe.

A.D. 1402: Mongolian ruler Tamerlane defeats Ottomans under Beyazıt I, setting back Ottoman expansion by a generation.

A.D. 1451: The Ottomans, under Mehmet II, capture Constantinople; the city is renamed Istanbul; the Ottoman capital is established there.

Ottoman Period 1453-1922

A.D. 1459-1517: The Ottomans conquer Serbia, Greece, Syria and Egypt. Selim I becomes Caliph (A.D. 1517).

A.D. 1520-1566: Reign of Süleyman the Magnificent. Height of Ottoman power and prestige; Ottomans conquer Rhodes, Baghdad, Hungary and Libya; the Mediterranean is turned into a Turkish lake.

A.D. 1571: Turks conquer Cyprus. First Ottoman defeat in the naval Battle of Lepanto by Christian forces.

A.D. 1669: Crete falls to the Ottomans.

A.D. 1699: Austria and her allies sign the Treaty of Carlowitz, the first Ottoman admission of defeat; Ottomans lose many central European territories.

A.D. 1854-1856: Crimean War ends in Russian defeat.

A.D. 1876-1909: Reign of Abdülhamit II.

A.D. 1878: Turco-Russian wars ends in Ottoman defeat; Serbia, Montenegro, Bosnia, Bulgaria and Rumania become independent; British govern Cyprus.

A.D. 1909: Abdülhamit deposed and exiled; Young Turks take power.

A.D. 1911-1913: Balkan Wars; Turks lose Macedonia and a section of Thrace.

A.D. 1914: Turkey joins World War I as ally of Germany. Russia, France and Britain declare war on Turkey.

A.D. 1915: Turkish forces, led by Mustafa Kemal, repel allied landings at Gallipoli.

A.D. 1918: Turks are driven out of Palestine and Syria by British forces. Turks surrender to the Allied Powers.

A.D. 1919: Italian forces occupy Antalya and southwest Turkey. French troops seize Adana and southeast Turkey. The Greek army occupies Izmir and invades western Anatolia.

A.D. 1919-1922: Turkish War of Independence. Greeks are defeated by the Turks and leave Anatolia.

Republican Period: 1923-

A.D. 1923: Treaty of Lausanne establishes sovereignty of modern Turkey, determines borders, and organizes the exchange of minorities between Greece and Turkey; Turkish Republic is declared; the Sultanate and the Caliphate are abolished; Mustafa Kemal Atatürk becomes first President.

A.D. 1925-1938: Series of westernizing economic and social reforms introduced by Atatürk includes: abolition of the *fez*, adoption of the western calendar, introduction of the Latin alphabet and women's rights.

A.D. 1946: Turkey becomes charter member of the United Nations; opposition parties founded. First general elections called.

A.D. 1952: Turkey becomes full member of NATO.

A.D. 1960: Cyprus becomes independent state; Military coup in Turkey.

A.D. 1961: Former Prime Minister Adnan Menderes and others are condemned to death.

A.D. 1971: Military topples government of Prime Minister Süleyman Demirel.

A.D. 1980: Military intervention led by Chief of Staff General Kenan Evren. Evren becomes head of state.

A.D. 1983: General elections are held. President Evren names Turgut Özal as Prime Minister.

A.D. 1989: Turgut Özal is elected President.

The story of human life in Anatolia is one of peoples who succeeded each other in irregular procession across the land. It is a story of varied and increasingly complicated levels of existence with each group building upon the houses and on the ideas of the previous inhabitants. People added 19 yards (17 meters) to the hill of Troy in the 3,000 years they occupied it. Users of stone tools were followed by users of both stone and metal; metal workers learned to mint standardized coins, the use of which improved lution, meant the difference between savage subsistence and the beginnings of human control of the environment.

More accurately, an important dividing line in the description of human development can be drawn at the time of the Neolithic Revolution, well before the advent of writing. Up until the appearance of the written word, our information is based largely on inference. Before it, we can surmise the general outlines; after, there is a crescendo of known developments, persons and events.

their business, and which continues to affect today's economy. Often the groups interacted with civilizations some distance away. The Miletian astronomer Thales was able to predict the eclipse of the sun in 585 B.C. because he knew about an 18-year periodicity which Babylonian astronomers had observed about eclipses.

Neolithic Revolution: The records of civilization in the Near East begin with a revolution, a turning point when people changed from being at the mercy of their environment to their becoming herdsmen of wild animals and cultivators of wild grains. This innovation, which is known as the Neolithic Revo-

The division is not a clear-cut one. Nor did it occur evenly everywhere. Perhaps it was stimulated by the warming of the earth's atmosphere after the last Ice Age.

The major areas of this revolution in the Middle East were the drainage basins of the Tigris and the Euphrates rivers, the Fertile Crescent. Much of this lies farther east than the province of this book, but the northwest point of that Crescent extends into the rich farmland of the Cilician Plain (today's Çukurova). Between Antakya and Silifke,

Above, wheat particles found at Karain Caves.

on the slopes of the Taurus Mountains, across the flat land to the west, and extending north along the Mediterranean Coast, archaeologists have found evidences of this change. Here fishermen, farmers and herders have left the clues with which scientists are piecing together the story of man's beginnings and his achievements.

Dates: Human life in the Middle East appears to go back about a million years. Only in the relatively recent past – perhaps 10,000 B.C. – did people begin using tools. And it was about 8000 B.C. before people started shaping their tools for specific purposes and controlling food production.

By 5500 B.C. people had metal tools; the first metal they used in quantity was copper – the Chalcolithic Period. At the same time, the original groups of people to live in primitive settlements perhaps were those who could harvest and store enough food to carry them through winter.

The next advance came with the discovery of how to make bronze. The Bronze Age, when this metal was shaped into strong tools, commenced around 3200 B.C. Copper, lead, nickel and arsenic are abundant in Anatolia, but archaeologists are not sure where the tin, which was needed to combine with copper to make bronze, came from. It may have been mined in the Taurus Mountains or it may have been imported from Mesopotamia.

Social changes: A metalworking industry meant a permanent settlement, some division of labor and some kind of social organization along with trading arrangements. With this advance, village life became more complex; buildings were constructed for purposes other than just habitation.

The Bronze Age lasted about 2,000 years. During that time writing was invented and brought into Anatolia by foreign Assyrians around 1900 B.C. The use of iron, with its superior strength, was introduced into the area around 1400 B.C. and established the Iron Age.

The theory associated with iron is that its abundance meant eventually that cheap weapons were available to the masses who then used them against their neighbors. The invading "Sea Peoples" at the turn of the first millennium destroyed civilizations, causing a major regression to a more primitive type of living in western Anatolia – a period described as the "Dark Ages."

Indo-European invaders: The Middle and late Bronze periods (2000 to 1000 B.C.) are known largely from the finds in Troy. The beginning of the period was marked by waves of Indo-European invaders, some settling peacefully and taking on many of the customs of the indigenous groups, others causing considerable destruction to the cities in their paths.

The Battle of Kadesh, which was concluded with a treaty of political alignment between the Hittites and Egypt, was fought on the Orontes River south of Antakya in about 1285 B.C. This established the Hittites as an internationally dominant kingdom and set a northern limit to Egyptian influence in the Middle East. The Trojan War between the Greeks and the Trojans ended in about 1250 B.C., probably opening Anatolia to invasion by another wave of barbaric tribes.

Beginning about 700 B.C., more accurate dates can be assigned to recorded events. Cimmerians from the Caucasus sacked Gordium around 690 B.C.; Tarsus was ravaged by the Assyrian Sennacherib at the same time. Lydians plundered Smyrna (Izmir) a hundred years later, and King Croesus was defeated at Sardis by the Persian King Cyrus in 546 B.C., beginning the period of Persian influence. Persian control of the western coast and influence of Persian art lasted until Alexander the Great's conquests between 334 and 323 B.C.

The Ahhiyawans: The written record of past events in Anatolia started in about 1900 B.C. when the Assyrian merchants living on the outskirts of the Hittite capital of Kanesh (near Kayseri) sent letters to their business associates in Mesopotamia. These letters were inscribed in cuneiform on clay and then baked in an oven. In them are references to people such as the Ahhiyawans who were living at the time on the coast.

The earliest group of people living in Anatolia for which we have a name is the Hattians. When they came and where they came from are a mystery. They were a non-Semitic, non-Indo-European group who were influential enough to give the name of their land to the next invaders who probably called themselves Nesians.

The Nesians, one of the many ethnic groups who invaded the area apparently from the east, established one of their capitals at Hattusa (Boğazköy) and another at

Kanesh (Kültepe). Their ruler styled himself "King of the Hatti;" they and their Indo-European language are known, with some oversimplification, as Hittite.

Lycians of Xanthus: The invasion of these Nesians, or Hittites, coincided with the arrival on the coast of the Ahhiyawans who seem to have come from the west and with whom the Hittites had commercial relations. They may have been the people whom Homer called the Achaeans; if so, more connections – business, military, cultural – between the Hittites, the Trojans and the Greeks may be uncovered. The Ahhiyawans appear to have been an early Greek colony living around Miliwandas. (Can this be Miletus?) Another Hittite influence on the coast shows in the record that during the reign of King Suppiluliumas the Hittites fought the Lukka nation, presumably the Lycians living around Xanthus.

The Hittites were apparently present on the coast as far north as Izmir, although their settlements up to now are known to be single sites. A stone statue of a Hittite still guards the pass at Karabel east of Izmir; there is a relief of a "Mother of the Gods" on Manisa Dağ. This scattering of remains has made archaeologists wonder what the Hittites were doing so far from Hattusa or Kanesh.

Another, possibly different, pre-Indo-European group was known as the Pelasgians. They were present in northwestern Anatolia before the Trojan War. Their name suggests that they came from the sea; however, that may merely describe them rather than being what they were actually called. According to Homer, who is the earliest source for such information, the Pelasgians were allies of the Trojans. Herodotus locates their capital on the Sea of Marmara.

At least two other peoples living on the Mediterranean coast of Anatolia at the beginning of this period used Indo-European languages: the Assuwans who spoke Luwian and the Hurrians.

Anatolian coastal districts: The names of the districts in Anatolia at one time indicated political identities and dominance. At present they describe the areas in general geographic and cultural terms. Starting in the north, the coastal regions are usually referred to as Thrace, the Troad, Aeolis, Lydia, Caria, Lycia, Pamphylia and Cilicia.

Thrace originally included all of today's European Turkey and stretched into Bulgaria and Greece. Greek mythology says Orpheus, who charmed open the gates of Hell with his playing of the lyre, was born on the shores of the Hermus (Meriç) River, the boundary between Turkey and Greece. Thracian invaders – or Phrygians – are probably the ones responsible for the destruction of Hattusa about 1180 B.C.

About 1160 B.C. the Phrygians, known also as the Mushki, appeared and grew in power on the eastern borders of Ionia and Aeolis. They may have brought about the downfall of the Hittites. Their contribution to life on the coast included their improvement of the trade routes known as the Royal Roads, one of which went east from Izmir through Dorylaeum (Eskişehir), Ankara and Boğazkale; another slightly south led from Sardis through central Anatolia and the Cilician Gates; both eventually ended at Susa, now a ruined city in western Iran.

The golden touch: The Phrygian King Midas was so rich that everything he touched turned to gold, including his beloved daughter. To rid himself of this fatal curse, he bathed in the Pactolus River which flows past Sardis and from which King Croesus got his gold. (Incidentally, British archaeologists are speculating that the ass's ears which Apollo gave Midas when the king preferred Pan's pipes to Apollo's may be a combination of two well-known medical conditions: abnormally long ears, and an excessive growth of hair on the edges of the ears.)

Phrygians are credited with inventing the frieze. They were known for their music; the Phrygian mode was supposed to be stimulating; its cadence may have been preserved through early hymns. (The Lydian mode was considered to be decorous; the Ionian mode, which the western major scale is based on, was called "wanton." The Aeolian harp is one on which the wind performs.)

Phrygian power was interrupted when the Cimmerians from the north invaded Anatolia briefly about 700 B.C. The Cimmerians may have gone off with Midas' treasure since no gold was found in his presumed tomb. The Phrygian Empire was absorbed into the Lydian Empire, and then it passed into Persian control. Under the Attalids it was part of the Pergamene Empire.

The Troad: At one time the northwest

corner of Anatolia covering what is now the province of Çanakkale was called Lesser Phrygia. By classical Greek times it was the Troad. The first person to establish a city in the Troad, according to legend was Teucer, a king who came to the mainland from Lesbos. His son-in-law was Dardanus, the hero of the Dardanelles. (Teucer's great grandson was Tros, to whom we owe the name Troy.) The Dardanians were allies of the Hittite King Mutwatallis in the Battle of Kadesh. They fought a few years later on the side of the Trojans.

The habitation of Troy from 3000 B.C. to A.D. 300 has given archaeologists a sequence against which to measure other sites.

Levels I through V in Troy belong to the early Bronze Period. The buildings were made of mud brick on top of stone foundations in the shape of a megaron, a long rectangular building with an entry porch.

From the time of Level II on (circa 2400 B.C.), Trojan potters used a wheel. This they must have learned from the people who lived in northern Syria or in Cilicia who had been using it before. Pottery similar to what was found first in Troy II has later been discovered in many places near the coast north of Izmir. Two kinds of jars are common at this

Above, arched gateway at Castabala Hieropolis.

level, one of them in a semi-human form, the other with two shapely handles. These are kinds found also in Tarsus and Yümüktepe (Mersin).

Treasures of Priam: The people living in Troy II were skilled in working with metals to make weapons, saws, jewelry and vases. The influence of their artistry spread over western Anatolia, Crete, Thrace and into the Balkans. It was the objects they valued and tried to save from a fire that archaeologist Heinrich Schliemann believed were the treasures of Priam.

By Troy V potters were using a red or a reddish-brown slip. Sometimes they put a reddish cross on the inside, a mark which has been on pots in Tarsus (and the Hittite city of Kanesh) and which suggests a link between those places. Also, bronze was manufactured from this time on.

The fortified city of Troy VI, lasting from about 1900 to 1300 B.C., is similar to Hittite forts: the engineering techniques of offsets (ledges) and columns to add strength to the walls were used in Hittite Alişar and Boğazkale. These Trojans seem to have been newcomers to the area, probably one of the Indo-European invaders. Their pottery was a gray "Minyan" ware, perhaps originally an Anatolian rather than a Greek design as was once thought.

Homer's epics: Troy VIIa, built on top of the earthquake ruins of Troy VI, was destroyed during a huge fire in about 1250 B.C. Most archaeologists identify this event with the war between the Trojans and the Achaean invaders from Greece who are remembered in Homer's epics.

Following that war a number of groups of people apparently scattered, founding cities along the Mediterranean Coast. Of these, some Pamphylian cities claimed a Trojan background: Perge, Aspendos and Sillyum (but not Side which is of later date).

The pottery in Troy VIIb is knobby like that which was being made in central Europe around the same time rather than anything made in Anatolia; thus it would seem that people from Europe were coming south into Anatolia. Troy VIIb also was destroyed by fire – probably in the course of another war brought on by invaders – around 1180 B.C.

Troy VIII (700-334 B.C.) was called Ilion; very little exists of it. Troy IX was not an important town except to pilgrims who came to its Temple of Athena to pay homage to Homer and his epic.

Aeolis was settled by the first group of people who were uprooted from their land in Greece by invading Dorians toward the end of the second millennium. Pushed from Thessaly and Boetia, the Aeolian refugees settled first in the area around Old Smyrna (Izmir). They probably moved in on an already-resident group who may have been Hittites, themselves earlier immigrants. Undoubtedly the Aeolians intermarried with those residents. The Aeolian territory extended from the Gulf of Edremit towards the Bay of Izmir.

Its cities included Pitane and Cyme on the coast, but by far its most important city was Pergamum (Bergama), which for a hundred and fifty years under the Attalid kings, rivaled Egypt in political power and cultural brilliance.

Whoever the natives were, the Aeolians were shortly supplanted by the Ionians who migrated after the collapse of the Achaean kingdom of Mycenae sometime before 900 B.C. Their geographic influence reached from a bit north of Izmir south to Miletus. During the eighth and seventh centuries B.C. they led in the development of civic organization with the Panionic League of 12 cities. They sent out a number of colonies to the shores of the Dardanelles, the Marmara and the Black Sea.

Their cultural influence was even more impressive. The Temple of Diana in Ephesus, an architectural masterpiece, and the Mausoleum in Halicarnassus (today's Bodrum) were two of the Seven Wonders of the Ancient World.

The historians: On the coast, the earliest historians were Ionians. They lived at the time of the Persian dominance, but their works contributed not to Persia, but to the importance of the Greek language and to the growth of Greek/Hellenistic analytical thought. (Even yet their name in Turkish identifies Greece as "*Yunanistan,*" the land of the Ionians.) Three of the historians were from Miletus: Cadmus (circa 540 B.C.), sometimes confused with a Phoenician god and credited with inventing letters; Dionysius, and Hecataeus (circa 500 B.C.). The latter began his history remarking, "I write as I deem true, for the traditions of the Greeks seem to me manifold and laughable." Xan-

thus of Sardis and Herodotus of Heraclea (Latmus) were precursors of the "Father of History," Herodotus of Halicarnassus (485-425 B.C.).

Lydia (Is this Lud of the Old Testament?) was a bit inland; its center was Sardis. Caria was around the Bay of Cos. Lycia is the land south of a line drawn from Antalya across the mountains to Köyceğiz.

The Lycians who around 1400 B.C. were raiding Cyprus from Crete settled temporarily in Miletus. Then they moved south to the area around Xanthus. During the Battle of Kadesh, Lycians fought on the side of their fellow Anatolians. Later, according to Homer, soldiers fought with their leader

Serpedon on the side of the Trojans from faraway Lycia and "the whirling waters of Xanthus."

Native stock Anatolians: The Carians and the Lydians asserted that they were native stock Anatolians. They were probably right, but their importance did not develop until they were stimulated from outside Persian and Greek influences.

The Carian and Ionian centers included Miletus, Knidos and Halicarnassus. Up until 500 B.C. they dominated Greek rational thought. Besides the historians, a remarkable number of philosophers were born in Miletus. Thales, the forecaster of the eclipse, also confounded his critics who claimed that philosophers could not be successful in business. He predicted a bumper crop of olives, cornered the market, and made a killing. Anaximenes and Anaximander searched for the basic principle of the universe; the first said it was air, the other claimed it was limitlessness.

As for Halicarnassus (Bodrum), one of its famous sons was Herodotus. Another man whose name still resounds was the good King Mausolus whose sister-cum-wife built a splendid mausoleum for him when he died about 352 B.C. Two queens named Artemisia ruled in Halicarnassus. Both were remarkably adept as captains of their ships in

That point is known for its treacherous seas; the new residents constructed a causeway joining the point to the hilly island to the west. In this way they created a double harbor, one south and one north, saving some ships from having to round the point in a storm. About the same time of their move, the Knidians acquired the statue of Aphrodite by Praxiteles which attracted many tourists to their city.

The Lydian capital was Sardis. Lydians appear to be associated around 800 B.C. with the Etruscans who showed up then in Italy, having come from the east perhaps because of a famine. Three Lydian kings, Gyges, Alyattes and Croesus, are particularly well

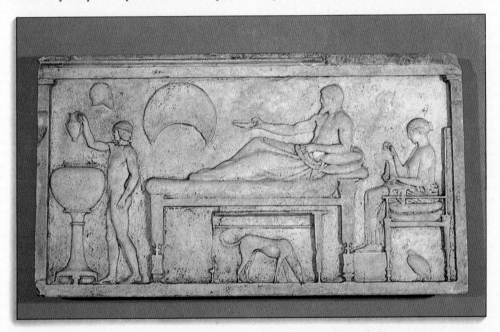

sea battles, the first against the Persians in 480 B.C., the second (widow of Mausolus) against the Rhodians in 351 B.C.

Statue of Aphrodite: Knidos was founded by the Dorians, the group who had pushed the Ionians and Aeolians out of Greece and then were pushed out themselves. As a coastal city, Knidos was troubled by pirates, and when it drove the pirates off it sent offerings of thanks to Delphi. In about 360 B.C., the city moved from its first location (near present-day Datça) to the tip of the peninsula.

Left, bust of Hermes, the messenger of God. **Above**, blissful family life in antiquity.

known: Gyges began his career as a prime minister in about 700 B.C., but having assassinated his king in order to save the queen's honor, he took the throne and set about expanding his holdings.

Under King Alyattes, the Cimmerians were defeated. They had invaded Anatolia from the northeast and killed Gyges. (Following their defeat they retreated to the Crimea.) By occupying the Phrygian lands left unattended in the Cimmerians' wake, Lydia came in contact with Persia and aroused the greed of its kings.

Minting coins: The Lydians under King Croesus reformed the monetary system. Previously, coins were an alloy, "electrum," made of varying amounts of silver and gold. The Lydians standardized the values of minting their own coins of pure metal, guaranteeing their quality and thus stimulating business. King Croesus was defeated by the Persian King Cyrus in 546 B.C.

Within a few years most of Anatolia was under Persian control, directed from Susa through their regional governors or satraps. That control continued for about two centuries. In general, it was a benign rule, the Persians mostly recruiting soldiers and levying taxes. One of their satraps, Pharnabazus, built a palace for himself in 546 B.C. on the shores of Lake Manyas east of Troy. His

Darius to engage them in a naval battle at Lade off their coast in which they were trounced. Darius went on to fight the Athenians only to be defeated himself at the Plains of Marathon in 490 B.C.

In 1982, a particularly exciting discovery of a shipwreck was made off the Turkish mainland at Ulu Burun south of Kaş. The contents of the shipwreck, dated about 1400 B.C., has expanded the knowledge about the cargo traded at this period and the people who had ties all around the Mediterranean.

The wreck held an amazing variety of objects: tin, glass and ostrich eggshells, for instance. Its cargo in large part was raw materials. Copper ingots – six tons of them –

palace garden was distinguished for its "paradise of birds" – a distinction that has lasted into the present times.

South, in Lycia, the many tombs from this period have made the region fascinating. They include pillar tombs (such as the Harpy Tomb in Xanthus with its original frieze now in the British Museum), house tombs and temple tombs (such as at Myra) and sarcophagi (as in Sidyma, Fethiye and Antiphellus/Kaş).

Ionian uprising: A rebellion by Ionians of Miletus led to their sacking the Persian stronghold of Sardis in 495 B.C. That in turn immediately provoked the Persian King

shaped like animal hides may have been molded in Ugarit in Syria just south of the Antakya border. Ivory may have come from Syria or India. Amber – a puzzle about what its commercial use was – seems to have come from the Balkans.

Nubian ebony: Some pottery came from Cyprus. There were vases from Mycenae and Crete, jewelry from Canaan, seals from Egypt, and ebony from Nubia. Some of the items from the wreck were identified from pictures on Egyptian tombs; one Mycenaean kylix-cup helped date the wreck because of its popularity during the 15th century B.C. A gold chalice indicated that part of the cargo may have been intended as a royal present. A gold scarab was inscribed with the name Nefertiti. The large amount of copper suggested that an army was to be equipped with bronze helmets and swords, but which war they were to be used in and against whom is not known.

The finds are lodged now in the Museum of Underwater Archaeology in Bodrum while study of the wreck goes on.

Cave man: Some of the early peoples in Anatolia lived in caves for at least parts of the year. These caves, particularly in Beldibi, Karain and Belbaşı in the Antalya region, have preserved evidences of the transformation in peoples' lives 8,000 years ago.

early period. The stone tools were carefully balanced and shaped to fit neatly in a human hand. Archaeologists have tried harvesting wild wheat with these kinds of tools and have decided that a family working for a month could bring enough to keep them going a year and with some to spare for barter.

Among the evidences of the changes that were taking place are the bones of domesticated animals, the sharp stones fashioned to fit sickle blades, the storage pits for harvested grain, and later the first man-built dwellings.

Elephants and hippopotamuses: The caves near Antalya have revealed, along with less exotic remains, evidences of species of ele-

Stone arrowheads discovered there are shaped with a tang to fit into a longer handle; they suggest that the people had begun to use both spears and bows. Tiny, sharp stones probably set along the edges of curved blades made sickles. These indicate the harvesting, but not yet the sowing of grain. Some of the blades still retain a patina which shows long time use. In both the Beldibi and Samandağ (west of Antakya) caves, scrapers and hand axes have been found from this

phants and hippopotamuses. The Samandağ Cave also contained bones of rhinoceroses, red deer, porcupines, oxen and boars. It is also possible that the first hunting and exploring by these people who lived in the caves were done as they sailed and fished along the coast.

Pictures painted on the cave walls and scratched on pebbles left in the caves are usually of hunting scenes. These may well have had a religious significance – a prayer for success in the search for food, or an offering of thanks to the spirits of the dead animals. Some have a timeless aesthetic value: a rock carving of a leaping stag at the

Opposite page: left, frieze of a naked man; **right**, woman with a lyre. **Above**, a scene of fighting from the Alexander's Sarcophagus.

entrance of the Beldibi Cave shows the grace of a master artist. The painting of hunting scenes seems not to have continued after the domestication of plants and animals, which lends strength to the supposition that the act was related to the need to insure a supply of food by an appeal to the gods.

Some time later cult statues, particularly of the Mother Goddess, appear in rooms that probably were used for religious or funerary purposes. They seem to have a link with similar symbolism in both Neolithic Çatal Höyük south of Konya and in Crete.

Pottery is predated by stone, wood and woven baskets and bowls. It appears that

Cilicia is today's Çukurova, the fertile plain south of the Taurus Mountains. In Hittite times it was known as Kizzuwatna. Olba (Uzuncaburç) was important in the Hellenistic Period. Among the ruined buildings is a third century B.C. Temple of Zeus with columns topped by Corinthian capitals still in place.

Tarsus and Mersin: Excavations at Tarsus and Mersin have unearthed handmade pottery which is like the early pottery found in the Karain Cave. Some of the earliest of these had patterns made by incising the wet clay.

The lowest level excavated at Mersin (Yümüktepe) revealed items from the Neo-

around 6500 B.C. the people on the coast learned how to make pottery from those who lived on the Anatolian plain. There is a strong similarity between the pots found in Çatal Höyük and the first pots of the Antalya region.

Pamphylia was the coastal country which included the cities of Perge, Aspendos, Side and Alanya. Aspendos appears to have had connections with the Lesser Hittite King Asitawandas of Karatepe; its fifth century B.C. name was Estweddiya. Side was founded in the seventh century B.C. by colonists from Cyme, an Aeolian city north of Izmir.

lithic Period. People had been living there earlier, but those levels have not been explored because they are under water. The walls of the Neolithic city were made of round pebbles perhaps from the stream bed or the sea. No mortar has been used; they were dry walls which have lasted longer than if they had been made of mud mortar which would wash out in a rainstorm.

Yümüktepe overlooked a trade route along the coast that went into central Anatolia through the Cilician Gates. The village was helped by the items, particularly obsidian, of that trade, and it must have loaded its own merchandise onto the caravans to be sold in the interior. Perhaps sea shells found in the palace temple in Hattusa came from here.

Importance of obsidian: Obsidian was probably more valuable than sea shells because of its hardness and its quality of flaking with a sharp edge. Obsidian is valuable to archaeologists now for another reason: it occurs naturally only in specific places around the volcanoes of Hasan Dağ, Erciyes Dağ and Karaca Dağ which are in the interior. When it appears in the early levels of Mersin and Tarsus, or in the Antalya caves, it indicates both with whom the people were trading and that they had developed some commercial skills.

tains was known in Hittite times as Kizzuwatna. It seems to have been a region of a number of petty kingdoms whose inhabitants used Hittite hieroglyphics for their inscriptions but who themselves did not speak Hittite. Kizzuwatna remained Hittite after the collapse of the central Empire under Phrygian attack.

Lesser Hittite sites: One of these lesser Hittite settlements was at Karatepe on the Ceyhan River north of Adana. Fragments of a Hittite-Luwian and Phoenician bilingual inscription found at the small citadel there have helped clarify some of the relationships among the Assyrians, the Urartians and the Late Hittite kingdoms.

Tarsus between 2700 and 2400 B.C. was a fortified town; its ruler was a minor king. Double-handled pottery produced there is like that found in Troy II and IV. Archaeologists say that probably this shape originated in Cilicia or further east around Islahiye and was carried north from there. A vase from Cilicia was found in the Fourth Dynasty tomb in Egypt, indicating a connection between those two areas too.

The southern slopes of the Tarsus moun-

Other evidences of the Hittites exist around Karatepe. South, near the village of Babaoğlan, is a castle (probably Roman in origin), and beside it is a rock carving of a man wearing the hat of a Hittite king. This suggests ties between Syria and the region of Hierapolis Castabala (now the village of Bodrum) a few miles beyond a bend of the Ceyhan River. Castabala is distinguished now by a medieval fortress. Castabala was its Roman name; its king Tarcondimotos fought for Mark Antony and was killed at the Battle of Actium. Castabala was a Roman city built on some earlier Greek and Hittite settlements.

Left, the Temple of Zeus at Aizanoi. **Above**, the amphitheater at Pamukkale.

ALEXANDER THE GREAT

When Alexander the Great began his campaign to conquer the Persian Empire and free the Ionian Greek cities of Asia Minor in 334 B.C., he fashioned himself in the likeness of Achilles and Heracles, both of whom he claimed lineage. In less than one year Alexander, leader of the League of Corinth and the Macedonian army, swept through Asia Minor, liberated the Greek cities, reestablished democracies, and introduced an advanced coinage standard that revolutionized trade and commerce. On his way to conquer the Persian Empire, Alexander paid tribute to his hero, Achilles, at Troy. Many historians claim that Alexander, on behalf of the Pan Hellenic cause in Asia Minor, sought to relive Achilles' triumph over the Trojans in Asia Minor.

After visiting Troy, Alexander confronted his first Persian army at the Granicus River (modern Kocabaş River near the Sea of Marmara). This decisive battle demonstrated his enormous personal valor and the brilliance of his military tactics. The Persians set a trap for Alexander by forcing him to ford the river at a point where the banks were extremely steep so that his troops had difficulty in holding close formations. However, Alexander courageously led his cavalry and broke the Persian line. Alexander was wounded badly by a blow through his helmet that reached the bone and while he was left unconscious his troops sorely beat the Persians, in addition massacring most of the Greek soldiers who fought for the Persians. Alexander recovered quickly and sent the 2,000 surviving Greek mercenaries to Macedonia to work as slaves in mines. His brutal actions demonstrated how harshly he would treat any Greeks who challenged him.

Persian panoplies: Alexander sent 300 Persian panoplies (sets of armor) taken at Granicus to Athens as an offering to Athena. The armor bore the inscription: "Alexander, son of Philip and the Greeks (except the Spartans) to the barbarians who inhabit Asia." Not only did this dedication

omit Sparta but it also omitted the Macedonians who made up the largest part of Alexander's troops. Alexander chose not to call himself King but simply son of Philip, paying respect to the Greek's love of democracy. Such reverence for Greek ideals was reflected in his policy of installing democracies in the newly-freed Greek cities which continued to be governed by a satrap in the Persian style.

From this victory he continued along the coast of Asia Minor, freeing Greek cities from Persian rule. He fought a long and difficult battle against the Persians at Halicarnassus (Bodrum). At Aspendos, the citizens requested not to be garrisoned and in exchange for this privilege, Alexander demanded a large sum of tribute as well as horses for his cavalry, for which Aspendos was famous. The citizens refused to meet his request and Alexander responded by demanding an even higher tribute, and taking all the horses he needed. As a rule, Alexander dealt severely with any city that stood in his way and fairly with cities that showed no opposition.

However, many cities such as Ephesus, Side and Phaselis willingly opened their doors and treasuries to him. In the Greek cities Alexander won popularity by establishing Greek-style democracies in place of the oligarchies which had ruled under the Persians. He left in place the Persian system of satrapies but placed finance in the hands of a separate person – usually a Macedonian or a Greek, but some Persians were included. Because he was continually short of cash, he insisted that each city join the League of Corinth and make "contributions" to his war time fund in lieu of providing ships and men. Consequently, the cities paid a tribute to Alexander equivalent to that under the Persian rulers.

Alexander's main achievement was to introduce Hellenistic culture to the east and change the map of the world forever. Alexander left garrisons in many Greek towns along the coast, encouraging intermarriage and an exchange of culture. Along with his army and navy, Alexander also brought with him artists, poets, philosophers and historians to record and commemorate his adventures.

Even though Alexander failed to establish an empire in Asia which would foster a brotherhood of peoples, his expedition successfully laid the framework for the spread of Greek thought and customs throughout Asia. The extraordinary centuries following his death are known as the Hellenistic Age. This era, from 323 B.C. to 30 B.C., was characterized by the demise of the Greek city-states and the establishment of large kingdoms, modeled on the Macedonian monarchy. This period saw the spectacular growth of trade and commerce as well as the development of a common culture made possible by use of the Greek language, and the adoptions of Greek institutions.

After Alexander's death, his newly-established empire dissolved and the successors, the Diadichi, battled among themselves for 20 years. Finally, three main kingdoms emerged: the Macedonians in Greece; the Seleucids in Syria; and the Ptolemies in Egypt. Control of western Asia Minor, however, fell outside of the three major empires, first ruled by one of Alexander's generals, Antigonus the One-Eyed, and later by another general, Lysimachus.

Monarchies: The new political order of this age was the large monarchical kingdom. These great monarchies, governed by autocratic rulers and vast bureaucracies, were in dramatic conflict with the Greek love of autonomy. Because the Greeks were a major source for the development and defense of the state, the kings allowed the Greek city-states to assume a degree of independence within the monarchical territories. Some Greek city-states combined to form leagues or federations such as the Ionian League.

The large political units encouraged international trade, fostered urban economies and led to the adoption of common law. The most important cross continental caravan route during the Hellenistic period began in India and stretched across the Persian Gulf to the Tigris, continued to Seleucia, the commercial capital of Asia, and finished at Ephesus. Olives, wine, sheep and grain were the most commonly traded agricultural products from

the Aegean Coast. Pergamum maintained a monopoly on parchment and textiles, particularly gold weave cloth. Miletus was the center for the wool industry.

Sculpture flourished in the Hellenistic Age in Pergamum and along the Aegean Coast. The Gauls who invaded Anatolia in the second century provided material for two innovative schools of art at Pergamum in the first and second centuries B.C. Sculptors depicted the Gauls as noble fighters.

Stoics and cynics: Strong interest in philosophy also grew during this period as the old gods of Olympus failed to satisfy intellectual curiosity. Although the Greeks and Hellenized natives continued to follow the old religions there was a concurrent growth of king worship, mystery cults and magic. The Stoics, the Cynics, the Skeptics and the Epicurians evolved reflecting a new growth of individualism and humanism.

The most important instruments facilitating the growth of philosophy in the Hellenistic Era were the new libraries established in Pergamum, Antioch and Alexandria.

Grandiose architecture: There was a trend towards the ornate and the grandiose in architecture during the Hellenistic period in Asia Minor. Due to a declining interest in religion and the city-state there was a significant decrease in the number of temples built. The new emphasis on ornate decoration was reflected in the popularity of the Corinthian order. Hellenized Greeks favored temples with an increasing number of columns and more elaborate sculpture on the column drums and volutes of the capitals. For example, the Temple of Apollo at Didyma (334 B.C.) was so immense that the cella was never covered but left open to the sky.

In summary, the Hellenistic Age was a period of much contradiction and complexity. While it represented a period of extensive material gain it was also a time of great poverty among the working classes. The forces of the day nurtured a new spirit of individualism and man believed himself more and more a citizen of the world. On the other hand, the advent of large monarchical kingdoms made possible a much more despotic control of the individual's life.

Left, bust and statue of Alexander the Great.

Although the Roman armies first set foot in Asia Minor in 190 B.C. for the purpose of defending Greece which was under attack from Antiochus III, this advance laid the stage for Rome's eventual domination of the entire Mediterranean basin. For many years, Rome cultivated strong alliances with kingdoms in Asia Minor, in order to protect its boundaries. In particular, Rome relied on Pergamum to control smaller kingdoms in Asia Minor and to act as a buffer state between Rome and the Seleucid Empire. Demonstrating its strong allegiance to Rome, Eumenes II of Pergamum supported Rome's campaign in Greece and Asia Minor. In the face of a strong enemy army at the final Battle of Magnesia, Eumenes' troops proved essential for the Roman victory. This decisive battle put an end to Seleucid rule in Asia Minor and Rome acquired the vast territory ruled by Antiochus III.

The Romans were reluctant to take on the governing of yet another large province so soon after acquiring Greece. Therefore they handed the province over to Eumenes who agreed to administer the kingdom and strictly adhere to Rome's foreign policy. This relationship insured that western Asia Minor was governed in the interest of Rome but the responsibility of rule lay with the Pergamene kings.

The last Pergamene king, Attalus III, was radically different from his predecessors. He was unpopular as a ruler and pursued his personal interests in botany and pharmaceutical sciences rather than responsibilities as king. He had no heirs. Therefore, to prevent the rise of petty tyrants who would likely take over in the absence of a strong rule, he bequeathed the royal possessions of Pergamum and the supremacy of western Asia Minor to Rome in 133 B.C.

Roman province: Rome responded to the bequest by immediately appointing a five-member commission to take control of the new province of Asia. When the commission reached Asia in 132 B.C., the country was in a state of civil war. The new government faced resistance from Aristonicus, an illegitimate son of Eumenes, who had the backing of the poor and the landless peasantry. In expectation of greater freedom under the Romans, the free cities refused to support Aristonicus. The cities had fought alone until 131 B.C. when an army was raised in Rome under the consul Crassus. The support of the city of Ephesus helped turn the war in favor of the Romans. In 129 B.C. Aristonicus was defeated by the Roman general Aquilius, who put down the final stages of the revolt and set about organizing the new Roman province of Asia.

Rome's political and economic policies for the new province of Asia resulted in hardship for most citizens. Annually appointed governors from Rome were largely uninformed and ignorant of local issues and citizens' needs. Moreover, the people did not feel the same reverence and respect towards the new Roman governors who, unlike their predecessors, were not patrons of art.

Exploiting the masses: While some of the governors including Aquilius made contributions to civil life in the province, a large number used their positions to exploit the citizens with extortionate taxes. For example, following the civil war when local governments were in a state of depression, high taxes were levied by the government in order to meet wartime expenses.

Through direct contacts with the Greeks in Asia Minor, Romans were greatly influenced by Greek religion and culture. Children of upper class Roman families learned to speak and read Greek. The Romans, fascinated by Greek literature and philosophy, translated Homer, and copied its forms in writing Rome's epic histories.

The founding of Constantinople as the new capital in A.D. 330 by Constantine I resulted in a shift of the imperial center to the east. The division of the Empire into East and West gradually assimilated Roman Asia Minor into the Greco-Anatolian world. By the time the western Roman Empire collapsed in the fifth century, the assimilation was complete, and the Latin Roman Empire had been replaced by the Greek-dominated Byzantine Empire, which lasted until the Ottoman conquest in the 15th century.

Right, Elizabeth Taylor as Cleopatra.

ANTONY AND CLEOPATRA

When Antony summoned Cleopatra to Tarsus in 41 B.C. to confront her with charges of scheming to support his enemies, the stage was set for one of the greatest love affairs in history, Antony's own tragic downfall, and the transformation of the Roman Republic to the Roman Empire. Antony was seeking to enhance his prestige in Rome, secure the eastern boundaries, as well as revenge Rome's only defeat at the hands of the Parthians. He was in desperate need of troops and money to campaign and conquer the Parthians. Cleopatra's objectives were nothing less than the restoration of the Egyptian Empire as it had existed under Ptolemy II Philadelphus. She was willing to trade the wealth of Egypt to Antony for support of the Roman legions. In his brilliant tragedy, *Antony and Cleopatra*, Shakespeare describes Cleopatra's dramatic arrival at Tarsus to meet Antony:

For her own passion,
It beggar'd all description: she did lie
In her pavilion cloth-of-gold of tissue
O'er picturing that Venus where we see
The fancy outwork nature: on each side her
Stood pretty dimpled boys, like smiling Cupids

Antony captivated: If Antony had not been captivated by Cleopatra the first time he met her in Rome when she was Julius Caesar's mistress, he was taken captive now. Antony delayed his plans to conquer the Parthians and the two returned to Egypt together where they spent the winter as lovers.

In 40 B.C. Antony returned to Rome to reestablish his position in the empire and resolve his differences with Octavian, ruler of the western half of the Roman Provinces. Also during this period he married Octavian's sister Octavia. Beginning with his absence in Egypt, Antony's power slowly declined while Octavian fortified his position within the empire, secured the western boundaries and won popular support. In order to reestablish his power in the east, Antony again waged war against the Parthians.

Four years after their last meeting, Antony summoned Cleopatra, this time to Antioch, in order to marshal support for his campaign. In return for Cleopatra's financial backing, Antony gave the Egyptian Queen part of Phoenicia and northern Judea and promised to wed her and legitimize her children. Antony was severely defeated and returned to Cleopatra who refortified him with money and supplies. Octavia, sent by Octavian, also came to Antony's rescue, but he sent her back precipitating a break between the two leaders.

Xenophobic fervor: Tensions between Antony and Octavian accelerated in 34 B.C. when Antony, celebrating victory in Armenia, staged a ceremony in which Cleopatra was pronounced Queen of Kings with Roman territories given to her children. Octavian destabilized Antony's position among the Roman legions by rousing xenophobic fervor against Cleopatra. In 32 B.C., Octavian declared war against Cleopatra.

Antony assembled a navy at Ephesus to prepare for battle with Octavian. He was once again assisted by Cleopatra, although she was of little help. She had little to gain from his victory against Octavian, for if Antony won the battle he would return to Rome in triumph, out of her influence and back into the arms of Octavia. What followed was the decisive battle at Actium in 31 B.C., where Antony realized his absolute defeat. Conquered and with no hope for a reconciliation with Rome, the lovers returned together to Alexandria where first Antony, then Cleopatra, committed suicide.

All along the Turkish Coast are places where the two lovers supposedly romanced. Antony purchased the city of Coracesium (today's Alanya) for Cleopatra to express his love for the Egyptian Queen. At Cedrae, an ancient island city in the Gulf of Gökova, Antony was purported to have transported the fine silt sand of its beach (known as Cleopatra's Beach) from the Nile to satisfy his lover. Travelers can also visit Cleopatra's Hamam in the Gulf of the Fethiye where the Egyptian sovereign allegedly built baths. These baths are now partly submerged as a result of earthquakes.

ST. PAUL AND THE SPREAD OF CHRISTIANITY

By foot over hot, dusty, steep roads, by jouncing horsecart, by rocky sailboat, St. Paul the Apostle journeyed the length of the eastern coast of Anatolia from Antioch-on-the-Orontes (Antakya) to Alexandria Troas (Odun Iskelesi south of Troy) during the middle years of the first century.

"I have been constantly on the road," Paul wrote. "I have met dangers from rivers, dangers from robbers, dangers from my fellow-countrymen, dangers from foreigners, dangers in towns, dangers in the country, dangers at sea, dangers from false friends. I have toiled and drudged, I have often gone without sleep; hungry and thirsty, I have often gone fasting; and I have suffered from cold and exposure."

Beginning with Antioch about A.D. 40, Paul's influence and that of the early disciples spread Christianity throughout the eastern Mediterranean. Three centuries later Christianity had become the major religion of Asia Minor.

The tentmaker: Paul was born in Tarsus, today a busy city in one of the richest agricultural regions of Turkey. As a boy he learned the trade of tentmaking. While studying in Jerusalem he was an accomplice in the stoning of Stephen, the first Christian martyr. But later, after seeing a vision of Jesus, he devoted himself body, mind and spirit to preaching Christ's word.

Paul's career as a disciple started when a follower of Jesus, Barnabas, called him to work in Antioch (Antakya) in A.D. 43.

The people whom Paul met in Antioch must have influenced his thinking. Of those attending the synagogue, there were Gentiles who had been attracted to the moral virtues they found in Judaism. Paul held firmly to the prime article of Jewish law: "The lord is our God, one Lord." While other Jews believed they could be faithful to the law only by keeping to their own community, for Paul, God's very oneness meant that Jesus, who announced God's kingdom, was calling to all the people. Thus Paul's mission came to be focused on the Gentiles.

Paul was not always successful. He resented it when his companions, John, Mark and Barnabas, found him overzealous. Even in some of the churches he started there were many who did not like him. He often ran afoul of the law and was imprisoned more than once for his beliefs.

Bitter experiences: In spite of all this, it has to be because of Paul's own bitter experiences and his inner certitude that he could understand and communicate across the ages his insight into Christ's teachings as the fulfillment of the law.

Considering that St. John wrote to the Christians in Laodicea (near Pamukkale), Thyatira (Akhisar), Sardis (east of Izmir), and Philadelphia (Alaşehir), which could have been on Paul's route between Galatia, Phrygia and Ephesus, it is quite possible that Paul had visited them in addition to Ephesus where we know he spent a lot of time. It is also possible that he went to the others of John's "Seven Churches of Revelation" (Smyrna or Izmir and Pergamum or Bergama as they are called now).

Places where he definitely stopped off at are exceedingly interesting.

Temple of Daphne: Antioch-on-the-Orontes (Antakya) was an important commercial and educational center, enriched by handsome public buildings. Known as a sports and recreation center, celebrations honoring Apollo were held at the Temple to Daphne in a sacred woods southwest of the city.

Among its bustling population of nearly a half million people was an important Jewish segment. Some of these people had fled Jerusalem during the persecutions of people who were friends of Stephen. In Antioch, the movement grew, and soon its members began using a name – Christians, the followers of Christ – to identify themselves.

Expulsion: From this church in Antioch, Paul and his companions set out to carry their message abroad. Sailing to Cyprus and then to Perge, Paul preached his first sermon to the congregation at the synagogue in Pisidian Antioch (Yalvaç between Konya and Afyon). The crowd he attracted was largely Gentiles, and the Jewish members so resented their intrusion that they got Paul and Barnabas expelled from the district.

The disciples then moved to Iconium (Konya). Again they preached to a large group of people, and narrowly escaped a plot to stone them. However, one young woman of Iconium, Thecla by name, was so captivated by Paul's preaching that she braved scorn and danger to follow him. A second-century book, *The Acts of Paul and Thecla,* was written about her exploits and names her Christianity's first female martyr. It also gives a description of Paul: he was short and bald, had hollow eyes and a hooked nose, but was so full of grace that he seemed sometimes like a man and sometimes like an angel. Thecla later lived as a nun and established a hospital at Ayatekla on the peninsula south of Silifke.

Paul, in his first journey, concentrated on

interior cities, in his next trips he spent longer periods of time in the major ports, hoping to convert people who would carry Christianity around the world.

Christianization of Europe: Paul was in Alexandria Troas, a thriving Aegean port just south of today's Odun Iskelesi, twice. The first time he didn't stay long. Church historians date the beginning of the Christianization of Europe to that call, although there already were members of the sect in

Above, mosaic of Jesus at Hagia Sophia Museum, Istanbul.

Rome. Maybe it was not a coincidence that Luke, with his concern for the western movement of Christianity, appeared in the story at this point. (It is unfortunate that the records of the apostles who worked in Egypt or in the East have not been preserved as Luke's account has been.)

When Paul was back in Alexandria Troas on his third journey, he and his friends stayed up talking late into the night. Suddenly a child who had been perched in a window fell out and landed three floors down on the ground. Paul dashed out to find the boy and was able to reassure his family that he was only badly shaken up. The discussions resumed where they had broken off.

Beautiful Ephesus attracted pilgrims from all over the Mediterranean because of its Temple to Diana. Its theater, its Temple to Serapis, its Celsius library, its odeon, its gymnasiums, to mention only some of the public buildings, give us today a sense of the wealth of community life when Paul was there.

Performing miracles: For two years Paul stayed in Ephesus teaching the word of Christ, converting people to Christianity, and performing his many miracles of healing. By then many people had joined the Christian community.

However, the silversmiths' trade in cult objects was hurt by Paul's condemnation of idols. The merchants created a serious disturbance during which a crowd collected in the theater yelling for hours, "Great is Diana of the Ephesians!" The demonstration threatened to turn nasty until the town clerk appeared to warn the crowd that while Paul was within the law they were not.

At the end of Paul's third journey he stopped in Miletus to visit the leading members of the church in that region. His farewell speech to his friends was full of wistfulness and affection as he reminded them of their long friendship and of how he had taught them everything he knew.

Paul was a controversial figure in the early church, partly because of the mixture in his teachings of Hebraic and Greek thought. The controversy over his teachings and his contributions to Christian dogma has not ended. But as important as his theology is his quality: a man who was passionately possessed to preach the news of the love of God as embodied in Jesus Christ.

In A.D. 1070, the advancing Seljuk Turks took Jerusalem from the Arab Fatamids, and in the following year they all but annihilated the Byzantine army at Malazgirt (Manzikert) and captured Emperor Romanus IV Diogenes. Within 20 years, the Seljuk armies had overrun most of Anatolia. Its army towered across the Bosphorus, casting a dark shadow over Constantinople itself (1092). The Byzantine Empire, which for seven centuries had held back Asian hordes, could no longer fulfill its historical mission as the European bulwark against eastern invasions. Constantinople itself was threatened.

Fearing the worst, Emperor Alexius I (1081-1118) joined Simeon, Patriarch of Jerusalem, in urging papal aid to drive back the Turks. The appeal was seconded by several prospering Italian cities: Pisa, Genoa, Venice and Amalfi. These Italian cities wanted to end Arab Moslem domination in the eastern Mediterranean and open the markets of the Near East to European trade.

Pope Urban II, dreaming of a united Christendom, took to the road in 1095, sounding out leaders and ensuring support for a crusade against the Moslem Turks. One cold November morning at Clermont in Auvergne, he made one of the most influential speeches in medieval times:

"O race of Franks! Race beloved and chosen by God!... From the confines of Jerusalem and from Constantinople a grievous report has gone forth that an accursed race, wholly alienated from God, has invaded the lands of these Christians, and has depopulated them...Jerusalem, that royal city, situated at the center of the earth, implores you to come to her aid.."

The First Crusade: Now, after centuries of argument, the two great faiths, Chistianity and Islam, resorted to war.

In the meantime, the Seljuk Turks, "the accursed race," did not speak of Crusades, but of Frankish (French) wars, or of the "Frankish invasions." In July 1096, Kılıç Arslan, whose father, Süleyman, was the first Turk to secure lands from the Byzantines, learned that an enormous number of Franks were en route to Constantinople. Not yet 17, Seljuk Emperor Kılıç Arslan already controlled most of Anatolia.

Now these Occidentals were nothing like the kind of enemy armies to which the Turks were accustomed. There were several hundred knights and a large number of foot soldiers, but there were also children and old people in rags, with strips of cloth in the shapes of crosses sewn onto the backs of their garments. This army looked "more like a wretched tribe evicted from their lands by some invader," thought the Turks.

Walter the Penniless: By the time the Crusaders, who set out from France in 1095 under Peter the Hermit and Walter the Penniless, arrived in Constantinople in 1096, they had been decimated by famine, plague, leprosy, fever and battles on the way. Byzantine Emperor Alexius welcomed them but could not provide enough food, so they broke into the suburbs and plundered churches, houses and palaces. In his haste to free Constantinople from these locusts, Alexius gave them ships to cross the Bosphorus and advance on Iznik where Kılıç

Byzantine icon from the Antalya Museum.

Arslan's bowmen awaited. The Seljuk forces marched out of the city and almost wiped out the First Crusaders. Walter the Penniless was among the slain while Peter the Hermit fled to Constantinople.

In 1097 new Crusader armies crossed the straits and besieged Iznik. Kılıç Arslan retreated only to face them in Sarhöyük (Doryleaum) near Eskişehir. "The Franks cut the Turkish army to pieces. They killed, pillaged and took many prisoners who were sold to slavery," wrote Ibn al-Qalansi, an Arab annalist from Damascus. "When this event, so shameful for Islam became known, there was real panic. Dread and anxiety swelled to enormous proportions."

In October 1097, the Franks were in Antioch, then Syria's largest city. Two years later, they occupied Jerusalem. "Wonderful things were to be seen," reported the eyewitness Raymond Agiles. "Numbers of Saracens were beheaded. Others were shot with arrows, or forced to jump from the towers; others were tortured for several days and then burned alive. In the streets were seen piles of corpses of men and horses." More than 70,000 Moslems were butchered and hundreds of Jews killed by the Crusaders.

Latin Jerusalem: Thus founded, the Latin Kingdom of Jerusalem lasted 44 years (1099-1143). In 1144, Zengi, a young slave-born *atabey*, or Seljuk military leader, recaptured Urfa for Islam. His successor, Nurettin, of equal courage and greater ability, took over. The Moslem resurgence compelled St. Bernard to appeal to the Pope for a new crusade. In 1147, the German Emperor Conrad III set out with his army followed by French King Louis VII. They took the route of the First Crusade. At Şarhöyük, where the First Crusade had defeated Kılıç Arslan, Conrad's army met the Turkish forces commanded by Seljuk Sultan Mesud I, and was so soundly defeated that hardly one Christian in ten survived.

The French army was decimated by starvation and Moslem raids. The collapse of the Second Crusade stunned Europe.

In the 40 years of peace that followed the Second Crusade, Nurettin spread his kingdom from Aleppo to Damascus. When he died, Selahattin Eyyubi (Saladin the Great) brought Egypt and Moslem Syria under one rule (1175). A four-year truce with the Latin Kingdom came to an end in 1188 when Reginald waylaid a Moslem caravan, taking rich booty and a number of prisoners, including Selahattin's sister. Saladin responded by attacking Reginald's army at Hittin. He then turned to Jerusalem, which fell after a siege.

The Third Crusade: Encouraged by the Italian fleet's domination of the Mediterranean, and Christian control of Tyre, Antioch and Tripolis, Emperor Frederick Barbarrosa set out for Jerusalem in the Third Crusade. The Turks quickly harassed his army and cut off his supplies; hundreds of Christian soldiers starved to death and the Emperor drowned (1190) while bathing in the Göksu River near Adana. Richard I (The Lionhearted), the newly crowned King of England, took over. Accompanied by Philip Augustus, the King of France, Richard reached and freed Acre (1191). At this time, Philip, ill with fever, returned to France. After a few indecisive battles Richard was able to advance within 12 miles of Jerusalem, but he too fell ill and sued for peace.

The Fourth Crusade (1202-1204) was led by the Venetian Republic, which agreed to the campaign on condition that it took half of the spoils of the conquest. However, the Venetian Doge had no intention of attacking the Holy Lands. Instead he aimed at conquering Christian Constantinople. The prospect of capturing the richest city in Europe was irresistable, and threats of excommunication fell on deaf ears. The Venetian fleet sailed for Constantinople, capturing the Hungarian port of Zara on the way. In the past, the Greek Orthodox Church of the Byzantine monarchy had offered little help, but had profited immensely from the Latin Crusades: it had regained most of Asia from the Turks and had been happily watching the mutual weakening of Moslems and Latins in their struggle for Palestine. But the time had come for them to pay.

The Venetian armada was before Constantinople on June 24, 1204. The Crusaders landed and set the city on fire. The blaze raged for eight days, spread through three square miles and laid a considerable section of the city to ashes. Soldiers looted homes, churches and shops. St. Sophia's great altar was torn to pieces for distribution of its silver and gold. Thousands of art masterpieces were plundered or damaged. The capture of Constantinople by the Latins prepared its occupation by the Turks.

51

Who, indeed, were these Turks that appeared in the western world, upset its traditions, changed its course and infuriated Pope Urban II into malediction: "that accursed race!"? Ancient historians called them the "scourge of God," and were terrified. Yet, even the most prejudiced admitted that they were not savages. They had a sense of honor and justice, and often proved themselves "more magnanamous than the Romans." They ate and drank moderately, lived and dressed simply, their only ornamentation being the delicate embroidery that attested the skillful fingers of their women.

Steppes people: The Turks originated from the steppes of Central Asia. Geologists tell us that today's arid regions of Central Asia were once much coveted land, nourished with great lakes and rivers. The recession of the last ice age dried up this area and as rainfall was insufficient to support the people, city after city was abandoned as men migrated in search of water. As late as 1868, some 80,000 inhabitants of western Turkestan, the "Turk country," were forced to leave because their region was being inundated by moving sand. Half buried in sand laid the cities of Başkara (Bactra) and Anav (Anau) where in 1907 Pumpelly unearthed the remains of a civilization which had cultivated wheat, barley and millet, used copper and domesticated animals. Pumpelly dated his findings to 9000 B.C. This meant the culture of Turkestan was very advanced by 5000 B.C., the year of the Egyptian Pyramids.

Historical records show the proto-Turkish tribes settled somewhere between the Ural and Altay mountains circa 1400-1200 B.C., about the time when Jewish tribes appeared in Canaan. They spoke one of the 14 "Turkic" languages, which are neither Semitic nor Indo-Aryan, but agglutinate in structure. Semi-nomadic, the Turks cultivated land, raised animals and worshipped a *Sky Tengrı* (*"tengri"* from "tien," the heavens; *"tanrı"* in contemporary Turkish) and other lesser gods of the sun, the moon, the earth, the

ancestors and the fire. Their beliefs differed sharply from Greco-Roman paganism. Turkish cosmology did not offer a scene where gods fought with man to keep him in his place, but provided a serene and fraternal relationship. In his capacity as the elder brother, *Sky Tengri* taught them every worldly thing they needed for survival, including how to light fire.

The history of Central Asia is no more than the story of the endless struggle of Turkish tribes for better pastures and water. As the desert expanded, the steppes shrunk, forcing the nomadic tribes to take refuge in oases and adapt to a settled life. Thus the region served as a *"vegina gentium,"* a peoples' womb, which raised kings and sultans to the civilized empires. However, there was another law at work: that the old empires eventually absorbed the invading Turks who settled to become a minority aristocracy. The two oldest civilizations of the world, the Chinese and the Persians, assimilated them so that within 50 years the invaders had become passionate defenders of their adopted civilizations and religions.

Islam: One such clan took its name from its leader, Seljuk. In A.D. 900, the Seljuk clan, like many Turkish tribes, adopted the Islamic faith and became the "Sword of Islam" against the Crusaders. Its dominions grew from victory to victory, until its descendants ruled Persia, Iraq, Syria and Asia Minor. A kindred clan under Ertuğrul, fleeing Mongol invasions in Central Asia, came and found military employment with the Seljuk Bey (Prince) of Konya, and received a tract of land to pasture its herds.

When Ertuğrul died (1288), he was succeeded by his son Osman (Othman), the eponymous founder of the Ottoman Empire. Seeing the Seljuks were too weak to stop him, Osman declared himself an independent bey of a mini-state in northwestern Anatolia. Between him and the Sea of Marmara lay a number of Byzantine cities. The most important among them, Bursa, surrendered to his son, Orhan, who made it his new capital (1326). Orhan took the title "Sultan of the Ottomans." The Byzantine Emperors made peace with him, gave him their daughters in marriage and allowed, begrudgingly, his son Süleyman to establish Ottoman strongholds on European soil. When Orhan Bey died in 1359, the Ottomans were well on their way to forming a dynasty.

Murat I (Ameurth) conquered most of the Balkans; Dimetoka fell to him in 1361, Filibe in 1363 and Sophia in 1389. He eased their submission by giving them a more efficient government than they had known under Christian rule, and made Edirne (Adrianopolis) his new capital. Beyazıt I, the "Thunderbolt" inherited his father's crown on the battlefield of Kosova, near Mitrovica, Yugoslavia in 1389. He besieged Constantinople four times. In his grandfather's traditions he married a Christian woman, Lady Despoina, sister of Lazerevitch, the ruler of Serbia.

Tamerlane: A new threat appeared from the East in the form of Tamerlane of Genghis Khan's stock. Tamerlane's army had recently taken Baghdad (1393), forcing its Arab sultan, Ahmed, to seek asylum with Beyazıt I. When Beyazıt refused to extradite Ahmed, Tamerlane entered Asia Minor. In 1402, the two kinsmen joined in battle near Ankara. A year later Beyazıt died a prisoner. Constantinople rejoiced, Christendom was saved from the Moslems by other Moslems for another 50 years to come. As Tamerlane's army marched back to Central Asia, Beyazıt's son, Mehmet I, reorganized the Ottoman state, which was in shambles. Mehmet I left his son Murat II to subdue Hunyadi Janos in the Balkans. When Murat II died after 30 years of rule, Christian historians ranked him among the greatest monarchs of his time.

Sultan Mehmet II, "The Conquerer," spoke five languages, excelled in mathematics and engineering, cultivated the arts, supported colleges and pious foundations. He is said to have equalled his father in culture and conquests, political acumen, and even the length of reign. It was to his cannons that Constantinople fell (1453), changing the course of European and Ottoman history.

In conquering Constantinople, the Ottomans took over a feature peculiar to the Byzantine Empire: one allowed to exist in the capital of colonies established by the European city-states of Genoa, Amalfi, Pisa, Venice, Ancona and Narbonn. Granted trading privileges and tax exemptions, these foreign enclaves were allowed to manage their religious and administrative affairs and to conduct their own legal and judicial business. The conquerer would not allow these foreign elements to retain their military strength. He dismantled their fortifications, but did not concern himself with the manner in which these Franks lived and traded. The capitulations of 1521 confirmed those privileges which the Venetians had enjoyed under the Byzantines. This was followed by those concessions granted to France (1536) and England (1580). In addition to commercial and navigational rights, these treaties allowed the European powers to appoint consuls in the Ottoman dominions and gave them jurisdiction in civil matters over their own nationals. Subsequent French capitulations gave the French kings the right to protect every Roman Catholic of non-Turkish nationality in all parts of the Ottoman Empire.

Millet system: Thus arose the most characteristic administrative feature of the Ottoman Empire: the millet system. Millet is the Arabic word for "nation," and in this case it meant the sultans granted varying degrees of autonomy to their non-Moslem subjects. The millet of Rum (Romans), for instance, consisted of those who obeyed the Greek Orthodox Patriarch, and the Armenian millet of those subject to the Gregorian Armenian Patriarch. The development of the system meant that the Turks themselves became members of a millet – millet of Islam, for sure, but a minority amongst Arabs, Kurds and the rest! The name "Turk" came to denote a vulgar brethren back in Turkestan. In 1828, a Scottish traveler, Charles MacFarlane, would say that the Turks "indeed consider our word Turk insulting. I remember seeing a poor Greek well kicked for exclaiming 'Turkikos!' where he thought no Turk would hear him!"

The steppes had supplied the sultans, but the Ottoman melting pot had engulfed the horsemen so fast that of 292 grand viziers of the Ottoman Empire, only 78 could claim Turkish parentage.

Sultan Mehmet the Conqueror died (1481) at the age of 51, just when his army seemed to be on the verge of conquering Italy. A contest among his sons gave the throne to Beyazıt II, a reluctant warrior who nevertheless managed to build an armada of 270 vessels and destroy the Venetian fleet off the coast of Greece. In 1512, he left his throne to his son Selim I.

The Grim: Sultan Selim I, known in the west as Selim The Grim, despised his father's pacifism. He started out by campaigning against Shah Ismail of Iran who had raided the Turkish frontier. Capturing Tabriz, he made northern Mesopotamia an Ottoman province. He then turned his army against Syria, Arabia and Egypt (1517) and carried the caliphate to Istanbul. Thereafter, the Ottoman sultans, as caliphs, also became spiritual leaders of the Moslem world.

Süleyman the Magnificent succeeded his father as sultan at the age of 26. Francis I had them would be to resist God." Three years later, Süleyman returned and unsuccessfully besieged Vienna (1539). On the way back to Istanbul, his army ravaged southern Austria. He returned west again (1539), where Venice bore the brunt of his assault, losing its possessions in the Aegean and the Dalmatian Coast (1540). Four years later, at the age of 72, the master of Egypt, North Africa, Asia Minor, Palestine, Syria, the Balkans and Hungary was dead. The Ottomans were the strongest power in Europe and Africa.

Until Süleyman's death, the only limit to Ottoman advance seemed to be determined by their ambitions. Then there set in, at the end of the 16th century, a period of standstill,

been proposing since 1516 to the European powers that they should utterly destroy the Ottoman state and divide its possessions among themselves as infidel spoils. Süleyman himself supposed that the best defense was offense. In 1521, he captured the Hungarian strongholds of Szabacs and Belgrade. In 1523 Rhodes fell. Hungary joined the Empire in 1526, amidst cheers from Protestants, for Luther had urged the Protestant princes to stay home, "for the Turks were obviously a divine visitation and to resist

Above, Ottoman Janissary band plays martial music.

when the Christian powers began to challenge Turkish supremacy. Following a temporary revival, under the vigorous Köprülü family of grand viziers, of military ardor and success which terminated in the second siege of Vienna (1683), stagnation and decline set in. The Peace of Carlowitz (1699) marked the beginning of the end of the Ottomans. The next blow came with the Treaty of Küçük Kaynarca (1774) signed with Russia, now consolidated under the House of Romanov. Soon the Russians opened the Black Sea, which for two centuries had been a Turkish lake, to commerce and navigation. Within a decade, Crimea and Caucasia were under Russian rule.

The decline continued into the 19th century, despite reforms of the armed forces, and establishment of a Council of State, a Penal Code and a State bank, institutions that were to prove abortive in practice.

Iron Fist rule: The 1877-1878 Russian War was a disaster not to be forgotten. The empire lost most of its European possessions. Greece had already gained its independence (1830). With Sultan Abdülhamit, the Ottomans wooed the Moslem nations under their rule and found a new ally in the west: Germany, which helped build the Baghdad Railway, a project that facilitated traffic to the holy cities of Arabia and reinforced the

army invaded Izmir. Three days later Mustafa Kemal Pasha (later named Atatürk), the victorious commander of the Turkish forces at Gallipoli, arrived at the northeast Black Sea port of Samsun and began the three-year national struggle for independence.

Under Kemal, Turkish nationalism was ignited, the Greek army was defeated and the French were pushed back. Italy withdrew its troops. The allied powers signed an armistice in 1922. The Treaty of Lausanne (1923) recognized Turkey's present boundaries, ended the capitulations and allowed for the exchange of minorities between Greece and Turkey.

The Republic: Turkey was proclaimed a

Smyrne

Le port et le Mont Pagus

Turkish ruler's position as Caliph. For 30 years he ruled with an iron fist, keeping the country out of major foreign wars, but Abdülhamit could not cure the ills of the empire. In 1909, Abdülhamit was toppled. The Committee of Union and Progress, which replaced him with a puppet sultan, convened Parliament. But soon the empire was plunged into one war after another, culminating with its defeat in World War I, in which it had sided with Germany.

Istanbul was occupied by the British, while the Italians seized Antalya and the southwest coast, and the French occupied the Cilician coast. In May 1919 the Greek

republic on October 28, 1923, and Mustafa Kemal was elected its first president with Ankara designated as the capital.

Sweeping reforms were carried out by Kemal to westernize the nation. The Sultanate was abolished and the Caliphate suppressed. Atatürk replaced the Sharia, the Islamic Holy law, with civil, trade and criminal codes adopted from the west. Turks adopted last names.

In 1925, the *fez*, the symbol of Islamic Orthodoxy, was banned, replaced by the *şapka*, the western-style hat with a brim. Atatürk said of the *fez*: "It is a badge of ignorance, indifference, backwardness and hostility to civilization." He urged Turks to dress like westerners because "it would help them think like westerners."

In 1928, the Latin alphabet replaced the Ottoman script, severing Turks' ties with their past. The government in 1934 prohibited the use of the honorary Ottoman titles *ağa, efendi, bey,* and *pasha*, and banned the playing of oriental music on Turkish state radio – a ban that was to be repealed. It also prohibited the wearing of religious garb in public.

Womens' rights: Isolated from men and treated as second-class citizens during the Ottoman period, women in the republic were now encouraged to mix with men at parties,

Turkish acquaintance, a gentleman of the old school who touched neither alcohol nor coffee and kept his palate additionally uncontaminated by abstaining even from tobacco. For drinks at the meal my friend's host provided only water; but the water was of four different kinds, each served in a different carafe: one from the sweet waters of Europe, one from the sweet Waters of Asia, the others respectively from Beykoz and Yeşilköy. He asserted that each of these waters had a special flavor and quality and recommended one for the fish, another for the *pilav*, the third for the sweet and the fourth for the fruit. This episode took place during the brief Caliphate of Abdülmecit,

Vue des Quais et la Poste Hellénique
Ἄποφις Προκυμαίας, Ἑλληνικὸν Ταχυδρομεῖον

attend public functions, take jobs in the civil service and go to the theater. Even beauty contests, unthinkable in the past, were encouraged. In 1932, a Turkish woman was crowned "Miss World." Turkish women were granted suffrage in the same year and 18 were elected deputies in 1936.

An English observer summed up the reforms this way: "One evening between the World Wars, a friend of mine, then representing a leading London newspaper in Constantinople, was invited to dinner with a

Left, Izmir in the 19th century. **Above**, "Infidel Izmir" during the Greek occupation.

when Turkey retained the forms, at all events, of an Islamic state. The host was perhaps exceptional in his connoisseurship of the finer points of water-drinking, but he was still a normal Turk in his abstention from liquor. A bare quarter of a century later the Turkish government, claiming that in its Anatolian provinces originated some of the earliest wines made by man, was inaugurating the export of Turkish wine of good quality as a permanent national industry. There can be few more striking illustrations of the change in the outlook of the Turkish state brought about by the Revolution of Mustafa Kemal."

ISLAM

Throughout touristic towns along Turkey's Aegean and Mediterranean coasts in the early hours of the morning after the discos and bars have sent their last customers home, another part of Turkish life begins. From the smallest village in the east to the capital of Ankara to the tourist city of Marmaris, *muezzins* ascend to the tops of minarets to call faithful Moslems (*ezan*) to morning prayer.

The muezzins wail from the minarets:

"Allah (God) is the great. Allah is great. I do testify that there is no god save Allah."

The Turkish population is 99 percent Moslem, mostly Sunni. Since the 1920s, due to Kemal Atatürk's religious reforms, Turkey has been a secular state. Therefore religious freedom is guaranteed to all non-Moslems. During the Ottoman Empire a large number of minorities practiced various religions. Today, a small community of Sephardic Jews remains in Istanbul and groups of Greek Orthodox, Armenian Orthodox and Catholics are scattered across the country.

Although Islam is the dominant religion in Turkey, it is practised in a wide variety of ways. It isn't surprising to see an elderly woman in traditional Moslem garb, the *çarşaf*, covered from head to toe in black, with her teenage daughter decked out in blue jeans and a Michael Jackson t-shirt walking side by side. While the Koran, the Moslem holy book, forbids alcohol consumption, Turks of all ages drink *rakı* and wine in restaurants and bars. In the southern resort towns, discos and restaurants with Turks wearing the same scanty clothes as other Europeans on holiday, can be found next to mosques.

Secular Turkey: Atatürk, the architect of modern Turkey, believed firmly in a secular state. He abolished religious law and instituted in its place secular law. Also Islam was

removed as state religion and the day of rest was changed from Friday to Sunday like the Christian West. He also created a secular school system. The Roman alphabet replaced the Ottoman script, which was based on Persian and Arabic, further separating Islam from education.

However, since the 1980s there has been an increasing interest in Islam. The 1982 constitution reinstated religious education in primary and secondary schools as a reaction to the growing militancy on university campuses in the late 1970s. This was followed by a considerable increase in the number of government-controlled religious schools to educate teachers and clergy for the mosques. The strength of Atatürk's belief in secularism as a founding principle of the state is so deeply ingrained in the fiber of the whole country that any dangerous tilt toward Islamic fundamentalism seems highly unlikely.

There are two major religious holidays on the Islamic lunar calendar. Since the lunar calender is approximately eleven days shorter than the Gregorian, Moslem holidays begin earlier each year. *Kurban Bayramı* (Sacrifice Festival), the most important religious holiday of the year, is equivalent to Christmas for Christians. The festival observes God's intervention when Abraham wanted to sacrifice his son Isaac to God. According to Moslem belief, Allah ordered Abraham to slaughter a sheep instead of his son. *Kurban Bayramı* is a four-day religious affair. Several days prior to *Kurban Bayramı* shepherds drive flocks of sheep into the cities to be sold for slaughter. On the first day of the *bayramı*, men go to the mosque early in the morning for prayer. After prayer, the head of the family slits the sheep's throat, skins and butchers it. A simple meal of lightly spiced sauteed meat from the animal, called *kavurma*, is prepared in most homes. One-third of the meat is given to the poor, one-third or less is eaten by the family and one-third is given to relatives and friends.

Rigorous fasting: *Ramazan* (Ramadan) is the month of rigorous fasting where nothing is drunk or eaten between sun up and sunset. The fast is broken with flat round *pide* bread bought hot from bakeries at sundown. This is followed by complex meals of favorite foods, eaten in extra large quantities. Just before dawn drummers go through the streets waking the faithful so that they can eat before sunrise. Many restaurants and shops will be closed for large parts of the day during *Ramazan* but it is still possible to find food. It's best to be discreet although many non-Moslems and moderate Moslems will be eating in public.

The month of *Ramazan* ends in a three-day national holiday, known as the Sweet Holiday, or *Şeker Bayramı*. Sweets such as *baklava* and *lokum* (Turkish Delight) are given as gifts.

perform the five required daily prayers; those who are rich enough must pay legal alms once a year called *zekat*; fast during the holy month of *Ramazan*; and perform the holy pilgrimage to Mecca at least once in a lifetime if one is in good health and has the financial means.

Whirling dervishes: Whirling men in long white robes, their arms extended, dizzying only to the observer – they are the Mevlevi dervishes, members of an Islamic mystic order who perform the *Sema*, a religious dance accompanied by holy music.

It is a dance of ecstasy during which they reach a union with God. During the dance, the dervishes turn left around their own axis

Prayers which start at 4 a.m. are repeated five times a day, becoming a dominant feature of Islamic life. Yet many Turks only go to pray on *bayrams* (religious holidays) or for some even rarer than that. Moslems do not have to go to the mosque to pray. Often shopkeepers spread out their small prayer mats in the direction of Mecca and pray.

Five pillars: The requirements of Islam, which literally means submission, are few and simple. For a believer to be a perfect Moslem he submits to five principles: the first, and most important, is to bear witness that there is no God except Allah, and Mohammed is his prophet. The others are: to

while circling the ceremonial area symbolizing the movements of the planets around the sun. The palm of the right hand faces the sky and the left is turned toward the ground, signifying man receiving from God and contributing to the people. The eerie ceremony is best seen during the week of the Festival of Mevlana in Konya, south central Turkey, in mid-December.

Mevlana Celaleddin Rumi, the great mystic poet, philosopher and founder of the whirling dervishes, was born in Ballkh in Central Asia in A.D. 1207. He emigrated to

Modern women also pray, <u>above</u>.

Konya, the capital of the Seljuk Empire, which is still the center of the mystic order. He preached to his disciples a union with God through music and dance. After his death in 1273, his followers, the Mevlevis, became closely connected with the ruling Ottomans. Not only did sultans marry Mevlevis but the order appealed to the urban classes who were interested in the intellectual ideas and the possibility of the mystical union of man with God, especially during times of political and social instability.

Circumcision: Decked out in a fancy white suit, fur trimmed hat, cape and sparkling attachments, a young boy is led smiling by his mother to become a circumcised Moslem. Boys are typically circumcised at an early age, four to six, but it's more common in large towns to perform the operation at birth and celebrate the occasion later. After the actual operation in a hotel, circumcision house, or even hospital, a lavish party with close friends and family is held. The boy receives many gifts and money which is usually placed in an envelope and tucked under the pillow of his circumcision bed. Sometimes mass circumcision parties are held, especially for orphans or boys of poor families, with one *fenni sünnetçi* (professional circumciser) carrying out as many as 1,000 operations in one session. The best known *sünnetçi* in Turkey, Kemal Özkan of Istanbul, claims he can perform a "bloodless operation."

As varied as religious practices are in Turkey so are marriage traditions. Attending a traditional village wedding is one of the most exhilarating social events one can experience in Turkey. For sure it is one of the longest events, typically lasting three or four days. Marriages are held in the autumn after the crops have been harvested and the families can spare the time and the lost labor of their daughters.

The couple is first married by an *imam* (Moslem priest) who comes to the bride's house and performs a short ceremony that includes prayer and an explanation of the marriage vows. All women in the wedding will have the palms of their hands and finger tips reddened with henna (kına) to bring good luck.

Separate parties: The women in the wedding have a party separate from the men where they dance and eat to celebrate the marriage of their friend. The men also gather on the same or following day. They also dance, sing, as well as imbibe vast quantities of *rakı*. Often guns are brought out and fired into the sky with a few tragic mishaps occurring now and then. The Turkish women wash the bride at the village *hamam* or her home and then she is carefully dressed in wedding clothes that include veils and numerous layers of colorful cloth. The groom's friends go to the bride's house to ask for her hand and are usually refused until they give a gift to the family.

The groom climbs to the roof and breaks an earthenware jug which scares away evil spirits. Finally the bride is shown to her new bedroom where she waits for her husband. When she enters she again asks for a gift, usually a gold bracelet or chain, and then before they sleep they pray together.

In large towns and cities, much of these traditions have been abandoned and replaced by a party given in a restaurant or tea garden. All couples must also have a short civil wedding according to modern Turkish law.

Birth and death: A new baby is named only after the whole extended family has been consulted. Usually a baby is named after a relative. The grandparents promise to give the child a gift that will grow, such as a poplar tree (*kavak*). Babies are always dressed with a piece of blue stone or glass that purportedly wards off the evil eye. This is not part of Islam but of folk belief. Many adult Moslems also wear the blue eye for the same reason.

When a Moslem dies he or she is carefully washed by someone of the same sex and placed on the bedroom floor. The body is then wrapped in a 16-foot-long white burial cloth. First it is taken to the mosque and put on a special stone catafalque in the courtyard designed for coffins. After the regular prayers, the *imam* leads special services for the dead before the coffin is taken to the cemetery, often shouldered the distance by male relatives of the deceased.

It is common to see religious men with hands behind their backs counting a *tespih* (worry beads) in long and endless motions. Worry beads, similar to Catholic rosaries, come in all sizes and colors. They are sold near mosques or in shops that sell Korans and calligraphy.

Visiting Ottoman Turkey in 1893, Lady G. Max Muller, wife of a British M.P. wrote: "We had expected to see all nations here, and we had indeed! It was as if the Tower of Babel has just fallen, and its inhabitants were pouring down the streets of Shinar. The sharp-featured Semites, the almond-eyed Mongols, the Arayans."

A careful eye will note that the Turks still come in all features! Not surprising, perhaps, when one considers that the country is not only a bridge between Europe and Asia, but also the former nucleus of an empire which extended from Vienna to Tabriz, and from Crimea to the southern tip of the Arabian Peninsula.

Melting pot: When the World War I defeat resulted in the loss of imperial territory for the Ottoman Empire, forcing the Sultan's subjects to take refuge within the present boundaries of the Turkish state, the ancient melting pot enjoyed still more ingredients. The refugees from the Balkans, as well as Russia, the Arab states and the Aegean Islands brought with them their ways of life and further enriched the culture.

One important feature that contributes to that variety is that Turkey is a peninsula which occupies a 300,984-square-mile (781,000-square-km) area, approximately three times the size of Great Britain. The major part of the country consists of high plateaus. The topography and the climatic conditions differ widely from one region to another. Temperatures of -40°F (-40°C) can occur, while days of over 113° F (45° C) are not uncommon. The result is that as the figs and grapes ripen on the Aegean Coast, Erzurum in the northeast may be overwhelmed by a snowstorm! Put it in another way, as the westerners enjoy a good swim, easterners are still wearing their overcoats and rubber boots. No wonder then, that the population (nearly 60 million) is heavily concentrated in the west and along the coast where the biggest cities are situated.

When large segments of population from the rural areas learn about the pleasures of

urban life from television or movies, or from direct observation via cheap public transportation, they decide to live in the cities. The same factors that cause heavy migration of peasants from the villages into the cities in the rest of the world are at work in Turkey too. Its causes in Turkey would appear to be high rural birth rates and decreasing death rates resulting in greater human pressure upon the land and increasing mechanization of agriculture. As urbanization accelerated, especially after World War II, housing short-

ages became severe, and *gecekondus* (squatter houses, shanty towns or overnight houses) mushroomed around the suburbs of major Turkish cities like Izmir and Adana.

Turkish shanty: Like all social problems, the Turkish *gecekondu* has some aspects which are universal and some which are distinctively Turkish. Perhaps the most distinct thing about the *gecekondu* is that it appears to occupy an intermediate position between the situation in England and the situation in India. In all three countries migrants from rural areas require housing. In England, the government builds houses for them, administered by the municipalities. In India, they

Preceding pages: women folk dancers. **Left**, a village beauty. **Right**, a city beauty.

camp in the streets. In Turkey, they build their own houses – ramshackle hovels on the peripheries of cities – without asking the state to pay for any of the construction or building materials or for their labor. Whole *gecekondu* cities are known to have been built within two or three years at these sites. But these *gecekondu* towns are built on somebody else's land, most often on state-owned property. "Were it not for the land problem, one can argue that this is the cheapest and most efficient form of low income housing known anywhere in the world," notes Professor C.W.M. Hart of the University of California. These slum houses, however, upset town planning schemes. The

proved themselves as a family. The parents are satisfied with that advance themselves, but they hope and pray and plan for their children to climb up the next rung of the social ladder, from peasant *gecekondu-dweller* to university graduate in two generations. It does not appear that putting schools in every village in Turkey and factories in half of them would stem the tide. "Why wait a hundred years for that to happen?" say the *gecekondu* people. "It's much easier and quicker to move to the city and build a *gecekondu*. There you will find not only factories for work but decent schools for your younger children."

Nowhere in coastal Turkey is the

frustrated authorities become more and more certain that nothing can be done in these cities unless the newcomers return to their hometowns. Unless a reverse migration can be started, municipal officials in many cities argue, the beautiful maps of new housing and town planning projects of cities will perish even before they are completed.

Unbelievable as it may seem to the upper and middle classes of Izmir and Adana who pass the *gecekondu* areas with a shudder, an overwhelming majority of the people who live in these areas firmly believe they are better off than they were in the villages they came from. They are sure they have im-

gecekondu problem as acute as in Adana, the country's fourth largest city and the industrial, agricultural and commercial hub of the south. The city's population has been growing at an alarming annual rate of 6.5 percent because of migrations from the rural areas of eastern Turkey. Expecting its population to double to two million by the year 2000, Adana's municipal authorities are building a new city to the northwest, rehabilitating the slums and moving some of the urban poor to the new neighborhoods.

The exodus: In Adana, where 85 percent

Above, men celebrate at a circumcision.

of the housing are substandard structures without proper drinking water, sewers and electricity and where the highest number of malaria cases is reported in Turkey each year, the majority of the *gecekondu* people are of Kurdish and Arab descent who migrated to the region at one time as seasonal cotton or fruit pickers and decided to stay. They came in waves mainly from the southeast provinces of Diyarbakir, Urfa, Siirt, Mardin, Adıyaman and Van where unemployment figures reach 30 percent of the work age population, employment prospects are grim, and the land is too arid for farming. The exodus from the rural areas to Adana and other big cities of southern and western Turkey continues from these and other areas of Anatolia. The migration from that part of Turkey, officials predict, will end only when a series of hydroelectric dam projects on the Euphrates and Tigris rivers are completed and begin irrigating the arid steppes between the two rivers of southeast Turkey.

Travelers to the Çukurova region can see many of these seasonal migrants with their tents pitched along the main highways, always displaced, working for a pittance and exploited by the big landowners, known as the *ağa*. These seasonal agriculture workers – Turkey's Okies and Arkies – follow the farming season, planting cotton and other crops in the spring, picking fruits and vegetables in the summer and harvesting cotton in October and November. They usually return to their families in the villages during the winter after the crops have been harvested only to come back in spring.

An interesting fact is that on the west coast, though nowhere else in Turkey, perhaps over half of the *gecekondu* people do not come from Anatolia at all. There are two other sources for the *gecekondu* population, which when combined at least equal or outnumber the Anatolians. One of these groups is the *göçmen*, the immigrant group, whose members were born, or whose families originated, outside Turkey. The other group are the people displaced as a result of extensive road building, slum clearance and urban renewal projects, as in Izmir.

Refugees galore: The older *göçmen* groups are grandchildren of Turkish refugees who fled their homes in the Balkans as a result of various wars from 1878 onward, and the contracting boundaries of the Ottoman Empire. One can find residues of every conflict that Turkey ever fought since the Crimean War 1854-1856, living in pockets of *göçmen* settlements scattered throughout the country, not only in the *gecekondu* of cities but in the countryside as well. Most of the inhabitants of smaller towns and farmers of Thrace, European Turkey, are of *göcmen* origin. During the Russian-Turkish War of 1878, nearly 1.5 million Turks living in Bulgaria fled to the present boundaries of Turkey.

Nearly 500,000 Turks from Greece were exchanged for Turkey's 1.5 million Greeks in 1923, as part of an agreement between Ankara and Athens ending three years of hostilities. These Turks were settled all over the country, but mainly concentrated in the western part of Turkey, including the Aegean and Mediterranean where they were given the properties left by the migrating Greeks.

The relatively new group are Turks from the Balkan countries of Greece, Romania, Bulgaria, Yugoslavia, Albania and the Aegean Islands who arrived after World War II. Most of them were given farming land in Anatolia, which they were required to cultivate for at least ten years. Some of the farm lands given to these immigrants were either sold or abandoned as soon as the ten-year limitation was up and these Balkan Turks too flocked to the cities.

Migration continues: The migration from Greece, Yugoslavia and Bulgaria to Turkey, which is still going on, is perhaps the most interesting. Typically, these people are Turks by ethnic origin, Moslem by religion, who find residence in the three countries intolerable whatever their economic conditions there. Rather well-off families from the Greek province of western Thrace, where 150,000 Turks still live, have been known to sell their farms and move to Turkey because of the Greek government's discriminatory policies against ethnic Turks. Often they move to the city and buy a *gecekondu* for which they pay up to T.L. 20 million without a land title deed. The money thus paid represents the life savings of such a family which would be wiped out if their farms were to be demolished by Greek authorities.

The most recent migration was the arrival of nearly 330,000 Turkish refugees from

Bulgaria in 1989, in what has been described as the biggest population movement in Europe since World War II. About one million Turks continue to live in Bulgaria. The Bulgarian government expelled these Turks, who had been protesting their forced assimilation into the Slavic society. Most of these Turkish refugees have been distributed throughout the country, but nearly one-third have moved to Bursa, a province in western Turkey. Some of these Turks have returned to Bulgaria since the fall of Bulgarian Communist Party chief Todor Jivkov, hoping that the political reforms sweeping that country and Eastern Europe will also benefit them.

In addition to the immigrants from the Balkans there are also recent arrivals from Central Asia, many of whom escaped communist China by way of Pakistan. These East Turkestan Turks, resembling the primordial Turks who conquered Anatolia in the 11th century, with slanted eyes and oriental features, have moved primarily into the cities of western Turkey, including Istanbul.

The Yörüks: Visitors to the Turkish Coast will often encounter nomadic tribesmen leading their camel caravans along the highways. These are the Yörüks. During the hot summers, the Yörüks camp out in the high mountain plateaus that surround the coast. In winter, they come down into the valleys and the coast. The Yörüks were nomadic Turcomen warrior tribes that ventured into Anatolia after the Seljuk victory over the Byzantine army in 1071 at Malazgirt and settled in the more remote areas of western and southern Turkey. Their name was derived from the Turkish word *"yürümek,"* to walk, which appropriately describes their way of life as wanderers.

They can be spotted principally in the coastal foothills of Muğla and Antalya provinces and also farther east in the Mersin and Adana provinces. In spring time, they hold a *panayır*, a kind of spring festival that is a continuation of the Greek *panegyria*, or religious holidays. During the *panayır*, a time of much fun and merriment, the Yörüks pitch tents, sell handicrafts, handmade carpets and food, and play the *davul* and *zurna* (the drum and the oboe) and dance.

The Yörüks are famous for their colorful costumes, tents, delicate embroideries and fancy flat weave wool carpets, the most famous of which are the *kilims*. They also produce fine pillow covers, saddlebags and sacks. The best collection of Yörük artifacts can be seen in the ethnographic section of the Antalya Museum.

Coastal minorities: Travelers to the Turkish Coast will also from time to time come across members of the non-Moslem minorities, the Greeks, the Jews, the Catholics and the Armenians.

A few hundred Greek farmer families still inhabit the Turkish Aegean islands of Gökçeada (formerly known as Imroz) and Bozcaada (Tenedos) – their existence, their own schools and religious practices are guaranteed by the 1923 Treaty of Lausanne. Some of these families operate pensions and restaurants in these islands and produce wines.

The region's Jewish population is concentrated in Izmir, Turkey's third largest city, where there are about 2,000 Sephardic Jews, but small clusters of Jewish families exist in Adana and Antakya, near the Syrian border. Jews have lived in Anatolia since Alexander the Great's time. But not until 1492, when Spain expelled Jews during the Inquisition, did large numbers settle in the Ottoman Empire. Welcomed by the sultan partly for their wealth and business acumen, the refugees became influential merchants and diplomats. For centuries, the Jews went to their own schools, the *Yesivot*, and spoke *Ladino*, or Judeo-Spanish, a mixture of medieval Spanish and Hebrew that in time contained words of Turkish, Greek and French origin. Today, older Jews are still fluent in *Ladino* and speak Turkish with a heavy accent. But few young Jews speak *Ladino*, even at home. And many Jewish families send their children to Turkish schools to learn flawless Turkish. Only one course in elementary Hebrew is taught at the *Yesivot*, but no instruction is given in *Ladino*, or Jewish history and literature. Most Turkish Jews are prominent industrialists and businessmen. There are many educators, artists, musicians and distinguished journalists among Turkish Jews.

Esoteric sect: One esoteric sect is the Dönme (which means Apostates in Turkish), a Jewish group that converted to Islam in the 17th century. The Dönmes, who number several hundreds in Izmir, are followers of the "False Messiah" Sabatai Zevi (1626-1676), a mystic Jewish leader who preached the Kabala and claimed he would lead the dispersed Jews back to redeem Israel. Zevi's mystical views about Israeli statehood came 200 years before the birth of Theodor Herzl and Zionism. Over one million Jews from every social class and in every country in Europe, Asia and Africa hailed him as their deliverer, though he was disavowed by conservative Jews as a paranoid personality who had hallucinations. Zevi was born in Izmir in a house that still exists in the Kemer-altı shopping district and is considered holy by Dönme adherents. The Sultan, seeing Zevi's movement a danger to his empire, imprisoned him and ordered him to abandon his faith or face death with his followers.

Christians from the West and was never strong among natives. With the exception of the Armenian Catholics, they were not incorporated into the millet system during the Ottoman period, and had to rely on the protection of France, Italy and England. Many Catholics, such as the Italians, Maltese and French, in fact, maintain their European citizenship, though some have adopted dual citizenship. A great many of the British and French Catholics living in Izmir belong to the class known as the Levantines. Nearly all have been born in Turkey and in many cases their families have lived in the country for several generations. Their retention of European citizenship is often the only con-

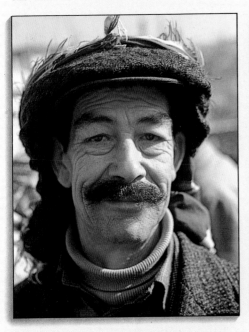 

Zevi, to the dismay of his supporters, converted to Islam. His hard core backers followed suit and became Moslems. Dönmes are outwardly Moslem, but in secret observe certain Jewish rites, but in no way do they associate with the Jews, whom they describe as *kafirs* (infidels). The rejection is mutual.

An estimated 2,500 Roman rite Catholics who live on the Turkish Coast are concentrated in Izmir and Adana. With one or two exceptions, the Turkish state has never considered Catholics as Turkish citizens, mainly because the Latin Church was confined to

nection with the nation from which they originated.

A final Christian group that lives on the Turkish Coast are the Armenians who number about 5,000. The Armenians, who are Gregorian Orthodox Christians, live mainly in Adana, Iskenderun and Antakya and in other scattered communities in the Hatay province.

Ethnic jokes: The joke that goes around these days in Turkey about the Turks is that they are made up of two essential elements: the leek-eaters and the zucchini-eaters. The leek-eaters are those who come from the wrong, that is the western, side of the Meriç

Left, a camel trainer and **right**, a peasant girl.

(Maritsa) River, which separates Turkey from Greece. The zucchini-eaters are the Anatolians who are further divided into two: the lovers of *lahmacun*, a pizza-like pastry, and those who claim they would eat anything caught from the sea, even if it were their own fathers! Put in these terms, the coastal line starting from Istanbul all the way down to Antalya, to the point where the hot *kebabs* of southeast Turkey begin to take over, is occupied by the leek eaters. The connotation is that these people are all but vegetarians who consume "any thorn or weed" that comes their way. The thorn is of course the artichoke, and the weed is the endive, cooked in olive oil, which eastern Turks would not

constructing the hotels and holiday villages of the Turkish Coast. They also control the bakeries of Turkey. Other Turks say the Laz have the ability to smell where money can be made. Making up affectionate jokes about the mercurial Laz, designed to disprove their claims to be geniuses, is a national pastime. One popular Laz joke is: What did one Laz say to the other Laz who was hammering at the wrong end of a nail? He said, "That nail belongs to the opposite wall, you fool." However, the Laz don't take that lying down. It is said that upon watching a Zeybek, a national folk hero from Muğla, dance the slow rhythm of the *aksak*, a popular dance, a Laz was heard to comment "Given so much

touch! (Try the delicious *istifne salad* in the Isle of Cunda off Ayvalik, on the Aegean, and see for yourself!) Cold food is unthinkable in the east where the diet is based essentially on cereals and *kebabs*.

Consumers of *hamsi* (anchovy) in the eastern Black Sea Coast look down upon both. As far as they are concerned they owe their superior intelligence and agility to that protein rich seafood! Immediately recognized by their fair skin, red hair, blue eyes, and large noses, the Laz completely dominate the construction business of Turkey, building the makeshift apartment buildings replacing the *gecekondu* in the cities and

time to decide where to place his foot next, even my old father could do this dance, for heaven's sake!"

Turkish women: Contrary to popular belief, the ordinary Turk did not keep a harem. Nor was the Islamic license to polygamy a rule. That a woman's place was, and to a large extent still is, at home, should not be understood as the patriarchal system of, for example, Rome, where the man, as indisputable head of the family, had the right to be the judge, jury and executioner of members of his family. Latife Tekin, a prominent Turkish woman novelist, puts the Turkish case this way:

"In our society, a woman's place is at home. This means she reigns at home. Man belongs to the streets; he rules in the world outside. Men are alienated, lonely and tense at home. Women feel the same outside. That's why they never leave the house unless fully armored, that is, dressed to their teeth.

That the men are seen as extra elements in the house, and that they are shooed to coffee houses are the overt manifestations of this fact. The men's and women's realms compete fiercely, wildly. I remember my mother kissing the door when my father left. My mother, our mothers, may be rightly called radical feminists as they never forfeited their territory in favor of men's. Anatolian is a closely knit family, with children who leave home only upon marriage, and grand parents who do not know what an old peoples' home is.

The young enjoy the loving umbrella provided by the family and they should, for in this day and age it is often that those above 21 are still being taken care of by their families! While the practice is the main deterrent against the current ills of drugs and alcoholism that strike the young in the western countries, it demands upholding of the old values and rules of behavior. More often than not, you will find that men who have raised children of their own will not, as a sign of respect, smoke (certainly not drink) in

women refuse to buy their final garment, the funeral shroud, with their husbands' money. They bring it with them as part of their dowry, bought for them by their mothers or grandmothers."

Very much like the ancient Anatolian mother goddess Cybele, the Turkish woman mothers her son and husband. If that means having to provide for them as well, she works outside the home, tilling the fields and harvesting crops with other women. The reward

Left to right: a Turkish girl carries her sister; old woman embroiders new designs; a farmer with gold teeth smiles; a Yörük with his camel.

their fathers' presence.

Yet, industrialization does not permit niceties and is breaking down the traditional family system. Once out of their own realm, the home, women should not expect to be pampered. At the end of a hard day's work, riding at the back of an overcrowded city bus, the young are too tired to leave their seats to the elderly who should not be out on the streets at that time of the evening anyway. Urbanization, which in final analysis alienates people, helps to hide the wavering from communal sanctions and codes of behavior. The end result is pollution in both senses of the word.

Adana kebab, Mevlana candy, Izmir köfte and Bodrum's *mantı* are some of the unique regional specialities from Turkey's Aegean and Mediterranean coasts. Today's Turkish cuisine reflects the extent of the Ottoman Empire which spanned from North Africa, through parts of the Middle East, the Balkans, and in Europe to the gates of Vienna. The legacies of the Ottoman and Seljuk courts include a rich selection of appetizers, soups, meat dishes, vegetable dishes, elaborate desserts and, of course, Turkish coffee.

During the Ottoman Empire, Istanbul, Izmir and Bursa were centers of sophisticated court cuisine due to the influence of European foods and the cosmopolitan lifestyle of the people. Even though soldiers and administrators from the major cities, particularly the janissaries, traveled and worked throughout the country they did not facilitate an exchange of cuisine with the rural areas. Until the establishment of the Turkish Republic in 1923, cuisine in the rural areas reflected the nomadic lifestyle and meat-eating traditions of the Turkish people who originated from the Asiatic steppes.

After the collapse of the Ottoman Empire in the early 1900s Turkish cuisine underwent a metamorphosis. With the establishment of the young republic, flocks of Anatolian villagers migrated to the major cities and regions along the coast, and brought their regional produce, cooking and eating habits. Also a flood of Turks living overseas returned to Turkey with food needs. Turks from Crete and Greece brought cooking techniques for seafood to the Aegean Coast. Middle Eastern spices and condiments were introduced to the eastern Mediterranean Coast by Turks from Syria.

Fresh ingredients: Turkey is one of the few countries in the world which produces enough food for its own needs. From the major cities in Europe to the smallest village near the Russian border, travelers can find open-air markets selling an abundance of fresh produce, homemade yogurt, honeys and jams. The market atmosphere is frantic, jubilant and festive – shoppers give the impression of visiting the market for the first time, greeting each other warmly, enthusiastically selecting their products, and bargaining furiously over every melon and fresh fruit. The crowd is easily moved by the aggressive salesman, whose marketing techniques include tempting the exhausted customers with wedges of juicy watermelon, chunks of soft creamy cheese, and handfuls of shiny, salty black olives.

Dining out in Turkey is an epicurean's delight. The palate is privilege to a most unique combination – the great tradition of the Turkish kitchen and flavor of fresh ingredients. In the early morning hours along almost any coast you can find fishermen gathered on the wharves munching on hot *simit* (a roll of bread shaped like a lifesaver and covered with sesame seeds) and drinking their first tea, guarding the catch of the previous night and exchanging adventure stories like their ancestors did a millennia ago as they wait for seafood restaurants to buy fresh fish directly from them.

Mornings in Turkey begin best on a sunlit balcony with a sumptuous Mediterranean breakfast. A typical breakfast both at hotels and in restaurants is a fairly substantial meal consisting of *beyaz peynir* (white cheese), honey or jam, black olives, boiled eggs and piles of fresh Turkish bread which resemble Italian loaves. In Antalya, the traveler will be lucky if he is served a local speciality known as *patlıcan reçeli* (eggplant jam), miniature eggplants preserved in sweet syrup, which is spread on bread or mixed in yogurt.

Eggs menemen: You can easily have a light breakfast of coffee and cheese toast at any cafe. For a more substantial breakfast, visit a *Süt İş* (milk shop). These small restaurants, catering to the morning crowd, specialize in various kinds of milk and egg dishes. One popular breakfast dish is *menemen*, a delicious concoction of eggs, peppers, tomatoes and cheese, served in a pan and accompanied by small buttery buns called *poğaça* and various kinds of cheese *börek* (layered pastry leaves cooked in the oven). *Süt İş* shops also create a variety of smooth milk-based

Preceding pages: grand buffet lunch at a Turkish resort. **Left**, fish and *shish kebab*.

puddings and sweet desserts, such as *sütlaç* (rice pudding), *tavuk göğsü* (breast of chicken pudding) and *aşure*, (Noah's pudding).

Turkish black tea, brewed until intensely strong and bitter and then diluted with water, is drunk with plenty of sugar throughout the day from small tulip-shaped glasses. Many foreigners find that Turkish tea helps counteract some of the oily Turkish dishes. Tourists will be offered tea wherever they have to wait, from carpet shops to the local market. It's considered an affront to the host if a guest refuses refreshments. For something lighter, try apple tea, the best of which is made from dried apples and petals already sweetened, or *ıhlamur*, a linden tea highly touted as a remedy for upset stomachs.

Turkish coffee, with its peculiar muddy grinds at the bottom of the cup and strong taste, is famous around the world for its use in forecasting the future. However, it is not as readily available as tea. When ordering coffee, the visitor should specify *sade* (unsweetened coffee), *orta* (medium sugar) or *şekerli* (extra sweet). The *çayevi* (tea shops), the social nerve center of every village and town, are generally frequented by men who leisurely linger over glasses of tea and play backgammon with lightning speed.

Lunch: Lunch is eaten between noon and two in various kinds of street side restaurants and *büfes* (sandwich stands). The most popular noon meal in Turkey is the *döner kebab*, layered lamb, ground beef and spices roasted on a vertical spit, and served thinly sliced over rice or in a roll with tomatoes, hot peppers and french fries. Generally, lunchtime restaurants in Turkey specialize in one kind of dish or cooking technique. For example, *kebab* houses (*kebapçı*) serve all sorts of grilled or baked meat dishes. The *pideci*, which is another speciality restaurant, serve freshly baked thick flat bread piled high with toppings such as cheese and eggs, *sucuk* (a spicy salami) or a mixture of the day's offerings.

Another favorite noontime snack is *lahmacun* (Turkish pizza), a thin crisp dough topped with ground lamb, onions, spices and served with ice cold frothy *ayran*, a fortifying drink of beaten yogurt, spring water and a dash of salt. *Lahmacuns* are sold on street corners but the best ones are usually found in *pide* shops – served crisp and hot out of the wood burning oven. *Lahmacuns* from Adana and along the southeast coast are especially tasty.

For those with a hearty appetite and more time to spend for lunch, a stop off at a *hazır yemek lokantası* (prepared food restaurant) will guarantee a substantial meal. These restaurants, offering a wide variety of hot traditional Turkish meat and vegetable dishes, don't need to advertise for they are easily found. From the street, the day's selections, unpretentiously displayed, can be viewed. A beaming *garçon* and other staff members will beckon the guest to dine inside as he strolls by. First the tourist should carefully examine the dishes, an array of meats, vegetables, *pilavs*, bubbling, roasting, and steaming in large steel containers over the stove and steam tables. Usually menus and price lists are unavailable, so selection must be made by pointing to the desired dish.

The kebabs: With great pride and flourish, the chef will serve generous portions, saying repeatedly *afiyet olsun* (bon appetit) and then stand firmly behind the customer waiting for verdict on his food. The meat dishes include several kinds called *kebabs*, such as *tas kebabı* (mutton with tomatoes and onions), *bahçivan kebabı* (a gardener's stew), or *köfte* (meatballs) such as *terbiyeli köfte* (meatballs in an egg and lemon sauce). Add to this *pilav* (rice), or spinach puree with a poached egg, or a dish of homemade yogurt and the meal will get the visitor through hours of sightseeing.

Dinner is eaten anytime between 7 p.m. and 10 p.m although many meals last until midnight. Restaurants are classified into two main categories, those serving meat dishes, and those serving seafood. Some, however, will have a combination of both. If you are feeling energetic, visit a *gazino* (a traditional nightclub) where you will be treated to a full night of food and drinks followed by belly dancers, singing and traditional Turkish music.

When eating at a restaurant, don't bother asking for the menu because usually there is none available and besides, the Turkish method of ordering is much more appetizing. It's best to follow the waiter to the kitchen where he will give a special viewing of the evening's choices. All the hungry tourist needs to do is indicate his choice by pointing at the dish.

A traditional dinner begins with *meze* dishes (appetizers), a dazzling variety of cold and hot treasures, ranging from salads to savory pastry to melons. Many Turks make a meal out of these appetizers. The traveler may choose to too because he may feel stuffed after consuming these rich tidbits. *Meze* dishes are typically consumed with the milky-looking drink called *rakı* –the national alcoholic beverage flavored with anise–served with water and ice. Turkey boasts three locally brewed beers as well, *Efes*, *Tekel* and *Tuborg*.

Appetizers: At a meat restaurant the *meze* usually include only vegetable and meat dishes. Cold *meze* dishes are brought to the

shouldn't be surprised to find vendors selling peeled fresh almonds mounded on a bed of ice, peanuts caked in salt, and of course, lottery sellers plying their wares among the tables.

One of the best *meze* dishes to look for anywhere along the the coast is *çiğ köfte* (raw meatballs) – they are Turkey's answer to steak tartare. Raw lamb, bulgur wheat and parsley pounded together create a tender, very spicy small meatball that is tempting even to those who don't usually eat raw meat. *Zeytin yağlı* vegetables cooked in olive oil and served cold make up a large category of *meze* dishes, such as stuffed green peppers, tomatoes, grapevine leaves

table by a waiter as soon as the guest has been seated. The waiter arrives with a tray or trolley piled high with small dishes which he proceeds to put on the table. You should stop him there and choose what he wants and send back the rest. Behind him another waiter is carrying a large salad – the customer should send this back if he doesn't think he can eat it. Other salads will be available that are more interesting, like shepherd's salad (*çoban*), white bean salad (*piyaz*), and *karışık turşu* (mixed pickles). If the restaurant is outside near a harbor, the tourist

Above, the chef slices *a döner kebab*.

and mussels. The vegetables or shells come bursting with a mixture of rice, pine nuts, currants and spices. Small lamb's brain served cold with lemon on lettuce are greatly sought after by Turks. There is also a variety of spreads for bread including *ezme* (a fiery hot tomato and onion *salça*, or paste), *haydari* (a thick garlicky yogurt dip), and *cacık*, a thinner version with slices of cucumber, olive oil and parsley, often served like a soup. Turks make amazing pickles out of every kind of vegetable and even some fruits. *Erik*, small green plums, are transformed into tart-sweet pickles that go well with olive oil-laden food. Turks also drink pickle juice. Southerners from Adana are especially fond of a dark red turnip juice, *şalgam suyu*.

Out of the more than 40 ways to cook the humble eggplant most of the best recipes are *meze* dishes. The simple *patlıcan salatası* made from coarsely chopped peppers, tomatoes, onions, and of course eggplant, must be tried. Diners at traditional Turkish food restaurants should sample the more complicated *imam bayıldı* (literally the priest fainted), a whole eggplant stuffed with onions, tomatoes amd swimming in a sweetish olive oil dressing, often eaten as a main dish. Simple eggplant puree is rendered sublime with bits of smokey eggplant skin. Eggplant

filling of crisp vegetables.

There are also triangle-shaped pastry stuffed with spinach, *pastırma* (cured beef); the most exceptional are stuffed with fish and mushrooms. One unusual hot *meze* is the *kadın budu köfte* (lady's thigh), an appropriately named meatball shaped like large Italian sausage made from lamb and rice and deep fried eggs. *Rakı* drinkers often eat a great deal of *Arnavut ciğeri*, Albanian-style lamb's liver served cubed and sauteed in olive oil and onions.

After the *meze* dishes, or as an alternative, the diner may order from a variety of traditional Turkish soups, usually thickened with flour or bulgur wheat and garnished with a

slices also come fried topped with yogurt or accompanied by green peppers.

Böreks: Like many foreign diners in Turkey, you may confuse the arrival of another massive tray of dishes, this time piping hot, with the main course. But these are just the appetizers. Among the most traditional are the *böreks*. Similarly named cheese and spinach pastries are served at breakfast or lunch in *börekçi* cafes and from street carts. At dinner you should try *sigara boreği*, tightly rolled cigarette-shaped layered pastries stuffed with cheese, deep fried and served piping hot. A version called *Çin boreği* are Chinese-style spring rolls with a

fresh squeeze of lemon juice. Year round Turks try several varieties of lentil soups made with bulgur wheat, rice and vegetables. *Adana çorbası* is a vegetable soup with meatballs and chickpeas. In the summer it's best to try tomato soup, created from the ripe juicy tomatoes of the southern coast, or *balik çorbası*, fish soup. In winter, Turks across the country savor *tarhana çorbası*, made from yogurt curds and flour that is mixed with broth, very popular in Denizli. Special restaurants serve an unusual soup called *işkembe çorbası*, made from lamb's tripe and served with plenty of garlic and vinegar, highly recommended by the locals as a remedy for a *rakı* hangover.

Meat dishes: If the traveler can resist consuming too many appetizers, the waiter will eagerly take orders for meat. In addition to a large number of *köfte* appetizers, a variety of grilled meatballs of various sizes and spiciness is available, including *kaşarlı* (with cheese) and *sebzeli* (with vegetables). Customers should save some of their cold appetizer dips to use as a good sauce. Also they can order a mix grill including *pirzola* (lamb chops), *böbrek* (kidneys) and *ciğer* (liver).

An *ocakbaşı* is a restaurant specializing in grilled meat. Similar to a Japanese sushi bar, guests are invited to sit and watch the food being barbecued over coal. The most popu-

after its creator, the Iskenderoğlu family in Bursa, is another Turkish specialty of layered *pide* bread, slices of *döner*, spicy tomato sauce, yogurt and burnt butter.

Many *kebab* dishes are cooked in the oven (*fırın*) such as lamb *tandır*, leg of lamb cooked slowly until it falls apart and *kağıt kebab*, lamb meat cooked inside a paper package fragrant with thyme, onions and garlic. *Güveç* is the name for various stews which are roasted in a slow oven and served in individual earthenware pots, such as layered lamb *güveç* made with onions and eggplant, chicken *güveç* served with baby okra, tomatoes and peppers, and shrimp *güveç* baked in a light tomato sauce and covered in

lar grilled *kebab* is *cöp şiş*, tiny pieces of skewered meat grilled and served with flat thin bread, onions and tomatoes. *Şiş kebab* (*shish kebab*), famous around the world, is made from chunks of lamb or beef – but tourists should look for the unusual and delicious regional *kebabs* often found at each *ocakbaşı* and meat restaurants. In Adana, the fiery hot mixture of ground meat grilled on a skewer called *Adana kebab* is a must. If a less spicy version is desired, choose *Urfa kebab*. *Iskender kebab*, named

melted cheese. Circassian chicken is a creamy dish made with shredded chicken in a walnut sauce that is reminiscent of the creamy white skin of the sultan's highly prized Circassian harem women.

Seafood: Fish restaurants along the coasts are replete with their own unusual *meze* specialities that have developed from the stock of seafood recipes brought back by Turks returning from Greece and innovative chefs enlarging their repertoire of dishes. Visitors to the region will find many of the cold *meze* dishes common in meat restaurants as well as an array of seafood salads, such as octopus salad marinated in lemon

<u>Left</u>, fish, cheese and *rakı*. <u>Above</u>, stuffed grape leaves and radishes.

juice especially good in Bodrum and in Marmaris, pickled sea bream, and shrimp salads.

Two popular hot seafood *meze* specialities are golden fried *kalamar* (squid) rings and *midye tava* (mussels) served with a special sauce. In tourist areas various kinds of seafood *börek*, a mixture of the local catch wrapped in leaves of tender pastry, have been added to the menu. Sardines wrapped in grapevine leaves and grilled is an unusual dish eaten primarily in August when sardines are plentiful.

As a rule, Turkish chefs grill and bake only large firm fleshed fish. The best season for eating fish is from early autumn to late

the coast near Mersin, is *balık doldurması*, a stuffed pike with rice, pistachios, and spices bursting from the fish. Along the Mediterranean jumbo shrimp, meaty and tender, are grilled with garlic and butter – these are highly prized by the locals for their unusual size and taste. The Turks also enjoy eating spiny lobsters which they grill and serve with butter and lemon.

Vegetables find their way into Turkish cooking in *mezeler*, pickles, salads and stews of meat and vegetables. They are also eaten separately in side dishes, such as pureed spinach, broad beans marinated in olive oil and white beans in light tomato sauce. Turks only eat vegetables that are in season, grown

spring but fish is fairly expensive in Turkey, so the price quoted by the waiter will probably be a per kilo price and not a portion price.

Flatfish: Along the Aegean Coast tasty *ton balığı* (small tuna) are best simply grilled and served with lemon. Sword fish caught in deep water are often grilled on skewers with tomatoes, green peppers and onions, while smaller *dil* (sole or flatfish) are grilled whole. One of the best fish from Izmir is the *trança* (halibut) which is cooked in the oven (*buğulaması*) with tomatoes, peppers, onions and *kaşar* cheese and served in the pan. This dish is usually shared by several diners. Another unusual dish, found further down

locally and of high quality. Wandering through any village market you will witness Turkish women selecting with care fruits and vegetables that have just been picked. After a tour of the market you will know what to order for a vegetable dish at a restaurant in the evening. If sweet peas are in season as in early summer or baby okra or the sweet pimento peppers of the south in the autumn, order these and you will be highly satisfied. Unusual twists added to the stock of Mediterranean recipes include the Turkish version of Greek *mousaka* made with layers of cauliflower instead of eggplant, stuffed marrow that are spiced with dill and mushroom caps stuffed with *pastırma* and cheese. Marrow is also used to stuff *börek* in Afyon and Denizli, and eggplant *börek* is common in Mersin.

Turkish cooking knows no limits when it comes to preparing rice, and other grains in *pilavs*. *Pilav* is the quintessential Turkish food. *Pilav*, originating in China, made its way along the ancient silk road west through Turkestan to Anatolia. There are over one hundred recipes for hot rice, bulgur wheat and *kuskus* (egg dough in small pellets). Dishes are cooked with butter or olive oil and the simplest is plain rice served with chickpeas called *düğün pilavı* (wedding rice), popular all over Turkey. If you like liver try

season – figs, water melons, peaches and apricots - sliced and arranged artfully on a plate, or one of the more elaborate and tempting Turkish desserts. Many restaurants do not make their own dessert and instead the diner can finish his meal over Turkish coffee while a waiter races to the local *pastane* (pastry shop) to buy you something fresh. Most meat restaurants have a selection of milk-based puddings and sweet desserts. Ice cream is popular along the south coast – favorite flavors include regional ripe fruits and nuts. The Bamyacı Ice Cream Parlor in Alanya is perhaps the most well- known ice cream maker in Turkey. The parlor serves two dozen flavors,

iç pilav, rice cooked with currants, nuts, bits of liver and flavored with cinnamon. *Mantı*, often called Turkish ravioli, are tiny lamb filled dumplings cooked in broth and served with a garlicky yogurt sauce and butter steeped in red peppers. These small packages, popular when the weather turns cool, should be enjoyed by all traveling companions together because of their intense garlic content.

Dessert anyone? After a rich Turkish meal the only room left may be for the fruits in

Left, *Adana kebab*. **Above**, *baklava*, a Turkish pastry.

including *Kahramanmaraş* ice cream. This is made by pounding milk for hours with a long metal peg. In Antalya look for cinnamon cones filled with ice cream and dipped in chocolate. Antalya also hosts some of the best pastry shops specializing in *baklava* with pistachio and *kaymak* (clotted cream) baked inside layers of flaky pastry.

Bodrum boasts golden morsels called *lokma*, which are fried doughnuts drizzled with syrup sold from stands which line the white streets. With Turkish coffee, the weary traveler can try one of the sweet, heavily flavored Turkish liquors or the local brandy and cognac.

The words,"Wanna buy a Turkish carpet? Come into my shop, it won't cost you anything. Just have a look," may be the first words that a tourist hears in the bazaars or on the streets of Turkey. Whether the salesman knows much English or not, these sentences are spoken eloquently and persuade the sometimes unwary customer into a purchase even when there was no intention of buying.

Handwoven carpets and flatweaves are perhaps the most available and widespread sale items in Turkey. Admired worldwide, Turkish handwoven coverings – for walls, floors, even tables are the best known of Turkish export items.

Turkish rugs are most easily found in tourist areas – sold in large commercial shops, small boutiques and even on the street. Carpet salesmen can be the most aggressive and, at the same time, the most hospitable of all salesmen in Turkey. Tea – regular or apple – or coffee is always part of the ceremony involved in the purchase of a carpet. The salesmen pull down from the numerous orderly piles literally hundreds of carpets which they throw at the feet of potential customers, one by one, with studied aplomb. And as the traveler soon learns, every salesman is an "expert."

Historical background: Oriental carpets have for centuries been considered works of art. Great speculation over the origin of knotted carpet weaving and the earliest dates of flatweaves is an interesting intellectual exercise. Suffice it to say that in Central Asia the Turkic nomads were most influential in the origin and spread of this art and they are maintaining that position of prominence even today. Along with the fame of the oriental carpet is the newly discovered and recognized fame of the less classical flatweaves or *kilims,* as they are generally called.

Unlike its competitors for the tourist market – ceramics, copperware and recently, leather goods – a woven item lives and grows

with association. Purchasing a woven item is akin to buying a friend for life. Each woven piece is the unique expression of the weaver which becomes the unique expression of the buyer and user. Quality carpets and rugs, like good wine, age gracefully if they are taken care of; the color and gloss become heightened in the carpet, the motifs and color harmony of the flatweaves mellow and gain warmth. Muted colors often result from the aging process, a quality that many carpet sellers feel enhance the value.

Learning where to find carpets and *kilims,* and how to judge their authenticity and quality does not require volumes of research or a special knowledge of history, although the more one learns about Turkish carpets the more one will undoubtedly want to know. Here are a few basics about Turkish carpets. These handmade articles which can be classified as textiles from the weaving and knotting process are basically of two kinds, the knotted carpet and the woven flatweave. Highly decorative, both are used as covers, and are produced on a loom with a warp (the continuous threads through the fabric) and a weft (the filler).

Preceding pages: at the carpet farm in Milas. **Left,** weaving a *kilim.* **Right,** nimble fingers work on a rug.

Knot power: The knotted carpet is made with the double Turkish or *Gördes* knot, a strong, durable knot which is tied around the warps with its ends clipped to make the resulting pile. Checking whether a carpet has been tied with this knot is very difficult once the carpet has been woven so one can only take it on faith. The *Sina* knot, common in Persian carpets, is an alternative and does produce a finer carpet since the knot is tied around a single warp rather than the double warp as in the Turkish knot.

The number of knots per square centimeter is a guide to the fineness of the carpet; the more knots the finer the carpet. The more knots the finer the weave, and generally terns are produced as the weaver winds colored weft yarn around pairs of warps. *Cicims*, *zilis* and some types of *sumak* are woven using three elements, the warp and weft and colored extra-weft wrapping or "float" yarns. In the weaving of a *cicim* usually two women work together, one at the back of the rug and one at the front. They pass the weft yarn through the warp threads working simultaneously on both sides in a "semi-wrapping" technique. The *zili* displays a "weft-float" brocading technique.

Expressing culture: Flatweaves and knotted carpets are true expressions of the indigenous culture of Turkey. They are woven throughout Anatolia and the coastal regions

speaking, the stiffer the carpet backing. A silk carpet may have 100 knots per square centimeter and can go up to 900 knots in a square centimeter. Wool carpets will have fewer with a standard of 36 knots per square centimeter.

Flatweaves or flatwoven rugs are generally called *kilims* because of the common weaving technique, but these can be further classified as true *kilims*, *cicims*, *sumaks* or *zilis* depending on the type of weave. A true *kilim* is made with a *kilim* "slit-tapestry" weave. The end result is a slit produced between the different colored areas of the rug. In the *kilim*, technique motifs and pat- by the women and young girls. They are a traditional expression of a people and their way of life and at the same time are still part of the economy of many Anatolian families. The environments out of which flatweaves and knotted-pile carpets come are different. To understand this is to understand the richness of each of the traditions which developed independently side by side. Those who weave one do not care to, nor do they traditionally, weave the other. The producers of both are artists in their own right.

Flatweaves are traditionally woven in the

Above, carpet weaving amongst ruins.

home for domestic use and result from the cultural need for coverings and containers for the nomadic tribal groups. They are lighter and more flexible compared to knotted carpets and besides being useful as wall hangings and floor coverings they appear as numerous other articles: *heybes* (saddle bags), *yastıks* (pillow covers), clothing or grain sacks, seat covers, horse trappings, cradle covers, etc. Unlike the knotted carpet which has always been a sales item to the West, or to the Turk as an investment, flatweaves have only recently begun to be produced as a sales item.

Flatweaves in general carry a great deal of symbolism and can reflect a historical context that experts now claim goes back as far as the Neolithic Period in Anatolia. The implications are social, ethnic and cultural. Some of the finest examples of these are still being woven by the Yörüks and the Avşar Turkmen of the Oğuz clan which came to Anatolia with the Seljuks in the 14th century. These groups, originally nomadic, migrated through the ages throughout Anatolia and in some places still maintain their identity and old customs. To them must be attributed the honor of having preserved some of the finest examples of flatweave art.

Symbols of life: Thus we can see that flatweaves were functional to the way of life of the Turkic nomads who migrated from Central Asia to Anatolia. They were produced to meet the needs of their living conditions – portable, functional for a tent life, practical. The women used the products easily available in their handicraft – wool and animal hair, which they made themselves. In the matter of the decoration and composition, traditionally the end product had to bespeak the very existence from which they had emerged. The motifs are a reflection of their life, and their understanding of it. This meant that a young girl may record in her weaving her concerns about finding a husband, marrying, having a family and living a long life with an assured peaceful death. The motifs traditional on the flatweaves record a story and symbolize a heritage not in writing but in weaving.

Güran Erbek, a Turkish art historian, has put it this way: "According to the Anatolian beliefs, the prayer cloth woven by a young maiden to be used by her future husband has a special meaning. The motifs produced by winding the threads around the warp present an expression of her expectations for the future: happiness, reproduction and a long life. Motifs comprise a language for the women and young maidens. Their happiness, sorrow and desires are expressed through those motifs. It is through those motifs that they display the thoughts which they cannot transform into words, which are considered inappropriate when uttered. A tomb stone on a *kilim*, generally perceived as death, is a way of saying 'I'd die if I ever have to part from my beloved.'"

Times have changed but *kilim* motifs and patterns are still personal – individually and tribally, and have changed little through the ages. As mentioned, originally they were an expression of the spiritual and religious elements in the lives of the tribal groups. The very names which continue to be used to identify them are an indication of this heritage. The meaning may not have the original significance now but as they have been passed from grandmother to grandchild they become an expression of what the weaver is. This is not as true of carpet weavers who have traditionally woven for middlemen and are given cartoons (patterns on squared paper) to weave from.

Traditional motifs: Some of the common traditional nomadic motifs still being used on flatweaves today bear out this fact: *elibelinde* (hands on hips) symbol of motherhood and fertility probably derived from the Anatolian mother goddess figure; *koçboynuzu* (ram's horn), a sign reflecting fertility, heroism, power and masculinity; *aşk ve birleşim* (love and union), an emblem related to the oriental ying-yang symbol for the harmony between male and female; *el/parmak/tarak* (hand/finger/comb), symbols to ward off the evil eye or to insure protection in birth and marriage; *nazarlık* (evil eye), a representation against the effect of an evil glance; *çengel* (hook), another symbol against the evil eye; *yılan* (snake), *ejder* (dragon), *akrep* (scorpion) all symbols indicate a desire for protection from nature, also they are signs of happiness and fertility; *kurt ağzı, kurt izi* (wolf's mouth, wolf track) protection against the wolves, the predator of sheep; *hayat ağacı* (tree of life), these stylized trees and plants stand for the desire for immortality and life after death; *çiçek* (flower) stylized motifs of roses, carnations, tulips and hyacinths reminiscent of the Garden of Eden; and *kuş* (bird) motifs evoke many things – women, love, joy, happiness, power and strength. These and many others are related to the everyday life of rural villagers or nomads and speak of their condition. No wonder they have continued to be used.

It is interesting to note that the word used by village women for motif is *"gelenek,"* which actually translates as "tradition;" a word which evokes considerably more meaning and emotion.

In knotted carpet weaving many of the same themes are used but they do not carry the same symbolic intensity of meaning. Those designs most suited to the knotting technique are used. Also, carpet designs have been more formal, emphasizing floral and complicated geometric patterns and all of these have been influenced by market tastes. Thus they have changed through the ages.

The dyes: Traditionally, weavers of both the knotted carpet and flatweaves spun their own yarn from the wool of their own sheep, and also dyed it. These dyes were natural dyes from leaves, bark, roots and fruit. Often the processes were family secrets. This practice in time has given way to use of chemical dyes. Distinguishing whether the dye used is natural or artificial in a given piece can be determined over a period of time and exposure to sunlight. Natural dyes are more highly treasured by carpet buyers as more authentic as they don't fade easily. Carpets dyed with artificial colors fade fast. One should ask a salesman if the dyes in the piece are natural or artificial, but only a real expert can dare challenge the answer and prove it.

Some experts suggest that when buying a carpet the customer should lick the corner of a handkerchief and rub it over a spot on the backside of the carpet. If it comes off colored, the dye, whatever its source, is probably not fast. This certainly is an indication that the piece will mellow with age!

The content of the warp and weft is important in the value of a handmade article. Wool – machine or hand spun – cotton, natural silk and artificial (floss) silk, camel or goat hair, can all be used. The inclusion of animal hair is infrequent but is characteristic of the flatweaves of certain tribal groups' products and the mixture of elements is more common and is used to give strength and texture rather than artistic effect. Yörük weavers use a great deal of goat hair. Some authorities claim that pure, long haired lamb's wool makes the best woven pieces. Yörük weavers prefer this. The wool from the sheep which graze on the high plateau is softer, stronger and more lustrous because of the climate and food in a grazing area.

Types and sizes: The types and sizes of knotted carpets are not strictly uniform although there are general categories. The following dimensions can help serve as a guide: *yastık* (cushion cover) 40 x 25 centimeters (small) or 100 x 60 cm (large); *çeyrek* (medium size) 135 x 60 cm; *seccade* (prayer rug) 180 x 120 cm to 200 x 130 cm. A group of larger carpets include *karyola* (bed size) 220 x 150 cm or *kelle*, 300 x 200 cm; *taban*, which is larger than six square meters; and *yolluk* (runners), come in various widths and lengths.

Flatweaves vary greatly in size and shape depending on the type. Often the shapes are defined because of the maximum width of the horizontal loom which is portable and particularly suited to the nomadic weaver.

Most carpets and flatweaves have been traditionally related to a geographic area. Sometimes they also carry the name of the group which produces them. Thus names were and continue to be carried with this nomenclature. This is changing both in interpretation by experts and also in the actual production within a given geographic area. Given motifs and styles in various carpets (especially the flatweaves) can now be produced in different sites quite independent of a geographic location. This is more true of the flatweaves.

Individual expression: Actually the original designation was probably incorrect since specific motifs, patterns and color combinations were more likely to be the expression of an individual tribal group and moved with this group as it migrated. There are of course exceptions to this. As commercialism begins to get the upper hand the conglomerate of varieties will be more evident.

The beauty of Turkish weaving design in both carpets and flatweaves is a function of color, motifs and overall composition. Its common characteristic is the repetition of geometric units. A central theme may dominate, surrounded by complimentary motifs. A favorite composition of carpets is a central diamond or medallion or two or three fringed by other motifs. On the carpets the central unit is usually contained in a border or borders. In flatweaves motifs generally are arranged on either a diagonal or vertical/horizontal axes and the composition is confined within parallel stripes extending the length of the piece.

Some nomadic groups known as Yörüks, such as the Karakeçili, Saçkarali, Sarıkeçili and Honamli, still weave their own types. The Karakeçili in the Balıkesir-Kütahya region weave their typical group designs as do the Yüncü Yörüks. The latter group mainly winters in the south on the skirts of the Taurus Mountains but spends their sum-

rounding areas continue south to Denizli, Isparta down to Antalya. Some *parmaklı* (finger) *kilims* common in Eskişehir, Afyon and Kütahya continue as far as Isparta and Burdur, but don't go further south. The *elibe-linde* motif, widespread in central Anatolia appears quite uniquely in a typical theme of the Antalya region. The *gülbudak* rose motif on the other hand is unchanged throughout the country.

Hereke silk: In Hereke, just east of Istanbul on the Sea of Marmara, the finest woven carpets in Anatolia are produced. That is, they are made with quality control and have the most knots per square centimeter. Hereke carpets are of two types, wool and

mers in the pasturelands between Egridir and Lake Burdur. The groups originally moved or were moved from their lands in central and eastern Anatolia during various upheavals in the Ottoman period. Thus the designs have migrated with them.

The effect of these migrations, the heritage of earlier periods – perhaps Neolithic, Phrygian – and those earlier motifs brought in from the western islands can be seen on western flatweaves. The snow-tooth-edged diamond designs common in Eskişehir, Afyon, Kütahya, Afyon, Nevşehir and sur-

Above, giving the sales pitch at a carpet shop.

pure silk. The wool carpets generally have 36 knots per square centimeter while the silk range from 100 to 196. Their designs are mainly copies of classical floral Turkish or Persian carpets or new creations by contemporary designers. At one end of each carpet the name Hereke is woven in. In earlier times this was in Arabic script.

Carpets from the Çanakkale region near the Dardanelles are generally woven in the villages of Ezine or Ayvacık. Many still have traditional designs dating to the 16th and 17th century famous *"Holbein"* carpets, so called because the rugs were depicted in several of Hans Holbein's paintings. A typical composition consists of one to three rectangular medallions surrounded by geometric motifs usually on a red field or, rarely, on a yellow field.

Bergama carpets have geometric compositions similar to the Çanakkale ones, but the colors are darker shades of red and blue. Kozak carpets are also related but are smaller in size. They may have *mihrap* (prayer) niches, single or mirrored in the middle field. In structure the knots are thick and visible and give the carpets a soft texture.

Brighter colors: Yuntdağ carpets, though similar in composition, have brighter colors such as strong green and even sometimes purple. The most familiar design is two by

dominate not only the prayer niches but also in the borders. Present production, though good, does not match the earlier masterpieces. The weave is always fine, 16 to 36 knots in a square centimeter. Sometimes these carpets have a cotton warp.

Yatak carpets: Çal (Denizli) is famous for its traditional large-sized Yatak carpets. Using strong yellow, black, blue and some red on a cotton warp, they exhibit a long, shiny pile. The field of the carpet is plain with scattered rozettes and squarish forms. The traditional carpets are rare today and hard to find.

Karakeçeli carpets do not belong to any specific region but are woven in western

three or four squares of different colors formed by intersecting bands.

Yağcıbedir carpets are woven in the Balıkesir region mainly in the settlements of Yörük tribal groups, the Yağcıbedir. These carpets are easily recognizable because the main colors are dark red, dark blue and ivory. The single or mirrored prayer niches are filled with stylized leaves, flowers and stars. These all have both a wool warp and weft.

The towns of Kula and Gördes were particularly famous in the 18th and 19th centuries. Even today they are known for their finely woven and elaborately designed prayer rugs *(seccade)*. Floral forms pre-

Anatolia in the Manisa, Kütahya, Balıkesir and Eskişehir regions by tribal segments of the Karakeçeli. The characteristic features of their carpets are a lustrous long and soft pile in red, blue and white and a composition of multi-hooked diamond shapes. Closely related to these are the Yüncü carpets formerly woven by nomad Yörük or Yüncü tribal segments in the Balıkesir region. Generally they are of finer weaves and have double multi-hooked diamond motifs.

Usually Milas carpets have either a single prayer niche or two or three narrow mirror

Left, an ancient rug. **Right**, a modern silk carpet.

image niches with stylized floral forms. The older carpets were bright red, blue, green and yellow but today the common colors are soft brown, beige, yellow and pastel shades. The warp can either be wool or cotton.

Döşemealti carpets: The most important carpets of the Antalya region come from the villages of Kovacik and Şağıoba in the Döşemealtı region, the latter being the common name for the whole group. The yarn for both the weft and warp is of plateau wool and the predominant colors are red and blue, the dyes being produced from the local plants.

The Dobağ Project of the University of the Marmara which is trying to introduce natural vegetable dyes in the area around Balıkesir has been most successful in encouraging the women to continue their home production with better dye stuffs. An example of the new interest in the preservation and recreation of carpets and *kilims* is *TEH*, Turkish Hand-woven Carpets. This new project under the supervision and guidance of the Ministry of Culture and Tourism specializes in the production and sales of Turkish handwoven knotted-carpets and flatweaves. With the aid of computers, historic woven pieces have been collected in photographs, coded, classified and catalogued and in some cases reconstructed from museum fragments or even paintings and are being handwoven by expert weavers using natural dyed yarns of shetland, merino, sheep's wool and silk.

Güran Erbek, the author of the beautiful sales catalogue of flatweaves for this project, mentions that the research on specimens and motifs – in particular their meaning, took the research team to 9,000 villages where they interviewed 110,000 weavers. The collecting and bringing to light of the thoughts of these village women in itself is indicative of the high regard now being shown for this unique Anatolian art form.

The Net group: The setting up of commercial centers for the production and sales of carpets and rugs is a way to meet the economic challenge. One such is the Tavas Center built by the Net Group of Companies, one of the world's largest producers and exporters of carpets, just 14 miles (24 km) from Denizli. The center, besides its vast sales area, includes dyeing, designing and weaving workshops where local village girls presently weave on 80 looms. Net, which operates the Bazaar 54 chain of gift shops

and carpet sellers, also has a commercial carpet production center in Sultanköy, near Kuşadası. Net also produces quality pure silk carpets at a workshop in suburban Istanbul. These kinds of centers are not unusual in urban settings, and are now becoming part of the scene at touristic crossroads.

The most unique carpet display center in the world is undoubtedly the Ildız Carpet Farm, near Bodrum, six miles (10 km) from Milas. Set up by the Ildız Company, a large producer and carpet exporter, it is the world's only carpet farm. Ildız opened the farm in 1984 to revive carpet making in Milas, a traditional weaving center. It is located in a dry, almost rain-free region.

At the farm, experts wash and dry under the sun tens of thousands of handmade wool carpets manufactured or bought by the Ildız Company, an Istanbul-based concern which owns the Tribal Art Carpet Shops chain. Ildız, which operates 3,000 looms throughout Turkey, specializes in the manufacture of pastel-colored Milas wool carpets, using natural root dyes. The 17-acre farm is capable of drying as many as 20,000 carpets at one time. The best time to visit the farm is in the early summer when thousands of carpets are spread out on the ground, like a huge colorful mosaic.

The carpets are brought there from the different villages of Milas, Bodrum and other Turkish cities. Their backsides are burned until they become charcoal black. The carpets then are washed with a special shampoo and vinegar, dried in a gigantic centrifuge, and spread out under the sun for as long as three months. The colors of natural dyed carpets don't fade, but some of the artificial colored ones do so quickly. The carpets are classified into five catagories according to the degree of color fading and then priced. Carpets whose colors have faded sell at lower prices.

A recent survey of changing village social patterns has revealed that instead of a decrease in the number of village women weaving, there is an increase. With greater mechanization of the agricultural processes and an increase in demand as well as better labor reimbursement standards, the women are turning to weaving in order to supplement their village income. This helps them gain a sense of individual worth and personal income in a highly inflationary economy.

ANTIQUITIES SMUGGLING

Since the days of Henrich Schliemann and his discovery of Troy, Turkey's antiquities have been plundered by treasure hunters, crooks and smugglers, all out to make a fast buck.

Visitors to such places ranging from the Metropolitan Museum in New York City and the Dumberton Oaks Museum in Washington D.C. to the Pergamum Museum in East Berlin and the Louvre Museum in Paris will find thousands of ancient artifacts that were illegally exported from Turkey.

Turkish archaeologist Mehmet Önder says there are as many Turkish treasures in foreign museums as there are in Turkey.

"What cocaine smuggling is to Bolivia, antiquities smuggling is to Turkey," Thomas P.F. Hoving, the former director of the New York Metropolitan Museum, once told a newspaper interviewer.

Turkey has been the home of 38 civilizations, ranging from the Hittites to the Turks. With an estimated 20,000 monuments and sites of archaeological importance in Turkey registered with the Ministry of Culture, the country has the richest deposits of subterranean and submarine antiquities in the world. Many of these ancient sites are located in uninhabited, isolated areas. They have not yet been excavated or protected, leaving them open to treasure hunters and smugglers. Turkish officials say that the smuggling of Anatolian antiquities will continue as long as there is a demand for old art objects.

Illicit exports: "The illicit export of antiquities is still going on in Turkey," Ekrem Akurgal, a distinguished Turkish archaeologist and a senior member of the Turkish Historical Society, said in a recent interview. "The enormous demand for historical art objects by rich people in developed and prosperous countries is the major factor encouraging clandestine digs and illicit commerce of antiquities." Akurgal said the invaluable remains of the great civilizations of Anatolia are "national property" and must be uncovered only by experts, and "art objects must be left where they originally stood."

In some cases in the 19th century, the rape of Turkey's archaeological wealth was tacitly approved by weak Ottoman sultans, kowtowing to western European governments. European diplomats, abetted by their governments, removed tons of statuary, entire buildings and city walls from ancient sites along the Turkish Coast.

Charles Fellows, who served as the British Consul in Asia Minor in the 1840s, with the support of the British Navy, carried off many exquisite pieces of sculpture and entire friezes to the British Museum in London,

from ancient ruins on the Turkish Coast. Two of the most magnificent items he stripped and removed that are now exhibited at the British Museum are the Nereid Monument, a magnificent Lycian tomb, and the original reliefs of the famous Harpies Tomb, both from Xanthus in southwest Turkey. The reliefs of the Harpies Tomb show the foul smelling female monsters carrying away dead children.

The Mausoleum: Another collection from Turkey that found its way to the British

Above, removing amphoras from the sea bottom is considered an act of smuggling.

Museum through government-sanctioned trafficking of antiquities is: the remains of the Mausoleum of Halicarnassus, one of the Seven Wonders of the Ancient World, including 17 slabs of Amazonamachy (a battle between the Greeks and the Amazons) and the statues of King Mausolus and his wife Artemesia the Younger.

Modern day Turks reject the Ottoman government's giveaways and demand that all relics found in Turkey which have been stolen should be returned.

The Turkish mafia: Authorities believe that the Turkish mafia, with its strong international drug and gun running connections, is involved in the smuggling of antiquities from Anatolia, using poor peasant farmers and treasure hunters and bribing officials for illegal digs. The Culture Ministry says there are more than 100 treasure hunters in Turkey, of which only a few are officially sanctioned to excavate in narrowly confined plots of land. Most of the treasure hunters use sophisticated metal detectors to locate old coins. Once the objects are taken out of the country they are sold to major art dealers in Europe and the United States and then sold to private collectors or museums.

Fake statues, coins and busts abound, and even experts have difficulty in distinguishing forged objects. These fakes can be found anywhere in Turkey from the Covered Bazaar in Istanbul to various sites along the coast.

Retaliatory steps: The Turkish government has begun to take retaliatory steps to get many of the antiquities back, including taking foreign museums to court and threatening to suspend current excavations by American and European archaeologists. It has tightened regulations governing private treasure hunting and severely increased the penalties for individuals convicted of smuggling antiquities. A person convicted of antiquities smuggling could face a prison sentence of from five to ten years.

It has also restricted scuba diving in the Aegean and the Mediterranean to reduce the smuggling of treasures from shipwrecks. Diving, for instance, is strictly forbidden where ancient shipwrecks exist. The Institute of Nautical Archaeology, an affiliate of Texas A.M. University, has mapped out more than 125 ancient shipwrecks along the Turkish Coast.

Using diplomatic pressure, the government succeeded, for instance, in getting East Germany to agree to return 7,400 Hittite cuneiform tablets that had been taken out of the country by German archaeologists at the turn of the century from the Hittite city of Boğazköy, near the central Anatolian provincial capital of Yozgat, for cleaning and coding. During 1940, Germany returned 3,000 of the tablets, but after World War II, the remaining tablets stayed in what then became East Germany.

The Kharun treasures: Turkey has also sued the Metropolitan Museum for the return of a 2,600-year-old collection of gold and silver antiques, known as the Kharun Treasures. The 189 pieces were initially dug up in the western Turkish province of Uşak by villagers in 1966, and sold to an international antiques dealer who eventually sold them to the museum for $1.7 million.

Ankara is also trying to get art collectors in the United States to return 1,900 silver coins, known as the Elmalı Treasures, that were removed from a village near Antalya.

Turkish authorities, however, have never been able to recover the gold treasures removed by Heinrich Schliemann. The treasures ended up in Berlin and were believed to be destroyed during the bombing of the city during World War II. Nor has the Turkish government been able to persuade the East German authorities to return the relics stripped from Pergamum in the 19th century and now exhibited in the Pergamum Museum in East Berlin. One of the most important buildings that was removed stone by stone and rebuilt at the Museum is the so-called Altar of Zeus, a magnificent temple of the Hellenistic period.

The Dorak affair: The most spectacular artifacts smuggling in recent years took place in the late 1950s and was known as the Dorak Affair – so named since the unusual gold jewelry were from the village of Dorak near Bursa. The incident tarnished the reputation of James Melaart, a controversial British archaeologist, who claimed that a Greek woman showed him the treasures in Izmir. The treasures were never found, the woman disappeared, and the authorities, suspecting Melaart's involvement, permanently suspended his excavations at Neolithic sites in Turkey. Melaart was suspected of smuggling the artifacts out of the country.

"A sense of freedom in the heart of nature" has come to be the motto of a number of holiday villages which have sprouted along the Aegean and Mediterranean shores of Turkey. Not long ago for most Turks vacationing meant visiting friends and relatives in some other city. With the start of the tourism development, the concept of vacationing began to change. In the summers, Turks started going to seaside resorts in the wake of the construction of hundreds of hotels and pensions on the Turkish Coast.

go to the Turkish vacation resorts in search of the basic four S's: sun, sea, sand and sex.

In the early 1970s, Club Méditerranée of France, Italy's Valtur Tourism Organization and the Turkish state tourism concern, Turban, were the first to open sprawling, vacation village resorts in what were then little known, rarely visited romantic settings in Turkey, such as Foça, (north of Izmir) and Kemer (south of Antalya), Kuşadası (south of Izmir) and Marmaris. Today these sites

The four S's: The development of holiday villages in the 1970s and 1980s came as a novelty. In Turkey, as in other countries, the idea of holiday villages was born out of peoples' longings not only to enjoy the sea but increasingly to get away from the noise, pollution and the humdrum of big cities. Holiday villages are characterized by remoteness from most of the blessings of modern life, such as crowds, television and elevators. To overworked, tense city people, vacationing at a holiday village represents an opportunity to get away from all the stress and return to nature, where humans were originally meant to live. Europeans tend to

are bustling resorts offering dozens of five-star accommodations.

The pioneers: Since the mid 1980s, sparked by Turkey's tourism boom, more than two dozen holiday villages have gone up along the Turkish Coast, mostly Turkish-owned, modeled after Club Med, but less sophisticated than the pioneers. In 1988, there were 40 holiday villages in Turkey with a bed capacity of 20,300. Construction is continuing on another 60 resorts that will double Turkey's vacation village bed capacity by the end of 1992. Most of the villages are rated first class, such as Club Letoonia, in Fethiye, now operated by Club Med, but there are several "second class" resorts that provide fewer sporting activities and less hedonistic living.

Even the big name, international hotel concerns are getting into the act. The Ramada Renaissance Antalya is one example of a hotel which has gone holiday village.

Most of the vacation villages have been built around Antalya and the lower Aegean coastal strip, which is famous for its stunning surroundings and favorable climate with an average 300 days of sunshine in a year.

A Tourism Ministry license is needed to establish a holiday village. Official regulations state holiday villages must be set up "in

a suitable touristic area or close to archaeological sites while providing various sporting and recreational activities next to comfortable accommodations and satisfying food."

Horses and donkeys: With competition growing everyday, the villages try to outdo one another with an array of sporting activities, including tennis, windsurfing, rowing, waterskiing, bicycling and sailing. Sometimes organizers have horse and donkey riding expeditions and hiking tours into the

Left, lights flicker at a coastal holiday village. **Above**, the Golden Dolphin Hotel in Çeşme.

nearby mountains. One holiday village, soon to be established in European Turkey, will have an 18-hole golf course open to international tournaments.

These recreational activities whether inside or outside the villages, are cleverly aimed at making the guests enjoy themselves and spend more money, contributing to the organizations' profits.

Another way to keep people out of their rooms is to make the rooms small, rather dark. A room to sleep or change in, and nothing else.

Children's heaven: A blessing in most of the Turkish-run holiday villages is that, unlike their foreign counterparts where sometimes children below the age of seven are not accepted, these are heavens for little children. The Tourism Ministry requires the Turkish villages to have special play areas and safe, shallow swimming pools for kids.

To protect the guests and maintain a clubbish atmosphere, holiday villages don't allow outsiders to enter the premises and security is strict. Vacationers at holiday villages regard highly the buffet-style food served in the open. They relish the rich variety of cuisine served with emphasis on fresh salads, vegetables and local dishes.

The Marmaris Holiday Village is considered the best in the Turban chain, which operates 22 villages, hotels and marinas, all of which are up for privatisation. It is located near the resort town of Marmaris at the confluence of the Mediterranean and Aegean. With 230 bungalows scattered among pine trees and pink and white oleander shrubs, the Marmaris Holiday Village is a favorite haunt for upper class Turks.

Flamboyant businessman: The luxurious Martı Holiday Village nearby is owned and operated by Halit Narin, a flamboyant textiles magnate and president of the Turkish Employers Association, and generally serves an upper class clientele. Resembling a medieval château from the sea, the Martı has spacious bedrooms with mini-bars, colorful curtains on windows with matching bed covers.

Along the beautiful stretch of beach from Kemer to Antalya are dozens of villages, including Club Salima, the Ramada Renaissance, Club Alda, and further down on the eastern coast, Club Robinson and Club Scandinavia.

Surf's up in Turkey and there are a dozen ways to make a splash along its coastline as this aquatic playground aspires to be *"California gibi"* (like California, like wow), offering a plethora of hydra-hype. Choose your weapon: catamarans, lasers and windsurfers skim in between waterski boats and sea cycles, which dodge bobbing snorkelers who float in fear of careening banana boats, forever on a collision course with noisy jet skis, the bane of the beach.

If the water gets too crowded, rise above it all, strapped onto a parachute and yanked to the sky by speedboat, for a gull's-eye view of the bikinis and local sand sharks below.

Beach Blanket Bingo: It was only a matter of time before Turkey created its own version of Beach Blanket Bingo. The arrival of acid color surfer shorts in every mom and pop shop from Ayvalık to Iskenderun was a hint that day-glo Body Glove suits were just a tidal wave away.

In general, watersports have become the domain of the holiday villages which line Turkey's coast and which offer offer a wide range of sports activities and instruction patterned after the Club Med concept. Available sports activities include waterskiing, windsurfing, sailing, snorkeling, canoeing and usually one gimmick – the conspicuous rubber water weenie, ridiculous sea tractor or geriatric paddleboat. Some clubs offer scuba diving, like Club Alda in Beldibi, Kemer, which offers PADI diving instruction taught by PADI certified teachers.

Where the clubs do differ, unfortunately, is in their attention to safety. In their haste to attract package tours, many resorts use inadequate sports equipment and untrained staff. Club Alda maintains safety is its number one rule and is Turkey's only member of Club Intersport, a Swiss sports organization which presides over Club Alda's activities and staff. Club Alda prohibits parasailing on its rocky beach but adventurers can set sail next door at Club Salima or the Ramada Renaissance Resort.

Sea life abounds: Scuba diving is gaining popularity in Turkey, especially off the coast of Marmaris where the confluences of the Mediterranean and Aegean meet.

Foreigners must always be accompanied by a Turkish dive guide and diving must be within posted legal boundaries. Much of the country's coast is off-limits to underwater activity in order to preserve its rich history, as priceless antiquities: amphoras, statuary and shipwrecks, dot the shoreline. To dive within the law, ask the local tourism office for the government's diving *"harita."* Don't push your luck: if you are seen even wearing diving equipment in restricted areas, chances are you'll be invited to spend the

night in jail.

Dive centers are located along the coastline in major tourism centers but not all are recommended by professional divers. Centers that received the thumbs-up include Companie and Barracuda in Bodrum, the dive center at the Turban Resort in Marmaris, and Heinz and Gabi's center at the Akman Hotel in Çamyuva, Kemer.

PADI certified: The Scuba Shop in Istanbul is a good place to start if planning a dive in Turkey. The PADI certified staff runs all levels of instruction and can arrange your dive excursion or put you in touch with a recommended center along the Aegean or

Mediterranean. Before making a dive with your guide, ask to see credentials: either a PADI or CMAS card and an updated Turkish diving license (*Rehber Balık Adam Lisansı*). Turkey has three decompression chambers, should the unfortunate need arise. One is in Bodrum, the other in Çeşme and the third at the naval complex in Çubuklu, Istanbul. But, like many other things, they are only as good as the people who operate them.

River rafting has not yet surfaced as an organized sport in Turkey although two rivers are excellent potential for white-water fun. Club Robinson in Side offers one-day "float trips" down scenic Köprü Çayı (Bridge River) near Selge. Guests float

rafting gear, but if you have your own equipment, contact Silifke's Tourism Office for assistance in planning a river trip. Find out if a permit is required to enter the river and take a local guide along who not only swims, but knows the river well. Don't forget Barbarossa's fate – wear a life jacket. (The German Emperor drowned while bathing in the Göksu.)

Windsurfing has become an art form along Turkey's beaches as carnival-colored Fanatic and Mistral sails cut graceful arcs across the bays and coves. The Gümbet area of Bodrum is an ideal spot with a number of sheltered bays that channel steady winds. The area is full of shops that specialize in the

down the river in small rubber boats, passing under the shadows of vertical canyons and cliffs and stopping periodically for picnics and water games.

Barbarossa's fate: The Göksu River flows from the Taurus Mountains to Silifke on the coast, slicing through one of the most beautiful valleys in Turkey. The river is ideal for rafting excursions but tour agencies have been slow to capitalize on its currents, leaving the fun to local children and kayaks. There aren't any places in Turkey that rent

<u>**Left**</u>, marine life as seen by scuba divers. <u>**Above**</u>, champion windsurfer takes time out.

seemingly impossible sport.

Bird watching: Perhaps the most favored of all sports is "bird watching," a seasonal, predominately male recreation which reaches its hormonal zenith at Kadınlar Plajı (Women's Beach) in Kuşadası. During summer, hundreds of Speedo-clad hopefuls jam the beach, cheek to cheek, on a less-than-respectful sightseeing mission. (*Topless tourist var mı?*) The few unfortunate women who end up on this stretch of sand become the center of undesirable attentions as the boys leer, lurk and lunge while vying for viewing position. Even squids have better manners.

Be it to enjoy the flowers, the birds, the insects, the landscape, or just the silence of a stretch of untouched beach, visitors traveling along the Turkish Coast will surely get their share of the best of Turkey. Although many areas, especially on the Aegean Coast, have been recently converted into modern tourist resorts, a score of deserted and mostly clean bays, beaches and real Mediterranean maquis (shrub lands) can be discovered by individuals who leave the better known and trodden pathways. Hundreds of books the size of this guide would not be enough to describe all the beautiful natural sites and abundant wildlife found on the Turkish Coast. But here are highlights of places where nature, rare birds and wildlife can easily be observed.

Bird watchers' paradise: Starting off in northwestern Thracian Turkey is Lake Gala, near Enez, on the Meriç (Maritsa) delta, separating Turkey and Greece. The area is rich in rare birds, including the Shag *Phalacrocorax aristelis*, the Bittern *Bautaurus stellaris*, the Glossy Ibis *Plegadis falcinellus*, and the Greyling Goose *Anser anser*. Bird watchers from all over the world come to this area to observe these endangered species.

Foreigners must get permission from the kaymakamlık, the county commissioner's office in Enez, to go on a bird watching expedition in the border area. The Turkish-Greek border is one of the most heavily guarded regions in the country. Trekkers should also avoid taking cameras and remember the fate of two eccentric British bird watchers who were detained in Enez for two months in 1983 on charges of espionage, after they were caught taking pictures of rare birds in a military zone. (The two men were later freed.)

Bird migration route: The Dardanelles is one of the world's main routes for bird migrations. Together with the Bosphorus, it is the only place in Turkey where Europe and Asia are separated by a narrow stretch of open water. This is important for the large migratory birds which, in order to save energy, use uprising warm air – the so-called thermals – to soar to high altitudes and then to glide downwards, thus traveling many miles with-

out beating their wings once. These thermals only occur above narrow straits and this explains why large, soaring migratory birds like storks and birds of prey converge at those bottlenecks. During August, September and October, large numbers of birds may be seen flying over the Dardanelles on their way from northern Europe to warmer climates for the winter. A good strong pair of binoculars will help the bird watcher observe the seasonal migration.

When you cross the Dardanelles by ferryboat, you might notice small groups of flying birds which follow the bends of the strait, flying so close to the water's surface that their wings seem to touch the waves. These are Shearwaters, until recently called Manx Shearwater but now generally referred to as Yelkouan Shearwater *Puffinus yelkouan*. Although for probably thousands of years these amazing birds have been flying every day from the Black Sea to the Aegean and vice versa, their exact breeding places are still unknown. Ornithologists (bird scientists) assume that the Yelkouan Shearwaters breed on the cliffs of the Black Sea and that their main feeding grounds are in the Aegean, necessitating hundreds of miles of travel each day.

Environment endangered: Traveling further south brings the nature observer to large stretches of maquis, the more original type of Mediterranean vegetation, which covers an area that begins at the Bay of Edremit and continues south as far as Izmir Bay.

Maquis is in fact a low shrub community, consisting of small trees and bushes two to four yards (two to four meters) high, ideal for nesting of some bird species, such as the Little Bustard *Tetrax tetrax*. Some typical plant species found in this region are Cistus species, tree heather, rosemary, thyme and juniper. Maquis is used extensively by the local inhabitants as a source of fuel wood, animal fodder and dye for clothing.

Unfortunately, in many places this vegetation has been replaced by more stony areas with low rounded bushes, caused by irresponsible cutting of the original shrubs and subsequent overgrazing by sheep and goats that stunts the recovery of most plants and trees. If the degeneration cycle intensifies further, environmentalists argue that most of the shrub will disappear, turning the region into true steppe country. If water were to flush down the top soil quickly, it would create a land that is of no use for men and wildlife; but fortunately, this stage is encountered only sporadically on the Turkish Coast.

Swampy marshland: One of the least known but most rich bird sanctuaries of Turkey is the Çamaltı Tuzlası, a big swampy marshland along the northwestern part of Izmir Bay. Heavy industrial pollution in Izmir Bay is threatening the 182 bird species known to live, breed or winter in Çamaltı Tuzlası. This

and thin, straight bill, and the Avocet *Recurvirostra avosetta*, known for its long legs and upturned bill. Izmir municipal authorities have given priority to the clean up of the Bay of Izmir and have instituted a project which includes a new sewage system and dredging the bottom of the bay.

One of the most endangered wetlands on the Turkish Coast is the Küçük Menderes (the Little Maeander) River delta between Izmir and Ephesus, around the district known as Pamucak. A dozen hotels have already gone up and others are under construction – activity that is likely to scare away many of the rare birds that breed there. The region is a breeding ground for the

marshland is a wintering ground for the graceful Flamingo *Phoenicopterus ruber* – as many as 3,000 flamingos were counted in the area recently by Turkish ornithologists, and the Dunlin *Calidris alpina*, large flocks of which come down to the area while migrating from tundra lands in Northern Europe.

Other birds that nest in Çamaltı Tuzlası are the Black-winged Stilt *Himantopus himantopus*, unmistakable with long pale red legs

Preceding pages: white pelicans in the Göksu delta. **Above**, the kingfisher, commonly encountered on the coast.

Squocco Heron *Ardeola ralloides*, a brownish bird that spends its days perched on tree tops.

Anatolian leopard: South of Izmir, after Kuşadası is the Dilek National Park on the Dilek Peninsula. The area consists of high peaks, deep canyons, and has a rocky coastline. This area was one of the last known habitats of the Anatolian Leopard *Panthera pardus tulliana* that still lived in the 1970s but that has become virtually extinct due to human pressure. The Booted Eagle *Hieraaetus pennatus* is a breeding bird found in the national park's pine forests, and there are several breeding pairs of the Peregrine Hawk

Falco Peregrinus. Outside the breeding season Eleonora's Falcons *Falco eleonorae* can be seen nesting on the rocky islands off Dilek Peninsula. Part of the National Park is managed for tourism.

A little further to the south is the Büyük Menderes (Maeander) River delta. A large part of the delta has been cultivated with cotton as the principal crop. The Menderes River has attractive vegetation, including the characteristic tamarix, trees or shrubs with slender branches and feathery flower clusters, common near salt water and often grown as a windbreak. The Menderes River delta is the breeding place of, amongst others, the Dalmatian Pelican *Pelicanus cris-*

ciconia and the Little Egret are some of the birds that breed and winter along Bafa Gölü, famous for the ruins of Heraclea and the Sanctuary of Endymion. Villagers who inhabit the eastern shores of Bafa Gölü are known to hunt birds on the lake as well as in the mountains, threatening bird populations in the area.

The Bodrum region is a renowned resort that, regrettably, now suffers from uncontrolled building development. The coastline is covered with houses and hotels, some of which drain off their sewage untreated into the Aegean.

Marine turtles: The complex wetland system comprising Köyceğiz Lake, the reed

pus, an endangered species with a world population of less than 2,000. In winter, the delta holds large numbers of wintering waterfowl, including many species of duck, geese and Great White Egrets *Egretta alba*. The delta is a famous hunting area, and the subsequent disturbance of all wildlife has been noted by national and international environmentalists as immense.

South of the Büyük Menderes River, but north of Bodrum, is Bafa Gölü, a lake region at the foot of ancient Mount Latmus, known today as the Beş Parmak Dağı (The Five Finger Mountain). The Short-toed Eagle *Circaetius gallicus*, the White Stork *Ciconia*

beds and marshes between Dalyan and the beach at Iztuzu, form a unique combination of different habitats encountered nowhere else in the Mediterranean. Apart from its ecological importance, the area is certainly one of the most attractive places on the Turkish Coast. The Iztuzu Beach is a major breeding ground for the Loggerhead Sea Turtle *Caretta caretta*, and in 1986 and 1987 the national and international conservation movement succeeded in stopping the construction of a 3,000-bed hotel on the beach. Noise and lights from the hotel, environmentalists argued, would endanger the newly-hatched turtles, which would get lost and head inland instead of seeking the safety of the sea.

In 1988, the area was declared a Specially Protected Zone by the Turkish government. During 1989, the state Environmental Affairs Office, in cooperation with a German conservation organization (AGA) and the Turkish Society for the Protection of Nature (DHKD), took additional measures to protect the magnificent Loggerhead Sea Turtles. A demarcation line on the beach protects the nests with the eggs, buried about 20 inches (50 centimeters) under the surface, and no- one is allowed at night on the beach during the July-September breeding season. The adult female loggerhead may weigh 300

A walk along the 2.8-mile (4.5-km) long Iztuzu Beach is rewarding, starting off on the eastern tip and ending in the west where one can get a lift from a fishing boat to Dalyan village. During the high season, volunteers from DHKD show videos on the life of the sea turtles in an information center in Dalyan, and informative leaflets and posters are handed out in the village and on the beach.

More turtles: The Dalaman Beach area, further southeast holds even more turtles than the Dalyan area. It is completely unprotected, according to a report prepared by the World Wide Fund for Nature. The only tourist development on this long beach is in the

to 400 pounds (136 to 181 kg.) The female nests three or four times in a single season.

Any kind of housing or hotel development that would drive away the female turtles and upset the hatchlings is prohibited. In 1989, the breeding success of the turtles was remarkably high, and the Dalyan story can be considered a big victory for conservation that serves now as a model for other areas and countries with important nesting beaches for marine turtles.

<u>Left</u>, pegs show bathers where marine turtles' eggs are incubating and mark the no-entry zone. <u>Above</u>, a marine turtle wades ashore.

Sarıgerme region. But Dalaman River, which empties into the beach area, is being severely polluted by wastes from the state Seka paper plant. The pollution, the report says, threatens the health of both turtles and humans, requiring immediate solution.

Just south of Antalya is the Olympus National Park, a large scenic area covered with pine and cedar forests, which is good for trekking and mountain climbing. Until recently, the National Park extended all the way down to the sea to protect one of the last breeding sites of the Monk Seal *Monachus monachus*, a 10-foot-long marine mammal that has become extinct in most Mediterranean countries in recent years. The Monk Seal needs coastal caves with an underwater entrance, and is extremely sensitive to human disturbances like fishing and dynamiting.

The Turkish population of Monk Seals is estimated at a mere 30-60 animals, yet Turkey ranks as the second most important country in the Mediterranean for the *Monachus monachus*. Objectionably, the coastal strip within the National Park has been given away to touristic development, and undoubtedly the Monk Seal won't be able to withstand the increased human presence. This will be another site lost for the Monk Seal, and one step further towards its extinction in Turkey.

The Bey Mountains southwest of Antalya also contain an abundance of the European Ibex *Capra ibex ibex*, an agile wild mountain goat with long, upturned horns. The European Ibex population, however, is being depleted because of hunting, environmentalists say.

Göksu delta: Near Silifke is the Göksu River delta, one of the most prominent wetlands on the Turkish south coast and undoubtedly one of the most important wildlife areas in the entire Middle East. The delta is situated on a peninsula and the beaches are of great importance for two Mediterranean species of sea turtles, the Loggerhead Sea Turtle and the Green Turtle *Chelonia mydas*. It is also here that the Purple Gallinule *Porhyrio porhyrio* has its sole breeding ground. Other rare birds that breed in the delta include the Marbled Teal *Marionetta augustirostris*, the Graceful Warbler *Prinia gracilis* and the White-breasted Kingfisher *Halcyon smyrnensis*.

For wintering waterfowl the area is of international importance. Two main lakes, Akgöl and Paradeniz Gölü, and adjacent steppe and sand dunes are the main features in the western part of the delta, while large portions of the northern and eastern parts of the delta are under cultivation. Recently the Göksu delta has been threatened by uncontrolled housing projects, mainly holiday villages, and the construction of shrimp and fish farms. Conservation organizations try to stop most of these undesirable developments that will certainly disrupt wildlife. In the long run "wildlife tourism" will prove to benefit the local people more than the standard hotel development.

People who want to visit the Göksu delta must follow the main road from Antalya to Adana that passes Taşucu and Silifke. Just after Taşucu, beyond the paper mill, turn right and follow the road along the sea. After 1½ miles (two km), you will see a holiday village on the left, located between Akgöl and the sea. All you need to do is hop over the sand dunes to search for Akgöl and its bird life amongst the reed beds. From the east, Paradeniz Gölü can be reached from the village called Kurtuluş.

The Çukurova delta: The Çukurova delta, south of Adana, was formed centuries ago by sediments brought by the rivers Seyhan, Ceyhan and Berden. Originally the delta was a wild area of which large parts were inundated with water annually after winter, and every time a thin layer of fertile sediment was deposited. During the 1950s, most of the river banks were embanked, and large marshes and lakes drained to fight malaria and to obtain farmland.

Now the Çukurova delta is Turkey's primary agricultural breadbasket, with cotton the chief crop. Extensive irrigation networks and other agricultural measures, such as intensive use of pesticides, have converted the Çukurova delta largely into an artificial area. Fortunately, the Çukurova delta still provides large stretches of unspoiled salt and freshwater marshes, dunes, beaches and lagoons. The main lagoons, with beautiful scenery, are Tuzla Gölü, Akyatan Gölü (easily accessible from Karataş) and the Yumurtalık Oil Terminal Complex (only to be reached from the village by that name, in the east). Total beach length is 69 miles (110 km), and many beaches serve as breeding sites for the Loggerhead Sea Turtle and the Green Turtle.

From an ornithological point of view, the Çukurova delta is of immense importance. It is home to large populations of Marbled teal, Black Francolin *Francolinus francolinus*, and one of the largest populations in the Mediterranean of the Kentish Plover *Charadrius alexandrinus* with about 3,000 breeding pairs. During April and May the region is extremely good for the observation of the migration of White Pelicans *Pelicanus onocrotalus*. In spring, no less than 7,000 pelicans can be seen on their way to breeding grounds in Europe. In winter, more than a staggering 100,000 waterfowl can be present at the main lakes.

Amongst the mammals that make the delta their habitat is the Egyptian Mongoose *Herpestes ichneumon*.

The natural parts of the Çukurova delta are threatened by the ever-advancing agriculture. The enormous accumulation of chemical fertilizers, herbicides and pesticides used in an uncontrolled way in the farmlands will certainly be detrimental to the environment in the long run. A greater potential threat may come from the oil refineries and transshipment ports in the Gulf of Iskenderun, east of the delta, and leaks from oil tankers plying the Mediterranean. The treated sewage and industrial wastes), over-hunting (mainly in the coastal wetlands) and increased number and mobility of tourists. Rapid touristic development of the coast is often glossed over by pointing to the needs of local people, but counter arguments to this are firstly that in many cases the big money in newly explored regions is earned by investors from far away cities and not all by the local people, and secondly that inquiries amongst tourists show that they come to Turkey to enjoy its historical and natural richness.

So for healthy development in the long term, there is the need to be extremely careful with what's left on the Turkish Coast. The

sea current is westerly, parallel to the coast. One major accidental oil spill might devastate all natural life in the Yumurtalık lagoons, the largest and most original part of the region. The establishment of an action plan in case of emergencies is urgently needed.

As can be gathered, there are considerable environmental problems on the Turkish Coast. The natural beauty and wildlife are directly or indirectly threatened by uncontrolled building development (houses, hotels, apartments and roads), pollution (un-

A griffon vulture flies overhead.

example of Spain's Costa Brava, where the tourist boom went wild and where local people are left with expensive hotels on a coast that has been destroyed forever, should certainly not be repeated on the beautiful Turkish Coast. Environmentalists feel strongly that lessons should be learned and careful tourism planning is needed to protect the environment, develop travel industry and boost the economy.

One way to control development is through proper legislation. It is hoped the Turkish government will soon establish a general management plan for the entire Turkish Coast.

Few coastlines in the world can boast the range of natural beauty, history, sporting and cultural resources, industry, and health facilities that the Turkish Coast does. You can enjoy the thermal baths of Kestanbol, try hang-gliding around the Assos cliffs, drink the wine of Bozcaada, study the displays in the Çanakkale and Bergama museums, watch the yacht races at Ayvalık, and taste spicy *kebabs* in Adana. You can explore the pits of Heaven and Hell or visit ancient sites like Pergamum, Ephesus and Karatepe. For serene vacations, visit the deluxe holiday villages in Kemer, Kızkalesi, and Kuşadası, noted for its Genoese castle. From the large petrochemical industry at Aliağa to the boy carrying tea on his swinging tray, the Turkish Coast offers variety, color and entertainment, as well as many opportunities for business and relaxation.

Sailing the coast: Sail down the gulfs of Gökova and Fethiye, two of the most magnificent bays in the Mediterranean or explore Bodrum's unique Museum of Underwater Archaeology. Located in a Crusaders' castle, it has the world's oldest known shipwrecks. Go scuba diving in waters that have sunken cities and rich marine life, and swim along a coast where Antony and Cleopatra once roamed together as lovers. In Milas, south of Izmir, tour the world's only carpet farm, where tens of thousands of carpets are washed and dried under the blazing sun to test their quality. In Demre, visit the Church of Saint Nicholas, where the original Santa Claus delivered sermons.

The Turkish Coast is highly indented with many deep bays, rocky promontories and miles of sandy beaches, ideal for sailing, swimming and windsurfing. It is also one of the most fertile regions in the world. The inhabitants make their living by growing and selling sun flowers, potatoes, olives, cotton, citrus fruit and figs. Some of the tastiest fish and seafood is caught along the coast. Highly recommended taste treats are sardines in towns on the Dardanelles, and giant shrimp in Iskenderun.

The Turkish Coast begins at the sleepy market town of Enez on the Turkish-Greek border and ends in Antakya, ancient Antioch, near the Syrian frontier. European Turkey includes the wide Saros Bay with its fine beaches and the Gallipoli Peninsula, scene of a World War I military campaign, and the Dardanelles, which separates the European and Asian shores of Turkey's Aegean.

The towns on the Çanakkale Peninsula, such as modern Çanakkale, are located on ancient Troad. The sites of Troy, Alexandria Troas and Assos of antiquity are found in this region. Further south is the Aeolian Coast with the resort towns of Dredmit, Ayvalık and Foça, with its many hotels and holiday villages.

Gateway to Ionia: Izmir, which stands about halfway down Turkey's Aegean Coast, is the nation's third largest city and second biggest port. The metropolis is also the gateway to Ionian cities like Claros, Ephesus, Priene, Miletus, and the remains of the monumental Temple of Apollo at Didyma. The resorts of Çeşme and Kuşadası are just a two-hour drive from Izmir.

From Kuşadası, travel inland along the fertile Menderes (Maeander) River Valley to the flourishing market towns of Aydın and Denizli.

Beyond the Menderes River to the south lies the province of Muğla, which in ancient times was called Caria. The resort towns of Bodrum, Datça, Marmaris and Fethiye lie in this region.

Rough Cilicia: An imaginary line east of Marmaris brings you to Turkey's Mediterranean Coast with its touristic hub in Antalya. The ancient cities of Perge, Side and Aspendos, with its stupendous Roman theater, beckon the traveler. After Alanya, the coast was known as Rough Cilicia because of its jagged, inhospitable shoreline. The town of Anamur with its magnificent Castle dominates the central Mediterranean. Rough Cilicia finally gives way to the fertile plain known as the Çukurova with its bustling cities of Mersin, Adana and Iskenderun and Antakya, ending the tour.

THE NORTHERN AEGEAN

The Turkish Northern Aegean stands on two continents, Europe and Asia, and is divided by the Dardanelles, the ancient Hellespont. Due to the lack of information about this region, it is one of the least known and underdeveloped touristic areas of Turkey. Only few foreign travelers go there, mainly to explore the ruins of Troy. Nevertheless, it is an enchanting region. The European part lies on the southwestern edge of the landmass known as Trakya or Thrace. It includes the areas around the Bay of Saros, the Gallipoli Peninsula, the Dardanelles and Gökçeada, Turkey's largest island. This area stretches from the farming community of Enez on the Turkish-Greek border to the charming village of Seddülbahir at the tip of the Gallipoli Peninsula, scene of intense fighting during the 1915 Gallipoli campaign. Gökçeada is one of Turkey's few Aegean islands. The 3,000 Aegean Sea islands, many of which hug the Turkish mainland, are mainly Greek territories.

Inland, Thrace is an agricultural breadbasket with gentle rolling hills and fields of sunflowers, potatoes, mulberry bushes, fresh fruit, vegetables and tobacco. Wine is made from grapes produced in the region. The population is homogeneous. Most of the inhabitants are farmers and fishermen. There are also descendants of Turkish refugees who fled from the Balkans during various wars fought between the Ottoman Empire and Czarist Russia; a great many are children and grandchildren of Turks who came from Greece during the population exchanges between Greece and Turkey starting in 1923.

Fish galore: *Sardalya* (sardines), *ton balığı* (Turkish tuna) and *kefal* (gray mullet) are caught in abundance along the Dardanelles and the Bay of Saros, canned at the town of Gelibolu, and then exported. The Dardanelles is a strategic body of water that connects the Aegean with the Sea of Marmara, the Bosphorus

Preceding pages: sunflower fields in Thrace.

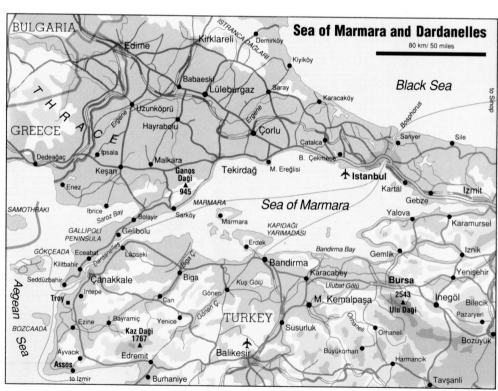

Sea of Marmara and Dardanelles

80 km/ 50 miles

and the Black Sea. Shaped like an S, the 42-mile (68-km) long waterway is known for its swift, erratic currents that make navigation hazardous. Sometimes dense, impenetrable fog descends on the Straits without warning, endangering shipping. The Dardanelles, which is less than a mile (1.2 km) wide at the narrows, is the only warm water outlet for the Soviet Union and other nations on the Black Sea.

The Asian part of the Turkish Northern Aegean is the region that is immediately south and southeast of the Dardanelles, an area that lies within the boundaries of the province of Çanakkale. This bulging landmass, known to the ancients as the Troad, is the northwest corner of Anatolia. Çanakkale, the provincial capital, is the biggest city in the region.

The Troad includes many famous sites from Homer's *Iliad*, including the ruins of Troy, and the burial mound of Achilles, which was honored by Alexander the Great before his invasion of Asia Minor and Bozcaada (Tenedos),

where the Greeks withdrew to induce the Trojans to receive the wooden gift horse. The highest mountain in the area at an elevation of 5,810 feet (1774 meters) is the legendary Kaz Dağı (Mt. Ida), where Paris gave the golden apple to Aphrodite, thus precipitating the ten-year Trojan War.

Fascinating sites: Many other fascinating sites dot this area, including the ruins of Sestus and Abydos on the Dardanelles. The legendary Leander swam the Hellespont nightly from Abydos to visit his lover, the priestess Hero, in Sestus, guided by a torch she put on the shore. He drowned one night in a storm when the winds extinguished the torch. Hero, in her sorrow, plunged into the water and committed suicide. Aristotle, the father of logic, taught for three years at Assos, near the modern resort town Behramkale, facing the gorgeous bay known as Edremit Körfezi and the Greek island of Lesbos. In the west is Alexandria Troas, a once bustling city with a population of several hundred thousand, now in ruins.

THRACE

Turkey's Aegean Coast begins at **Enez**, a farming community situated on the Meriç (Maritza) River along the Turkish-Greek border. In classical times, Enez, or Ainos as it was called, was a flourishing port city. Due to the silting of the Meriç, Enez is now two miles (three km) from the Aegean. In 481 B.C. on his way to Thermopylae and Salamis, the Persian King Xerxes visited Enez. Alexander the Great and his army also marched through Enez in 334 B.C.

Enez, an important commercial center during Roman times, was linked to the *Via Egnatia*, the overland route that connected Rome to Byzantium. With the fall of the Roman Empire, Enez was plundered by various barbarian tribes. In 1384, the town came under the rule of Genoese merchants. The Ottoman Turks conquered the city in 1456.

Medieval fortress: The ancient city lies beneath the modern settlement, a town of 3,000 people with a small square and court house. There is virtually no remains of the ancient period save for an imposing medieval fortress.

The walls and a column of a cathedral remain standing to the left of the town's gate. The presence of a minaret base and a stone *minber* (an Islamic prayer pulpit) indicates that the structure was used as a mosque during Turkish rule.

Near the ramparts, travelers can see a depression that was once a chapel. Afif Erzen, an Istanbul University archaeologist who has excavated the site, found two graves beneath the chapel. About 200 yards (180 meters) outside the main gate are the remains of an underground church, and nearby is the **Türbe of Has Yunus**, the tomb of the Turkish naval admiral who conquered Enez.

Birds galore: The **Meriç River** delta with its neighboring **Lake Gala** is a breeding ground for many bird species. Its marshlands are favorite grounds for Turkish duck hunters. The area, however, is in a military zone. Photography is strictly forbidden.

Enez has no adequate hotels, and therefore travelers who want to spend the night in the region are advised to stay in **Keşan**, a town 39 miles (62 km) east.

Enez is best reached by driving from Istanbul, a distance of about 163 miles (260 km). The trip takes about four hours. There are regular bus services also from Istanbul. Motorists follow the Sea of Marmara on E5/100 highway past the town of Silivri, turning left on the E25/110. The road continues inland after Tekirdağ along rolling farmlands. They then would turn left on route 550 to Keşan and take the secondary road to Enez. Travelers arriving in Turkey from Greece and Bulgaria at Ipsala or Edirne can take route 550 to Keşan to travel to Enez.

NATO war games: A dirt road which follows the **Bay of Saros** back to Keşan has some of the finest beaches of Turkey. The whole region is the setting for annual North Atlantic Treaty Organization (NATO) war games, beginning the last week of September and lasting usually one month. The maneuvers include amphibious landings along the Bay of Saros, parachute drops near Keşan and mock inland tank battles.

From Keşan, route 550 continues to the narrow, rocky **Gelibolu** (Gallipoli) **Peninsula**. The first town that one comes to is **Bolayır**, which dominates the narrowest point of the isthmus from the top of a hill just off route 550. The Aegean, the Sea of Marmara and the Dardanelles can be seen from Bolayır. A public park with cypress trees off the main square contains the **Tomb of Gazi Süleyman Pasha**, the warrior son of Ottoman Sultan Orhan who led the Ottoman forces across the Dardanelles in 1354, giving the Turks a permanent foothold in Europe. Süleyman Pasha, who died in 1389, is buried with his faithful horse. A smaller grave nearby is the **Tomb of Namık Kemal** (1840-1888), a fiery nationalist poet, playwright and journalist who spent much of his time in prison and forced exile because of his patriotic views.

The hill is honeycombed with con-

Left, a peasant woman looks out of her window in Thracian Turkey.

123

crete pillboxes which were used as gun emplacements during World War I. A farm road continues along the top of the hill to **Çimpe Kalesi**, a Byzantine fortification which eventually became Süleyman Pasha's stronghold. Further southwest is the promontory known as **Namaztepe** (Prayer Hill), just above the cove where the Ottoman troops first crossed the Dardanelles from Anatolia under Süleyman Pasha's leadership. When the Ottoman soldiers reached Europe, they held a mass prayer at this point, which is now commemorated with a simple monument.

Piri Reis: The road continues for about 10 miles (16 km) to **Gelibolu**, a picturesque town famous for its sardine canneries and numerous Ottoman monuments. A regular ferryboat service takes passengers and cars across to Lapseki on the Asian side of the Dardanelles. The waterfront has a protected wharf, lined with small fishing boats, and remains of an eighth-century Byzantine castle. In the main square on the waterfront is the **Bust of Piri Reis** (1465-1554), the great Ottoman admiral and mariner from Gelibolu whose map of the coast of the Americas in 1513 confounds today's geographers because it was drawn only a few years after Columbus discovered America. Piri Reis drew the map, which is now in the Topkapı Museum in Istanbul, in color on a gazelle hide.

Other sites to visit in Gelibolu are the 15th-century open air mosque known as the **Namazgah**, located on the lighthousepoint. Nearby is the **Tomb of Karaca Bey**, the standard bearer of the Turks as they liberated the town in the 14th century. Near the grave is the **Cenotaph of Hallacı Mansu**, a famous Moslem dervish whose real grave is in Baghdad. Another landmark is the **French Cemetery**, where French soldiers killed during the Crimean War (1853-1856) are buried. Next to it is the **Tomb of Sarıca Pasha**, a 15th-century Ottoman governor of Gelibolu. The last monument in Gelibolu to see is the unpretentious **Tomb of Sinan Pasha**, a commander of the Ottoman navy.

The town square at Eceabat.

124

The road continues along the Dardanelles past **Cumalı Çayı**, a stream formerly known as **Aegospotami**, where the Spartan navy under Lysander defeated the Athenian Fleet in 405 B.C., ending the Peloponnesian War in one of the greatest naval battles in history.

Battle sites: Before the road reaches Eceabat, a road forking to the right goes to **Gallipoli Campaign battle sites** around the Sarı Bayır mountain range and Suvla Bay, and includes numerous Australian, New Zealand, British and Turkish war graves, such as those at **Anzac Cove** and **Lone Pine**, **Conk Bayır** (**Chunuk Bair**) and **Kabatepe** (**Gabatepe**).

On a slope by the point known today as Akbaş Limanı is the ancient settlement of **Sestus**.

The town of **Eceabat** has several pleasant outdoor fish restaurants and a stunning view of the Dardanelles. A regular ferryboat takes passengers and vehicles across to Çanakkale. The village of **Kilitbahir**, with its heart-shaped fortress, is directly across from Çanakkale, and a small launch ferries cars and commuters across the Straits.

The road continues along the Dardanelles and then inland to **Alçıtepe** (Krithia), a village which has a privately-owned war museum with a collection of mementos of the Gallipoli Campaign. The magnificent **Mehmetçik Anıtı**, the Turkish War Memorial commemorating the 100,000 Turkish soldiers killed during the Dardanelles campaign stands on a hill at Morto Bay. Underneath the memorial is a small war museum. Nearby is the unkempt French War Cemetery.

The **Tumulus of Protesilaus**, who was the first Greek soldier to have fallen in the Trojan War, is said to have been located nearby. But it is said to have been destroyed during the 1915 fighting. The Commonwealth **Cape Helles War Memorial** overlooks the village of Seddülbahir and its castle at the tip of the Gallipoli Peninsula. Several British war cemeteries are located in the Cape Helles region.

Scene from Kilitbahir village.

THE GALLIPOLI CAMPAIGN

The calm blue sea was "absolutely red with blood" for a distance of 50 yards from the shore. It was "a horrible sight to see." Red ripples washed upon the beach and everywhere the calm surface of the water was whipped up into a ghastly discoloured foam by thousands of falling bullets. The sun was shining.

From Alan Moorehead's *Gallipoli.*

Such was the description of the massacre that took place at the Cape Helles Allied landing site known as V Beach, on April 25, 1915. It was given by British Commodore C. R. Samson as he flew in a reconnaissance plane over the battle site where the Turks held up units of the British 29th Division.

Nearly 50,000 Allied troops went ashore that day at seven different beaches along the Gallipoli Peninsula in Europe, and Kumkale, on the Asian shore of the Dardanelles, beginning an eight-month military campaign aimed at defeating the Ottoman Turks in the Great War.

At V Beach, three heavily-armed and well-trenched Turkish companies, led by a courageous sergeant by the name of Yahya Çavuş, held back overwhelming numbers of British forces for more than 24 hours, slaughtering the first waves of soldiers as they hit the beach. Entire battalions, including the Royal Dublin Fusiliers, the Royal Irish Rifles, were almost annihilated, losing most of their officers and over 60 percent of their men in the first day of fighting. Yahya Çavuş and all of his men were killed.

Turkey enters war: Shortly after the outbreak of World War I, Ottoman Turkey sided with Germany and Austria. The Allied powers, Britain, France and Russia, felt that Turkey, weakened by successive Balkan wars, could be forced to accept peace by a decisive show of strength launched against it. The allies believed that a peace with Turkey would free the stranglehold

against Russia and influence the neutral Balkan states to join Serbia in assaulting Austria. The action chosen was to dispatch an Allied fleet to the Dardanelles. The objective was to destroy the Turkish defensive lines and force a passage into the Sea of Marmara and threaten Constantinople.

On February 19 1915, the fleet took up position and began its bombardment of the outer defenses. The attack caused panic in and around Constantinople, the Turkish capital.

Bombardment resumes: On February 25, the fleet resumed its bombardment of the forts with a lot more precision and effect. By March 4, the outer and intermediate forts had been demolished and the way was open for a major assault on the inner forts.

At the beginning of March the fleet began its attack on the inner defenses. At first the shelling caused confusion amongst the defenders but, in fact, little damage was done to the permanent defenses. However, by March 12 the situation looked very grim for the Turks

Left, Mustafa Kemal observes enemy positions during the Gallipoli Campaign. **Right**, the Turkish War Memorial at Morto Bay.

127

and the German High Command considered defeat imminent. A quote from Admiral von Tripitz summed up the German feelings, "It is a dangerous situation. The capsizing of one little state may affect fatally the whole course of the war."

On the morning of March 18 the British fleet, reinforced by a French squadron, reopened its attack on the inner forts with the intention of forcing a passage through the Narrows. To the Turkish defenders, the sight must have been awesome as it was the largest armada ever assembled. At first, the Turkish defenders retaliated valiantly but were gradually silenced and by mid-afternoon the situation had become very critical.

Disaster strikes: With victory in sight, the battleships moved in for the kill, and it was then that disaster struck. First the *Bouvet*, a French battleship, exploded and disappeared with most of her crew. Within minutes, three major British warships had either joined her at the bottom of the sea or had been disabled.

At this point, the fleet withdrew in the belief that it was being attacked by either mobile shore batteries or land launched torpedoes. Later, it became known that a small Turkish minelayer, the *Nusret*, had penetrated the British screen and had laid mines which had gone undetected. These were responsible for the damage done to the fleet.

Fortunately for the Turks, the Allies were more concerned with their naval losses than with resuming the attack, and did not appreciate how close they were to victory. The assault was abandoned and a new campaign was planned involving a joint operation between the navy and the army. The latter was to land on the peninsula, to overcome the Turkish defenders and then occupy and control the Dardanelles.

Anzac landing: The first landings by Allied troops took place at 5 a.m. on April 25, 1915, as the Anzacs (Australian and New Zealand Army Corps) set foot in what proved to be the wrong place. Even so, the troops advanced steadily against light opposition up the

Scene from Turkish trenches.

ridges of the Sarı Bayır Mountain Range. Turkish coastal troops were fleeing in terror. Fortunately for the Turks, at this point, a young Turkish Colonel, Mustafa Kemal, later known as Atatürk, appeared on the scene. Kemal, commanding the Turkish Army 19th Division, arrived ahead of his troops, stopped the fleeing soldiers and asked why they were running away. They replied that the "*Ingiliz*" (British) were coming and they had no ammunition. Kemal's answer was, "You can't run away from the enemy." He ordered them to fix their bayonets and lie down. Seeing this the Australians also began entrenching. "This was the moment of time that we gained," Kemal was to write in his memoirs.

The Turkish officer was the first commander to recognize the importance of the heights of the Sarı Bayır Mountains as holding the key to the entire Gallipoli Peninsula. He quickly ordered his troops to occupy the heights and counterattacked with his two best regiments.

The fighting raged on for many days as both sides attacked and counterattacked on the slopes. Although it cost many lives, no progress was made by either side. The Turks held the higher ground and the Anzacs were confined to a small perimeter around the beach, precariously clinging to the sides of the mountain.

Johnnie Turks: Gradually, both sides developed a great respect for each other which bordered on affection, as typified by the Anzac's description of the enemy as "Johnnie Turks" and their refusal to use gas masks, saying that, "The Turks won't use gas. They are clean fighters." And neither side did.

The landings by the British and the French at Cape Helles had mixed results. On some beaches, such as V Beach, the Turkish opposition was murderous, but on others it was nonexistent. Overall, the landings were successful but the leadership was poor and the advance was uncoordinated. In general no advantage was taken of opportunities offered. Over a period of months, and after many frontal assaults against

enemy trenches defended by machine guns, the Allied line was pushed forward at great cost. However, the Turkish position grew stronger while the Allied attacks gradually weakened until both sides were exhausted and stalemate resulted.

Basically the campaign, like many others in World War I, was marred by unimaginative leadership, culminating in a series of costly mistakes and lost opportunities.

Suvla landings: In August the Allies endeavored to break the impasse by landing troops at Suvla Bay, just north of the Anzac positions. The landings were a complete surprise and were virtually unopposed. Again, bad leadership ruled the day and the advantage was not seized and, after heavy losses, the position was deadlocked.

By late 1915 the Allied General Command had concluded that further military operations on Gallipoli had very little chance of success and that the army should be withdrawn. The evacuation was probably the most imagina-

urkish roops repare to lepart for iallipoli from stanbul.

tive and successful operation of the whole campaign. Between December 1915 and January 1916, the whole army was evacuated from the peninsula with few casualties, although tons of equipment were abandoned.

So ended a passage in military history that still captures the imagination. It was the baptism of fire for the new nations of Australia and New Zealand, and it demonstrated the courage of the Turkish soldiers. It also created a Turkish hero, Mustafa Kemal, who had a higher destiny to fulfill. For the Allies, Gallipoli was a calamity and saw the fall from favor of many high-ranking officers and politicians. Some reputations were made, but many were lost. The Dardanelles venture was to serve as the model for the evacuation of Dunkirk and the invasion of Normandy during World War II.

The peninsula and its close environs mark the graves of approximately 110,000 men. Of these 34,000 were British or Commonwealth troops, 9,000 French and 66,000 Turkish.

Gallipoli today: In 1918, after the armistice, British troops occupied the peninsula and controlled the Dardanelles until forced by the Turks to leave in 1922. The battlefields of 1915 were, where possible, made safe and the allied dead laid to rest in carefully prepared cemeteries where they fell. Memorials to the Allied dead were raised at Cape Helles, Lone Pine, Conk Bayır and Morto Bay. There are Turkish monuments all over the peninsula but the largest now dominates the headland at Morto Bay.

The main World War I battlefields are all situated towards the south of the peninsula, Anzac and Suvla Bay on the Aegean shore and Cape Helles on the southern tip. There are several companies in Çanakkale, Eceabat and Gelibolu offering tours of the area but, for the individualist, the best way to see the sites is to obtain a map and, using the yellow Commonwealth Graves Commission signs as a guide, find the cemeteries which mark the main areas of fighting.

Suvla Bay is situated in a natural horseshoe of hills extending south of Anzac Cove. The dominating feature of these hills is Conk Bayır, which overlooks both Anzac and Suvla. On a clear day the **New Zealand Memorial**, which sits on top of this hill, can be seen from long distances.

Lonely beach: Suvla is best approached from the coast road heading north past Anzac Cove and Arı Burnu (the Cape of Bees). Lala Baba, the southernmost extremity of the battlefield is signposted to the left. Further on is another left turn that skirts the salt lake and leads to **Green Hill**, **Azmak**, **Hill 10**, and **Anafarta**, the major foci of the battle in this area. The lonely beach at Suvla is very welcoming with fine, yellow sand and a clear, blue sea. It is an excellent setting for camping and spear fishing.

The best approach to Anzac is to take the road that leaves the main coastal highway just north of Eceabat. It goes west and is signposted Anzac Koyu, Gökçeada or Kemalyeri. In the distance is the tree-covered ridge marking the

The Lone Pine Memorial commemorates the Australian dead.

site of the Anzac battlefield. On the right hand side of the ridge is the Kabatepe War Museum, which has a good collection of war artifacts and old battle photographs.

Traveling from the museum toward the sea one soon sees the Commonwealth War Graves Commission signposts indicating the various cemeteries. One can follow the high ground which was, in general, held by the Turkish defenders, or go down towards the sea. The former route gradually climbs to Lone Pine and the **Australian Memorial**. Still climbing, the road passes through what was no man's land and the remains of trenches and tunnels can be seen on either side, the Turkish to the right, Anzac to the left.

A short distance farther on is the **Nek** with its Turkish Memorial. In the distance and higher up is Conk Bayır and the New Zealand Memorial. Beside the memorial is a pyramid of cannon balls and Turkish trenches which marks the spot where Mustafa Kemal supposedly gave his legendary order: "I don't order you to attack, I order you to die. In the time it takes us to die other troops and commanders can come and take our places." Below the brow of the hill is a large Turkish memorial, shaped like an open hand. From Conk Bayır, one has a complete view of both Suvla Bay and the Dardanelles. It was here that Kemal led the Turkish defense. The tours tend to return back to Anzac Cove. A new Turkish Memorial now stands with the following eloquent words spoken by Atatürk in 1934 inscribed on its façade:

"Those heroes that shed their blood and lost their lives..

You are now lying in the soil of a friendly country.

Therefore rest in peace.

There is no difference between the Johnnies and the Mehmets to us where they lie side by side here in this country of ours..

You, the mothers,

who sent their sons from far away countries wipe away your tears;

Your sons are now lying in our bosom and are in peace.

ANZAC Beach Cemetery.

After having lost their lives on this land they have become our sons as well."

Cape Helles is best reached from Kilitbahir and Alçıtepe, where there is a private war museum. South of Alçıtepe the British and Turkish War memorials dominate the horizon. The Commonwealth War Graves Commission signposts are up everywhere. The road to the memorial passes the French Memorial.

Westward from Alçıtepe is a track leading to the **Nuri Yamut Turkish Memorial**, situated at Zihindere, or Gurkha Bluff. The center of intense fighting in 1915, this area claimed 10,000 Turkish soldiers. There is still evidence of the tragedy and it is not unusual to find bones and other relics in the fields.

The Cape Helles Memorial overlooks the village of Seddülbahir and its fortress and V Beach. Nearby is an unpretentious cemetery for the valiant Yahya Çavuş and his men.

THE TROAD

The Troad is the ancient designation for what today is called the Biga or the **Çanakkale Peninsula**. It did not have a firm boundary, but extended inland along the Dardanelles covering about the same area as the present-day province of Çanakkale.

Çanakkale, located on the Asiatic side of the Dardanelles, is the center of the province of the same name. By car it's about six hours from Istanbul. There is a marina for yachtsmen who want to tie up here.

Çanakkale sets the pattern for the area with its ties to ancient, Ottoman and modern history. First Xerxes and Alexander the Great built bridges of boats as they moved their armies across the Straits (the Hellespont). Probably those bridges reached between the narrowest point of Abydos (Nağra Burnu north of Çanakkale) and Sestus Akbaş north of Eceabat). The Straits has challenged such swimmers as Leander and Lord Byron to conquer their waters.

The Çimenlik Fortress Museum (formerly the Sultaniye Fortress) which one sees just west of the ferry landing at Çanakkale was built in 1452 by Mehmet the Conqueror. Süleyman the Magnificent repaired it. Later the Queen Mother Hatice Türkhan (who later completed Yeni Cami in Istanbul) restored it and the heart-shaped **Kilitbahir Fortress** directly across in Europe. With these two castles the Turks controlled the passage through the Straits when the Allied Fleet tried unsuccessfully to force its way through in the World War I Çanakkale Naval Battle on March 18, 1915, a prelude to the Gallipoli landings. Reminders of that day are visible in the damaged walls and the several cannons placed around the park. A replica of the minelayer, **the Nusret**, is firmly docked on the terrace wall.

On a hill, on the European side of the Dardanelles, facing Çanakkale, is a figure of a giant Turkish soldier with the inscriptions taken from a poem by Necmettin Onan entitled "*Dur Yolcu*" or "*Stop O Passenger*", commemorating the Gallipoli Campaign. Roughly translated it reads:

"The earth you thus tread unawares is where an age sank. Bow and listen.

This quiet mound is where the heart of a nation throbs."

Fresh seafood: Near the ferry landing are restaurants where you can savor the fresh seafood specialities in a leisurely meal. A daily ferryboat service takes travelers to **Gökçeada**, the island of **Imroz**, from Çanakkale, as well as from Karatepe, on the Gallipoli Peninsula. But as Gökçeada and the smaller Bozcaada to the south are in military zones, foreigners wishing to go to either island need to first obtain permission from the Vilayet Binası (the provincial governor's office). Both islands are inhabited by Greek farmers. Today they are known for their beautiful beaches, two fortresses and a pleasant, bucolic existence.

Regular ferryboats also operate be-

Left, relaxing after a hard day's work. **Right**, a vase from the past.

tween Çanakkale and the village of Kilitbahir and the town of Eceabat, across the Dardanelles from the boat landing. In the main square, the clock in the tower sounds the hours. A tree-shaded promenade extends northeast along the sea front. Stately houses on the hill to the north date from the 19th century when Çanakkale was a busy international commercial center. The exports of those years (valonia oak [tannin], cereals, lumber, wine and pottery) are still important to the economy of the city. The name by which it is now known comes from the quantities of ceramics and terra-cotta (Çanak in Turkish) which continue to be made in the region.

Travelers to Çanakkale should visit its old **Aynalı Çarşı**, or Bazaar with Mirrors, near the town's center, for souvenir hunting.

Just south of the main part of the city near the E24/500 road to Izmir is the **Archaeological Museum** (open 9 a.m. to noon and from 1:30 p.m to 5 p.m. every day except Monday). Here are displayed finds from sites around the Troad: graceful, decorated vases from Troy, coins, gold wreaths, small statues from various sites, goddesses with ornate headdresses.

The Dardanus Tumulus: Leaving Çanakkale and traveling south, the first site that you come to is that of the **Dardanus Tumulus**, indicated by a yellow sign showing a turn off the main highway. (Or it can be approached from the road to Güzelyalı.) After following a dirt road for about a mile one finds the walled entrance to the family tomb in the midst of a pleasant pine grove.

Dardanus, the mythical hero after whom the Straits was named, came originally from Samothrace where he had been caught in a flood. By good fortune he was able to float across to the mainland on a skin bag. His luck continued and he married the daughter of Teucer, the first person to found a city in the region. Dardanus' grandson was Tros; when Tros became king the people and the land took his name. Or so they say.

Playing backgammon at Behramkale.

The beach of Dardanus continues on to **Güzelyalı**; the whole area makes a pleasant summer vacation center. Hotels, camping spots, pensions and restaurants are varied, good and plentiful, and the swimming and surfing are excellent. In Güzelyalı, the **Tusan Hotel** is an excellent place to spend the night. The **Emre Family Pension**, owned by the *muhtar* (village headman), provides inexpensive accommodations with friendly service.

From Çanakkale or Güzelyalı one can make day excursions to various sites in the area; here you can relax on the beach, paint the changing colors of the sea and the mountains, or enjoy the hospitality and stories of the families who have chosen to live here year-round.

Trojan war heroes: A tour west of Troy around the plain begins with the side road which forks off to the right to **Kumkale** just south of Intepe. If one keeps to the shoreline one sees – at least in the distance – several tumuli considered to be monuments of the heroes of the Trojan War. Some of them are in a military zone and therefore not open to tourists; some of them have revealed graves or identities of actual or legendary heroes, and each has enough Hellenistic shards scattered about to keep the legends alive.

The **Tomb of Ajax** is near the village of Yeni Kumkale on the east side of the Küçük Menderes River. Emperor Hadrian believed when he found the bones of a very large man near here which had been exposed by the sea that he was seeing the mortal remains of Ajax. Therefore he picked them up reverently and had a new tumulus cast up over them.

Shortly beyond Yeni Kumkale, and over the dikes that line the river, is the **Castle of Kumkale**. It is presently a military post. A fierce battle during the Dardanelles campaign in 1915 concentrated on the Kumkale Fortress located on the point where the Dardanelles begins. Soldiers who died fighting are memorialized with a monument.

Mound of Achilles: The road turns south at Kumkale and at once the two tumuli attributed to Achilles and to his friend Patroclus are visible on the coast. Again the area is in a military zone. South of them is **Cape Sigeon**, and then the **Tumulus of Antilochus**, the one who carried the news of Patroclus' death to Achilles. On the sea west of Yenişehir is **Beşiğe Tepe**, perhaps the Tumulus of Penelaus, one of the Greek warriors. Items from here in the Çanakkale Museum date from the same time as Troy I – about 2500 B.C. They include a necklace of gold and semiprecious stones, some loom weights and a curious four-handled pot.

Not far from **Üveycik** is a prominent dark hump of a much later date than the five Trojan War heroes; it is known locally as **Sivri Tepe** and may be the tumulus of the Emperor Caracalla's friend, Festus.

The port of Odun Iskelesi is the jumping-off spot for Bozcaada, the island of Tenedos. Ferries carrying passengers, trucks and a few passenger cars take normally a bit less than an hour for the twice-daily crossing.

Selling wool handbags and carpets in the Northern Aegean.

Bozcaada is the island behind which Agamemnon hid his ships while the Trojans tore their city gate down so they could tug the clumsy horse inside.

Venetian crusaders: The main harbor of the island in bygone years was guarded by a handsome fortress built perhaps first by Venetian Crusaders. Genoese and Byzantine architects had a hand in it before Mehmet the Conqueror and Süleyman the Magnificent added to it. In addition to the towers and curtain walls, which were restored by the Turkish Ministry of Culture and Tourism in 1965-70, it encloses the remains of a mosque, an infirmary, barracks and an arsenal.

The island is 26 square miles (42 square km) with long stretches of golden sandy beaches. Bozcaada wines are famous throughout Turkey, and much of the sunny island is planted in vineyards.

For a completely relaxing vacation, the island offers plenty of comfortable, not-too-expensive hotels and pensions with many restaurants serving fresh fish and good local wine. Bicyclists should enjoy the roads here.

Alexandria Troas: Somewhat less than three miles (five km) south of Odun Iskelesi on the mainland are the scanty ruins of **Alexandria Troas**. The city's founding is recent relative to most of the places on the coast. Started at Alexander the Great's orders around 330 B.C. it had its heyday under the Roman Empire. Its ancient baths can still be seen today. Alexandria Troas was successful as a city because it was a port (known today as Dalyan). However, that location caused its downfall: because it was so accessible from the sea it was frequently plundered.

St. Paul's Journeys: To those who want to trace the missionary journeys of St. Paul, Alexandria Troas is of interest because he visited it twice. His first stay was short: here he had a vision of a Macedonian calling to him to come preach to people across the Aegean. The second time St. Paul was in Alexandria Troas was towards the end of his third journey when he stayed there for a week with some of his friends. From Alexandria Troas St. Paul continued by land to Assos.

The thermal springs of **Kestanbol** next to Alexandria Troas have been a center of healing for as long as people have lived in this area. The 150-bed capacity establishment attracts those from the Çanakkale region who are seeking relief from problems like rheumatism, gout, skin and bone diseases, heart and nervous disorders, and metabolism imbalance.

Neandria's ruins lie between Alexandria Troas and Ezine on Mt. Çığrı. The city walls, built probably in the fifth century B.C., can be traced. Capitals of its seventh-century B.C. temple are in the Istanbul Museum. They are much like the capitals from Larisa. Neandria lost its residents to Alexandria Troas when the latter was founded.

Between Kestanbol and **Gülpınar** the road goes past several seaside camping spots and another hot spring with colorfully stained rocks at Tuzla. The lack of development there contrasts to that at Kestanbol.

Many yellow signs point to **Apollo Smintheon** (Chryse) where there is a second century B.C. temple in the town of Gülpınar. Smintheus is one of Apollo's several names. It means "the killer of mice," and refers to the legend that Teucer (Dardanus' father-in-law) built his first city here where mice gnawed his men's bowstrings.

At the far southwest point of the Çanakkale peninsula stands the dark fortress of **Babakale** (Lefton). An inscription at the entrance to the castle reports that early in the 18th century this was a place where hated and evil pirates dwelt. It adds thankfully that Mustafa Pasha got rid of them. Mustafa Pasha went on to build a mosque, a Turkish bath and a fountain in Babakale. Tourism and mining are the main activities of the village now.

One can approach **Assos** (Behramkale) by sea (there is a yacht marina in the harbor at the foot of the hill) or by road from Gülpınar, Ayvacık or Küçükkuyu. The most dramatic way leads from Ayvacık through the pretty pine forest near Paşaköy from where there is a view of the acropolis in the distance. Near Behramkale is a 14th-century Turkish bridge arching over the stream to the side of the road.

Aristotle and Assos: Assos was established about 1000 B.C. by Aeolians from nearby Mitylene. In keeping with the history of the area it was ruled successively by Lydians, Persians, Pergamenes, Romans, Byzantines and Crusaders until Sultan Orhan took it over for the Ottomans in 1330. During the fourth century B.C. its ruler was the eunuch Hermias, who was trying to be the philosopher king of his teacher, Plato. Aristotle taught here for three years and married Hermias' adopted daughter. Assos was the port from which St. Paul boarded the ship which took him to his last visit with the elders of the church in Miletus.

The craggy peak of Assos was surrounded by a wall; the care with which it was built is evident in the sections that stand today. The theater, council chamber, gymnasium and agora are marked with signs. Archaeologists are busy with some reconstruction of the Temple of Athena, built about 530 B.C. This temple is interesting to art historians because of its combination of Doric capitals and an Ionic frieze. Parts of the latter are distributed among the Paris, Boston and Istanbul museums.

Much of the organization of Assos resembles that of Pergamum: the main temple was on the acropolis, the gymnasium and the agora with its arcades and the theater built into the side of the hill were below the temple area. The wide view from the acropolis is more dramatic than that of Pergamum because you can look out across the deep blue sea to the Greek island of **Lesbos** or **Mitylene** (Midilli in Turkish) about six miles (10 km) away.

A fledgling Bodrum: The atmosphere in the restaurants and hotels at the harbor of Assos is that of a fledgling Bodrum. Some of the same elements are present: a historic site, a harbor, an artist colony, good swimming and lots of sun, and closeness to major cities to make it an accessible retreat.

The bridge to Assos.

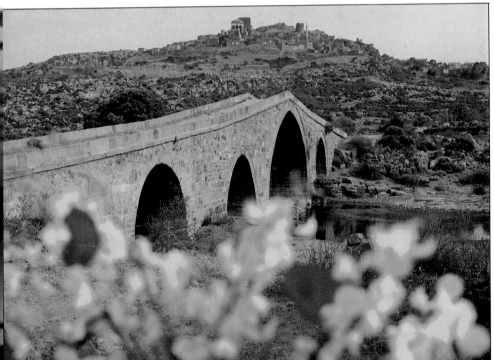

TROY AND THE TROJAN WAR

A beauty contest, a big war with lots of heroes on both sides, the best publicity ever written, and then a treasure hunt to find the hidden gold – what a perfect combination Troy makes for a place to stir one's blood!!

To see Troy is to share for a moment in the excitement of soldiers clashing swords and shields, of the dust beneath their horses' hooves whitening their faces, of the smell of their sweat at the end of a day of hard fighting.

Schliemann's world: **Troy**, an ancient city in northwestern Turkey, was excavated by a German businessman, Henrich Schliemann, who revolutionized scholars' ideas about classical history. The city is a series of levels, some on top of each other – most levels difficult to distinguish – that go back 5,000 years to the Early Bronze Period. It is where the story of the Trojan War took place. Most significantly, it is remembered as the setting for much of the greatest poetry ever composed, Homer's *Iliad* and *Odyssey*.

Ancient ruins, excavators, Greek myths, epic poetry – there is much to Troy. Each of the parts is fascinating, but none by itself makes full sense.

To see Troy (or Truva in Turkish), it is easiest to start from is Çanakkale, a port on the Dardanelles 20 miles (30 km) northeast of the site. You need to take the E24/500 highway toward Izmir. After passing Intepe, he needs to take the country road that forks to the right with the yellow sign pointing toward Truva.

In ancient times, the low hill of Troy overlooked a plain close to the fork of two rivers, the Scamander (Küçük Menderes) and the Simosis (Dümbrek). Since then the bed of the Scamander has moved slightly west and the hill has risen due to the accumulation of debris for centuries.

Wooden horse: The approach to the site is protected by a fence, along with gift shops, soft drink bars and the museum ticket window. Your imagination is immediately teased by the wooden horse at the entrance. You can climb into the horse, pretend that it is about to be tugged inside the walls of Troy and shout as you come to capture the sleeping Trojans. But would anyone now fall for that trick?

Many of the items found in the excavations are presently displayed in the Archaeological Museum in Çanakkale. These include a terra-cotta sieve from Troy II, graceful stemmed goblets from Troy VI, and a black-glaze vase decorated with an owl from Troy VIII. The last often reminds visitors of Schliemann's complaints in his book *Ilios* about "innumerable owls, which built their nests in the holes of my trenches; their shrieks had a weird and horrible sound, and were especially intolerable at night."

The general tour around Troy leads first to the massive tower in the strong wall of Troy VI, up through the east gate, and past the carefully constructed houses from Troy VI to those more carelessly made in Troy VII.

The Trojan Horse, now a symbol of peace.

Wine-dark sea: From the top of the hill you can look out to the Plain of Troy and beyond to Homer's "wine-dark sea," the Aegean. The next thing that comes in sight is Schliemann's great north-south trench. Northwest of a paved ramp and against the wall of Troy II is the place where Schliemann found gold. The part of the treasure that he sent to Berlin disappeared during World War II, but a few pieces which the Turkish government placed in the Istanbul Archaeological Museum, remain.

Some speculate that the west gate, beyond where the treasure was found, is the gate that was enlarged so that the wooden horse could be hauled into the city.

The Roman theater was built on top of the Troy VI walls. The main city gate next to it, called the Dardania Gate, was guarded by a tower. This tower, or the one by the east gate, could be where Andromache fainted to see Achilles drag her husband by his heels in the dust.

Schliemann's biography: Henrich Schliemann was one of the first persons in recent years to ask where Troy had been and what was still there. From early childhood, Schliemann was inspired by Homer's epics and determined to prove that Troy was a real city. Poverty, disease, shipwreck, fire and the loss of his sweetheart didn't deter him from his goal. Starting as a grocer's helper, Schliemann taught himself English, French, Russian, Arabic, Latin and Greek. He memorized the whole of the *Iliad* and the *Odyssey*, and a number of books in other languages, too. He worked hard as an importer of indigo. Then he went to California and struck gold. He happened to be there when the state joined the Union, so he became a citizen of the United States. At last he was independently wealthy. In 1871 he began the excavations for which he is most famous.

To see Troy is to exult with Schliemann at his moment of truth when he found the city, and pried out of the dirt what he believed was Priam's glistening goblets and earrings. To see Troy is also to see old stones and dry weeds, to be disappointed that Schliemann left so much rubble and so little order. People are often tempted to ask what all the fuss has been about. To begin to make sense of the site it helps to have a map of the many layers and a good guide.

Nine levels: Schliemann thought that there were seven levels of city in the tumulus which he dug. He recognized two more levels later, and archaeologists have sorted out many more distinct periods; nine levels are still used for reference. However, so much has been built on top of and using bits of previous cities that one can excuse Schliemann for being confused.

The people who occupied the bottom layer (Troy I) lived in the city around 2500 B.C. They left implements of copper, lead, stone, terra-cotta and bone, enabling archaeologists to determine that they made their pots by hand. Not much else is known about them except that they lost their homes in a huge fire.

The residents of the second level (Troy II) who built their city a few years after the fire, enjoyed several improvements. They seem to have been the same people or relatives of those who lived in Troy I, although there were important differences. Could the disaster have inspired an international emergency relief project that brought in new ideas? Among these were the potter's wheel and the kiln. The artisans of Troy II were skilled in the making of gold, silver, copper and tin – none of which existed in the neighborhood. Thus they must have been engaged in commerce with other countries.

Treasures of Troy: This is also the level which Schliemann believed was Priam's Troy. His excitement upon seeing the first glimmerings of gold reverberates through his description. Schliemann instructed his workmen to take a break to prevent them from seeing his treasure. He cut into the dirt and rocks with his knife at the risk of the wall collapsing above him. With the help of his wife he packed the treasure into her shawl. Together they smuggled it into their house and later out of the country.

At first Schliemann claimed that someone had collected the hoard in a box and had tried to escape with it. Trapped, perhaps by fire or an enemy, the Trojan abandoned it at the city wall just as the fire brought the adjacent royal house down on top of it, he said. Later, having found four more caches of treasure near by, Schliemann decided that the gold had fallen from the upper story of the palace and been hidden for centuries.

Schliemann's discovery drew worldwide attention and fired up the imagination of archaeologists. People accepted the idea that, however fictional the ancient gods and goddesses may have been, Homer had told the story of a real event and people. Schliemann's work opened up the productive field of archaeology. From thenceforth, the search was on to uncover more and more of the treasures hinted at in classical literature.

The obsession: A quotation on the title page of Schliemann's book, *Ilios*, hints at how often he recited to himself Homer's *Iliad*, mulling over it for clues that would lead him to the right place. In Andrew Lang's translation the lines read, "yet will we twain, even I and Sthenelos, fight till we attain the goal of Ilios; for in God's name are we come." With later, more skillful excavation, archaeologists were able to conclude that Troy II predated Homer's city. It is still not known for certain what destroyed the city Homer wrote about, but one explanation offered is that warriors (perhaps from Central Europe) invaded and conquered it.

The archaeologists have likewise felt that with Schliemann's huge trench Troy suffered another catastrophe. He was the first to dig there; scientists have profited by what he uncovered. But he destroyed too much in his singleminded purpose of finding only the city. Or was he merely looking for gold?

After Troy II, waves of migrations continued for 400 years while the less prosperous cities of Troy III, IV and V came and went.

Genetic change: Archaeologists have not determined what happened between Troy V and Troy VI that caused the later city to flourish. Did some genetic change occur because of the marriage of the two peoples – the natives and the invaders?

Troy VI (about 1300 B.C.) was the height of Troy's splendor. Perhaps a balance had been reached among the different residents in their skills of government and commerce. It was in the city-states which developed then that each man learned to exercise his responsibility for the political, ethical and aesthetic life of the community. This was an improvement in the history of human relations that apparently came out of nowhere.

Stately city: Troy VI was a stately city for its time. It was bigger than the cities it covered up. Its houses were well built and arranged in an orderly fashion. Its walls are sturdy and placed with a keen eye for defense. Its citizens did a lot of trading with Crete and Cyprus: they must have been good sailors.

Professor Ekrem Akurgal thinks that Troy VI was the home of Priam of the *Iliad*. He and American archaeologist Carl Blegen think the city came to an abrupt end in 1275 B.C. due to an earthquake rather than a war.

About a generation later the city of Troy VII (which was less well built) was sacked and gutted, probably by Achaean invaders. Smoke from the fire can be traced on the stones of Troy VII. The late George Bean, who taught classical history and archaeology at Istanbul University for 25 years, and Professor Blegen put Priam's city at this level. Was this time lapse between the earthquake and the fire the reason why Homer thought it was a long war? Akurgal suggests that it was Troy's power and her threat to mainland Greece that brought the war upon her. He also suggests that without the earthquake which weakened her defenses the city could not have been taken.

In the two events – the earthquake and the fire – are found several more puzzles about the story of the Trojan War.

Was the *Iliad* about Troy VII? That epic gives no reference to the final capture of the city. Did Homer not know who won the war? Had the earthquake been forgotten?

The Odyssey: Then there was the *Odyssey*, which does not include the wooden horse and the capture, and Troy VII. Does this mean that Homer did not compose both epics? Or did Homer compose several works – now lost – which covered the whole story?

Was the fall of Troy the critical event which opened the rest of the Mediterranean to attack by the Sea Peoples and which brought on the Dark Ages, beginning about 1200 B.C. when civilizations of Anatolia, including the Hittites, were lost? What happened to the well-organized people who had built Troy VI? Was their leader an enlightened despot who ruled them with such harsh discipline that the survivors of the earthquake hated him? Did they assign the guilt for their misfortune (translated into the gods' displeasure) to him and thus do everything in their power to revert to former, less sophisticated behavior?

Myth and reality: Why the wooden horse? Was there a connection between the belief that Poseidon created the first horse and the opinion that the Trojans were famous for taming horses? A connection between the belief that Poseidon caused earthquakes and the story of the downfall of Troy? Would the passage of time have so mixed myth and reality that history reported that the impregnable city (Troy VI) could only be destroyed (Troy VII) by a divinely-related horse (read Poseidon's earthquake)? Or was this simply Homer's poetic license?

The cities of the next level, Troy VIII, lasted about 500 years, and the most important building during that time was the Temple of Athena.

Troy IX, the city enlarged by the Romans who thought that they were going back to their roots, was inhabited until about A.D. 400. Its importance decreased when Constantine located his capital city on the Bosphorus rather than on the Dardanelles.

The story: For a romantic, to see Troy is to imagine the most beautiful woman

Troy's tiny amphitheater.

of all time, her bright robes blowing about her, with Paris, hot from battle, leading her to his perfumed bed.

The legendary background of the Trojan War was the curse on the family Atreus (whose sons were Agamemnon and Menelaus) for cannibalism. The more immediate mythical instigator was the goddess Eris (Discord) who did not get invited to a wedding that she wanted to attend on Mt. Olympus. Piqued, she tossed a golden apple among the guests inscribed with the words, "for the fairest." By rank and prestige, Zeus should have decided who got the apple, but he did not relish handling all the jealous women who would lose. Rather, he turned the honor over to Paris, the handsome son of King Priam of Troy.

Paris had been spending his days on Mt. Ida, south of Troy. The three goddesses who most wanted the apple went to the bother of finding him there. Here, Zeus's wife tried to bribe him to give it to her by offering wealth and power. Athena, one of Zeus's daughters, promised glory and fame in war.

Judgment of Paris: But in the beauty contest Paris decided that the goddess of love, Aphrodite who was also Zeus's daughter, was "the fairest." Her reward for the prize was that, instead of being stuck with sweet, innocent Oenone to whom he was pledged, Paris won Helen, the sultry, sophisticated and experienced wife of Menelaus, King of Sparta. Considering the criterion he had to use, and that he was a mere mortal (the most intelligent of animals – and the most silly, according to his fellow Anatolian, Diogenes), Paris made the best of a difficult situation. The story does not say whether or not he knew what his choice would mean.

However, Menelaus must have had some premonition of the trouble he was getting into by marrying a much-sought-after beauty. Helen had her pick of all the eligible men in Greece, and had settled on Menelaus, perhaps because she thought she preferred an older man. At their nuptials Helen's father had all her suitors swear to stand by her

An Embankment in Troy

husband if anything happened to her.

Paris sailed to Sparta and was welcomed by Menelaus. In Euripides' *Trojan Women*, Helen called him a "Seed of Fire" and exclaimed, "O, a Goddess great walked with him then." As soon as Menelaus had turned his back, Paris ran off with Helen, "bearing unto Troy destruction for a dower," according to the play *Agamemnon* by Aeschylus.

When Menelaus discovered that he had lost his wife, he called on his friends to fulfill their promise. Not all of them were eager to help him at the outset. Odysseus, king of Ithaca, did not want to leave his wife Penelope and their son so he pretended he was insane. Achilles' mother knew that her son would be killed if he went to Troy so she put him in a dress and made him play with a bunch of girls.

The war begins: It took a couple of years for the Greeks to get themselves organized and outfit all their ships – a thousand by poetic count. As soon as the Greeks reached Troy the war began. Almost at once Hector (the son of Priam and the brother of Paris) killed the Greek Protesilaus. According to an oracle, that death determined the outcome of the war, for the side to lose the first man was destined to be the ultimate winner.

The war dragged on for many years turning at times in favor of the Trojans, at times in favor of the Greeks. Homer's *Iliad* takes up the story towards the end of the tenth year. The beginning introduces the brilliant, swift-footed Achilles who is angry at Agamemnon, an anger that was to lead to the deaths of many heroes. Their quarrel was over a slave girl.

On the Trojans' side Hector has often been seen as the most sympathetic of Homer's characters. He embodied courage, integrity, tenderness and sorrow as he fought a war which had been thrust on him.

Family bliss: Hector's – and Homer's – kindness is illustrated in a scene between him, his wife Andromache, and their son. As Hector was leaving for the day's battle, Andromache accosted him, to remind him that he faced dangers and he had responsibilities to their family, as demanding as those of the defense of Troy. Hector replied that honor in war (he would have chosen Athena in the beauty contest!) was more lasting than personal comfort. Then – in a very human touch – he reached down for his son. But the boy cried at seeing his father's battle gear. So Hector took off his gleaming helmet with its horsehair crest and, laughing, kissed his son and tossed him in the air.

The end of the war came when the Trojans were so successful that they started to burn the Greek ships. Achilles, who was still sulking about the slave girl and threatening to pull out, finally let his best friend Patroclus wear his armor in battle. The sight of Achilles' shield was enough to frighten the Trojans away, but Patroclus was killed by Hector.

Achilles' wrath: Stung, Achilles forgot his anger at Agamemnon. He resumed his soldier's role to revenge his friend's death by killing Hector. Gloating furiously, he tied Hector's feet to his chariot and dragged him around and around Patroclus' tomb.

The *Iliad* ends with the funeral rites for Hector after Priam managed to get through the Greek lines and ransom his son's body. Helen joined Andromache in the dirge, lamenting her involvement in the war and mourning for Hector's gentleness of heart, calling him "of all my brethren of Troy far dearest to my heart!"

Homer picked up parts of the story in the *Odyssey*, reporting that shortly thereafter Achilles himself was shot in the heel – the only vulnerable spot on his body – and killed by Paris.

Paris too was mortally wounded by Philoctetes. He died when Oenone, a nymph whom he had abandoned for Helen, refused to heal his wound.

Horse gift: The death of such a hero appeared to the Trojans reason enough for the Greeks to give up. They had folded up their tents and taken their ships off. As a parting gesture, they left a toy on the beach for the Trojans to play with – a wooden horse.

Laocoon tried to warn his friends about Greek gifts, but he and his son were mysteriously swallowed up by a sea monster, so no-one believed him. The Trojans pulled the horse inside the city for safekeeping and spent the night celebrating their easy victory. In the dark the Greek soldiers slipped out of the horse, the Greek fleet returned and Troy fell in flames. The Greek leaders took many of the Trojan women prisoners. Odysseus, for instance, took Queen Hecuba. Cassandra went to Agamemnon. Polyxena, the daughter of Priam, was taken by the ghost of Achilles and was slain on his tomb. Andromache was claimed by Neoptolemus.

The Greeks scattered to their homes. Menelaus took Helen back with him. Helen, the declared reason for the war, remained uncriticized and as desirable as ever. One explanation of this seeming impossibility was that Helen had really spent the war untouched in Egypt, but it took a lot of convincing even for Menelaus to buy that one. In Euripides' play *Helen*, she greets him effusively on his arrival in Egypt:

Hail to thy wife's restored at last!
upon which Menelaus responds,
Wife indeed! lay not a finger on my robe.

Euripides' more generous portrayal of Helen is in the *Trojan Women* in which she points out to Menelaus that had Paris chosen Athena in the beauty contest, Greece would have fallen to the Trojans:

...thus my love
Hath holpen Hellas. No fierce eastern crown
Is o'er your lands, no spear has cast them down.

Odysseus sailed around for ten years barely escaping many dangers as he tried to reach Ithaca. Homer related the events at the end of his journey when he overcame the suitors who had been pestering his clever, patient Penelope to marry again so that one of them could become king.

Homer's life: From ancient times everyone who has spoken Greek or who has been acquainted with the culture of the northeastern Mediterranean has known Homer. It is generally accepted that he was a poet who lived in 850 B.C. (about four hundred years after Troy VII) and breathed art into the epics of the *Iliad* and the *Odyssey*. He was a resident of Asiatic Turkey, born in Izmir. His native tongue was Greek. Tradition says that he was blind.

Homer worked with material that was so well known that he had only to refer to Helen or to Hector for his hearers to fill in the rest of the story. Thus there had to be a large body of lore already existing on which he drew. Homer did not use the complete story of the Trojan War; instead he selected what would suit his subject, using the common myth as his framework.

Homer probably intended both the *Iliad* and the *Odyssey* to be recited or sung, not read. Perhaps the occasions for their performances were festivals at court; perhaps they were recited on the presumed anniversaries of Hector's death, or of Odysseus' homecoming; perhaps there were contests for the best recitations. The earliest known written texts existed about 550 B.C. which means that for maybe three hundred years they were passed by memory from one person to the next. One wonders how much was changed during that time.

Early tourists: Among the early tourist visitors to Troy was Xerxes who made a big sacrifice at the Temple of Athena, but who was then defeated at Salamis. Alexander the Great followed him. He believed that one of his ancestors was Achilles. Alexander, just before beginning his Asiatic campaign, offered a sacrifice at the Tomb of Protesilaus, near Cape Helles, to ensure that he had better luck than the first Greek Prince who fell in the Trojan War. He also picked up a piece of armor in Troy which he thought had been at the Temple of Athena since the Trojan War.

At the time of Julius Caesar – about 800 years after Homer – Virgil took up the story of the Trojan War. In his *Aeneid*, he followed the hero until Aeneas, a Trojan prince, founded Rome. One of Virgil's last desires was to see the place he had written about.

The Crusaders left Troy alone, but Dante, who was their contemporary, chose Virgil to guide him through the Inferno and into the Purgatory. With the Renaissance, no European gentleman was considered educated who did not know the classics.

Even more than Dante, Goethe in the 18th century drew on Homer and Virgil. His works, *Iphigenie auf Tauris* and *Achilleis*, to say nothing of his heroine Helen in Faust, were created out of their influences.

The inspiration: The story of Troy presents a number of puzzles. For one, after fighting so hard for so long, why did the Greeks go meekly home? Even the archaeologists see no evidence that they made any use of their conquest. That raises the question of what the war was all about. Was it over the control of the Dardanelles? Theirs was not the last army to fight over the Straits. Was it because the Trojans were so rich from the commerce that passed through their land that others wanted to rob them? Or was it just over the beautiful Helen – as the story seems to say.

There may be some things about Troy that were easier for ancient Greeks to accept than they are for us. They were closer to the time of the Trojan war. They did not have to be persuaded that Achilles and Hector really lived. They knew exactly where Troy was and where their heroes were buried. They did not have to sweat in school to learn a language that no-one spoke anymore. They could go to a temple-museum and marvel at the trophies from the war: shields, swords, perhaps even Achilles' heel.

The image: That image – perhaps to see Troy at its deepest level is to remember Homer's *Iliad* and *Odyssey*, the epic poetry the ancient world considered so great that it was sacred. On these two works the Greeks based their judgment of human behavior. On these two great books is great Western Literature still judged. No European literature is known to be dated earlier than Homer; few Western writers have come close enough to the richness of his language, the breadth and glory of his humanity, the tenderness and detail of his observations of the world.

Turning point: However overgrown with myth, Troy is a real place. It can be visited; the stones which were scarred with smoke of fire from the devastation can be seen and touched. No matter how interpreted, one or several battles took place here which marked a turning point in Western history and thought.

Of all writers who have been touched by what happened here, Homer most perfectly preserved these conflicts between freedom and responsibility, between the weakness and nobility of humanity, between evil pride and heroic striving. His portrayals of people, of their emotions and their appetites, grandeur and frailties, above all of his own humanity, have illuminated the lives of people throughout the ages. In that illumination, Troy still lives.

A path cuts through Troy's walls.

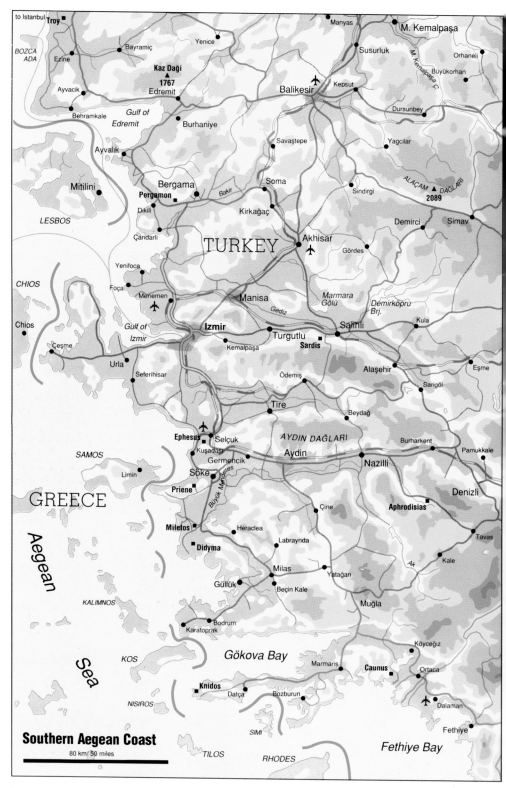

Southern Aegean Coast

80 km/50 miles

148

THE SOUTHERN AEGEAN

The southern Aegean Coast of Turkey begins at the southern slopes of Kaz Dağı (Mt. Ida) of the Trojan legend and ends at the beautiful Bay of Marmaris. The region has miles of unspoiled beaches, ruins of hundreds of classical sites unmatched anywhere in the world, pristine fishing villages and empty coves ringed by pine forests. It also includes exciting resort boom towns such as Ayvalık, Çeşme, Kuşadası, Bodrum and Marmaris. Turkey's third largest city, Izmir, stands halfway down the coast.

The northern part of the region was known as Aeolia with its capital at Pergamum, which was the regional capital of the Roman Empire.

Famous citizen: Special information is also provided about the towns of Ayvalık, Foça and Çandarlı (Pitane), whose most famous citizen was Arcesilaus, disciple of Plato and founder of the New Academy.

Ayvalık's name would appear to mean a stand of quinces (*ayva*), more probably, the source is the name of a local mussel, *ayvada*. The Greek word for the same mussel, *kydonia*, was once the name of the city. This is in keeping with the seafoods which have made Ayvalık a great attraction.

Today Aeolia has become a playground for foreign travelers seeking sun, sand and relaxation. Hundreds of hotels, holiday villages and resorts have opened along the coast, stretching from Edremit (the ancient port of Adramyttium Thebe) to Izmir.

While there are citrus fruit orchards, cotton fields and large stock piles of lumber around Edremit and Burhaniye, the major crop of the region is olives. Magnificent groves, some with gnarled trees several hundred years old, stretch for miles along the highway and disappear up and over the distant hills.

Izmir, Turkey's second largest port, is the gateway to the ancient province of Ionia, which has 55 historical sites, including the ruins of Ephesus, which was a magnificent city during the Hellenistic Period.

In 1952, Dame Freya Stark, a distinguished British travel writer, visited all 55 sites, and came across only one other foreign tourist. Today as many as two million foreign tourists visit Ephesus every year.

Villagers along the southern Aegean Coast raise fighting camels. Camel wrestling is a favorite spectator sport of the region. The Super Bowl of camel wrestling takes place in January when Turkey's top fighting camels slug it out.

The region southeast of Ephesus is the winding Menderes (Maeander) River Valley with many significant archaeological sites, including Priene, Miletus, Didyma. One of the world's geographic wonders is located at Pamukkale, which is famous for its white calcified water cascades and hot baths. Aphrodisias, which lies in the heart of the cotton-growing fertile Menderes River Valley, is becoming another Ephesus as archaeologists, funded by the National Geographic Society, make new discoveries at the site that was known as the "Florence of the Roman" world.

Native people: The southernmost region of the Turkish Aegean lies within the boundaries of the province of Muğla. In antiquity the region was known as Caria and was inhabited by the Carians, an independent and indigenous people known for their skills as mariners. The Carians fought the invading Persians and Greeks and were conquered by both.

The most important remains of the Carian civilizations are the Mausoleum of Halicarnassus in Bodrum (one of the Seven Wonders of the Ancient World), the Gümüşkesen Mausoleum in Milas and the holy shrine of Labraynda in the hills of Mt. Latmus, today's Beş Parmak Dağı. Bodrum, considered by many the St. Tropez of Turkey, is an exciting town with hundreds of nightclubs and discotheques that appeal to the young.

The southern Aegean offers boating cruises in the Gulf of Gökova. The area is also known for sponge fishing.

AEOLIA

Somewhere between Assos and Edremit the region of the Troad stops and that of Aeolia begins. **Mt. Ida** (Kaz Dağı), the home of the nymph Oenone and her childhood sweetheart Paris, has associations with Troy; Mt. Ida slopes into Aeolian ports of Küçükkuyu and Akçay.

The Thunder God: Near Küçükkuyu a yellow sign points to a **Temple of Zeus** about three miles (five km) off the highway and just before the village of Adatepe. A bumpy dirt road leads up the mountain to an outlook on the crest of the hill. There, half hidden in pine trees and fluttering talismanic rags, is the tomb of a locally revered holy man. Behind it is an old altar. Zeus the Thunder God would have had a grand view of the entire Bay of Edremit and Lesbos (Greek island) from this perch.

The Edremit coastline, including **Altınoluk**, **Akçay** and **Ören** has become a summer recreation area with vacation centers scattered among tourist attractions. **Edremit**, a city of more than 30,000 people, is near the ancient port of the Adramttium Thebe. Edremit is a sister city with West Germany's Piding.

Ayvalık, about 31 miles (50 km) south of Edremit, is a major center for processing the region's olive oil and its related products. Ayvalık is renowned for its natural beauty and narrow Greek-style streets. While the date for the city's founding is unknown, shards from the Hellenistic, Roman and Byzantine periods found there indicate the existence of a city in ancient times.

Some historians estimate the founding of modern Ayvalık to the 14th and 15th centuries. One of the first references to the island of Alibey (Cunda), was by a 16th-century Ottoman Admiral, Piri Reis, in his book *Kitab-ı Bahriye*. Under the 1923 Lausanne Treaty, Turks from Macedonia, Crete and Lesbos traded places with Greek residents there.

On its beautiful coastline is an archipelago of 23 islands around **Ayvalık Bay**. Of them, **Alibey Adası** (Cunda) a picturesque island known in Greek as Moshonis (the fragrant one) a picturesque island, is tied to the mainland by a mole. Regular bus and ferryboat services run between Ayvalık and Alibey Adası.

Another long beach is **Sarmısaklı** south of Ayvalık, where you can find every kind of popular recreation associated with sand, sun and water.

Satan's table: Beyond the two-star Murat Reis Hotel a road leads up to **Şeytan Sofrası** (Satan's Table), an area with a delightful panoramic view of Ayvalık, its islands and the bay. The outlook was supposedly named Şeytan Sofrası because of its spellbinding sun rises and sunsets and the belief that devils gathered to dine every evening at this spot. A giant footprint near the hilltop restaurant is said to belong to Satan.

South of Ayvalık is **Çandarlı**, formerly known as Pitane, a city on a thumb of land located about six miles

Left, a blue wagon stands in the street. **Right**, selling the day's catch.

(10 km) west of the main road. Pitane was the northernmost city in the Aeolian League. Little of its history is known beyond the broad outlines of the area. Pottery bits discovered in the excavations at Patane are in museums in Istanbul, Izmir and Bergama.

In Ottoman times the city was the home of the grand Vizier, Çandarlı Halil Pasha, who opposed Mehmet II's goal to conquer Constantinople. When the city fell, Mehmet executed the Grand Vizier for treason.

On the southwest side of the narrow peninsula a well-preserved Crusader castle built by the Genoese in the 13th or 14th century occupies what may have been part of the ancient Greek wall.

Pergamum's port: Continuing south on the highway you first go past **Elaea**, the port of Pergamum, indicated only by a small yellow sign pointing down a dirt road to Iskele. The city wall parallels the highway. The next Aeolian city is **Gryneum**, identified on some maps as Çıfıt Kalesı. This low promontory has no marking. It can be found between Yenişakran and Çaltıdere. The presumed ruins of a Temple of Apollo are not much to see, but they are far enough off the road from Gryneum to be a pleasant pinic spot.

Myrina is on the north bank of the Güzelhisar rivermouth; its double hill is visible from the highway. Hellenistic terra-cotta statues discovered there are in the Istanbul Museum and in the Louvre.

Aliağa (south of Myrina) was once a small village whose inhabitants had used stones of Myrna and Cyme to build their houses. Now its residents number 18,000, and it is the location of Tüpraş Crude Oil Refinery, the PETKIM Petrochemical Complex, the Izmir Iron and Steel Works and the nearby Industrial Free Zone.

The ancient port of **Cyme** (Namurt Koy) is off the highway about three miles (five km) off Aliağa towards the village of Çakmaklı.

Amazon legend: Cyme (sometimes spelled Kyme), an important city in Hellenistic and Roman times, derived its name from a legend about an Ama-

zon. Its rulers contributed to fleets of Darius and Xerxes when the Persians ruled the land. It also paid more taxes than Ephesus or Miletus – a sure sign of prosperity – when it belonged to the Delian League. Excavations by Italian archaeologists have uncovered some old buildings. Parts of the harbor mole and imprint of a theater are visible.

A scenic, winding road goes past Yeni Foça and Eski Foça, 24 miles (38 km) off the main road from Aliağa (or more directly from the turn north of Menemen off the main highway). Phocaea (Eski Foça) is near the north end of the broad Izmir Bay.

The ancient residents were well-known as navigators. Their ships were powerful, swift 50-oared vessels capable of carrying 500 passengers. Merchants of Phocaea had business with Egypt, with Amiscus (Samsun) on the Black Sea, and with the colonies of Phocaea, which by the sixth century B.C. were established in the Mediterranean, among them Marseilles and Nice. Two associations with the French con-

Sunset at Seytan Şofrasi.

tinue: the figurehead on the prow of Phocaean ships was a rooster, supposedly related to the french *coq galoise*. Club Méditerranée has a resort village a short distance north of the city.

Seals and Phocaea: Different explanations have been offered for the name of Phocaea which means seal in Greek. One theory is that seals were common in the areas around Phocaea. Others suggest that the outline of one or several of the small offshore islands resembled the animal.

The Genoese who ruled Phocaea in the 13th century built a fortress. In the 14th century the Genoese began alum mining operations at a site about 13 miles (20 km) away and moved therefore to Yeni Foça (New Foça). The Ottoman Turks conquered Phocaea in 1455 and built the **Fatih Mosque**.

Eski Foça, which hosts a music, folklore and a water sports festival in June, has a touch of Old World charm.

Four miles (seven km) east of Eski Foça on the Izmir road next to a stream is a massive, stepped pyramid-like fifth or fourth century B.C. rock tomb called **Taş Kule**. As no inscriptions have been found, it has not been determined which king was buried there.

On a hill behind the town of **Burumcuk** are the ruins of a fifth century B.C. city, identified by some as **Larisa**. (It may actually be Cyllene, and the true Larisa may be at Yeniköy on the hill north of Burumcuk. The site includes city walls, a palace, wells and tombs.

Menemen, population 24,000, is a county capital and market town situated on the Gediz (Hermus) River. There is an old han in the center of town, an old Ulu Cami (great Mosque) and a monument to Kubilay, a soldier who died in a religious uprising in 1930. Menemen is in the midst of a tobacco and cotton growing region, and its many shops sell harnesses, handles for spades, wooden churn and hemp rope. The pots and baskets found in abundance on the highway are well known Menemen products. Menemen also gives its name to a tasty dish of tomatoes, green peppers and scrambled eggs.

The resort town of Ayvalık.

THE OLIVE OIL INDUSTRY

An olive grove is one of those magical places where it seems you are never alone, as if your footsteps caught woodland spirits at play, sending them hiding among the twisted trunks of every tree.

The olive tree stands firmly rooted in history, with references dating to the sixth millennium B.C., and throughout time, ancient cultures tapped the power of this special evergreen and its perfect fruit to produce light, medicine, food, cosmetics and sacred oils.

A staple of the Turkish diet for centuries, the olive is revered even today for its important role in the country's economy, as Turkey is the world's fourth largest producer of *zeytin yağı* – olive oil.

Nearly 86 million olive trees thrive in Turkey; 75 percent of these blanket the rolling hills along the Aegean Coast, while the remainder grow in pockets on the Mediterranean Coast, Sea of Marmara and southeastern Anatolia.

Big business: Turkey is home to five major olive oil producers, including Komili and Tariş, a government cooperative, and nearly 4,000 independent producers who operate from neighborhood factories using old-world methods and machinery. In towns like Ayvalık, Muğla, Izmir, Edremit and Çanakkale, olive cultivation is a big business requiring serious commitment as farmers wait nearly two to five years for a new tree to bear fruit and almost 20 years before it reaches maturity. Orchards are a long-term investment and regarded as a measure of wealth, with groves handed down through generations.

Turkey's olive producers and farmers are eager to set tourists straight on the subject of authentic Turkish cooking, good naturedly accusing "big city cuisine" of false advertising by using cheaper vegetable oils instead of the real thing – virgin olive oil.

In 1989, Turkey produced 120,000 tons of olives, adding $180 million to its cupboards. Export revenues reaped $45 million. Libya and the Soviet Union are the country's number one and two export markets respectively.

Harvest time: In early spring, Turkey's orchards ignite with green flowers which in May bear tiny fruit that is nurtured by sun and *imbat*, the steady warm west wind. In autumn, when the fruit changes color from green to reddish-orange to black, the harvest begins. The harvest season is heralded by the arrival of workers and their families who travel from inland villages and set up temporary camps on olive farms.

The workers "milk" the fruit off the trees, handpicking and dropping it into straw olive baskets. Sometimes, short poles are used to hit the tree branches, sending the olives down onto a soft net. Handpicking is slow, labor-intensive and very costly, but few alternatives exist due to the delicate nature of the olive; even the slightest bruising can result in spoiled fruit and bitter oil.

Upon delivery to the factories, olives are hand-graded to remove debris and damaged fruit. Next a washing and crushing cycle separates the stems and the pits, leaving a thick olive pulp which is made into a paste and squeezed through a press. The resulting oil and water mixture is then decanted to capture the pure virgin oil. It takes five kilos of olives to produce one kilo of oil.

Oil tasters: Before being placed in underground storage, the oil must pass the final trial: the taste test. No scientific techniques are needed, just a good nose and sharp taste buds determine the oil's fate. Professional tasters are employed by producers just for this purpose. To one oil connoisseur, whose culinary expertise has been called upon for 40 years, olive oil is simple: it's either very good or it's very bad, and it's a smile or a grimace which indicates the thumbs up or down.

Olive oil is sold in two ways in the Turkish consumer market-place. Virgin olive oil, the finest oil from the first pressing, is labeled, *Naturel Zeytin Yağı*. This chemical-free oil has an acidity of less than 0.1 percent. A less expensive oil, labeled, Pure Olive Oil, or Riviera Type, is widely distributed in the Turkish market and despite its name, is actually a mixture of chemically-refined crude olive oil (from later pressings) and a smaller amount of virgin olive oil.

All is not golden in Turkey's olive oil industry these days, as coastal areas are faced with a pollution problem caused by the indiscriminate dumping of *karasu* (black water), the high nitrogen by-product of olive oil production. Illegal disposal of sewage has residents in a panic. Ayvalık is one resort town which is seeking to remedy the situation to protect its tourism business. Present plans call for the relocation of Ayvalık's many small olive oil factories from the city to another site where new plants and a modern treatment facility will be built.

Although science is now proving what the ancients knew long ago – that olive oil promotes healthy bodies and minds – olives seem to have lost their popularity with Turks.

Consumption decline: Industry officials attribute a ten-year decline in domestic consumption to competition from newer vegetable oils, such as corn and sunflower, which entered the Turkish market with promotions promising lighter, more modern and less expensive oils.

Turkey's producers are hard pressed to reverse the trend and have been working closely with the International Olive Council, of which Turkey is a member, in an effort to launch an ad campaign, pitting the high qualities of olive oil against vegetable oils.

Olive oil has a clear case as it's the only oil which can be consumed in its natural state, and is medically-proven to help fight cholesterol, as well as aid digestion, bone formation and brain function.

The ancients didn't need science to prove what magic they had in their silvery green groves. Sophocles knew what he was talking about when he referred to the olive tree as "the tree that stands unequaled, that can not be surpassed, that bursts forth again and again."

Olives for sale.

PERGAMUM

As the capital of a fast-growing empire, as a center of art and religion, as a Mecca of healing, Pergamum in the Hellenistic Period was most impressive. That which remains of it now – ruined buildings, history, legends – attracts visitors by the hundreds of thousands. As a walled city on a peak it had a commanding location when it was ruled by Philetaerus and his successors in the third and second centuries B.C.; as the citadel today, people look up to it from afar wondering at its power; they gaze down from its heights with awe. It was and is a magnificent site.

History: Pergamene kings claimed descent from a certain Telephus who, according to myth, ruled the area at the time of the Trojan War (1250 B.C.). Archaeological information, including the discovery of shards, shows that the earliest settlement occurred some time later, around 800 B.C. The whole area

came under Persian control after Cyrus defeated Croesus in 546 B.C., but there are no records mentioning Pergamum by name. Following Xenophon's exploits leading his 10,000-man mercenary army in an ill-fated campaign against Persia, he cooperated with Sparta in ruling Pergamum briefly in 400 B.C., and for that he lost his Athenian citizenship.

Pergamum's real importance began after Alexander the Great's death in 323 when Lysimachus, one of his generals, left a large amount of money there under the stewardship of his officer, Philetaerus. Lysimachus was soon killed in battle, and Philetaerus claimed the treasure as his to use for the good of the city. From 281 to 263 B.C. he expanded Pergamene control over the cities northward to the Sea of Marmara by offering gifts of money and prizes. Philetaerus also constructed many magnificent temples and new buildings in the city.

Philetaerus' successor, his adopted son Eumenes I (263-241 B.C.), was able to maintain his position only by buying off the Gauls. They had come from Europe to Anatolia in 279 as mercenary soldiers for the King of Bithynia and had acquired a reputation for being unbeatable, unruly, fierce and warlike. The sculptors of Pergamum were to use the Gauls as models for their many works of art.

Attalus defeats Gauls: Eumenes' adopted son, Attalus I (241-197 B.C.) decided to take care of his troublesome neighbors, the Gauls. Before the battle, he used a bit of psychology on his own men. In the usual religious service the surprised priests discovered the words, "Victory for the King," written on the sacrificial animal's liver. Only after Attalus' emboldened soldiers had defeated the Gauls did he confess that he had written the words backwards on his hand and stamped them on the liver as he was helping the priest.

It might not be sheer coincidence that the idea and the know-how of writing on skin – parchment – is attributed to a Pergamene ruler at about his time. When Alexandria put an embargo on papyrus

A statue of a Pergamene Goddess.

to stunt the growth of the rival Pergamum library, scribes found they could use both sides of the parchment sheets and that pages were easier to handle than long rolls.

During Attalus' reign the influence of Rome began to be felt in the area when he gave Rome a sacred black stone from Pessinus that was worshipped as the Mother of the Gods.

Ties with Rome: Attalus' successor was Eumenes II (197-159 B.C.). He brought Pergamum to its height of power and cultural attainments. To his credit are the Temple of Zeus, the library and gymnasium and the lower agora. Eumenes continued to cultivate good political relations with Rome and reap the benefits. When the Romans defeated Antiochus the Great, the king of Syria, in the Battle of Magnesia in 190 B.C., they turned over most of the Syrian lands to Eumenes. Thus in less than 100 years the Pergamene Empire had expanded from a tiny city-state to take in the Aegean Coast of Anatolia as far south as the Maeander River and as far east as present-day Konya.

Eumenes was succeeded by his brother, Attalus II (159-138 B.C.). Attalus further cemented Pergamum's ties with Rome, consulting with its rulers on major political and economic decisions, regional problems and conflicts. Attalus spent most of his years warring with his neighbors, including the Kingdom of Bithynia, northeast of Pergamum. When Attalus II died at the age of 81, his nephew Attalus III succeeded to the throne of the Pergamene Empire.

Attalus III reigned only for five years (138-133 B.C.). He was more interested in botany than in politics, writing a book on agriculture which became a reference for the Romans. His specialities were medicinal herbs and poisons which he tried out on condemned prisoners. He ensured his place in the history books by giving his whole kingdom to Rome, shocking the Pergamenes and effectively ending the Attalid dynasty.

Rebellion: The bastard son of Eumenes II, Aristonicus, led an uprising

Modern Bergama as seen from the ruins.

against Rome, organizing disenchanted elements, mercenaries and slaves. At first Aristonicus was successful, defeating a Roman army led by a consul. But within three years the Romans had put down the rebellion.

Pergamum's last attempt at independence took place in 88 B.C. when it served briefly as the headquarters of Mithridates, King of the Pontus and an avowed enemy of Roman expansion in Asia, who invaded the Aegean Coast of Asia Minor to liberate the Greek-speaking cities. Hundreds of Latins were murdered in the streets. But Roman legions, led by Pompey the Great eventually expelled Mithridates and repossessed Pergamum.

Province of Asia: The Republic of Rome organized the larger part of the Pergamene kingdom into the Province of Asia. However, Rome was not experienced in administering overseas territories, and made a bad job of it at first. Troubled by the insensibility to art in the capital, many of its sculptors moved to Aphrodisias, which became the art center of the ancient world.

When Rome became an empire, the provinces in Anatolia in general were better administered. The emperors took a more personal interest, and many visited Anatolia, starting with Augustus. Trajan's father had been governor of the province of Asia (which included Pergamum). Caracalla received medical treatment at the Asclepieum after a bad accident at Gallipoli (A.D. 214). In gratitude he had the Temple of Dionysus covered with marble, and got himself proclaimed the "New Dionysus." In time, the inhabitants of Pergamum moved down from the hilltop fortress to the plain below. The fortress walls were left in a derelict condition and pillaged for stones.

People moved down from the hilltop fortress such as that at Pergamum, leaving the walls untended. In time they picked up the squared stones to build their own houses.

Church of Revelation: Members of the Christian church in Pergamum were criticized by St. John at the end of the first century for various heresies and were told that they lived where Satan's throne was found. Pergamum's reputation, however, grew over the years because one of the Seven Churches of Revelation existed here. Under the Byzantine Empire, Pergamum was a bishophric. Its importance diminished after the center of power moved from the Aegean coastline to Constantinople in A.D. 330.

Pergamum was ravaged during the seventh-century Arab invasions. The Crusader Henry of Hainut who was Latin Emperor of Constantinople (1205-1216) took Pergamum in 1212 from the Byzantine Emperor, Theodore Lascaris, who was trying to rule from Nicaea (Iznik).

Early in the 14th century it became a part of the Seljuk Empire and then the Ottoman Empire, at which time Pergamum took its current Turkish name, Bergama. The new city was rebuilt below the acropolis hill after Tamerlane's army destroyed Bergama in 1402 during its brief, bloody rampage through Anatolia. Ottoman control re-

A Roman statue at Pergamum Museum.

sumed until the town was occupied in 1919 by the invading Greek army for three years.

Since 1923, Bergama has been under the control of the Turkish Republic. Bergama, with a population of 40,000 today, is the capital of the county of the same name in Izmir Province.

Archaeology: The historic buildings from the Hellenistic and Roman periods of Pergamum, which are of interest to tourists, are located in three separate areas: the acropolis, the present town and the Asclepieum or medical center. It is common to start one's visit with the acropolis because from that height one gets a panoramic view of the old city and the relationships of the various parts, and also because the oldest buildings are there.

The highest point of the acropolis in the Hellenistic Period was controlled by the army. Here were placed the barracks and the arsenal, giving the guards the maximum survey of all sides. The Palaces of the Kings sheltered just below. Those buildings today have not even their bare walls standing.

The **Temple of Trajan** is in striking contrast to the palaces because of restorations being directed by German archaeologists. The white marble columns and flooring of the surrounding enclosure help create a sense of majesty of the people who lived in this part of the ancient city.

It is the only building in this area that does not date back to the Hellenistic times. It was begun during Trajan's reign (A.D. 98-117) and completed by Hadrian (117-138). Contemporary practice deified the Emperor; statues of Trajan and Hadrian found there are now displayed in the Pergamum Museum in East Berlin.

Slightly below the Temple of Trajan is the **Temple of Athena**. Its courtyard acted as a kind of museum where works of art and curiosities were displayed, many of which were offerings to the goddess. The Doric temple has six columns on the ends and ten on the flanks. The Temple of Athena, as of those in other western Anatolian cities – Izmir, Miletus and Erythrae – was the most important shrine in the city. In Pergamum, it was related to the Parthenon, according to archaeologist Ekrem Akurgal. Among the bronze statues probably located there were two commemorating the Pergamene battle with the Gauls. Marble copies now in Rome show the "Dying Gaul" and the soldier stabbing himself after having killed his wife to escape capture. Both statues are of the noble foe, the enemy whose courage and devotion raised the struggle above savagery.

Rich library: The entrance to the Library of Pergamum was through the upper entrance of the Temple of Athena, an appropriate association with the goddess of wisdom. Pergamum was one of the centers of ancient learning, and its library once rivaled the great Library of Alexandria, according to ancient chronicles. The library is supposed to have contained 200,000 volumes, but there is a question of where they were all stored since the ruined building seems to have been big enough for only one-tenth of that amount. The library is famous for its rich collection as well as its destruction. Its demise, caused partly by a fire and partly by reactionary Moslem clerics, deprived later generations of much Hellenistic culture. The library continued in its importance as a depository of learning until a love-struck Mark Antony gave most of the volumes away to Cleopatra to take to Alexandria.

In the seventh century, the Moslem Caliph Omar, reasoning that the books were either inconsistent with the Koran and impious, or, if consistent then unnecessary, ordered them all destroyed in Alexandria, according to the late historian George Bean.

The Palaces of the Kings stood east of the Temple of Athena and served as the residences of the various Pergamene kings including Eumenes. It was surrounded by the barracks for the kings' guard of honor and soldiers working in his office.

Just 30 feet (10 meters) below the palaces were arsenals, five feet-long buildings constructed parallel to each other, which played a pivotal role in the defense of the ancient city. The barracks and the Command Tower, built during the reign of Attalus I, stood just above the arsenals. Little or nothing remains of these sites.

The Temple of Zeus, the biggest temple in Pergamum, was protected from a fate similar to that which struck the library. Germans in the 19th century took it out of the country stone by stone and reconstructed it in the Pergamum Museum, now in East Berlin, saving some of it from being destroyed for construction materials. Turks, however, argue that the temple and other Pergamene relics were smuggled out of the country and should be returned to their place of origin. Nevertheless, German archaeologists are planning to rebuild the Temple of Zeus in Pergamum using casts taken from the original temple in the East Berlin Museum.

The two friezes, that of the mythical adventures of Telephus and that representing the Battle of the Gods and the Giants, were sculpted at the summit of artistic excellence in the Hellenistic Period. The Telephus Frieze interests art students because it is an early attempt to give a realistic perspective and physical setting to the figures. The technical skill exercised in carving the marble with such finesse, the knowledge of anatomy, and the sense of drama vividly conveyed in the scenes place these marbles among the world's masterpieces.

The Temple of Zeus is the largest of the buildings on the acropolis. Since it was dedicated to both Zeus and Athena (and perhaps to the rest of the Greek pantheon), it would more correctly be known as the Great Temple. Popular ascription of this as "Satan's Throne" (admittedly a dramatic site at which to point) probably lessens St. John's more general condemnation of the Roman government.

Located next to the Temple of Zeus is the upper agora which was surrounded originally by two – and three – story colonnaded porticoes.

The **Pergamum Theater,** impressive now in its size and acoustics, stretches up the side of the hill for 80 rows of seats and could hold 10,000 spectators. When there was a performance a wooden stage and backdrop were erected above the orchestra; these were dismantled at the end of the performance or at the end of the season. Above the center of the lower landing stood the king's box, which was completely made of marble. The Temple of Dionysus associated with the Pergamum Theater (immediately north of the stage) was dedicated to Dionysus, the god of wine and entertainment who was believed to have inspired the first drama. Sacrifices for the actors and their performances were held there before the plays began. The building was impressive and pedestrians walking by could gaze with admiration.

A long promenade runs south of the stage where people walked, conversed, made business arrangements, and enjoyed the view.

Temples galore: Below the acropolis in the south side of the hill are less official buildings, among them the **Temple of Hera**, the **Temple of Demeter**, the **Temple of Asclepius**, the lower agora, and the gymnasium on three levels. Perhaps most of the worshippers at the Temple of Demeter were women who held special celebrations at night with torchlight parades.

In the gymnasium the upper building was for young men, the middle building was for adolescent boys, and the lowest was for young boys. As with other gymnasiums, this was a place for both athletics and academic studies. The complex included an auditorium which seated 1,000 people and a number of baths. It was in use into the fourth century. There was a ceremonial hall in the eastern part of the gymnasium for receptions, prize givings and other official functions. Next to it was a kind of prayer room where the emperors were worshipped. Water to the gymnasium was pumped from the northern mountains. The middle terrace includes the foundations of a temple dedicated to the patron gods of the gymnasium, Heracles and Hermes.

Pause to look at the construction of the vaulted stairway as you walk down from the gymnasium to the Hellenistic House of Attalus and the lower agora.

Water supply: Consul Attalus was a man of means. The water from the cistern in his house supplied the fountain in the agora below him. Among the official records found in this agora is one that announces the rules concerning the use and maintenance of the water supply – a matter of supreme importance in the defense of a city on a hill, particularly one which can be blistering hot in summer. (The new **Kestrel Dam** northwest of the acropolis is evidence of that continuing importance. Pipes from a water supply in the mountains follow much the same path as the Hellenistic aqueduct.) A hint of the personality of this Attalus can be found in the inscription on the wall of his living room inviting his friends to come and enjoy life with him.

The ancient buildings of the lower city date from the Roman Period. The biggest is the **Kızıl Avlu**, or Red Court, built over the channel of the Bergama Çayı (Selinus River) during the reign of Hadrian. The red color one sees now is of the bricks which originally were faced with patterned marble rather than all pure white stone.

Even without the brick color and the heavy walls, the building has a completely different feel to it from the temples on the hill. The many places for ritual ablutions and the paired male-female caryatids which held up the roofs of the porticoes indicate that the religious practices observed here may have been to honor the Egyptian gods who were popular in Roman and early Byzantine times, such as Osiris, the god of the underworld and the dead and husband of the fertility goddess Isis. Osiris was related to the Greek gods of the underworld, Pluto and Hades. The Kızıl Avlu was constructed in the second century. During the Byzantine Period the basilica was used as a church dedicated to St. John. One of the towers is now a mosque.

Battles among crocodiles: The Roman amphitheater, which straddles a tribu-

Olive trees burst through the Great Altar at Pergamum.

tary of the Bergama Çayı, is one of the very few such structures existing in Anatolia. When realistic sea battles among crocodiles were to be staged, the river was dammed. Also in the valley of the Bergama Çayı was a stadium and a theater, both having been constructed during the Roman period. Neither the amphitheater, the theater or the stadium have been excavated by archaeologists. These places are best approached on foot. From one of the gates of the theater a road began that led southwest about half a mile (one km) to the **Asclepieum** or medical center. (The present road starts in the center of Bergama.)

As you approach the grounds of the Asclepieum, you will see the old road (the columns were added during Hadrian's reign), the central yard with the small theater to the far right behind more columns, and on the left the stone and brick ruins of some other buildings. Almost immediately in front of one is a rather short broken marble column decorated with snakes twining around a laurel branch – the caduceus, the sym-bol of the medical profession during ancient times.

Psychotherapy: Treatment at the Pergamene Asclepieum consisted of a combination of herbal medicines, physical therapy, psychotherapy, diet, baths, massage, music, sports and intellectual stimulation. A lively account of some of the practices is found in the writings of the hypochondriac, Aelius Aristides, who was a patient in Pergamum for 13 years at the time of the institution's most famous physician, Galen. Patients at the Asclepieum slept for brief periods on the ground in the sanctuary: this was termed "incubation"; the dreams which they had were interpreted by the doctor-priests who then prescribed a treatment. Among the cures were mud baths followed by running naked around the temples. The theater and a library housed in the northeast corner of the courtyard helped the patients to while away their recuperation time.

During one bitterly cold night, the staff had Aristides smear himself with mud and run three laps around the temples. He finished by washing off the mud in the sacred fountain.

The institution was so popular that even many Roman senators and merchants came to the Asclepieum for treatment and to see Galen for a check-up or for just plain relaxation. Women who could not bear children would visit the place, hoping medical treatment would result in miracles. One woman, according to a dubious ancient account, was pregnant for five years but could not deliver her child. But after she slept one night at the Asclepieum, and had a vision of the God of Medicine, she at once gave birth to a five-year-old son.

Anatomical procedure: Galen, whose great 16-volume medical treatise, *On Anatomical Procedure*, parts of which have survived to these times, was a specialist in anatomy, human dissection and internal medicine. The bulk of the first nine volumes of his work has survived in Greek and Arabic and constitutes our main knowledge of ancient medical practices. Although he was a

Haircut for a young lad.

highly scientific man, Galen worshipped heathen gods like Asclepius, believed in dreams and portents and even ascribed to absurd folk medicines that bordered on quackery.

The circular building to the immediate left of the entrance to the courtyard was the **Temple of Asclepius**, the Roman god of medicine and healing and son of Apollo, the god of music, youth and poetry exemplifying manly youth. It was a small copy of the Pantheon which had been built about 20 years earlier.

South of it and slightly outside the line of the south portico was the round two-story treatment building with a number of separate rooms. It was linked to the sacred pool near the theater by an underground passage. Probably people stretched out on its roof (now collapsed) to sunbathe.

The Bergama Museum was built in 1936 to house the finds in the area uncovered since then. It contains a small reproduction of the Temple of Zeus as one would see it in Berlin. A number of pieces of the Hellenistic, Roman and Byzantine periods collected here merit close attention. The items include statues, friezes, ceramics and coins. The museum also includes an ethnographic section of regional costumes, handwork and armaments.

The modern city of Bergama is remarkably unspoiled by its illustrious past and the large numbers of foreigners who spend their time and money only on its history. While the residents are conscious of this concern, many are engaged in the ordinary businesses which support a city and in the agricultural industry of the area. There is a long-standing International Bergama Fete every May and June. Good restaurants, hotels, and camping facilities (one in connection with a hot spring) are available. Shops display onyx items; some offer the famous hand-woven *Yağcı Bedir* Bergama carpets, produced in the nearby mountain villages. The dominant colors of these carpets are dark blue and red. The deep blue of the Aegean gives the basic color.

Snapshots anyone?

IZMIR

With over two million inhabitants Izmir is Turkey's third largest city and second largest port (after Istanbul). It is a cosmopolitan city created by Turkey's most European-thinking citizens directing an influx of rural Turks seeking a better life. In addition to its European ambience, fostered by fine shops, modern hotels, high-rise apartment buildings, and facilities integral to shipping, Izmir offers pleasant surprises to its more independent visitors. Walking through its less affluent streets you may chance upon a colorful folk dance performed by transplanted villagers or a man prompting his rabbit to select the piece of paper with your fortune written on it. Although Izmir's commercial stature resembles Europe, it remains Turkish in spirit and hospitality.

Izmir's position as Turkey's leading exporter has deep historical roots. Ancient Izmir's commercial development was facilitated by its location, on a deep-water harbor at the end of the Golden Road, a trade route which passed through Lydia, Phrygia, the Hittite capital of Hattusa, and then Mesopotamia. Izmir became a center for shipping in Ottoman times, after the port of Ephesus was abandoned. During the past 500 years, minority groups such as the Greeks, Sephardic Jews and Levantines have been indispensable in expanding Izmir's trade in figs, cotton, olive oil, steel and textiles.

Infidel Izmir: Moslem Turks liked to describe the city as *"Infidel Izmir,"* because the city's inhabitants before the 1923 population exchanges were overwhelmingly Christian Greeks. No Greeks remain there today. As religious fervor wanes in the secular state of Turkey, Izmir is now praised, at least by locals, as Turkey's most cosmopolitan and western-oriented city. Izmir's prominence as an eastern Mediterranean emporium is illustrated by the **Izmir International Fair**, which begins each August 26 at **Kültürpark.**

Izmir is home to NATO's Allied Land Forces Southeastern Europe and Sixth Allied Tactical Air Force headquarters, which guard western Europe's southern flank. The city is obviously patriotic, as indicated by the prominent location given to **Cumhuriyet Meydanı** (Republic Square). Located only a block from Izmir Bay and near Izmir's best hotels, this square features a **Monument of Atatürk** riding a horse and pointing toward the sea. This monument epitomizes the end of an era, for Izmir was the last large Turkish city to be liberated from Greek occupation forces. Izmir celebrates the anniversary of its liberation on September 9.

Two hundred yards (183 meters) east of Atatürk's statue, on the Gazi Osman Bulvarı, is the entrance to the luxurious **Büyük Efes Hotel** with the city's main Turkish Airlines Office located in the arcade below. This showpiece of modern Izmir will be rivaled by the nearby Hilton Hotel in the early 1990s. Near the Atatürk Statue, facing the main Post Office, is the four-star **Pullman Etap Hotel,** considered to be the second best

Left, Mosaic at Ildiri. **Right**, strolling at Kuşadasi Camp.

165

Izmir

500 m / 0,3 miles

Izmir Bay

Kültürpark

St. Jean (Cathedral)
Alsancak Istasyonu (Alsancak Station)
Atatürk Müzesi (Atatürk Museum)
ALSANCAK
Atatürk Caddesi
Sehitler Caddesi
Kibris
Ali Çetinkaya Bulvari
Talatpasa Bulvari
Sair Esref Bulvari
Ziya Gökalp Bulvari
Pilevne Caddesi
Atatürk Cumhuriyet Bulvari
Vasif Çinar Bulvari
Cumhuriyet Meydani
Atatürk Monument
Pasaport Iskelesi (Ferry Boat Pier)
Se Nevresbey Bul.
PTT
THY
City Terminal
Büyük Efes
Turizm Danisma Bürosu
Botanical Gardens
II. KÜLTÜR
ISMET KAPTAN
Açikhava Tityatrosu (Open Air Theatre)
Zoo
Bozkurt Cad.
Bulvari
Mürselpasa Bulvari
BASMANE
Gaziler Caddesi
Basmane Istasyonau (Basmane Station)
Fevzipasa Bulvari
Corakkapi Camii (Mosque)
Mirkelam Kervansarayi (Caravan-sary)
Belediye Saray (City Hall)
Hisar Camii (Hisar Mosque)
Anafartalar Caddesi
Konak Camii (Konak Mosque)
GÜZELYURT
NAMAZGAH
Kemeralti Bazaar
Agora
SAKARYA
Balikuyu
Hasan Tahsin Monument
Anafartalar Cad.
Konak Saat Kulesi (Konak Clock Tower)
Salepcioglu Camii (Salepcioglu Mosque)
MIMAR SINAN
Dr. M. Ender Cad.
Mimar Sinan C.
I. KÜLTÜR
Dr. Refik Saydam Bulvari
Osmanpasa
Necatibey
Fettibey Bulvari
Halifziya B.
Gazi Bulvari
Kemalettin Cad.
Sair Esref Bulvari
Sehit Fettibey B.
Cumhuriyet
Atatürk Cumhuriyet
Caddesi
to Istanbul

Izmir Bay

IMBATLI
Anadolu Caddesi
Zübeyde Hanim Caddesi
Atatürk B. Caddesi
SOGUKKUYU
KARSIYAKA
Kemalpasa Cad.
Gürsel
Ferry
Cemal

Izmir Bay

Atatürk Heykeli (Atatürk Monument)
Pasaport Iskelesi (Ferry Boat Pier)
PTT
Gazi B.
Fevzipas
Konak Camii (Konak Mosque)
Hisar (Hisar
Belediye Saray (City Hall)
Ferry
Konak Saat Kulesi (Konak Clock Tower)
KONAK
Kemeralt Bazaar
Tityatrosu (State Theater)
E. Ü. Atatürk Kultür Merk (E. Ü. Atatürk Cultural Centre)
Devlet Opera ve Balesi (State Opera and Ballet)
TURGUTREIS PARKI
CICI PARK
Iki Ces Camii (Iki Ces Mosque)
Yolu Caddesi
MECIDIYE
TURGUTREIS PARKI
Asansör
Archaeology Museum
KOCATEPE
Estelpasa Caddesi
Yesillik Caddesi
Sahil Mihatpasa
PARKI
Rakim
Kemal Caddesi
Halide Edip Adivar Caddesi
MURAT REIS
Inönü
BAHÇELIEVLER
BAHAR
Uluönder Caddesi
Ordu Caddesi
Eski Izmir Caddesi
GÖZTEPE PARKI
Mustafa Caddesi
Mihatpasa

Izmir

1300 m / 0,8 miles

Inönü
Gazaler Hasan Tahsin Cad.
Firlz Ordu C.
Polat Caddesi
Yildiz
DOGANAY
ESENDERE

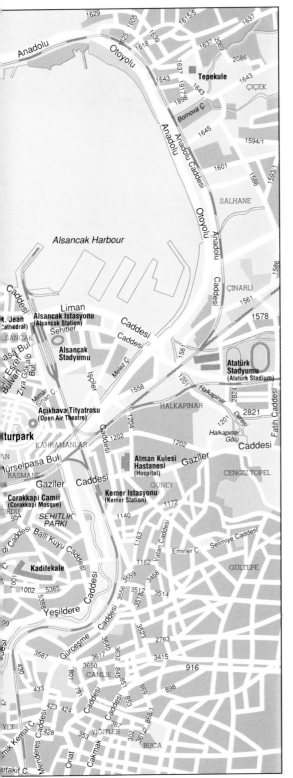

in Izmir. Of the many hotels located along Fevzi Paşa Bulvarı, the three-star **Hotel Hisar** near the Basmane Train Station and the 9 Eylül (9 September) entrance to the Kültürpark, is the best.

A walk along **Atatürk Caddesi** north of Cumhuriyet Meydanı is especially interesting at dusk. Along this bayside promenade, known also as Kordon-boyu, lined with palm trees are numerous souvenir shops, hotels, restaurants and government buildings.

Near the French Consulate and NATO Regional Headquarters are outstanding seafood restaurants like the **Orfoz** or **Imbat**. The former provides an ideal place to watch the sun setting over Izmir bay and the lowering of the flags of the 16 NATO countries. The latter is named after the *imbat* or ocean breeze which cools down sultry summer afternoons. At night this street is closed to traffic in order to permit pedestrians and seafood lovers to fully enjoy their respective pleasures.

Jewish quarter: Continuing along the promenade (Atatürk Caddesi) one soon reaches the prestigious **Alsancak** district of Izmir. Many of Izmir's most elegant shops and boutiques are concentrated in the area northeast of the Atatürk Museum and the Alsancak Iskelesi, a ferryboat landing. Gold, leather, and almost anything else can be purchased in the old **Jewish Quarter** at the western end of the **Kemeraltı Bazaar** near the Hisar Mosque.

Izmir also offers plenty of public and religious structures worth visiting. Chief among the public monuments is the **Konak Square** with its lavishly decorated Moorish **Clock Tower** and its **Monument of Hasan Tahsin**, a Turkish journalist who was the first casualty in the fight against the Greeks who invaded Izmir in 1919. The monument, showing the patriotic Tahsin firing a gun at the Greeks, is also referred to as the Ilk Kurşun Anıtı (**The Monument of the First Gun Shot**). Just north of this statue are the buildings of the **Belediye** (Municipal government) where Turkish art is displayed. Across the street is the **Vilayet Binası** (Provincial Governor's office) where elaborate flag lowering ceremonies occur daily, snarling downtown traffic badly for half an hour. From the nearby docks, ferryboats take 15 minutes to cross the bay to Karşıyaka, a suburb which offers seafood restaurants and views of Izmir's shimmering city lights.

City mosques: Perhaps the two most interesting of Izmir's many old mosques are the **Kemeraltı Mosque** and the **Hisar Mosque**. Built in 1672, the Kemeraltı Mosque, also known as the **Hacı Mehmet Ağa Camii**, is a modest but attractive building located on Anafartalar Caddesi in the heart of the Kemeraltı Bazaar. The narrow street leaving this mosque is crowded with shoppers looking for all manner of merchandise. Built in 1598, Hisar Mosque is the oldest and largest Moslem shrine in Izmir.

Located just outside the courtyard in front of the mosque are two nurseries and a small tea garden under an old sycamore tree. Locals believe that young women were sold as slaves in the **Kızlarağası Hanı**, a caravansary and market building behind (southwest of) the tea garden. The most delicious ice cream in Izmir is served at **Abdul Menan**, two blocks toward Fevzi Paşa Boulevard from the Hisar Mosque.

Of the seven original Christian churches (communities) of Asia Minor mentioned in Revelations, only Izmir's still flourishes. The church dedicated to Saint Polycarp, martyr and fourth bishop of Izmir, is located at the corner of Necatibey and Kâzım Bey boulevards. The nine-day ritual honoring St. Polycarp begins each February 14. The original church at this site dates back to 1625. Today's exquisitely decorated **Church of Saint Polycarp** dates to 1929. Visitors will find the contrast between its humble exterior and opulent interior is unforgettable.

Just 165 yards (150 meters) southwest is the **Santa Maria Church** built in 1667. Franciscans administer this modest church located at **Halit Ziya Bulvarı**, Number 67, a block south of the **Tourism Information Bureau**.

The Archaeology Museum: Located on a hill southeast of the Government Theater and Conservatory (opera) and next to the Devlet Hastanesi, or state hospital, the three-story **Archaeology Museum** contains numerous statues, artifacts, ceramics and frescoes from Greek and Roman sites throughout the region (including Claros, Belevi, Erythrae, ancient Izmir, Sardis and Ephesus). It is advisable to visit the museum before touring such archaeological sites. The exhibit describing Bayraklı, or ancient Izmir, explains the cuneiform tablets excavated at the Hittite site of Kültepe. These indicate that the original name of Izmir was *Tismurna*. Sometime after 1800 B.C., the prefix was dropped so that the placename Smurna remained. Izmir is the Turkish pronunciation of *Smurna* or Smyrna.

Next door is the **Ethnographic Museum**. A two-story structure which opened in 1985, the museum contains a wealth of old Ottoman and Turkish artifacts, including coins dating to 1389, weapons, carpets, household furnishings, embroidery, jewelry, and exhibits describing production of wood printing, pottery and evil eyes (*boncuk*) made of glass. Exhibits on camel wrestling and military commanders typical of western Anatolia (e.g. Efe and Zeybek) are fascinating.

The Velvet Castle: Those accustomed to exercise may begin climbing the slopes of **Mount Pagus** from the area near the Basmane Train Station. As one approaches the summit, the winding streets seem to get narrower and the houses smaller. Friendly children and quaint houses make the climb to the **Velvet Castle**, Kadifekale, pleasant. Concealed inside the western walls of Kadifekale are three acres of pine trees, a children's playground, a soccer field and botanical gardens. Doves singing early in the morning make this center of ancient Izmir especially idyllic. A Byzantine cistern is nestled amid pine trees. From the western ramparts of the ancient fortress there is a splendid view of downtown Izmir and the harbor. At night the tea garden hosts live music. Just east of the tea garden several

women busily weave brilliantly colored yarn bags on black-strap looms.

Many of the houses you see around Kadifekale and in the hills surrounding the city are illegal squatter houses, known as *gecekondus* (night landings). A vast majority of these houses were built by waves of peasants arriving from the countryside.

A Hellenistic settlement around Mount Pagus (at the summit of which is Kadifekale) began after 334 B.C., as a result of Alexander the Great's command. Kadifekale was connected to the agora by a Roman road. From its northeastern gate the road leading south went to Ephesus. The western ramparts, with round, Byzantine watchtowers on a Hellenistic foundation, have been fortified by several successive conquerors (Greeks, Romans, Byzantines, and Ottomans). These walls are wonderful places for strolling, watching sunsets over the wide bay, and contemplating ancient Izmir.

Construction of the Hellenistic city on top of Mount Pagus was allegedly commanded by the Goddess of Vengeance (Nemesis) in a dream of Alexander the Great in 334 B.C. Alexander, however, didn't apply the goddess' mandate to resettle the Smyrnaeans in the new city. The project finally began under Antigonus in 300 B.C., but it was Lysimachus, conqueror of Ephesus, who completed Smyrna's resettlement by 288 B.C. After relocation around Mount Pagus was accomplished, Izmir became the 13th member in a confederation of Ionian cities (the Panionic League). Izmir's population then exceeded 100,000 and the historian Strabo praised it as the "most beautiful city in Ionia."

Agora: The remains of the agora are located on a tract of land in downtown Izmir, one mile (1.6 km) southwest of Kadifekale and half a mile north of Konak Square. The original state agora also dates to shortly after Alexander the Great's dream. The agora included a temple, a marketplace and an indoor meeting place where business and politics were discussed. From an altar to Zeus in the center of the agora fragments of statues of Demeter, Poseidon and Artemis (hardly recognizable) have been reassembled. The statues of these three nature deities are now displayed in the Izmir Archaeology Museum.

An unusually severe earthquake in A.D. 178 forced the Romans to rebuild the Hellenistic agora. In the middle of the agora was a marble square. Along the northern gallery 17 columns of what was once a 540-foot (165-meter) long, three-story marble edifice remain. Daily business was conducted inside this basilica-style structure. In the center gallery was the entrance. On the ground floor were arched galleries and 26 shops. The agora itself was on the first floor. The section with columns standing on steps was the second floor. The third floor was destroyed, except for fragments of beams connecting two columns. At the northwest corner, a marble staircase takes you underground to an impressive vaulted basement where piped water runs continuously. Nearby are the remains of the aqueduct built 2,000 years ago. Commercial activity today is especially brisk only 330 yards (300 meters) south of here in the picturesque Kemeraltı Bazaar, which begins in the courtyard of the Kemeraltı Mosque.

Success in exporting and rapid industrialization have obliterated or transformed the rest of Izmir's legendary sites. The **Baths of Agamemnon**, where this great king and his soldiers may have recovered after the Trojan War 2,500 years ago, are still used in treating various ailments. The baths are now administered by the **Balçova Hot Springs**, located eight miles (12 km) west of Izmir, near Inciraltı. Those expecting to visit Homer's birthplace near the banks of the sacred Meles River will find that **Diana's Baths** are now enclosed by Izmir's waterworks, east of the Sümerbank factory off the Altın Yol (Golden Road). Homer is said to have written his epic poetry, the *Iliad* and *Odyssey*, in a cave near Diana's Baths (**Halkapınar Suyu**) where a statue of Artemis was discovered.

Izmir's history: Archaeological evidence from Tepekule suggests that

Izmir was inhabited by 3000 B.C. Now concealed in the industrial zone at the northeast edge of Izmir Bay, the oldest level at Tepekule (Hill Tower) at Bayraklı is contemporary with Troy I. This site was inhabited for 2,000 years by Hittites or Lelegians before Aeolians from the Aegean islands began colonization about 1000 B.C. In 800 B.C. Ionian Greeks displaced Aeolian Greeks. By 600 B.C. Tantalos, the tyrant who ruled ancient Izmir, was buried in a round tomb almost 100 feet (30 meters) in diameter and a magnificent Temple of Athena had been built. Following two invasions launched by Lydians before 500 B.C., Ionian Izmir lay dormant for 200 years, until Alexander the Great and his successors relocated it.

After 129 B.C. Izmir was ruled by Rome and it continued to flourish. Christianity was introduced to Izmir by St. John, or by St. Paul after A.D. 53. The fourth Christian bishop of Izmir, Saint Polycarp, was a direct disciple of St. John. Polycarp, who wrote "the love of money is the root of all evil," was burned at the stake in the Izmir Stadium, in A.D. 153 by order of a Roman administrator. Nevertheless, Izmir's Christian community has persisted until today.

Seljuk Turks controlled Byzantine Izmir from 1078 to 1097, the year Crusaders captured it. In 1261 the Genoese were granted control over Izmir. But, for the next 200 years Izmir was hotly contested by various factions of Christians and Moslems. Izmir remained under Ottoman rule from the time of Sultan Mehmet I until it was occupied by Greeks in 1919 as part of World War I spoils. The Turkish Republican Army, led by Atatürk, forced Greek evacuation and liberated Izmir on September 9, 1922. The evacuation culminated in a great mysterious fire that destroyed the city. Historians recently discovered documentary evidence indicating that it was Armenian insurgents living in Izmir, that set the city ablaze. For nearly seven decades, Turks and Greeks had accused one another of burning the city down.

Life on the Kordonboyu Avenue.

THE IZMIR INTERNATIONAL FAIR

Izmir's International Fair is an annual extravaganza which tastefully showcases the latest technological and commercial achievements to stimulate export of Turkish products and import of essential items. Moreover, numerous artistic and cultural activities promote international understanding and appreciation of human diversity. By attracting visitors from Turkey's rural areas and from urban centers around the world, the fair provides for an international exchange of ideas as well as goods. It strengthens Izmir's reputation as Turkey's most cosmopolitan city and Turkey's commitment to rapid development and entry into the European Community.

Beginning in 1936, with the sixth Izmir International Fair, the fairgrounds, or Kültürpark, has hosted the colossal trade fair and various smaller fairs. The fairgrounds occupy half a square mile (one square km) in the heart of downtown Izmir and are surprisingly uncrowded in the mornings. They provide an oasis with abundant shade beneath numerous trees, an amusement park for children, tennis courts, jogging trails and cycling lanes, two outdoor theaters, a zoo and plenty of inexpensive restaurants. The fairgrounds also house the regional offices of Turkish Radio and Television.

Visitors to Izmir can get to the fairgrounds easiest by returning to the Basmane Train Station and walking along Anafartalar Caddesi past 9 Eylül Meydanı (9 September Square) and entering the fairground through the 9 Eylül Gate, which faces the square. There are four other gates: the **Lozan** (Lausanne) **Gate**, which faces the Lozan Meydanı (Square) three blocks away from the 9 September University, the region's main institution of higher learning; the **Montrö** (Montreux) **Gate**, facing the Montrö Meydanı which is connected to Cumhuriyet Meydanı by Şehit Nevresbey Bulvarı;

The Izmir International Fairgrounds.

the **26 Ağustos** (August) **Gate** in the north and the **Cumhuriyet Gate** in the east, both of which face Dr. Mustafa Ender Caddesi.

The fair's queen: From August 26 to September 10, exhibits from more than 25 countries and Turkey, are open to the public between 3 p.m. to 11 p.m. daily. Turkish exhibits are open an additional ten days, until September 20. Evenings are boisterous with excitement and crowds. Many rustics with their peasant wives and children mill about the exhibits wondering with amazement at the new technology. Locals and tourists alike enjoy the best in Turkish entertainment, with belly dancing, floor shows and solo music performances available nightly, and watch Izmir's most talented and gorgeous women competing for the honor of being crowned "Queen of the Fair."

Some of Turkey's leading female and male vocalists have performed at the Izmir Fair, including the lusty blond Sibel Can, a belly dancer turned vocalist; the shapely Güngör Bayrak, an actress famed for wearing see-through dresses; and Bülent Ersoy, a controversial young male singer of classical Turkish tunes who once underwent a sex change operation; and Ibrahim Tatlıses, the Elvis Presley of Turkey and the "King of Arabesque" music.

In addition to shopping and being entertained, visitors to the fair can meet people from countries throughout the world. The non-Turkish exhibitors in the 58th annual fair in 1989 included the United States, the Federal Republic of Germany, Belgium, Czechoslovakia, Palestine, France, South Korea, Netherlands, Iraq, Iran, Sweden, Switzerland, Turkish Republic of Northern Cyprus, Libya, Hungary, Pakistan, Poland, Rumania, the Soviet Union, Sri Lanka, Syria, Tunisia, Yugoslavia, the Philippines, England, Thailand and Italy, as well as international organizations such as NATO and UNICEF.

Each country or organization has its own pavilion. Countries may include exhibits from 20 or more different private companies or state-owned enterprises. Within the pavilion space allo-cated to a particular country the exhibits may change from year to year. More than 1,100 non-Turkish companies, including well-known corporations such as BMW, Bosch, International Business Machines Corp. (IBM), Coca Cola Corp., KLM Royal Dutch Airlines, Air France, Samsung Electronics and Renault participated in the 1989 Fair.

Turkish products: Turkey's exhibitors include about 250 privately owned companies displaying furniture, clothing and textiles, banking services, books and magazines, fruit and vegetables, dairy products and hundreds of industrial products. Among the best known domestic exhibitors are Arçelik, a manufacturer of home appliances, television sets and refrigerators; the Turkish subsidiary of Chrysler, which produces trucks and diesel engines in Turkey; Kent, a producer of confectionery; Kütahya Porcelain with its exquisite ceramics and porcelain; and Tuborg, an Izmir beer and malt producer.

Also represented are about 80 companies affiliated with the Turkish Chambers of Industry, Commerce and Stock exchanges, 40 companies affiliated with the Development Bank of Turkey, and 35 official enterprises and cooperatives, including the Izmir-based Tariş, one of the world's largest agricultural cooperatives. Tariş produces and sells everything from cotton and yarn to Smyrna figs, sultana raisins and olive oil.

Turkish trade increases: In 1989, nearly three million visitors toured more than 2,000 exhibits. In addition to the exhibits, 21 covered pavilions housed hundreds of informative and visually attractive displays. Walking through the exhibits convinces one that commerce had made it a truly small world after all, and that Turkey's share in global trade is steadily increasing.

Tourists who plan to visit Izmir during the International Fair should book their hotels way in advance. It is very difficult, sometimes impossible, to find accommodations in the city during that period as tens of thousands of Turks from other parts of the country visit Izmir for the fair.

IZMIR'S MINORITIES

Izmir's affluent ethnic minorities have played an important role in the development of industry, banking and commerce in the city. What follows is a rundown on who these minorities are and their history.

Sephardic Jews: The Jewish community in Izmir may be 2,000 years old. In response to King Ferdinand's order expelling all Jews from Spain in 1492, Sultan Beyazıt II confided to his courtiers that the Spanish King had foolishly "impoverished his own land and enriched ours." Sultan Beyazıt's invitation to settle in the Ottoman Empire was accepted by thousands of Jews exiled from Spain and Portugal. By 1575 most commerce in the Ottoman Empire was controlled by Jews, and Spanish was the trade language of the Mediterranean.

Today the majority of Izmir's 2,500 Jews are still involved in commerce although it is estimated that less than half of them speak fluently the Spanish of Cervantes' era.

There have been two eras of exodus for Izmir's Jewry. During World War I, some 10,000 left Izmir for Latin American countries, such as Uruguay, Argentina and Mexico. Still, in 1927, 17,000 Jews remained in Izmir. After World War II most of them went to Israel.

Beth Israel: Among the numerous old synagogues of Izmir there are seven principal ones, the oldest and best preserved is the **Beth Israel** on Mithat Paşa Caddesi, number 265. Two of Izmir's older synagogues are located on **Havra Sokak** (street of the synagogues). A synagogue built in 1821 is located near the gold merchant's quarter of the Kemeraltı. Its amazingly unobtrusive exterior conceals a splendid interior. The monumental synagogue in the suburb of Karataş was built by the famous Rothschild family.

Most scholars agree that Ottoman Jews were better treated than their European counterparts. Izmir's Jewish community is already busy making preparations for elaborate festivities to commemorate the 500th anniversary of their residence in Turkey in 1992.

The Dönme: Sabatai Zevi, born in Izmir in 1626, triggered a scandal of international proportions. Izmir's Orthodox Jews were outraged when Sabatai proclaimed himself the Messiah in 1665. He attracted such an immense international following that the Sultan ordered him to convert to Islam or die. He defected from Judaism and converted to Islam.

Believers still exist. Sabatai's followers, called the Dönme (turncoats), live secretively in Izmir and Istanbul. Izmir's Jews condemn Sabatai as a "False Messiah" or charlatan who misled the gullible. "His name is cursed among us," one Jewish businessman said. Nevertheless John Freely, an American educator and travel writer who lives and works in Turkey, reported observing a few elderly Dönme worshipping in an old house in Izmir which they regarded as Sabatai's birthplace in his *The Western Shores of Turkey*. The house was for many years the

The Latin Church of St. Polycarp.

residence of Osman Kibar, the late conservative Mayor of Izmir who was himself a Dönme.

The Levantines: In 1581 an agreement between Sultan Murat III and Queen Elizabeth I granted a seven-year franchise to a group of English merchants known as the Levent Company. These original Levantines were responsible for introducing Europeans to coffee. They also exported Izmir's world famous figs, currants, dates, lemons, oranges, sultana raisins, carpets, textiles, jewelry and copperware. They and their descendants have contributed enormously to Izmir's commercial development.

Today there are 1,500 British residents in Izmir, most of whom are still exporting items such as dried fruits, tobacco, cotton, grapes and motor engines. They meet frequently and many of them worship together at the Church of St. John the Evangelist at the northern entrance to **Talat Paşa Bulvarı** in Alsancak. Two other Anglican churches, one at **Buca** and the other at **Bornova**, are still in use.

Italians of Izmir: The term Levantine has been rather loosely applied to all families of European origin, including French and Italian. Italians have long been active as traders throughout the region surrounding Izmir. In 1261 the Byzantine Emperor granted Italians from Genoa full control of Izmir. Although they lost political control of Izmir after 1320, their descendants still survive in the region. Today Izmir has only 80 Frenchmen, some of whom attend St. Joseph's School and worship at the Church of Saint Polycarp, where French is spoken.

Today only 1,300 Catholics live in Izmir, primarily of Italian descent. Izmir's chief Catholic churches include **Santa Maria**, the **Rosary Church** near Alsancak Iskelesi, **Santa Elena** in Karşıyaka, **Saint Anthony** in Bayraklı, and **Our Lady of Lourdes** in Göztepe. Mass is increasingly said in Turkish. About 100 children attend the private Italian Primary School and receive instruction in Italian.

Jews pray in a synagogue.

THE
IONIAN COAST

Heading west from Izmir on the highway to Çeşme one reaches Urla about 22 miles (35 km), after passing Inciraltı and Güzelbahçe. **Urla Iskelesi** is a small picturesque town half a mile (one km) right off the main highway. Along its tranquil beach are a few hotels and the ruins of the Ionian port of **Clazomenae**. Greek colonists from Peloponnesus settled on the mainland, just 1.2 miles (two km) southwest of where an indigenous population had lived. After the Ionian revolt, around 500 B.C., these Greeks moved out to the island in the bay for fear of the Persians. By order of Alexander a causeway connected the mainland to the island. Today a paved road links the mainland to the **Urla Hospital**, which specializes in bone diseases. Because of their proximity to the hospital, the ruins of Clazomenae aren't open to the public.

Çeşme, a quaint fishing village, and neighboring **Ilıca**, famed for its thermal baths, are booming. Their beautiful white sand beaches entice more visitors every year. During the summer season international travelers and residents of Izmir enjoy its daytime sun and nighttime fun. In early July, the Çeşme Sea Festival features art, music and sports activities. Çeşme is uncrowded and enchanting between the end of September and early June.

Çeşme is windy and picturesque, cooler and less crowded than Izmir. It offers plenty of shopping and sightseeing, with a bit of history to provide a break from boating, beaches, water sports and discos.

Stone castle: A tour of the **Genoese Fortress** overlooking the bay affords spectacular views of Çeşme, its harbor, and the Greek island of Chios. This impressive stone castle was built to protect traders originally from Genoa. Inside this 14th-century castle, a small museum displays Hellenistic and Roman Period artifacts.

Near the fortress are the ruins of an

Housing development at Erythrae.

18th-century inn or caravansary. In front of the fortress is a **Statue of Cezayirli Gazi Hasan Pasha** and a lion. For Turks the lion symbolizes bravery, and this monument commemorates Hasan Pasha's victory over the Russian navy which attacked the Ottoman fleet in the Bay of Çeşme in 1770. Across the street at the harbor, ferryboats carry passengers about nine miles (14 km) to **Chios**.

Numerous restaurants are located along the promenade at the edge of the harbor and others are situated along **Inkilap Caddesi**, the main street. At night, after this street is closed to traffic, restaurants like the **Imren** are especially enjoyable.

Turkish ambience: Those seeking more Turkish ambience will find it 1.6 miles (three km) north at **Dalyan**. This lovely village sits on a little bay where yachts anchor. Seafood connoisseurs congregate at several fine restaurants such as the **Liman** and the **Körfez Hotel and Restaurant**.

The ruins of **Erythrae** can be found near Ildır, a sleepy seaside village northeast of Çeşme. Erythrae is one of 12 Ionian cities mentioned by the historian Herodotus. Principal attractions include the ruins of **Athena's Temple** and a 10,000-seat theater. Between the temple and Ildır are ruins of a Roman villa, a mausoleum, and a wall belonging to the agora. On top of the hill are ruins of a 150-year-old Greek church and Athena's Temple.

Fishing villages: On the way from Çeşme, Kuşadası and Selçuk, there are numerous worthwhile but less publicized sites which can easily be reached by private transport or taxi. Leaving Çeşme and Ildır, traveling east toward Izmir, you reach a junction just before Güzelbahçe. A right turn here (onto route 505) will take you south to **Seferihisar**. At Seferihisar another right takes one to **Sığacık**, a pleasant little fishing village with an imposing Genoese fortress. Continuing southwest 1.2 miles (two km) one passes the white sandy beach of **Akkum**. The road forks left toward Teos, about half a

Çeşme as seen from the Castle.

mile (one km) away.

Teos, a prosperous Ionian port, was situated near one large and one small harbor. By 600 B.C. its wealth and location at the center of the Ionian region prompted Thales to propose that it be Ionia's capital city. His suggestion was never carried out. The inability of Ionian cities, Teos included, to unite politically left them vulnerable to Persian conquest. After the Persians were expelled from Ionia, Izmir lay dormant for 200 years, between 500 and 300 B.C., while Teos regained its prominence as a thriving port.

Teos declined after Romans gained control of Asia Minor, beginning with their naval victory over the Seleucid king, Antiochus III. This decisive battle was fought in 190 B.C. in the southern harbor of Teos.

The best preserved part of Teos is the **Temple of Dionysus**, located in an olive grove just off the paved road.

Other visible ruins include traces of the Hellenistic-era city wall, a Roman Period odeon and parts of a theater.

The prototype for Dionysus, the wine god, may have been Bacchus, of Lydian origin. The Lydians representing satyrs in processions of Bacchus dressed in goat skins and sang "goat songs" which may have inspired Greek tragedy. Since Dionysus was their patron, the Artists of Dionysus resided at Teos between 300 and 150 B.C. From Teos these professional actors and musicians performed at theaters and musical festivals throughout the Greek world.

Myonneus, Mouse Island, is nine miles (15 km) south of Sığacık. This landmark, known in Turkish as **Çifit Kalesi** (the Jew's Castle) is just north of Cape Doğanbey.

Traces of ancient walls remain on top of this steep and rocky fortress which once protected pirates from the Romans who attacked Teos. There is a causeway, visible only underwater, connecting the mainland to the citadel.

Lebedos was one of the poorest of the Ionian cities primarily because Ephesus and Teos had better harbors. The ruins are located just south of **Ürkmez**, on a

The ruins of Claros.

178

knoll overlooking an attractive sandy cove with a restaurant and camping facilities. There are hotels nearby at Ürkmez and Gümüldür.

From Gümüldür there are 11 miles (17 km) of scenic coastline before reaching the cliffs with the partially excavated ruins of Notium. Its ruins include a **Temple of Athena**, an agora, a theater and an extensive city wall.

Claros: Homer's hymn to Apollo indicates that the **Temple of Apollo** at Claros, 1.2 miles (two km) inland from Notium, was a famous sanctuary by the seventh-century B.C. At the southern entrance to the sanctuary six marble columns have been unearthed in a small canyon. The road entering this sanctuary was three feet (10 meters) wide and may have been connected to a harbor at one time.

A short distance north of the entrance is a large altar dedicated to Apollo, and a smaller altar to Artemis, his twin sister. Fragments of statues of Apollo, Artemis, and their mother, Leto, have been recovered.

West of the altars numerous columns, including their Doric-style decorated capitals, are plainly visible.

Colophon: Eight miles (12 km) north of Claros is the affluent Ionian city of **Colophon**, built on the mountain behind the quaint Turkish village of Değirmendere.

Colophon's strong navy, maritime trade and abundant farmland made it a prosperous member of the Ionian League. At its peak in the seventh and eighth centuries B.C., it even conquered Aeolian Izmir. Yet even its ferocious warrior-dogs and famous cavalry could not protect it from Lydian and Persian conquerors. It was ruled continuously by Persians until Alexander the Great. Although Colophon was rebuilt in 281 B.C., it was, even with its coastal ally Notium, unable to compete with the emporium of Ephesus. Its disappearance from history is so complete that even the ruins are insignificant.

The territory controlled by Colophonians extended east to the fertile plain of **Cumaovası**. From Colophon north to Menderes (formerly Cuma-

ovası) it is 10 miles (17 km). About halfway between them, to the right of the highway, is the central bottling plant of **Şaşal** drinking water, famous throughout Turkey. **Menderes** is a small town located on a plain where olives, figs, and grapes are grown. From Menderes it is only a few miles to the highway leading north to Izmir or south toward Torbalı and Selçuk.

Twenty-five miles (40 km) south of Izmir, in the middle of a rich agricultural region, is the town of **Torbalı**, where two small castles may soon be open to the public. Another nine miles (15 km) south, on top of a hill to the right of the highway, looms **Keçi Kalesi** (the Goat's Castle). This Byzantine fortress was built around A.D. 1200.

Selçuk is a small but thriving tourist center located near the church of St. John, the Isa Bey Mosque, the Artemision and the ruins of Ephesus. Its main attractions are the museum, the remains of an aqueduct near the train station (where steam-engine trains arrive), a partially restored Ottoman bath from

An Efe, a veteran of the Turkish War of Independence.

the 1370s and shops with onyx, carpets, leather and souvenirs.

Before visiting the ruins a trip to the museum (open daily from 8:30 a.m. to 6:30 p.m.) is highly recommended. In addition to the two famous statues of Artemis, there are numerous examples of funeral relics including Mycenaean bowls dated to 1400 B.C., a fresco and marble head of Socrates, a marble head of Eros, a bronze statuette of Eros riding a dolphin.

Tours of Ephesus and Meryem Ana, the purported last House of the Virgin Mary, can be arranged from Selçuk.

A short drive east of Selçuk is the quaint village of Şirince. It is still unspoiled by tourists. This small village, founded by Christians who left Ephesus around A.D. 600, is surrounded by pine-covered hills and orchards of olive and peach trees. Homemade wine can be purchased directly from enterprising villagers. There are three restaurants, plenty of old Greek houses, and two abandoned Greek churches to see.

Only 11 miles (18 km) from Selçuk is the chic coastal playground **Kuşadası**. From here organized tours of Ephesus can also be arranged. Tourist development at Kuşadası has focused on several long sandy beaches and lovely bays located at the center of a 16-mile (25-km) stretch of coastline.

Belly dancing: Kuşadası's most unique lodging is at the **Kervansaray,** situated in the heart of town in what was formerly the Öküz Mehmet Paşa Caravansary. This historic landmark has been lovingly restored and converted into a fine hotel. On the ground floor there are several shops, and a fountain in the middle of a courtyard. The buffet dinners served here nightly are animated by belly dancing and other forms of lavish entertainment.

From mid-April through October the water is warm enough to make swimming a delight. The most pristine beaches are located away from downtown, extending from Kadınlar Plajı (Womens' Beach) south to Güzelçamlı, and from the Tusan Hotel north to Pamucak.

Trees in full bloom with Selçuk Castle in background.

Visitors can hire yachts or sailboats at **Kuşadası Marina**. Daily boat tours around the coast are also available. Ferryboats leave daily for the Greek island of **Samos**, only one mile (two km) away. Windsurfing facilities and lessons are also available.

Except for Ephesus, archaeological sites are scarce. The village of **Pygela**, formerly situated a few miles north of downtown Kuşadası was founded, according to Strabo, by Lelegians and colonized by Agamemnon. The annual meeting place of the 13 Ionian cities comprising the Panionic League was 16 miles (25 km) south of Kuşadası, near the village of Güzelçamlı and the entrance to the **Dilek Peninsula National Park**. After the Byzantines granted trading rights to Italians from Venice and Genoa these Italian merchants shipped silk, saffron and other goods to Europe from Kuşadası. Under Ottoman control Kuşadası continued to flourish.

In addition to the Genoese castle on the island, there are two interesting Ottoman era structures built by the archi-

tect for whom they are named. The **Öküz Mehmet Paşa Mosque** is located near the Town Hall, east of the Öküz Mehmet Paşa Caravansary, which was built in 1613. This impressive stone inn provided safety and hospitality to travelers on the trade route culminating here. The open courtyard housed the animals serving the travelers who were lodged in second-story rooms. Connected to the mainland by a causeway 1320 feet (400 meters) in length is **Kuşadası**, Bird Island, from which this town took its name. This small island offers a restored fortress, a fine restaurant, a disco, a tea garden serving snacks and beverages, and magnificent views of the ocean and bay.

The Genoese Fortress at Kuşadası may have been built by A.D. 1500. Later it became the home of Hayrettin Barbaros, an Algerian pirate appointed grand Admiral by the illustrious Ottoman Sultan, Süleyman the Magnificent. In 1546 Hayrettin died rich and famous. He was 70 years old.

Left, Isa Bey Mosque at Selçuk. **Right**, the Basilica of St. John.

CAMEL WRESTLING

Every year in mid-January, the market town of Selçuk hosts the Super Bowl of camel wrestling. For two days during the Selçuk Camel Wrestling Festival, an atmosphere of gaiety and carnival excitement prevails in the town as the top male fighting camels of Turkey vie for honors, prize money and trophies.

Camel wrestling, or *deve güreşi* in Turkish, is the most popular spectator sport in the southern Turkish Aegean Coast.

Desert ship: Before the advent of automobiles, long-distance lorries, trains and jetliners, camels were the principal means of transportation in the Ottoman Empire and the Middle East. Camel caravans carried people and goods from one city to another across miles of deserts and wastelands. Because of its ability to withstand extreme heat and cold, survive long periods of thirst and hunger and stride in a swaying motion, the camel was affectionately described as the "ship of the desert."

Only Yörük Turks, an old-fashioned nomadic people inhabiting the mountain plateaus of coastal Turkey, still prefer camels to cars for public transportation. Travelers to the coast will frequently come across Yörük camel caravans.

Village herdsmen now basically train the beasts as fighters. These herdsmen don't race camels, a popular pastime in some Middle Eastern countries including Saudi Arabia, Kuwait and Yemen.

Camel wrestling is supposed to have started when herdsmen noticed male camels fighting over their females during mating season and turned the affair into a sport.

Weekend tournaments: Camel wrestling meets are held every weekend in many small towns in the provinces of Izmir, Aydin, Denizli and Muğla from January through March. During a weekend tournament, thousands of peasants from nearby villages descend on the towns to bet on their favorite camels and also to sell their produce and display carpets and other handicrafts.

Male camels wrestle as many as 30 times in one winter season, a time when the females are in heat. During the rest of the year they just munch on fodder, ruminate and require special handling. The upkeep of a beast costs an enormous amount of money, but ownership of a camel often brings prestige to peasant herdsmen – the same kind of prestige owning a flashy new sports car would bring to a young city Turk.

Not all camels can be trained as wrestlers. "Great wrestlers are born not made," says Hulusi Kanat, a camel trainer for 30 years and a professional announcer at camel fights. The best camels are those from Iranian mother camels, he says. Camels generally begin wrestling at the age of six, but it is not before the age of 15 that they become big and strong enough to be champions. Some old war horses continue wrestling to the age of 25.

The bulldozer: Turkey's 250 best fighting camels are known as *tülüs*. These camels can earn up to $1,200 and much more on side bets for their owners during each bout, when one camel is pitted against another. Each *tülü* is an awesome sight, weighing over a ton and standing six feet (two meters) at the shoulders and seven feet (2.3 meters) at the top of its hump. Each beast is recognized as a superstar in his own right and has a ferocious name, such as the Bulldozer, the Killer, the Quiltmaker, Deli Tülü (the Mad Camel), the Warrior, the Commando, the Conqueror, Kara "Black" Kemal, Kolombo, Felek (Fate), and Sulfur.

It is at Selçuk, two hours out of Izmir, where the top camels slug it out. Often, more than 120 camels participate in this extravaganza. Before the tournament begins, the Selçuk-Bodrum Highway, a major thoroughfare, is closed to traffic for about one hour as the owners parade their camels, decked out in colorful blankets, pompons, gold bangles and jewelry, through the main street. The camels also wear large cow bells that jingle as they stride through town.

The camels, frothing at the mouth at

the height of the mating season, are muzzled to prevent them from biting jealous rivals or human admirers.

After the opening ceremony in Selçuk, which includes speeches by the provincial governor, the mayor and vote-seeking politicians, the camels are marched to the nearby ancient city of Ephesus for the big meet.

Gladiators of antiquity?: The fights take place on the grounds of a ruined stadium, used during Roman times to feed Christians to the lions and for fights among gladiators. One writer has, in fact, likened the fighting camels to the "gladiators of antiquity."

Thousands of spectators, including women, jam the stadium and sit on the stone seats to watch the matches amidst the playing of drums, fife and folklore performances. Vendors sell popcorn, potato chips, nuts and *simit*, a Turkish sesame seed roll shaped like a doughnut, during the eight-hour program.

Two snorting, bellowing male *tülüs* are brought in. They stand at opposite ends of the stadium. The match begins only after a female camel struts between the two rivals to arouse their excitement and ire. Suddenly the two camels charge at one another like angry bulls, butting heads, bumping sides and kicking with their feet. Often the camels go into a dangerous neck lock or leg lock. The stronger animal tries to crush his opponent with his weight.

Each bout lasts about ten minutes after which two nine-men teams, each wearing red or blue color leather coverings, pull the animals apart with rope in a tug-of-war fashion. No animals are seriously hurt. The only injuries are bruises and bloody noses. The most exciting matches are among the top heavyweights.

Victory: To win, one wrestler has to knock the other down on his side, chase him out of the stadium or cause him to squeal a camel's version of "uncle." Otherwise the match is a draw.

In addition to prize money and earnings from bets, the animal owners get a camel trophy, a plaque and special handmade carpets.

Camels fight it out at Germencik.

EPHESUS

Left, the many-breasted Artemis. Below, Priapus, the fearless satrap, and his overgrown phallus.

In the sixth century B.C., when **Ephesus** was an affluent Aegean port, Heraclitus, the son of an Ephesian priest, dedicated his philosophical treatise called *Nature* to the Temple of Artemis (Nature Goddess or Mother Goddess). For this famous native son, the eternal flux or constant change he recognized as fundamental in nature was best symbolized by water and rivers. The gradual transformation wrought by the **Kaystros River** (Küçük Menderes in Turkish), which flows into the Aegean, epitomizes Heraclitus' theory and explains the demise of Ephesus.

The prosperity Ephesus enjoyed as a port of trade connecting Europe, Asia and Africa was dependent on its having a functional harbor. Ephesus began to decline when its harbor was ruined by the centuries of silt accumulation that occur at the mouth of the Kaystros River. Today the city lies three miles (five km) from the sea. The region lay nearly dormant from 1450 to 1950.

In its heyday, Ephesus was the most important commercial center in western Anatolia and had a population of more than a quarter of a million people. Inscriptions found by archaeologists described Ephesus as the "first and greatest metropolis of Asia."

British and Austrian archaeologists excavated the site in the 19th century. The Austrians smuggled out most of the relics found there, but returned the artifacts when the Ottoman government threatened to ban all future Austrian excavations in the Near East.

In recent decades its ruins have attracted tourists from all over the world. Ephesus is, in a sense, an international city again. Nearly two million foreign tourists visited the ancient city in 1989. The informed visitor to Ephesus may, with a bit of imagination, relive a moment of world history, and relearn a lesson about our species' abiding dependence upon Mother nature.

This Aegean port turned Asian metropolis has been home to various cultures and religions. Little is known about the earliest inhabitants of Ephesus. The Carians, whose most important city was Halicarnassus (Bodrum), evidently considered themselves natives of the region. Sometime later Smyrnaians, or an Amazon called Smyrna (Izmir), may have colonized Ephesus and Izmir.

Mycenaean pottery: The earliest archaeological evidence of human occupation of Ephesus is painted pottery of Mycenaean origin dating to 1400 B.C., which are on display at the Selçuk Ephesus Museum. These elegantly crafted Mycenaean bowls were widely traded, and appear at sites from Troy to Bodrum. It is unclear whether Mycenaeans settled in Ephesus or simply traded with a local population. At any rate, the city called Apasas in Hittite records of 1400 B.C. is surely Ephesus.

The Ionian region of Asia Minor in which Ephesus is located was definitely colonized by 1000 B.C. A political struggle for control of Athens prompted the Athenian colonists, led by Androklos, the son of Kodros, king of Athens, to establish Ephesus at the northern end of Mt. Pilon. Legend has it that Androklos built a temple dedicated to Athena at the place where a wild boar was killed, in compliance with cryptic instructions received from the Oracle of Apollo, which he consulted. The remains of this temple may be on the small hill just west of the Roman stadium. An effigy of the boar stood on the street in front of the temple for centuries in thanksgiving for the fulfillment of the oracular prophesy.

The Carians fought a losing battle against these Greek invaders but managed to kill Androklos. A shrine to him was built near the **Magnesian** (Manisa) **Gate**. His descendants ruled Ephesus for the next four centuries.

Rapacious king: The prosperity of Ionian Ephesus caught the eye of the rapacious King Croesus of Sardis. In 560 B.C. this Lydian king captured Ephesus and relocated its inhabitants in the area around the Temple of Artemis.

Statues of golden calves and beautiful column capitals, one of which bears his name, were Croesus' chief contribution to the Artemision (Temple of Artemis). He also had a fortification wall built around the city.

After the Persian King Cyrus defeated Croesus in 546 B.C., Ephesus was ruled by Persians as a satrapy. Although the citizens of Ephesus continued to trade and practice their religion freely they were obliged to pay extortionist tribute to their Persian masters. From 546 B.C. until 334 B.C, the Ionian region was in turmoil as Greeks and Persians fought each other. When Alexander the Great defeated the Persians on the southern shores of the Sea of Marmara at the Battle of the Granicus in 334 B.C., Ephesus was liberated and it became a quasi-democratic city. It was briefly dominated by the Ptolemites of Egypt before being annexed by the Attalid kings of Pergamum.

Roman Ephesus: Roman control of Ephesus began after 133 B.C. Although Ephesians joined in a successful revolt

The amphitheater at Ephesus.

against Rome in 88 B.C., Roman rule was quickly reestablished. In 27 B.C. the Roman Emperor Augustus proclaimed Ephesus capital of the Asian province. It was during this period that Ephesus became one of the largest cities in the Roman Empire; one of only three cities to have street lighting.

Roman Ephesus was a free city governed by two assemblies: one for ordinary citizens (*Demos*), the other for the *Boule*, a 300-member elite. Rich Ephesians could attain prestige by sponsoring public works and ceremonies. The most prestigious ceremonial duties, those of the *prytanis*, could be assumed by both sexes. The *prytanis* paid all expenses incurred in carrying out daily animal sacrifices, supervising all cults and insuring that the eternal fire honoring Hestia, goddess of the hearth, always burned in the Prytaneion.

When Emperor Hadrian visited Ephesus in A.D. 123, it was still a booming emporium and residence of the Roman governor of Asia. Most of the buildings visible today date from the Roman era

Modern folk dancing in the ancient theater.

when Ephesus had nearly 250,000 inhabitants. The buildings, fountains and monuments commemorate Roman administrators and Ephesians rich enough to sponsor public works. Following a devastating attack by a large Gothic fleet in A.D. 262, the grandeur that characterized ancient Ephesus began to wane.

Christians persecuted: During this era of decadence, Christians were persecuted for refusing to sacrifice animals and to worship pagan deities. The struggle between the pagan Roman religion and the monotheistic Christianity resulted in Christians being killed by lions in the same stadium where gladiators and wild animals entertained Roman audiences. It is believed that after Christianity was endorsed as the official religion of Rome, all the seats in Ephesus Stadium were destroyed. Today the stadium is the scene for the popular camel wrestling festival.

The legend explaining the **Grotto of the Seven Sleepers** illustrates the growth of Christianity. Around A.D.

250 seven Christian boys took refuge in a cave, located about 1,650 feet (500 meters) east of the **Vedius Gymnasium**. When they awoke, after 200 years of slumber, Rip van Winkle-style, Christianity had become the official religion and Emperor Theodosius II proclaimed that they had been resurrected. Several hundred graves dating to the fifth century, including those of the seven sleepers, and a church, were excavated in this cave.

Many biblical scholars believe that St. Paul's version of Christianity (one which was to become detached completely from its Jewish roots) differed significantly from that of St. John and his followers. Paul of Tarsus was a Roman citizen and a Benjamite Jew who did not know Jesus in Jerusalem. The fact that Paul persecuted Christians until his blinding vision on the road to Damascus (Acts 9:1-9) distinguishes him from St. John.

Flight from Jerusalem: There is evidence to suggest St. John and Mary left Jerusalem to escape the persecution that threatened them. If Professor Brownlee is correct in identifying John as Lazarus of Bethany, then the chief priests' decision to kill both Jesus and Lazarus (John 12: 9-11) would make the flight from Jerusalem a necessity. With its commitment to religious freedom and its already thriving Jewish community, Ephesus must have seemed a safe haven. At any rate, both Mary and John are believed to have lived and died here.

Paul's famous confrontation with Ephesians loyal to Artemis is one of a series of conflicts which culminated in his being decapitated on the outskirts of Rome in A.D. 64. It was then that St. John became leader of the **Church of Ephesus**. It is believed that John is buried under the church which now bears his name. By the fourth century, when a modest basilica was built over his grave, the glory of Roman Ephesus was gone. The harbor had silted up. Much of the marble used to build the towers and fortification walls surrounding the **Church of St. John** (completed around A.D. 550), located in the town of **Library of Celsus.**

Selçuk, was brought from the stadium where Christians were once tortured to entertain up to 70,000 spectators.

It is widely believed that the worship of Artemis was a continuation of the veneration of the Mother Goddess and fertility cult suggested by the statues of Cybele scattered throughout Turkey. Statues excavated at the farming community of Çatal Höyük in southcentral Anatolia are 9,000 years old. Yet if Artemis was indeed the mother of all animals, her prototype is likely to have its origins in hunting and gathering cultures. Perhaps the prototype is represented by the Venus figurines and human females depicted in magnificent cave art appearing at numerous sites in Europe and Asia more than 13,000 years ago. The oldest evidence of Cybele-Artemis worship at Ephesus is a plain wooden statue.

Artemis cult: The three well-preserved statues of Artemis on display at the Selçuk Ephesus Museum graphically illustrate the meaning this great mother once had. From the hips down to the toes on both statues, flowers and bees are visible. The belt of the **Great Artemis** (the one wearing the tall crown displayed at the western end of the hall) shows bees and flowers. Next to the **Beautiful Artemis** (displayed at the eastern end of the hall) is a headless statue of Artemis with bees and flowers on her chest. These icons of Artemis imply that the survival of plants and animals requires mutual dependence or symbiosis. Artemis was evidently the chief guardian and personification of harmony in nature. In worshipping Artemis, Ephesians proclaimed that living in harmony with nature was their central concern.

It is frequently asserted that the social structure of bees provided the model for the religious hierarchy entrusted with the worship of Artemis. The Queen Bee which reproduces the species is served by all others. At Ephesus there were hundreds of priests, priestesses and guards devoted to Artemis. The chief priest or Megaysos was in charge of receiving donations to and loaning

Temple of Hadrian.

money from the temple treasury. He and the other priests had their reproductive organs removed to become permanent celibates before assuming office. The priestess who assisted the Megaysos were virgins consecrated to Artemis (reminiscent of the six Vestal Virgins serving the Roman goddess of fire, Vesta).

Testes of bulls: Chastity, fertility and reproduction are key attributes of Artemis. Depicted on the breasts of both statues of Artemis are the testes of bulls which were sacrificed to her. Long misidentified as eggs, these testes symbolize fertility as well.

The necklace which adorns the Beautiful Artemis is comprised of the signs of the zodiac, indicating that she incarnated life and influenced the cosmos. Her association with life was also manifested in the right of asylum granted to criminals who came and sought refuge within the boundaries of the temple. Although such unconditional love of criminals upset many Ephesians, their request in A.D. 22 for an end of asylum

was not granted by Emperor Tiberius. Evidently the great mother was expected to demonstrate love for all her children.

The first Temple of Artemis was evidently destroyed by the Cimmerians who attacked Ephesus in the seventh century B.C. The oldest artifacts associated with this temple date to the eighth century B.C. and are in the British Museum.

The Great Temple: Built between 550 and 460 B.C., the first major temple honoring this queen of heaven and earth was magnificent. It was the largest structure ever built of marble. A total of 127 Ionic columns, each 20 yards (19 meters) high, sustained a roof enclosing a courtyard 163 yards (155 meters) long by 58 yards (55 meters) wide. On all four sides of the temple are two rows of columns. This **Temple of Artemis**, first located in 1869 by British engineer John Wood was even more impressive than the rival Temple of Hera in Samos and four times larger than the Parthenon in Athens. It was considered one of

Details from a sarcophagus.

the Seven Wonders of the Ancient World.

Besides the Temple of Artemis, the Seven Wonders included the Pyramids of Egypt; the Colossus of Rhodes; the Statue of Zeus at Olympia; the Hanging Gardens of Babylon, the Lighthouse at Alexandria and the Mausoleum at Halicarnassus.

The temple was rebuilt after it was burned down, allegedly on the very night Alexander was born in 356 B.C., by an Ephesian desperate for publicity. The second major Artemision, built between 350 and 250 B.C., was essentially identical to the first except that it was elevated on a base 3.3 yards (three meters) high with 13 steps.

The temple had to be reconstructed again after it was destroyed by Goths who attacked Ephesus in A.D. 125 and again in A.D. 262. With the growth of Christianity the cult of Artemis declined to be replaced perhaps by the adoration of the Virgin Mary. Marble from the Artemision was used in the construction of **Haghia Sophia** (the

grand **Aya Sofya** basilica in Istanbul) and the Church of St. John on the hill in Selçuk. Today only a single column rising out of a muddy pool reminds one of what was once one of the Seven Wonders of the Ancient World.

The **Fortification wall** and the original Magnesian Gate were built in the third century B.C. by Lysimachus. To appreciate the excellent Hellenistic workmanship on the wall, it's best to climb to the top of the mountain where the city wall is better preserved. After entering via the Magnesian Gate a north turn will bring the tourist to the remains of the **Eastern Gymnasium**, built in the second century. Just east of the Odeon stands the mostly unexcavated **Varius Baths**. Just south of the Odeon are the remains of the **State Agora** and the **Basilica**.

A rectangular temple built around 25 B.C. was located at the center of the State Agora. The pediment of this **Temple of Emperor Augustus** is now on display in the courtyard at the Ephesus Museum in Selçuk. The pediment

Relief of a flying goddess.

illustrates a legend described by Homer. Three allies of Odysseus are preparing to blind the Cyclops Polyphemus after Odysseus got him drunk with wine. The 170-yard long (160-meter) but narrow Basilica contained the statues of Augustus and his wife now seen at the Ephesus Museum. Located to the west of the Basilica is the **Prytaneion** where the eternal flame of Ephesus burned and where the two famous statues of Artemis were found.

Modern performances: The small theater or **Odeon** seated 1,400 and was built by a couple of rich Ephesians in A.D. 150. Although it was used for concerts, it was the political meeting place for the *Boule*. The people's assembly or *Demos* was convened in the well-preserved 24,000-seat Theater, where today modern folklore shows and plays are frequently performed.

Continuing west toward Curetes Street, to the north of Domitian Square, is the **Memmius Monument** built in the first century B.C. to honor Roman military commanders. The temple dedicated to Domitian (A.D. 81-96) is largely unrestored. To the east of the steps at the entrance to the **Temple of Domitian** stands a two-tiered column with reliefs. Just behind it is the cool **Inscription Gallery** where numerous documents pertaining to the history of Ephesus have been found.

About 111 yards (100 meters) west past the **Hercules Gate**, which marks the beginning of Curetes Street, between the Trajan Fountain and the Temple of Hadrian, are the remains of the **Scholasticia Baths**. These heated baths were built in the first century and were repaired frequently thereafter until about A.D 400. The last citizen to restore the baths, Christian Scholasticia, is commemorated by a statue. As in all Roman baths, hot, tepid and cold water was available in different rooms. Hot air circulated through baked clay pipes under the floors of the room. The taps provided hot and tepid water.

Next to the baths is a peristyle house that was the Brothel, indicating that **Mosaic in Ephesus.**

prostitution was institutionalized in Ephesus. The upper story of the house has been destroyed and only traces of frescoes remain. A mosaic in the dining room depicts the four seasons while a simple mosaic in the adjacent pool shows three maidens, a servant, a cat and a mouse eating crumbs. A tiny bronze **Figure of Priape**, a god with an overgrown phallus, was found in the brothel and now adorns the Ephesus Museum.

Public toilets: To the west of the baths is the Latrina or public toilets. Across the street from the entrance to the Latrina is the western entrance to the baths. Hidden to the right of this entrance is a 20-inch (50-cm) tall relief of Artemis. She is depicted there with an animal head facing right and holding a staff in her right hand.

The **Temple of Hadrian**, completed in honor of Emperor Hadrian by A.D. 138, is a visual feast. Behind the bases of four columns which once held statues of four Roman emperors rise four Corinthian columns. A richly-deco-

rated arch featuring the face of Tyche, the goddess of chance equivalent to the Roman Fortuna, crowns the two central columns. Above the door behind the central chamber stands a semicircular frontal depicting a bare-breasted maiden surrounded by flowers and leaves.

On the south side of Curetes Street, several elegant houses built on the slopes of **Bülbül Dağı** (Nightingale Mountain) have been excavated. These three-story structures had courtyards, running water, heating, mosaic floors and walls adorned with frescoes. Originally constructed during the reign of Augustus, these houses were frequently altered until the end of the seventh century. Two of these houses on the slopes are restored and may be entered by climbing the steps just across the street from Hadrian's Temple.

Celsus library: At the end of Curetes Street is the impressive two-story **Celsus Library**. Because it had to be built between the two older edifices, this structure was cleverly designed to

Inscriptions at Ephesus.

look wider than it really is. When Tiberius Julius Celsus, a famous Roman administrator, died in A.D. 114 his son had this library built as a monument and mausoleum. Celsus was buried inside an elaborately decorated marble sarcophagus found under a library wall. The interior of the library was spacious and housed 12,000 scrolls kept in niches designed to minimize damage from humidity. Eight Corinthian columns placed on a podium support elaborately-adorned frontals.

At the north side of the Celsus Library is the **Mazeus Mithridates Gate** which leads into the Agora. Its three passages are reminiscent of a Roman victory arch. The elegantly decorated frieze above the arch has three sections. Upon emancipation, two slaves, Mazeus and Mithridates, built this ornate gate to honor their former master, Emperor Augustus and his family. Beside the inscriptions in bronze to their master and his family is the stern warning: "Whoever urinates here will be tried in court." This admonishment reminded Ephesians that the agora or forum was to be entered reverently and not to be sullied.

The **Agora** or shopping center at Ephesus was a semi-sacred square where various stores were located. Merchandise displayed included locally-produced perfume, Arabic herbs, Anatolian wine, jewelry, foods, ceramics, and artifacts of bronze and copper. Women reputed to be the most beautiful in the East were sold here as slaves. Today only numerous columns standing at the perimeter of this large square meeting and marketplace remind one of the exchange of goods and ideas from three continents that once transpired here. Excavations currently underway will undoubtedly explain more about the original agora built in the third century B.C.

The Temple of Serapis is located at the end of a marble road which begins at the southwestern corner of the agora. This temple, under construction in the second century, was dedicated to Serapis, the Egyptian god of the under-

world and judge of the dead. Eight massive marble columns, each weighing 57 tons, lie in front of the temple ruins. After 547 B.C., when Ephesus was conquered by Persians, maritime trade between Alexandria and Ephesus must have been brisk. Numerous Egyptian statues and a peace treaty written on marble also confirm the connection between Egypt and Ephesus. In 299 B.C. the alliance between Egypt and Ephesus was cemented by the royal marriage between Lysimachus and Arsinos, an Egyptian princess.

From the Celsus Library the sacred or Marble Road goes toward the theater. Built into the western slope of Mt. Pion during the reign of Lysimachus, this impressive, well-preserved theater seats 24,000. Hellenistic plays were quasi-religious, dedicated to Dionysus, the god of wine and entertainment. Prayers and animal sacrifices preceded performances given by masked male actors.

During the Roman era, when St. Paul's provocative sermon to Ephe-

sians was delivered here, the theater was enlarged. St. Paul's challenge to Artemis worshippers, and Ephesian silversmiths whose livelihood depended on selling statues of Artemis and her temple, resulted in a riot in this very theater (Acts 19:24-41). The superb acoustics and stellar performers, among them Ray Charles, thrill modern audiences each spring at the Ephesus Festival. The top tier provides a panoramic view of the **Arcadian Way** leading west toward the ancient harbor.

The wide **Harbor Street** testifies to the grandeur that was Ephesus in the first century B.C. After docking at the harbor, dignitaries marched 1,650 feet (500 meters) along this marble-paved, arcaded road lined with statues, porticoes and public buildings. A recently-excavated inscription confirms that 50 lamps hung from columned porticoes on both sides of this street at a time when lighted cities included only Ephesus, Antioch and Rome. Between the theater and the ancient harbor, statues of the four evangelists were, in the fifth cen-

tury, placed on columns whose shafts are still visible. At the north side of this street are the ruins of the Theater Gymnasium, the Verlanus Sports Arena and Paleistra, the Harbor Baths and the Church of the Virgin Mary.

Nestorian heresy: Located to the north of the Harbor Baths, near the **Church of the Virgin Mary**, the first church ever dedicated to the Virgin Mary, is a long extensive ruin where the Third Ecumenical Council proclaimed in A.D. 431 that Mary was the mother of Jesus, the son of God. This council recorded that Mary lived and died near Ephesus, and branded Nestor, Patriarch of Constantinople, a heretic for his denial of the virgin birth. The church was converted from a school of higher education to a basilica in the fourth century. Because this basilica underwent two additional alterations, this narrow, elongated edifice now seems confusing. Near the northern apse is the large baptismal pool where the faithful were immersed and baptized inside what was once a circular baptistery covered by a domed roof.

After being expelled from Jerusalem, St. John and the Virgin Mary came to Ephesus. It is believed John's grave lies underneath the church erected by Emperor Justinian, who reigned from A.D. 527 to 565. Even before the construction of the **Church of St. John**, which stands near the Citadel of Selçuk, there was a Baptistery in use there. The circular pool where baptisms were performed had a marble floor and was originally covered by a dome with a glass mosaic.

Toward the eastern end of the church, at the end of the central nave just west of the apse, is the **Tomb of St. John**. The burial platform, two steps below the floor, used to be covered by a small dome. The marble mosaics adorning the platform have been restored. For several centuries this church was a shrine visited by pilgrims and by the sick and ailing who hoped the dust from the burial chamber would perform miracles and heal them.

The fortification wall which sur-

Praying at the House of the Virgin Mary.

rounds the church was built in the seventh and eighth centuries to protect Ephesus against Arab attacks. At the main entrance to the church, the **Pursuit Gate** and its adjoining courtyard were built according to an ancient Hellenistic strategy for defense. If the enemy penetrated beyond the gate they were trapped inside the courtyard which has no exit. In that position they could be killed by men positioned above the courtyard walls.

Turkish conquest: When the Turks arrived in 1304 all that remained of Ephesus was a small Byzantine village which was easily conquered. The **Isa Bey Mosque** is remarkably uncrowded and occupies a huge area at the western base of the hill where the Church of St. John stands. It was built in 1375 for the Seljuk sultan Isa Bey by the architect Ali Damessene. The mosque was subsequently toppled by an earthquake. Sometime soon after the Ottomans took over in 1426 Ephesus was utterly deserted. This double-domed mosque has been restored and has three chambers. Above the main entrance the last of three original minarets still stands. Surrounding the large inner courtyard are unusually high walls which were partially constructed with marble from Ephesus.

Magnificent views highlight the five-mile (7.5-km) ascent from the Magnesian Gate to the souvenir shops and restaurant located on the path leading toward the haven to which St. John brought the Virgin Mary after the Crucifixion. The visionary dream of a German nun, Catherine Emmerich, eventually inspired the search for the **House of the Virgin Mary** (Meryem Ana in Turkish), where Mary lived from A.D. 37 to 48. In 1891, a search party led by the Father Superior of the Lazarists discovered the House of the Blessed Virgin in a pine forest just before an *ayazma*, a sacred spring. Since its restoration in 1951, this house, which is used as a chapel, has been visited by two popes and millions of pilgrims, both Christian and Moslem.

The building is officially recognized by the Vatican and the Eastern Orthodox churches as the last residence of the Virgin Mary and is considered a holy shrine. Virgin Mary is also considered a Moslem saint. Pope John Paul, the Polish pontiff, held mass in the chapel when he visited Turkey in 1979 for theological unification talks between the Vatican and Orthodox Church Patriarchate in Istanbul.

Each year several hundred thousand pilgrims enter the chapel where Mary's icon stands. After drinking the healing spring water, devout pilgrims attach their prayers to a nearby wall. Chronicles have recorded many miracles, such as the curing of invalids, who entered the chapel on crutches and left discarding them.

In accordance with local tradition, as adopted by Pope Benedict XIV, each August 15 the mass commemorating the Assumption of Mary is celebrated in the surprisingly modest stone chapel. The 30-minute visit that Selçuk taxi drivers allow is certainly not sufficient to fully appreciate the serenity this shrine offers.

The nearby town of Kusadaşi.

THE MAEANDER RIVER VALLEY

The **Büyük Menderes Valley**, the site of many cities of antiquity including Miletus, Aphrodisias and Hierapolis, is one of the most fertile regions in the world. In summers, this broad, long valley, nurtured by the winding 365-mile (584-km) **Büyük Menderes** (the Maeander River of ancient times), is relatively dry. In winter, torrents of streams irrigate the valley, allowing peasant farmers to grow cotton, olives, citrus fruits and vegetables, graze cattle and sheep and raise poultry. In recent years, Söke, Aydın, Nazilli and Denizli, the main cities in the valley, have become cotton boom towns with high standards of living. Many farmers in this region own tractors, trucks and automobiles, sure signs of prosperity in this agricultural breadbasket. From the many twists and turns in the Büyük Menderes River, we get the verb "to meander" in the English language. According to ancient belief, the river's winding channel inscribed the entire Greek alphabet.

The quickest way to reach the Büyük Menderes Valley from Kuşadası is to take one of two minor asphalt roads through the verdant, undulating hills to **Çamlık**, a village and railroad switchyard station, on the E24/550 Izmir-Denizli highway. By turning right on the Izmir-Denizli highway motorists can drive to the valley below.

Carpets and cuisine: Near Çamlık is the commercial carpet weaving center of **Sultanköy**, operated by the Net group, Turkey's biggest producer and exporter of handmade Turkish carpets. At **Ortaklar**, the first town in the Büyük Menderes River Valley, turn left, take the E24/320 highway at the junction toward Aydın and Denizli. The junction is noted for its many one-man *kebab* stands, where you can enjoy a delicious *çöp sis* lunch or dinner. *Çöp sis* are tiny morsels of lamb meat roasted on coal barbecues along with tomatoes, peppers and onions.

Aydın, a sprawling provincial capital of 100,000 people, is 14 miles (22 km) from Ortaklar. Founded originally by an odd group of barbarian tribes from Thrace and the Peloponnesus, Aydın was known in ancient times as Tralles. It came under Carian and Persian domination in the sixth century B.C. Tralles passed into the hands of Alexander the Great in 334 B.C., and was later acquired by the Kingdom of Pergamum. In 129 B.C. it became a part of the Roman Empire. The Seljuk Turks ruled the city from A.D. 1186 to 1300. The Aydınoğulları princes controlled the city for the next 126 years before it was conquered by the Ottoman Turks in 1426. The city was held by the Greek army from 1919-1922, until its liberation by Turkish nationalist forces.

Ottoman monuments: Traces of ancient Tralles, which can be seen about a mile north of the present town, include scant remains of a gymnasium, agora and theater. The city itself has many Ottoman monuments, the oldest of which is the **Alihan Kümbeti**, a 14th-century tomb with the cemeteries of four

Left, bathing in the holy pool at Pamukkale. **Right,** a statue of a god in Aphrodisias.

Aydınoğlu notables, including Prince Ali Han. This structure is located in the **Üveys Paşa Mahallesi**.

Several 16th-, 17th- and 18th-century mosques are scattered about the town, including the **Ağaçarası Mosque**, the **Süleyman Bey Mosque**, the **Üveys Paşa Mosque**, the **Eski-Yeni Mosque** and the **Ramazan Paşa Mosque**. The 18th-century **Nuh Paşa Medresesi**, a u-shaped Islamic school of theology, can be seen in the city's **Köprülü Mahallesi**. Aydın's main street, **Adnan Menderes Bulvarı**, is named after the Turkish prime minister who was toppled in the 1960 military coup and executed in 1961.

Two towns on the E24/320 highway are **Nazilli** and **Kuyucak**. A country road forks to the right after Kuyucak toward **Karacasu** and Aphrodisias, passing though gentle rolling hills where shepherds graze their sheep.

The ruins of the fabulous Roman city of **Aphrodisias** are located near the village of Geyre, off the right hand side of the road. **Geyre** was once located amidst the ruins, and the villagers used many of the city's stones and statues to construct their houses. The village was relocated in the 1960s as a result of expanded excavations carried out by New York University archaeologists, led by Professor Kenan Erim and financed by the National Geographic Society.

School of sculpture: Tourism authorities say that Aphrodisias is likely to surpass Ephesus in size and splendor eventually as a result of Professor Erim's new discoveries and excavations. The settlement dates to well before 3000 B.C. A Carian city, Aphrodisias made its mark in history during the Roman Period, when it was sponsored by the emperors as a center of art, sculpture and religion. The city's School of Sculpture, where many of the Roman Empire's greatest sculptors conducted classes, turned out fine masterpieces from marble quarried in the foothills of the nearby **Babadağ**, a snow-capped 7,000-foot (2,102-meter) mountain.

Left, peasant woman in the Aegean. Right, a frieze from Roman times.

The **Aphrodisias Museum** houses many of the statues found during excavations by Professor Erim and his team. The most astonishing statue in the museum is of Aphrodite, the patron goddess of the city. Aphrodite's statue bears a striking resemblance to the giant statues of Artemis found in Ephesus, showing a close connection between the two deities.

Aphrodisias was the center of the cult of the Carian Aphrodite, from which the town got its name. Pilgrims from all over the Greco-Roman world visited the **Temple of Aphrodite**, parts of which still stand. The temple was transformed into a church after the Roman Empire adopted Christianity as a state religion.

The stadium: The magnificent **Stadium**, built during the early period of the Roman Empire, is perhaps the best preserved in the ancient world. The long, narrow stadium is rounded at both ends and has a seating capacity for nearly 25,000 people. A royal box is on the northern side of the stadium for visiting dignitaries from Rome. The stadium was the site of many athletic events including foot races. A semicircular ring on the eastern part was where gladiators fought.

Other buildings of note in Aphrodisias are a small odeon, where theatrical performances and public debates were held, a well preserved theater, an agora and a street with columns on each side, and the Baths of Hadrian. Two mounds at the acropolis hill were merely levels of earlier inhabitation. Pottery shards found here showed that Aphrodisias was one of the earliest settlements in the Maeander River Valley.

During the early Christian era, the name of the city was changed to Stavrapolis, or City of the Cross, to wipe out its affiliation with the pagan goddess Aphrodite. A series of earthquakes and invading armies destroyed the prosperous city. All that remained of Aphrodisias after the seventh-century Arab conquests of Anatolia was a village that took the name Caria from the

Riding
through
Aphrodisias
on
donkeyback.

ancient Roman province where it was located. In the Turkish period, the name Caria was corrupted and changed to Geyre.

Falcon crest: The country road climbs a mountain and then descends to Denizli, a provincial capital in the Büyük Menderes Valley. Just before Denizli is the village of **Tekkeköy**, famous for its roadside **Şahin Tepesi** (Falcon Crest) **Restaurant** on the top of a cliff overlooking a gorge. The restaurant serves a delicious lambs' stew dish called *saç kavurma*.

With a population of 170,000, **Denizli** is an important carpet weaving, mining and agricultural center. Specially bred Denizli roosters are world famous. Denizli was founded in the third century B.C. by Seleucid kings of Syria but it only developed during the Roman period. In 1094, the Seljuk Turks conquered the city, later incorporating it into the Germiyanoğlu Principality. The Ottoman Turks took over in 1428. Denizli ("sea" in Turkish) gets its name from an abundance of streams that run through the countryside.

The ruins of **Laodiceia**, ancient Denizli, are located four miles (six km) from Denizli. Laodiceia was founded by Antiochus I, king of Syria, and named after his wife, Laodice. The ruins include a stadium, gymnasium, aqueducts and a theater. The city was the center for one of the Seven Churches mentioned in the Book of Revelation. About five miles (eight km) from Denizli is the 13th-century **Akhan Caravansary**, a kind of motel that was located on the main caravan route in the Middle Ages and that served travelers visiting the areas.

The Cotton Castle: Pamukkale, which means Cotton Castle in Turkish, is one of the most spectacular natural wonders of Turkey. Located 14 miles (22 km) north of Denizli, Pamukkale is a cliff of white limestone cascades, tiers of stalactites and natural swimming pools formed over thousands of years by the deposits of mineral and calcium-rich hot streams which run down the hill. The cliffs resemble a fluffy cotton **Grazing among ruins.**

castle from a distance, especially if you are approaching the site from Denizli.

Pamukkale, situated next to the ruins of the ancient Roman city of **Hierapolis**, has always been known for its thermal springs. A profusion of tasteless hotels and pensions, which operate *hamams* (Turkish baths), have been built in recent years in the surroundings of Pamukkale. But the most popular spa continues to be the old **Pamukkale Motel** with its natural outdoor 35 degree Celsius spring pool where bathers swim throughout the year among toppled columns and marble blocks of the main street of Hierapolis.

The natural springs are believed to be therapeutic for persons suffering from coronary, respiratory and kidney ailments and rheumatism.

The Devil's Hole: The source of the springs is believed to be in a cave-like opening known as the **Plutoneum** or the **Cin Deliği** – the Devil's Hole – behind the hotel in the middle of the terrace of Hierapolis. In ancient times, this cave was believed to be the entrance to Hades, the underworld. Entrance to this cave is forbidden today because of its noxious gases and fumes. Death comes instantaneously to animals, such as birds, dogs and cats, lowered into this cave in baskets. The cave was linked by a passage to the nearby **Temple of Apollo**. In the past, soothsayers and priests were able to operate in this passage by holding their breaths.

The entire Büyük Menderes River Valley lies on the Anatolian fault, an earthquake-bound belt. Several of the towns in the region, including Denizli and Aydın, have been leveled in the past by land tremors. Many towns in the region have thermal and steam baths to benefit from the volcanic nature of the earth's crust below.

Hierapolis was established by the Pergamene kings in the third century B.C., but Attalus II, the King of Pergamum, bequeathed the city to Rome in 133 B.C. The city prospered during Roman times and three emperors visited Hierapolis during this period. But the city never fully recovered from three devastating earthquakes that rocked the site in the first century and the many wars fought nearby.

St. Philip's Martyrium: Other interesting sites in Hierapolis include two theaters, Roman Baths and the Martyrium of St. Philip, one of Christ's 12 disciples who lived and was martyred there. The necropolis of Hierapolis is one of the most extensive anywhere in Turkey, with hundreds of tombs in the hillside on both sides of the road west of the town. On most days peasant shepherds graze their sheep among tumbled masonry of the tombs.

About three miles (five km) west of Hierapolis is the **Karahayit Thermal Resort** with its *Kızıl Su*, a reddish mineral water geyser that gushes out of the side of the hill forming red and sulfurous deposits.

The return trip from Denizli to Ortaklar along route E24/320 is a four-hour drive. Halfway to Ortaklar is the unusual geothermal springs at **Çubukdağı** (also known as **Buharkent**, the Steam City). Hot steam gushes out of crevasses on both sides of the highway at Buharkent for several hundred yards, reducing visibility. Neither steam bath spas nor stations producing geothermal energy have been built at Buharkent.

To see the other sites of antiquity in the Maeander River Valley, motorists must turn left at Ortaklar on route 525 toward Söke, Milas and Bodrum.

Magnesia on the Maeander: The ruins of Magnesia-ad-Maeandrum (Magnesia on the Maeander) lie two miles (three km) from Ortaklar to the right of the highway. Aeolian soldiers from the original Magnesia in Greece who fought in Agamemnon's army during the Trojan War are believed to have founded the city around 1260 B.C. The descendants of the early founders claimed that Magnesia on the Maeander was the first city in Asia Minor to be colonized by the Greeks.

The city was always prosperous because of its closeness to the Maeander River and its nearness to the major trade routes. Because of its wealth, the city incurred the jealousy and wrath of its stronger neighbors. It was sacked twice in the seventh century B.C., first by the Lydian King Gyges and then by the Cimmerians.

Magnesia became part of the Persian Empire during the sixth century B.C., and Xerxes spent some time there preparing for his invasion of Greece. The city capitulated to Alexander the Great without a fight in 334 B.C. Finally it came under the domination of the Pergamene kings and Rome. It isn't known why the city was eventually abandoned during the Byzantine period, but it may have had something to do with the Arab invasions in the seventh century.

Themistocles: The most important historical figure associated with Magnesia was Themistocles, the Athenian statesman responsible for the big Greek naval victory over the Persians, led by Xerxes, at the Battle of Salamis in 480 B.C. Themistocles spent the last years of his life in Magnesia, having fallen from favor in Athens as a result of a political scandal and branded a traitor. Rather than serve Persian interests against his native Greece, the 65-year-old Themistocles committed suicide in Magnesia by drinking the poisonous blood of a bull. All that remains of the city are walls of some buildings, including traces of the Temple of Artemis and a theater and odeon.

Söke, a lively market town with a population of 50,000, is off the road. Prosperity has come to the town as a result of a boom in cotton production. The only historical monument of any significance in Söke is the **Ilyas Ağa Camii**, an old Turkish mosque that was restored in 1821. South of Söke, a country road turns right after the town of **Yenidoğan** in the direction of Priene, one of the most outstanding sites of the classical period.

Priene, one of the best preserved Hellenistic cities in the world, is perched on the side of a mountain off the road. The first thing that strikes visitors is the neat grid pattern layout of the city. Everything has been done on a small scale, compared to its neighbors Ephesus in the north and Miletus in the south, which emphasized bigness in their architecture. Lord Kinross, a dis-

Late afternoon in Pamukkale.

tinguished British diplomat, biographer and travel writer, who visited the site in the early 1950s had this to say about Priene: "Hellenistic in style, unpretentious in scale, Priene has a simplicity which few cities of Greece can equal."

While Miletus, its chief rival, grew fat on commerce and increased its influence with military might, Priene remained modest and unpretentious, devoting most of its time to the worshipping of the gods, sponsoring of sports events and cultural activities. Its population never exceeded 5,000 people at any one time.

Athenian colonists founded the small city-state during the Greek invasions in the 12th century B.C. Although a member of the 12-city Ionian League, Priene always felt a particular closeness to Athens, the mother city.

Seven sages: Priene's golden age was in the sixth century B.C. when the city produced one of the Seven Sages of Antiquity, Bias, from whom we get the English verb "to be biased." Bias was instrumental in codifying the laws of the city. Priene suffered severely during the Persian invasion of western Asia Minor. In 545 B.C. the army of Cyrus sacked the city, burning it down to the ground and enslaving most of its people. Priene joined the Ionian revolt against Persian rule in 499 B.C. by contributing 12 galleys. Alas the Persians soundly defeated the Ionian fleet off Lade, an island near Miletus and Priene, in 495 B.C., and sacked the city one more time.

During his military campaigns in western Asia Minor, Alexander the Great stayed in Priene for some time and financed construction of the grand Temple of Athena.

After Priene came under Roman domination, it lost its importance and was finally abandoned in the Byzantine period.

Sacrificial victims: Among the buildings in Priene visitors should see include the small **Greek theater** with five stone thrones in the orchestra for priests, and a special water clock to time speeches at public assembly meetings;

the massive **Temple of Athena** with many of its tumbled elephantine columns sprawling about; the **Council House** resembling a tiny theater; the **Temple of Demeter**, which had a sacrificial pit, where the blood of the sacrificial victims, often humans, were poured down as offerings to the gods of the underworld; and the **Stadium**, where foot races, boxing, the pentathlon and the pancratium, a competition resembling a combination of today's American-style Big Time Wrestling and Thai Boxing, were held.

For a city that was once a grand maritime power and which had a harbor that could hold 200 warships at one time, **Miletus** is a big disappointment to travelers visiting the site. The city was once located at the tip of a headland overlooking the Latmian Gulf. Today it is five miles (eight km) from the sea due to the silting of the Maeander River. The city isn't as impressive as either Aphrodisias or Priene.

A Mycenaean settlement existed there between 1400 and 1200 B.C.

Bathers at Pamukkale.

Later it was occupied by a mixture of Cretans and native Carians and was colonized by the Ionians. The historian Herodotus wrote that the Ionians, having brought no women with them, slaughtered all the male inhabitants and married their wives. The women of Miletus vowed never to sit at the tables of their husbands. It was ruled in succession by the Persians, Alexander the Great, the Romans, the Byzantines and the Turks.

By the eighth century B.C., Miletus had set up as many as 90 colonies in the Mediterranean, the Dardanelles, the Sea of Marmara and the Black Sea, and traded with Egypt, Africa and Greece.

Solar eclipse: Miletus was also a center for learning and intellectual enlightenment. It was the home of many learned men and philosophers and scientists, including Thales, Anaximenes and Anaximander. Thales, considered by many to be one of the Seven Sages of Antiquity, predicted the solar eclipse of 585 B.C. He also managed to calculate the height of the Egyptian Pyramids by measuring their shadows at the time of day when a man's shadow is equal to his height.

Miletus' steady decline began with the Ionian revolt of 500 B.C. against Persian rule which ended in defeat. The continuous silting up of the Maeander announced the city's death knell, and it was eventually abandoned. The most significant sites in Miletus are the grand theater and the Faustina Baths, the Byzantine Citadel, the Heroon (a monumental tomb), the Agora, the Byzantine Church, the Temple of Athena, and the Turkish Caravansary.

Labor strike: The world's first recorded labor strike took place in Miletus during the construction of the theater about A.D. 100. The construction workers, dissatisfied with the terms and conditions of their contracts, stopped working. The strike was settled when the sides sought the arbitration of the Oracle of Didyma.

The **Faustina Baths** are indeed splendid, consisting of a dressing room,

cold room (*Frigidarium*), warm room (*Tepidarium*), hot room (*Calidarium*), steam room (*Sudatarium*), boiler room and exercise areas (*Palaestra*). A reclining statue of the River God Maeandros and a statue of a lion can be seen in the *Frigidarium*.

The most remarkable and popular building in Miletus is the 14th-century **Ilyas Bey Mosque Complex**, built by Ilyas Bey, a prince of the Turkish Menteşeoğulları Dynasty that ruled the area before the Ottoman Turks. It includes a single-domed mosque, an attractive courtyard with cemeteries, an *imaret* (a place where poor people were fed), a convent for dervish mystics, and a public bath.

Didyma: The **Temple of Apollo** at **Didim** (**Didyma**), 11 miles (18 km) south of Miletus, is one of the outstanding buildings of the Greek world, not only in size but in architectural style as well. The oracle dates to the seventh century B.C., long before Ionian settlers arrived in the region. The cult was in the hands of the Branchidae family, who claimed to originate from Delphi, site of the great oracle.

The temple was destroyed by the Persians in the sixth century B.C. and by Alexander the Great in the fourth century B.C. The vast structure seen there today dates from about 300 B.C., built by Seleucus, king of Syria.

Its decline coincided with the growth of Christianity. Christians finally took control of the pagan building and constructed a church in its most sacred part.

In ancient times, emperors consulted the oracle for advice. Croesus, the king of Lydia, who once consulted the oracle, was told that a great empire would be destroyed if he were to attack Persia. In fact, it was Croesus' empire that was destroyed.

Across from the ruins of the temple is the **Kamacı Restaurant**, which serves delicious seafood, including sea bass. The area has many five-star hotels, holiday villages and pensions and a fine beach area known as **Altin Kum**, the golden sand.

The sprawling temple of Didyma.

CARIA

The region known as **Caria** of the Greco-Roman world corresponds roughly to the boundaries of the present-day province of **Muğla**, in southwest Turkey. The Carians, the earliest-known inhabitants of this region, were a native stock Anatolian people famed for their skills as mariners. Ancient chronicles say Carian sailors served in the navies of the Egyptian pharaohs and of Persian ruler Xerxes. Homer mentions the Carians in his *Iliad* as being "barbarous of speech." (Coincidentally, linguists have noted, the Turkish dialect spoken in this part of the country is the harshest in western Turkey.)

The region is one of the most popular travel destinations in Turkey for foreigners and Turks alike. It is rich in archaeological sites and its shores are among the world's best for yachting, sailing, scuba diving and other water sports. The local inhabitants earn their livelihood from tourism, carpet weaving and farming. Cotton, olives and citrus fruits are grown in abundance.

To reach the Carian hills from Didyma, motorists should drive along the attractive Akbük Bay to highway 525 and turn right. Lake Bafa, on the edge of the Beşparmak Dağı (Mt. Latmus of antiquity), is the beginning of Caria. **Beşparmak** means five fingers in Turkish and indeed the top of the rocky 4,557-foot (1,367-meter) mountain resembles the stubs of five fingers. **Lake Bafa** was once a part of the Aegean Sea. But the silting of the Maeander River has left it landlocked and a good 12.5 miles (20 km) from the sea.

The ruins of **Heracleia under Latmus**, one of the most romantic but least visited ancient sites of Aegean Turkey, cling to slopes of Beşparmak Dağı on the eastern side of Lake Bafa, running down to the village of Kapıkırı. The ruins can be reached by taking the country road that forks to the left after passing Lake Bafa. A yellow sign points in the direction of the ancient city.

Endymion and Selene: Heracleia is associated with the legend of Endymion and Selene. It has a **Sanctuary of Endymion**, a horseshoe-shaped temple honoring the shepherd demigod. When the Moon Goddess Selene fell in love with the handsome Endymion, a jealous Zeus put him to sleep. Selene then went to sleep with Endymion and bore 50 children, according to the legend. The sanctuary is located near the lake at the lower part of the village, facing a large trailer camp.

Heracleia also has a partly-submerged necropolis of tombs by the lake, an ancient market, a Byzantine church, the Temple of Athena and several miles of well-preserved defensive walls with towers that curve part of the way up Beşparmak Dağı. A number of monasteries are located on the mountain. Boats can also be hired in the village to visit the Byzantine churches and monasteries on the islands in the middle of Lake Bafa.

The next fascinating site on highway 525 are the ruins of **Euromos**, a Carian settlement just off the road, and its

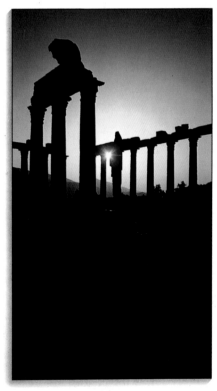

eft,
esting at
he
ümüskesen
Mausoleum.
tight,
unset at
uromos.

spectacular **Temple of Zeus** with its 16 columns still standing.

Labraynda: Before you enter Milas, a dirt road forks left into the rolling hills to the Carian sanctuary of **Labraynda**, a splendid site. The six-mile (10-km) drive up to the holy shrine is bumpy. The village, built on terraces, dates from the fourth century B.C. The hamlet is 2,300 feet (700 meters) above sea level.

The most important site at Labraynda is the **Temple of Zeus Labrayndus**, the god of the double axe, the patron deity of Caria. Located on an upper terrace, the temple is in ruins with columns and pillars strewn about the site. Behind the temple is the **First Andron**, a well-preserved building with a seven-foot (two-meter)-thick wall. The **Androns** – there are several at the site – were men's clubs, where the priests of the shrine gathered for social purposes. Next to it is a **residence** of the clergy.

Fortune-telling fish: The site also has a large tomb, with three sarcophagi inside, on the slope overlooking the temple. Mausolus and other Carian kings maintained at Labraynda a **Summer Palace**, which has not yet been excavated, but is believed to lie near the temple. The holy community also had a **Sacred Pool of Oracle Fish**, which were adorned with earrings and necklaces. According to early chronicles, the gold fish in the pool were capable of making yes and no prophecies by accepting or rejecting food offered after a question. The pool was located in what is now the **Ablution Hall**, along a wall at the lower terrace. Traces of the **Sacred Way**, an eight-mile (13-km) road linking Labraynda to ancient Milas can still be seen. A man from a nearby village operates a roadside teahouse at Labraynda and serves refreshments, sandwiches and *menemen*, a delicious rural-style scrambled eggs with peppers and tomatoes.

Milas, one of Turkey's leading producers of handmade wool carpets, is built on the side of a hill, right of the highway. The market town, known to the ancients as Mylasa, was once the capital of the Carian state, but was ruled successively by the Persians, Alexander the Great, the Romans, the Byzantines and now the Turks.

The most impressive monument in Milas is the Roman mausoleum known as **Gümüşkesen**, or the "silver purse," visible from every point in town. Located in a public park overlooking Milas, the monument is a smaller replica of the Mausoleum of Halicarnassus, with a pyramid roof supported by columns. It was built in the first century, and gets its Turkish name from alleged treasures hidden inside its crypt, which was long ago broken into but is now locked. A strange hole exists on the floor of the funerary monument surmounting the sepulchral chamber below. This hole, according to Richard Chandler, an 18th-century traveler, was used by family members of the deceased to pour libations of milk, honey and wine into the chamber to satisfy the spirit of their beloved one.

The ruins of a Roman temple can be seen near the **Belediye Binası**, the town hall, but all that remains standing is a

Tomb of Gazi Ahmet Pasha at Beçin Kale.

fluted column on an elevated marble floor. The **Tomb of Güveç Dede**, a minor Islamic saint whose name in Turkish means "Grandfather Casserole" can be seen in the **Hacı Ilyas District** of the town. Two 14th-century Turkish mosques, the **Orhan Bey Camii** (1330), and the more impressive **Firuz Bey Camii** (1397), also known as the Gök Camii with its pinkish marble façade, are located near the city center.

The double axe: One other fascinating site in Milas is the **Baltalı Kapı**, or the "Gate of the Axe," located on the main street, just off the state hospital (**Devlet Hastanesi**). Baltalı Kapı derives its name from the frieze of a double axe on its façade, symbolizing the divine Kingdom of Caria. The arched gate was in ancient times the beginning of the "Sacred Way" connecting Milas with the holy shrine Labraynda.

After leaving Milas the road reaches a junction. Highway 525 continues to head east toward the coal mining town of Yatağan and the provincial capital of Muğla. The other road heads towards the resort of Bodrum. A dirt road near the junction leads to **Beçin Kale**, an old Turkish fortification that has a stunning view of Milas and the valley. Beçin Kale is a 14th-century stronghold of the Menteşeoğlu Beylik, a Turkish dynasty that ruled this area before the Ottoman conquest in 1390. Beçin Kale is situated on a flat, rocky hilltop. The fortress, which is in a state of ruins, can be toured in 20 minutes. Just inside the gates of the citadel, on the right, is a flight of solid marble steps, believed to be part of an ancient temple.

Nearby is the interesting **Medrese of Gazi Ahmet Pasha**, an Islamic religious school named after a Menteşeoğlu statesman. The statesman, Ahmet Pasha, and his wife are buried next to each other in an open part of the *medrese*, and today they are considered to be saints by the local inhabitants.

Behind the *medrese* are the ruins of a mosque. This is an excellent picnic spot. A one-man beverage stand near the *medrese* provides refreshments.

Original site: Pottery shards found around Beçin Kale dating from the fourth and seventh century B.C. have led British archaeologist J.M. Cook to suggest that this was the original site for the ancient city of Mylasa, an assertion supported by the fact that the Carians built their cities on high ground, mainly for defense purposes.

The world's only carpet farm, the **Ildız Carpet Farm**, is located on the Bodrum-Milas Highway, six miles (10 km) out of Milas. At the farm, experts wash and sun tens of thousands of handmade wool carpets to test the quality of the carpets. The carpets are manufactured or bought by the Ildız Company, one of Turkey's leading carpet exporters and producers. Ildız specializes in the production of pastel-colored Milas carpets. Visitors to the carpet farm should ask the young attendants inside to unroll some Milas carpets.

Near the carpet farm a road forks right to **Güllük**, a fishermen's town with a pretty port and numerous pensions and small hotels. A Turkish-British company is building an international airport near Güllük to make the region more accessible to tourism.

Boats can be chartered from Güllük for a one-hour trip to the ruins of **Iasus**, a Greco-Roman city. Iasus can also be reached by a rough dirt road that turns west on the Izmir-Milas highway near the ruins of Euromos.

Peloponnesians from Argos, having fought a long and bitter war with the local Carians, colonized Iasus and surroundings. But the city, which prospered from its fishing industry and trade, was ruled successively by the Persians, the Athenians, the Spartans, Alexander the Great, the Seleucids, the Rhodians, the Romans, the Byzantines, the Knights of St. John and now the Turks. The town was sacked numerous times by the rival powers and its citizens were sold into slavery.

The principal ruins to see at Iasus are the land walls, a theater, a gymnasium, a council house, a Byzantine gate, a magnificent mausoleum and the **Temple of Demeter and Core**, and an agora. The island castle was probably built by the Knights of St. John.

BODRUM

The most international of Turkey's cities, **Bodrum** is renowned for its foreign restaurants, party town atmosphere and bohemian lifestyle. This combination is appealing, especially to young foreigners and western-oriented Turks, who flock there in summer. Bodrum has a population of only 13,000, yet it boasts one Indian, four Italian, and three Chinese restaurants. (Istanbul, Turkey's largest city, has a population of 7.5 million, but has only four Italian and three Chinese eateries, and no Indian restaurant.)

Sex city: In recent years, the town has attracted crowds of young British men and women, who come on cheap charter flights and package tours, looking for fun and romance. Visitors to Bodrum go swimming and sunning by day on the many nearby beaches. Come night, they gather at the town's many outdoor pubs, discotheques and bars to drink, dance and party till the wee hours of the morning. At these pubs love stories often begin. "Bodrum," local denizens are fond of saying, "is 30 percent sex, 25 percent love and 45 percent relaxation."

Located on the southeastern shore of the Bodrum Peninsula, the town is built on twin bays separated by the massive Castle of St. Peter. Tiny, white soapbox houses, characteristic of Bodrum, rise from the town and carpet the surrounding hills and mountains. The dark silhouette of Karaada, a virtually uninhabited Turkish island, can be seen at the mouth of the bay with the shadows of the Greek island of Cos in the distant horizon.

Sailing center: Bodrum's harbor is protected by a long jetty, and scores of yachts and sailboats are moored along the quayside. Dozens of restaurants serving seafood and small outdoor coffeehouses line the harbor. Bodrum has a 125-berth marina. The town is the most important starting point for the Blue Voyage, a delightful yachting cruise into the neighboring Gökova Bay.

Downtown Bodrum, starting from the foot of the castle and winding along the narrow **Dr. Alim Bey Caddesi** and **Cumhuriyet Caddesi**, bustles with activity in summer. These two connected streets are lined with lively bars, restaurants, tavernas, small stores and giftshops selling carpets, leatherware, local jewelry, handmade sandals and more. Young artists display their paintings on street corners, old men peddle colorful sponges, and vendors in traditional costumes sell *Kahramanmaraş dondurması* (ice cream).

The town has been a center for boat building since the days of Mark Antony and Cleopatra. Sturdy, luxury yachts, known as gulets, are built all along the Bodrum Peninsula, but the biggest shipyards are located at **İçmeler**, a ten-minute drive from Bodrum.

Knights and conquests: Bodrum has a rich 3,000-year history, replete with military campaigns, naval victories, knights and conquests. In ancient times the city was known as **Halicarnassus**. In 546 B.C. Halicarnassus, like most Anatolian cities, came under Persian domination. Sixty years later, at the time of the Persian-Greek wars, the city was ruled by a Carian dynasty whose most famous member was Queen Artemesia. When Xerxes, the Persian King of Kings, was preparing his invasion of Greece, Artemesia joined his forces contributing several fighting ships. During a naval engagement in 480 B.C. in which the Persian fleet was routed, Artemesia displayed unusual bravery, causing Xerxes to exclaim: "My men have shown themselves women and my women men."

The golden age: Halicarnassus saw its golden age under King Mausolus, a Persian-appointed satrap belonging to the Carian dynasty. Mausolus moved his capital (from Mylasa) to Halicarnassus, turning it into a splendid city. He died in 353 B.C. and was succeeded by Artemesia the younger, his wife and sister. Artemesia, who ruled for only three years, built a majestic tomb in her husband's memory, from which we get the word "mausoleum."

Alexander the Great arrived in Halicarnassus in 334 B.C. and conquered

Left, a windmill in Bodrum.

the city. After his death the city continued as a Greco-Roman city until A.D. 654 when it was completely destroyed by the Arab invasions of Anatolia, and wiped from the pages of history until the 15th century.

The Knights of St. John revived the city in 1402, when they were given possession of Halicarnassus by Tamerlane, the oriental ruler whose armies swept through Anatolia. The Knights built the Castle of St. Peter, after their patron saint, and named their city Petronium, from which the modern Turkish name Bodrum is derived. The Knights finally abandoned the city in 1522 when the Ottoman Sultan Süleyman the Magnificent conquered Rhodes, their stronghold.

Many Turkish writers and intellectuals have made Bodrum their home, the most famous in recent years being Cevat Şakir Kabaağaçlı (1890-1973), a British-educated Turkish writer nicknamed "Fisherman of Halicarnassus." Exiled to Bodrum in 1925 because of his unorthodox political views, Kabaağaçlı popularized the town through his essays, short stories and novels, attracting like-minded romantics, writers and artists.

Forsaken and isolated: Bodrum, in 1925, was a forsaken, isolated, tiny fishermen's village with a population of less than 2,000, which had no road connections with the provincial capital Muğla. Thus it took Kabaağaçlı, accompanied by *gendarmes*, nearly four months to arrive in Bodrum from Ankara, the capital of the new Turkish Republic. He trekked part of the way over mountain passes and trails that had not been used since the days of Alexander the Great.

Much has changed in Bodrum since the days of Kabaağaçlı. It was discovered by Istanbul's intellectual crowd in the early 1970s, who made it an "in place." Soon the country's *nouveaux* rich arrived, turning it into their summer hangout. Its fame spread and then came the international jet set. Celebrities like Barbra Streisand, Dustin Hoffman, Clint Eastwood and Jacqueline Onassis

spent vacations in Bodrum. Ahmet Ertegün, a Turco-American who owns Atlantic Records, one of the world's leading music recording companies, bought a house there, and his guests included the likes of rock star Mick Jagger, former World Bank President Robert McNamara and ballet star Rudolph Nureyev. Today the city is a veritable Turkish Saint Tropez.

The Knights of St. John: The most fascinating site to visit in Bodrum is the **Castle**, a well-preserved architectural complex. It was built between 1402-1503 by the Knights of St. John, an international Catholic military monastic order, also known as the Knights Hospitaliers of St. John of Jerusalem, the Knights of Rhodes and later as the Knights of Malta. The castle was used by the Knights to carry out raids on the Aegean Coast and served as a refuge for Christians fleeing Turkish captivity. To build the castle, the Knights used green stones, statuary, masonry and marble slabs from the nearby Mausoleum of Halicarnassus, which they found in

ruins, destroyed apparently by an earthquake sometime after the 12th century. The castle today houses the **Museum of Underwater Archaeology**.

More than 125 shipwrecks: The museum, located in several buildings in the courtyard, is one of the most impressive of its kind in the world. Opened in 1960, it contains the remains of the world's oldest known shipwrecks, discovered by scientists of the **Institute of Nautical Archaeology (INA)** along the Turquoise Coast. Founded in 1973 by George Bass, a renowned American underwater archaeologist, INA is an autonomous research organization affiliated with Texas A&M University. Using the Bodrum Castle as its headquarters, the INA has discovered and mapped more than 125 ancient shipwrecks off the Turkish Coast.

Right of the courtyard entrance is the **Bronze Age Hall.** It contains rich Mycenaean findings from a land excavation at **Musgebi** on the Bodrum Peninsula, dating from 2500 B.C. It also has bronze bars and amphoras recovered by

Yachts line Bodrum's harbor.

George Bass and his team from a 12th-century B.C. shipwreck.

Since 1982, Bass and his divers have been excavating the oldest known shipwreck, dating to the 14th century B.C., discovered by a sponge diver off Uluburun, near the town of Kaş.

Across from the outdoor teahouse is "**Shipwreck Hall**" which will soon be opened to exhibit the hull and cargo of an 11th-century shipwreck that was found at **Serçe Limanı**, a shallow cove near Marmaris.

A series of steps behind the Bronze Age Hall lead to the building displaying artifacts from the so-called "**Glass Wreck**." This exhibition contains hundreds of colorful, almost phosphorescent glass jars, bottles and vases, retrieved in 1977 from the Serçe Limanı shipwreck.

The **Italian Tower**, which was the residence of the Italian Knights, houses the **Coin and Jewelry Hall**, a wide collection spanning several centuries. To the left of the Italian Tower is the **French Tower**, where there are two Byzantine shipwrecks, dating to the fourth and seventh centuries.

In the farthest corner of the castle is the **English Tower**. On its walls are the coats of arms of Edward the Fourth, one of the members of the House of Plantagenet, the dynasty which ruled England from 1154 to 1485, and of the captains of the Knights, Sir Thomas Shefield and John Kendall.

The **German Tower**, where the German Knights lived, is now open to the public. To its left is the structure known as the **Snake Tower**. It gets its name from a snake's frieze on its walls, taken from the mausoleum, which symbolized the serpent shape that Zeus, the supreme deity of the ancient Greeks, took before adopting human form.

The Mausoleum of Halicarnassus can be reached by walking along Neyzen Tevfik Caddesi from the castle along the harbor. A right turn at Hamam Sokak after passing the mosque and a left turn at Turgutreis Caddesi brings you to the Mausoleum of Halicarnassus located on the left hand side of the street

Sailing off Bodrum Castle.

hidden by a wall. What remains today of the mausoleum – a foundation, a jumble of masonry and tumbled columns – belies its original greatness as one of the Seven Wonders of the Ancient World. The structure, built in the fourth century B.C., consisted of a high base, a peristasis of 36 columns, a pyramid of 24 steps, crowned by a quadriga, and a four-horsed chariot, according to ancient accounts. A small model of the mausoleum can be seen inside the enclosed area. The reliefs and colossal statues of Mausolus and Artemesia uncovered by British archaeologists in the 19th century are now displayed in the British Museum.

A short walk uphill along one of the narrow streets from the mausoleum brings you to the Roman **Amphitheater**, located on the other side of the Bodrum-Izmir Road, with a splendid view of the town and its castle.

Gümbet, a village with a long sandy beach, about three miles (five km) from Bodrum, is world renowned as a windsurfing center. In addition to windsurfing, water skiing, banana boat riding, canoeing, parasailing and sea biking are also possible.

The **Cemetery of Cevat Şakir Kabaağaçlı**, the author who made Bodrum famous through his writings, overlooks Bodrum from a hill between the town and Gümbet.

Chicken princess: The best restaurant in Bodrum is **Balık Restaurant**. Located on a side street off Dr. Alim Bey Caddesi, Balık Restaurant specializes in authentic Turkish food, including *tandır kebab*, lamb on a skewer cooked on a coal fire, *tavuk prenses* (chicken princess), a tasty chicken dumpling served with black peppers. It also serves delicious seafood such as octopus salad and *kalamar*, a fried squid.

A pub crawl, involving visits to several of the town's nightclubs, bars and discotheques on the same night, is the best way to enjoy Bodrum's nightlife, starting with the upmarket and immensely popular **Halikarnas Bar and Nightclub**, and working down toward Bodrum Castle. Halikarnas Nightclub,

eft, selling potatoes on market day, and right, inside a private garden.

with a grand view of the floodlit Bodrum Castle, caters to glamorous young foreign men and women and fabulously rich Turks, who breakdance to loud music from midnight to 5 a.m. The outdoor seaside disco resembles a Greek acropolis with an odeon and an amphitheater surrounded by columns. A jet of water bursts out of a fountain by the beach near the dance floor while psychedelic lighting is flashed from behind the stage.

The **Sensi Bar** on Cumhuriyet Caddesi provides pop music in a crowded atmosphere. For those who prefer folk music, **Beyaz Ev** (the White House), next door, may be the best bet in town. **Rick's Bar** further down, appeals more to British teeny-boppers than others. The popular Tanju Okan sings romantic melodies at **Big Ben Bar** (Cumhuriyet Caddesi), along the seashore.

The B-52: The crowded **Kavalye Bar** and the **Hadigari Cafe Bar** on Dr. Alim Caddesi should top off the night. The Hadigari, reputed to be the best bar in Turkey, is famous for the *B-52*, a pow-erful cocktail concoction that is supposed to be downed in one swig.

Daily boat trips are available from Bodrum to Cos and Datça. Boats working under the principle of a shared taxi also operate daily to Karaada and nearby beaches and coves for a small fee. Leaving the harbor at 11 a.m., these motor driven-boats, usually Bodrum-built *caiques,* are capable of taking on 30 people at one time.

Karaada, the dark island that guards the town's bay from a distance like a sentinel, is famous for its mud baths. "These baths," the Fisherman of Halicarnassus once wrote, "are capable of nearly resurrecting the dead." After allowing passengers a short mud bath and dip in the clear waters, the boat leaves for Ortakent. Left is the Greek island Cos. Bodrum is to the right.

The boat enters **Ada Boğazı**, a shallow body of water separating a minuscule island, Iç Ada, and Bodrum Peninsula. The boat only stops there on the return trip to allow for swimming and snorkeling. Ada Boğazı is often re-

Left, sandals on display, and _right_, glass bead jewelry for sale.

ferred to by the local populace as the "**Aquarium**," because its sandy bottom is rich in marine life. It then passes Çelebi Island and comes to **Ortakent Beach**. Dozens of restaurants and pensions are clustered on this half-moon beach.

On the return voyage to Bodrum, the captain follows the coastline, first passing two promontories on which stands the Aktur Holiday Villas, a luxurious complex. The next wide bay is **Bitez**, one of Bodrum's most popular seaside resorts, with windsurfing, swimming, sunbathing and banana boat riding.

The Hermaphrodite: The last cove before Bodrum is **Bardakçı** (glass maker in Turkish), which has a fine beach. Bardakçı is associated with the legend of the Hermaphrodite, the son of the Olympic deities Hermes and Aphrodite, who fell in love with the nymph Salmacis. It was in Bardakçı that Hermaphrodite and Salmacis were united in a single body, having both male and female sexual characteristics. The cove lives up to its reputation for sexual di-

versity even today. It is the favorite beach of Zeki Müren, a popular semi-retired transvestite Turkish singer who makes his home in Bodrum. In the summer, you can see the Liberace-like Müren wearing high heeled sandals and colorful clothes at his favorite coffeehouse at Bardakçı, surrounded by a flock of his gay admirers.

A number of uncrowded and less noisy towns and villages are located in the vicinity of Bodrum. **Gümüşlük**, at the western tip of the Bodrum Peninsula, is a gem of a village with fine fish restaurants and pensions gracing its shore. The ruins of the ancient city of **Myndus** are close by.

The town of **Turgutreis** has a number of fine hotels and pensions. The town's name is derived from a 16th-century Turkish naval admiral who was killed during the siege of Malta and was known in the west as Dragut. **Yalıkavak**, a pleasant village, is renowned for its sponge fishers. **Torba**, a quiet little settlement north of Bodrum, has two holiday villages.

Strolling in Bodrum in the afternoon.

SPONGE DIVING

When May comes to coastal villages on the Bodrum Peninsula, most of the men set sail in small wooden-framed boats in search of sponges that will eventually find their way into bathrooms of homes in western Europe, Japan, Canada and the United States. For five months, the fishermen comb the entire Turkish Aegean and Mediterranean coast for sponges.

In the past decades, Turkey, with its relatively unpolluted waters, has been the world's biggest producer of commercial bath sponges. Other leading producers include Cuba, Mexico, countries in the Antilles, the United States and Greece. Turkey's annual sponge exports have totaled an average 15 tons.

Until the present tourism boom and a fungus epidemic in 1986 killed many sponges off the Turkish Coast, sponge fishing was the main livelihood of most fishermen and their families around Bodrum. Many former sponge fishermen now prefer chartering their boats to tourists to sending young divers deep down into the sea in search of sponges. Nevertheless, many young Bodrum lads still follow their fathers' footsteps and begin sponge diving at the tender age of 14.

Way of life: Sponge fishing has been a way of life for people of the peninsula for nearly 3,000 years. The ancient Greeks used sponges for bathing, or scrubbing tables and floors, for padding armor. The Romans fashioned them as paint brushes, tied them to wooden poles and used them as mops and even substituted them for drinking cups.

Dubbed the "gold of the sea depths" because of their high value, sponges are porous, multi-cellular marine animals that grow geometrically. Sponges are generally found attached to rocks at depths of 33 feet (10 meters) to 234 feet (70 meters). Others occur in great depths. More than 5,000 varieties of sponges, mostly marine, are known in the world. A few varieties live in fresh waters.

Known in Turkey as *sünger*, sponges vary in shapes and sizes and may reach a diameter of three feet (one meter).

"The best sponges for commercial use are those with large holes that return to their original shape when pressed," says Selim Dinçer, a Bodrum marine biologist who has studied sponges.

Lifeline: A sponge fishing team usually consists of five divers, a captain and a cook aboard a 33-foot (10-meter) *tirandil*, a wooden-framed boat that is built in the Bodrum area. Each diver takes a turn under water. The average dive is two to three hours. Equipment consists of a wet suit, mask and regulator. Air is pumped by a regulator to the diver along a lifeline, described as a *nargile*, a hubble bubble or a *hookah*. This allows the fishermen to dive to depths of 500 feet (150 meters). But the further down the sponge divers go, the greater the dangers of getting the dreaded divers' disease, the "bends" – an ailment that can permanently impair, cripple and even kill healthy men. A diver suffering from the "bends" must be treated in a decompression chamber within 24 hours.

Often sponge divers find ancient shipwrecks and amphoras. In 1988, sponge divers discovered in the Gulf of Gökova the remains of two British World War II fighter planes with the skeletons of the crew inside. The two planes had been shot down in 1942 by the Germans.

"A living sponge looks more like a slimy piece of raw liver than like the familiar sponge of the bathroom," Ralph Buchsbaum, a prominent American biologist, wrote in his two volume book, *Animals without Backbones*.

When they are taken out of the sea, sponges are covered by a membrane and a gastric bag full of visceral fluids. They are left in the boat for some time to die, put in plastic bags and lowered into the sea again. After a while, the sponges are brought back up and trampled on to remove the membranes and other fluids. The remaining skeletons are washed, rinsed, dried and chemically treated to give the sponges a pleasant white or yellow coloring.

Right, drying sponges in the sun.

BLUE VOYAGE

The area between Bodrum and Fethiye which accounts for over 90 percent of the yachting activity of the Blue Voyage can be divided into three main sailing grounds, the Gulf of Gökova, the Gulf of Hisarönü and Sömbeki, and the Gulf of Fethiye. From Bodrum to Marmaris encompasses the ancient Carian Coast. From Marmaris to Fethiye lies the Lycian Coast, which extends as far as Antalya.

Planning a cruise: Unless you are prepared to spare at least three weeks, don't try to squeeze a Blue Voyage into the three gulfs in one cruise, for you will miss a great deal while making quick leaps from one stop to the next. A wise plan would be to divide the area into three separate travel zones and allocate a week to 10 days for each but by no means less than five days. A fortnight is needed to make the best of two zones. If pressed for time, it is better to spend it properly in one gulf and come back again for the others.

The essential spirit of the Blue Voyage is a leisurely communion with nature in the very seas where Western civilization bloomed. The Blue Voyage is not a glimpse-and-go package trip of look-alike bays. To the sophisticated traveler it is a bridge that leads to the souls and minds of the Pelasgians – the tribes of the sea – as Homer described them, who, though long gone, still haunt these shores. Unlike yachting holidays in other parts of the world, a Blue Voyage in the Aegean is a pilgrimage through 3,500 years of Western history, a homage to the past, and an understanding of ancient civilizations.

Fisherman of Halicarnassus: The **Gulf of Gökova** (also known as the Ceramic Gulf, Kerme Körfezı and Giova), is where it all began. Between the two World Wars, Cevat Şakir Kabaağaçlı, linguist, historian and a student of the classics, was sent on political exile to Bodrum. He fell in love with the tiny fishermen's village, adopted the acronym "Fisherman of Halicarnassus" as well as the local fishermen's way of life. He wrote continuously of his experiences, especially of sailing in the Gulf of Gökova. In about 30 years, Turkish intellectuals finally understood what this man was telling them and the Blue Voyage became "in" among the better educated. The Blue Voyage has evolved from a trip in a small sponge diver *caique* to a journey in a luxurious Bodrum-built gulet, a 48 to 67 feet long (14 meter to 20 meter) wooden-framed yacht with a rounded stern. Today, Turkey's intellectuals can hardly afford the Blue Voyage, and their exclusion has had an adverse effect on the journey: over commercialization.

The Gulf of Gökova extends about 35 miles (56 km) from east to west. The main places to see, however, cover a 20-mile (32-km) strip of territory on the northeastern corner of the Datça Peninsula. The northern shores of the Gulf of Gökova offer quite a few pleasant, picturesque anchorages dominated by the 3,000-foot (900-meter) Kıran Dağı, a mountain which drops to sea level in a sheer precipice.

A voyage to the Gulf of Gökova logically starts from Bodrum. Not only can provisions be obtained there and the necessary boats chartered, but maintenance facilities and communications networks also abound. The prevailing winds also make it easier to sail southward to Marmaris or eastward into the Gulf of Gökova from Bodrum.

Once the loading of provision, fueling, watering, selection of cabins, settlement of bureaucratic procedures for leaving the port are finished, the yacht is ready to sail forth.

Mud baths: The Blue Voyage begins at Karaada, the island famous for its mud baths. Karaada is three miles (five km) from Bodrum. The mud baths, located in a grotto, are rejuvenating. Bathers come out of the grotto looking like Indians on the war path, with red mud covering their bodies.

Just across the northern tip of Karaada is the small **Pabuç Burnu** (Cape Shoe), a good safe haven for late starters from Bodrum to spend the night. Another anchorage is **Kargacık Bükü**, where the incipient construction of a holiday complex mars its beauty. Another inlet south of it, **Alman Bükü** (German Cove), is quieter, though gusts of *meltem,* a brisk summer wind, may be disturbing at times. In all of these places, it is best to anchor out and tie a mooring line ashore from the stern, leaving lots of cable.

Orak Adası (Sickle Island), about 10 miles (16 km) east of Bodrum, is famous for its clear waters and abundant marine life. A derelict house stands in the middle of the bay facing north. Strangely, the island is also notoriously known for its gigantic rats.

Three miles (five km) east of Orak Adası is Alakıfla Bay, also called **Kise Bükü**, a degenerated version of the word "church" (*kilise*) probably because of the ruins of a monastery in the northwest corner. Monasteries in this part of Turkey were mostly built on ruined temples or necropolises of previous civilizations.

The pleasant hamlet of **Çökertme** decorates a picturesque bay near the beginning of the mountain range that culminates in Kıran Dağı. Çökertme, or Fesleğen (Basil), is a stopover either before or after the crossing of the gulf. In the hamlet are two restaurants, whose motorboats accost visiting yachts soon after anchoring and ask whether the yachtsmen wish to make reservations. The food served at the two restaurants are good and reasonably priced. Belly dancing, accompanied by lively music, is the night's entertainment. Handwoven carpets can also be obtained in the village.

Threatened environment: Between Çökertme and Akbük, there is little else to stop for. The ugly coal-fired **Gökova Thermal Energy Plant** with a gigantic smokestack, built in the mid-1980s despite strong protests from the international environmentalists' movement, stands at what was once the village of Türkevleri spoiling an otherwise scenic coastline. Once operational, environmentalists say, this plant will belch low grade coal fumes into the air and will pollute the entire region. It is incompre-

Map of the Blue Voyage routes.

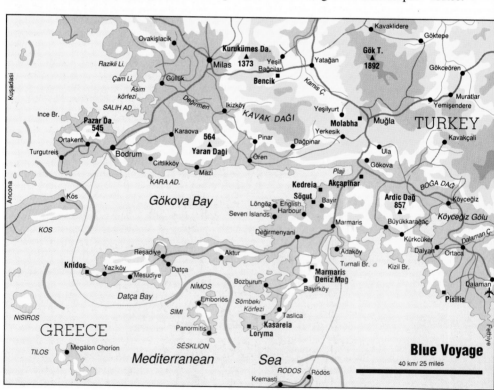

hensible why the Turkish government, which declared the Gulfs of Gökova and Fethiye environmental preservation zones, is preparing to destroy what it tries to protect for the virtues of obtaining energy. Concerned citizens hope that the decision to operate the power station will be revoked. Nevertheless, the smokestack will probably remain and, just as the ruined buildings of Hiroshima, will show the coming generations that contemporary civilization has its evil aspects too. One plan, proposed by President Turgut Özal, is to turn the plant into a five-star hotel, possibly as a face-saving measure.

Ancient Ceramus, now named **Ören** (which means "ruins") is a bad anchorage, but a cheaper center than Karacasöğüt. Various Carian, Roman and Byzantine ruins can be seen at Ceramus, including two temples and a church.

One of the magnificent, if not the most beautiful bays in the gulf, is **Akbük**. Once past Ören, yachts sail in the shadow of the majestic Kıran Dağı that tints the sea with a barely discern-

ible deep purple in daytime and gives off lapis lazuli glows as the sun sets. Young pine forests thrive on the vertical slopes of the mountain and Kıran Dağı looms above. After a seven-mile (11-km) cruise along this breathtaking coast, yachts arrive in Akbük, a fiord-like inlet. Smaller boats may find cosy temporary anchorages in a number of coves in Akbük. These coves, unsuitable for bigger yachts, are the least spoiled in the entire Aegean. Pine forests surround Akbük and Kıran Dağı looms above. A beach stands at the end of the bay with a restaurant that is much better than expected in such wilderness. However safe it may look, Akbük is plagued by troublesome gusts and squalls, which deflect from the mountain and can disturb a yacht at anchor. As in all Aegean anchorages, it is advisable to get tern lines ashore after laying a long cable.

Cleopatra's love nest: Did Cleopatra really frolic with Antony at the islands of **Cedreae** (Cedar), south of Akbük? It is not difficult to fathom how such a cosy place could be chosen as the venue of an imperial love tryst. The main island has one of the finest and, sometimes, the most crowded beach of Turkey, known as **Cleopatra's Beach.** According to one legend, Mark Antony had the beach's fine silt sand transported from the Nile River to satisfy Cleopatra's whims.

It is best to visit Cleopatra's Beach early in the morning or in the late afternoon as it is a regular haunt for tourist hordes coming daily from Marmaris.

This group of three islands was perhaps also the holiday resort of antiquity. Little archaeological study has been conducted in the city of Cedreae, on the main island, which has remains of a castle, and an amphitheater. **Yılan Adası** (Snake Island) in the north has a necropolis.

Architectural award: Very few skippers venture east of Cedreae and Akbük to **Gökova Iskelesi**, at the extreme end of the gulf because of the presence of shoals and insufficient protection from gusts off Kıran Dağı. Those that do, however, should visit the **Residence of**

Cruising off the Turkish Coast.

Nail Çakırhan, a Turkish poet and journalist, in the nearby village of Akyaka. Çakırhan is also an accomplished architect – a traditional-style garden house he built won him the 1983 Aga Khan Award for Architecture. For lunch or dinner, yachtsmen should try Cennet Restaurant, a pleasant eatery with old-style architecture by a natural spring.

The most logical place to anchor safely after Cedreae is Söğüt (often known as Karacasöğüt or Karaca Limanı), 25 miles (40 km) from Marmaris by road. One of the most magnificent bays in the Mediterranean, Söğüt has already attracted land developers and many private houses owned by rich Turks have been built near the pier. A noisy restaurant by the small pier keeps most yachtsmen up all night with music alaturka (Turkish-style) and belly dancing. Another calm wooded anchorage nearby is Çanak (Bowl) Bay.

English harbor: According to local lore, British naval vessels hid in Ingiliz Limanı (English Harbor), one of the bays interweaving the perfectly sheltered fiord-like Değirmen Bükü, during raids against the German-occupied Greek islands in World War II. One fact giving credence to the story is that entrance to the English Harbor is difficult to find. Another was the recent discovery in the bay by Turkish scuba of the remains of two World War II British military aircraft with skeletons inside. Villagers say the two planes were shot down by German anti-aircraft guns in 1942 from the Greek islands.

Six good anchorages exist in Değirmen Bükü. One is occupied by a restaurant which sells water and provisions. A delicious dish served there is oğlak çevirme, a baby goat skewered on charcoal. But if you are unaccustomed to goat's meat, this meal may give you an upset stomach and diarrhoea.

Three miles (five km) west of Değirmen Bükü is the well-sheltered bay known as Ballısu (Honey Water, a name derived from the nearby watering hole), which is a perfect anchorage.

Secret bays: The entrance to Löngöz

Boats tie up for the evening.

226

Fiord is half a mile (one km) west of Ballısu. Known also as Kargılı and Gözleme, Löngöz is a narrow tree-lined inlet surrounded by steep rocks ending in a marsh. Throughout the Blue Voyage, you will often hear groans and grunts at night. These are wild bears. In the past these beasts lived by the shore and threw stones at yachtsmen in protest of the noise they were making. Remarkable shots, the bears seldom missed. The bears have now taken to the deep forests.

Tuzla, a sheltered bay west of Löngöz, is a good anchorage, protected by a cookie-shaped island from the strong summer winds.

A classic stop of the Blue Voyage is at **Yedi Adalar** (Seven Islands), a secluded bay south of Tuzla. The bay is ideal for swimming, snorkeling, windsurfing and spear fishing. Visitors can pull out sponges, catch crabs and watch star fish pulsate.

Three miles (five km) south of Yedi Adalar is **Bördübet Limanı**, one of the safest and most pleasant anchorages in the gulf. In the north is the area known as **Amazon**, which is now occupied by a camping site. Amazon gets its romantic name from the race of female warriors that once inhabited these shores.

The **Bay of Büyük Çatı** (Big Roof), not to be confused with Küçük Çatı (Small Roof), a cove to the east, is popular among yachtsmen because it is safe from all winds. This was once a fisherman's watering hole. The remains of a basilica and other ruins that might have once been a monastery are to be found in the hills.

Körmen on the northern shore of the Datça Peninsula is a drab windswept harbor. But it is the main point of contact between Bodrum and Datça. Ferries carrying cars and passengers stop off here at least twice a day during the high season. In late September and early October, when shoals of albacorea, a distant relative of tuna flock into the gulf, almost all fishermen and yachtsmen in the Bodrum area cast their nets for a catch. Körmen then serves as a logical anchorage for the fishermen and yachts.

Another stop toward the end of the Datça Peninsula is **Mersincik**, another pretty cove.

Knidos, an ancient city situated at the tip of the Datça Peninsula, is usually the last stop before returning to Bodrum from a one-week to 10-day Blue Voyage in Gökova Bay. Knidos, strategically located along the major commercial sea route, was one of the most prosperous cities in the Dorian Hexapolis. It benefited from its safe harbor which sheltered ocean-going merchant ships. Knidos is famous among other things for the **Statue of Aphrodite**, the first ever of a woman in nude. Until the sculptor Praxiteles (390–330 B.C.) made Aphrodite's statue, the subject matter of all nudes were male gods. Even in ancient times, tourists flocked to Knidos to see the statue.

The fate of the Knidian Aphrodite is an enigma. Archaeologists can find no trace of her. One view is that the statue was destroyed in an earthquake. Otherwise it would not have escaped the plundering greed of 19th-century British archaeologists who, supported by the British Navy, removed tons of statuary from Knidos . The city was the home of Eudoxos, a fourth century B.C astronomer and mathematician who founded an observatory here which operated on the principles of modern geometry. Other wonders include two amphitheaters, the **Temple of Aphrodite** and many other buildings that are still being excavated by American archaeologists.

The ruins have a grand view of both the Gulf of Gökova in the north and the Gulf of Hisarönü in the south and the open sea in the west. A series of Greek islands, including Cos, Yiali, Nisiros, Khalki and Rhodes can be seen from the headland.

Three ramshackle restaurants serve fresh fish and lobster. As always, bargaining before ordering is recommended. The locals, whose proclivity to wine drinking is notorious, throw a dancing party every night in one restaurant for the benefit of tourists and themselves. **Baba's Restaurant** in front of the harbor serves delicious fried *barbunya*, a kind of striped mullet.

MARMARIS

Marmaris has come a long way since it was leveled by a devastating earthquake in 1957. The town, once a tiny fishermen's outpost isolated from the rest of Turkey, was completely reconstructed. Today Marmaris is Turkey's most popular resort with hundreds of pensions and hotels and noisy nightclubs. Often described as the "Pearl of the Mediterranean," because of its magnificent natural surroundings, Marmaris has become an important yachting center in recent years. Located in a long, wide bay, fringed by pine forests and fragrant oleander shrubs that cascade down to the shore from the surrounding mountains, the city lies at the confluence of the Aegean and the Mediterranean. The town is built around a 16th-century Ottoman citadel.

Marmaris can be reached in two hours by car from Dalaman International Airport, which is about 75 miles (120 km) from the town. A Turkish Airlines shuttle bus operates everyday back and forth from the airport to the town. Daily passenger buses carry tourists between Marmaris and most major Turkish cities, including Istanbul, Ankara, Izmir and Antalya. Regular boat services also operate between Marmaris and the Greek island of Rhodes, four hours to the west.

Marmaris has a population of 10,000 which swells to 50,000 during the long summer season when its hotels are completely booked and its streets crowded with Turks and foreigners alike.

Like Bodrum, Marmaris is very noisy in the evenings with a steady beat of amplified music coming from dozens of discotheques, bars and pubs. Visitors to Marmaris are advised to stay away from the noisy hub of the town for a good night's rest. They can always go into Marmaris by hiring a taxi or a motor launch or by taking the regular municipal trailer train, which is drawn by a big tractor and stops at every main hotel along the bay region. There are hundreds of reasonably-priced hotels and pensions around the town and in Içmeler Village. But the best hotel in Marmaris is the **Altın Yunus** (The Gold Dolphin), a five-star resort stretched out in a pine forest by the shore, three miles (five km) from Marmaris. The resort is owned by the illustrious Koç group, Turkey's largest industrial and trading company.

Turkish character: Marmaris has a distinct Turkish character, unlike Bodrum, nevertheless it is favored particularly by German and British tourists and wealthy Turks. The five-mile (eight-km) long, two-mile (three-km) wide **Marmaris Bay** is protected by two islands at its mouth, making it ideal for windsurfing, waterskiing and jet skiing.

Palm trees, banks, restaurants and souvenir shops line Marmaris' **Kordon Caddesi** and **Barbaros Caddesi** at the northwestern end of the bay. The main shopping center of Marmaris is on several side streets that run off **Cumhuriyet Meydanı** (Republic Square) and the **Atatürk Statue** in front of the cita-

Left, Marmaris Bay, and right, Atatürk's Statue in Marmaris.

del. These shops sell a range of goods, from carpets and leatherware to provisions for yachts. Most shops in Marmaris stay open till 9 p.m.

Silk carpets: The best place to buy carpets in Marmaris is at **Bazaar 54** near the marina. Bazaar 54 sells all brands of carpets. The Istanbul-based company, which specializes in the manufacture of fine, handmade silk carpets, can deliver carpets to customers anywhere in the world. Another carpet shop that may be worthwhile to check out is **Silk Road** on Barbaros Caddesi. Leatherware and sheepskin coats can be purchased at **Antilop Leather** on Barbaros Caddesi and at **Crocodile** in **Barış Çarşısı**, a bazaar.

The most famous product of Marmaris is honey, turned out by the thousands of bee keepers in the nearby villages, and sold in big jars by street vendors in the town. *Çam balı* produced by bees from the nectar of pine trees, is the tastiest honey of Turkey, far sweeter than *çiçek balı*, or flower honey.

A number of fine seafood restaurants surround the harbor, where fish and *meze* dishes are served. Several bars and pubs line Barbaros Caddesi, including **Akvaryum Bar** and **Physkos Bar**, which are excellent places to socialize with western-oriented Turks and foreign women, and to listen to music. There are seven discotheques in Marmaris, the best of which is at **Martı Holiday Village** in Içmeler.

Concrete jungle: Several charming luxury hotels and holiday villages are located in the more secluded spots of Marmaris Bay. But Marmaris has suffered from the construction of hundreds of tasteless apartment buildings and ugly concrete hotel apartment buildings that hug the shoreline, particularly around the town of Içmeler, on the other side of the bay, five miles (eight km) to the west, and Turunç, a village just outside the bay.

The **Old Quarter**, with its white houses on twisting lanes, is built on different levels on a rocky peninsula around the citadel, and is well worth a stroll. The citadel was originally con-

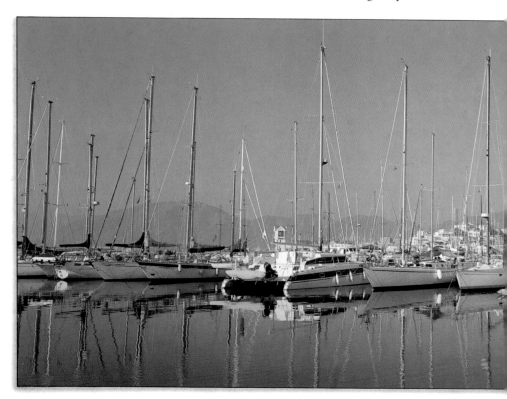

structed by Ionians who settled there in 3000 B.C. It was repaired by Alexander the Great in the fourth century B.C. and expanded by the Ottoman Sultan Süleyman the Magnificent in A.D. 1522 during a military campaign to conquer Rhodes. The marina, located on the other side of the peninsula, has 800 berths, and is operated by the Net group, Turkey's fastest growing private tourism outfit.

Flourishing center: The ancient city of **Physcus**, a deme of the Rhodian Peraea, was located at Marmaris and was a flourishing trading center. But nothing remains to be seen of this old settlement save for some walls located at **Aşar Tepe**, on a hill overlooking the town. The hill is a recommended climb only for photographers who want to get some spectacular shots of Marmaris.

Daily excursions: Day excursions by boat can be arranged from the town to the many deserted coves around Marmaris Bay. Yachts can also be chartered in Marmaris (there are three dozen travel agencies and charter companies here) for longer Blue Voyages to the neighboring gulfs of Bozburun, Sömbeki and Hisarönü.

The best way to get acquainted with Marmaris Bay and the outlying areas is to take a boating trip to Çiftlik (the farm). Motorboat launches, capable of carrying up to 30 persons, leave Marmaris quay, along Kordon Caddesi, at 9 a.m. The round trip costs less than $10 per person.

It takes two hours to get to Çiftlik, a tiny community outside the bay which has the best and cleanest beach around Marmaris. The easiest way to reach Çiftlik and the other villages on the rugged Loryma Peninsula is by boat as road connections are still woefully inadequate. The launches cruise along the northeastern part of the bay, hugging the shoreline, leaving behind Marmaris and its marina.

Paradise beach: To the left is **Günnücek Park** with its fragrant conifers. After rounding **Bedir Island**, the boat comes to a stop at a little hidden cove aptly named **Cennet** or Paradise,

Yachts in the marina.

which is surrounded by a lush forest of pine trees. Resembling a veritable Garden of Eden, Cennet is part of **Nimara Peninsula**, a bulging landmass that shelters the wide bay. The boat stays for only 20 minutes, allowing for a quick dive into the water and a swim to the sandy beach.

Once all the passengers have returned to the boat, the skipper will continue the voyage, rounding Nimara Peninsula and heading out to the open sea. Often the captain will take passengers behind the peninsula to the **Phosphorescent Grotto**, sometimes referred to as the Pirate's Cave. The boat can only partially enter the tiny cavern where the shiny bottom can be seen.

Leaving the grotto, the boat cuts across the sea to **Turunç Bükü**, a once lovely bay that has been ruined by the construction of many ugly hotels, noisy discotheques and bars, and sails to the next bay, **Kumlu Bükü**, which has just one hotel and a few pensions. Sometimes the boat will stop at both bays to disembark or take on passengers. Next the boat glides by a long, rocky coastline that is completely uninhabited, finally stopping off at **Gerbekse**, a charming cove with interesting ruins of several Byzantine churches, allowing the passengers to take a quick dip in its clear waters.

Spear fishing: The boat turns back and goes to **Çiftlik**, a bay which is protected by a craggy island on which an Istanbul businessman has built a castle-like summer mansion. The waters of Çiftlik's mile-long beach are crystal clear and clean, a place where snorkeling, swimming with a mask and spear fishing along the rocky shoreline is possible. Except for a big hotel that is under construction, several summer cottages and three farm house restaurants, the bay is deserted. The restaurants serve *shish kebab*, fish, salad and melons. The most pleasant of these is the one operated by the always smiling Mehmet Yılmaz and his big family, who are known for their hospitality and generosity. Yılmaz also operates on the beach an unusual outdoor drinking bar made from the remains of a *caique*. The

passengers are allowed two more hours of swimming before the boat begins its return journey.

Leaving Çiftlik, the boat passes Kumlu Bükü and Turunç Bükü and enters Marmaris Bay, stopping off at Içmeler, which has several big hotels, including the five-star Munamar Hotel and the nearby Martı Holiday Village, owned by Halit Narin, a flamboyant textiles magnate.

Continuing along the coast, the boat next passes the luxurious Altın Yunus Hotel, the Turban Holiday Village and the renovated Hotel Lidya. To the right is the **Floating Hotel**, usually docked by Keçi Adası, the Goat's Island, at the mouth of the bay. Authorities shut down the 300-bed hotel, built on a large steel-framed barge capable of maneuvering in the bay, in 1985 because it was discharging pollutants into the waters. The boat finally returns to Marmaris about six in the evening.

Environs: One of the most interesting side trips to take from Marmaris is to travel along Datça Peninsula to the

The old lady wiles away time by knitting.

ruins of **Knidos**, an ancient Carian city, situated 59 miles (95 km) west of Marmaris. Since some of the roads to Knidos are still in bad condition visitors should prefer a four-wheel drive for the three-hour trip. Especially at night, they should avoid driving on the treacherous highway, which weaves among dangerous cliffs. It's best to spend the night at Datça, an up-and-coming resort town facing the Gulf of Hisarönü. Motorists should bring spare tires before leaving as the bumpy roads to Knidos have flattened many tires.

Although difficult, the drive to Knidos is rewarding, just for its splendid scenery. After Içmeler, the asphalt road winds into the mountains for about 13 miles (20 km) only to drop gently to the fertile plains and the **Gulf of Hisarönü** below. The Datça Peninsula, a spiny, 45-mile (72-km) long, finger-like projection, separates the Hisarönü Bay in the south from the Gökova Bay in the north. The eastern part of the peninsula is verdant, covered by pine forest, valonia oak and olive trees.

Nighttime in Datça.

The easternmost part of the bay is silted and shallow and is known as **Keyif**, meaning "enjoyment and bliss." Soon the narrowest point of the Datça Peninsula is reached. It is appropriately named **Balıkaşıran** (the place where fish leaps across), for here the isthmus is less than a mile wide. When the Persian army invaded Asia Minor in 546 B.C. and subdued the Greek cities on the coast, the Knidians began building a deep defensive canal there to separate the Datça (Dorian) Peninsula from the mainland. To get an outsider's view about the project they consulted an oracle, who replied: "Dig not nor fence your isthmus: Zeus himself had made your land an island, had he so wished." With oracle's verdict, the Knidians abandoned construction, and the Persian army swept through the peninsula and conquered Knidos.

In the 19th century, English naval Commander Graves, who was surveying the area for charting, reported to have found signs of the canal, but archaeologists George Bean and J.M. Cook, who visited the site in 1950s could find no traces of the waterway.

Solar energy: The hidden fiord facing the Gulf of Hisarönü is known as **Bencik**, a favored anchorage among yachtsmen on the Blue Voyage. **Dişlice Island**, which means "Toothy" in Turkish, stands at the entrance of the inlet, resembling bared teeth from a distance. On the eastern end is a meteorological station and an unusual solar energy research institute, which blemish the solitude of the otherwise perfect fiord.

For the next 20 miles (32 km) the road is a series of hairpin turns into the mountains from which both bays can be viewed simultaneously from dizzying heights. A huge holiday village occupies the magnificent bays of Çiftlik and Kurucu Bükü.

Halfway up the peninsula, one reaches **Datça**, which has become a popular stopover for yachtsmen. The town has several colorful seafood restaurants, pubs and discotheques. Of the many pensions and hotels in Datça, the **Hotel Club Dorya**, on the tiny peninsula, is the best. Across the bay the Greek island of Symi, or Sömbeki in Turkish, is visible only seven miles (11 km) away. Daily ferryboats carry passengers and cars between Bodrum to Körmen, Datça's harbor village on the Gulf of Gökova. It is possible to take daily excursions from Datça to Knidos by boat on a shared-taxi basis. The boats stop off at a number of completely deserted bays, including **Domuz Bükü** (the Bay of Pigs), where tourists can plunge into the clear waters for swimming. A British-operated holiday village is there.

Almonds and olives: A few miles out of Datça, the road becomes unpaved and very rough as it climbs the rugged vertebrae of a new mountain chain, past villages, almond orchards and olive groves. It takes about one hour to reach the windswept Knidos from Datça.

The sleepy village of **Palamut**, eight miles (13 km) away, is the next settlement. Palamut, which means "bonito" in Turkish, gets its name from the abundance of fish caught in the bay. The village is the site for the ancient Knidian city of Triopium. It was in that ancient city that Dorian states held competitive sporting events in honor of Apollo, the Greek God of manly youth and beauty, that were precursors to the Olympic Games. An acropolis and some ruins are above the village, but it isn't really worth walking up the hill to see them. Palamut is famous for its fish restaurants which serve lobster. Its small harbor is good shelter for yachts seeking protection from the wind. A long strand of beach is good for swimming. The popular Emel Sayın, an attractive blond Turkish female vocalist who has a summer house in Palamut, dines often at the **Gangün Cafeteria**, a restaurant coffeehouse by the beach.

Knidos lies next to **Cape Crio**, the tip of the Datça Peninsula.

Another possible excursion from Marmaris is up the Loryma Peninsula to Bozburun, a picturesque village. The road is rough most of the way and motorists are advised to rent jeeps for this trip. The road to Bozburun, southwest of Marmaris, forks left at the end of the

Gulf of Hisarönü. The first village one comes to is **Hisarönü**, just off the road. The village, by the shore, has several pleasant pension-hotels, including the Kaplan Pansiyon and the Melba Pansiyon, an outdoor restaurant-coffeehouse and a campsite. The village is crowded during the summer months with British and German tourists.

The ruins of **Bybassus**, an important Rhodian deme, is located on the other side of the main road. The ruins include an acropolis on a steep rocky hill surrounded by a Hellenistic fortification.

The **Sanctuary of Hemitea**, built in honor of the goddess of healing, is located on a ridge of the mountain known as Eren Dağı (900 feet/274 meters) above the plain of Hisarönü. At this sanctuary pregnant women were treated by a method resembling hypnosis, described as "incubation," believed to relieve abdominal pains. All that remains of the sanctuary is the temple's platform and crumbling theater. In ancient times the annual Festival of Castabus was held there.

The day's catch.

234

The **Bay of Orhaniye**, a deep wide inlet of the Gulf of Hisarönü protected by Eren Dağı and clad with olive trees and pine forests, is a popular stopover for yachtsmen. There is a small boat landing and a motel **Keçibükü** (goat's bay), which is at the end of the Bay of Orhaniye, has a boat landing as well. A Byzantine fortress crowns the top of the small island in the bay and a long sand bar runs along the end of the bay. A pleasant club house and a restaurant are located at Keçibükü.

After Keçibükü, the road gets rough. Another dirt road forks left uphill about half a mile (one km) to a bucolic shaded grove known as **Şelale** (Waterfalls), where peasants serve special village *böreks* and grapes by a stream. Several waterfalls plunge down the terraces, forming the stream and a deep pool in which bathing is possible.

Oregano and laurels: The village of **Bayır**, located in the mountains on the main road to Bozburun, has a pleasant square shaded by a 600-year-old oak tree under which several teahouses provide refreshments for visiting tourists. The villagers are renowned for making *kekik yağı,* the oil of oregano, which grows wild in the mountains of the peninsula. *Kekik yağı,* locals say, has medicinal properties which help cure stomach ulcers, asthma, intestinal worms and eczema. The villagers also collect aromatic *defne yaprağı,* laurel leaves, used as a flavoring in preparing *shish kebab.*

The most charming village in the area is **Selimiye**, which has a Byzantine fortress at its entrance. The bay forms a natural harbor.

Bozburun is a little town of 2,500 people. The famous boat building center has in recent years become an important stopover for yachts on the Blue Voyage. The biggest hotel in town is the Akvariyum Tourism Facilities, owned and operated by Korel Göymen, a well-known social democrat politician. Boats can be chartered from Bozburun to the ancient site of Loryma at the tip of the peninsula and to Serçe Limanı, a bay facing the Mediterranean.

emple of
phrodite in
nidos.

MEDITERRANEAN COAST

The Turkish Mediterranean Coast begins east of Marmaris and ends at the Syrian border south of Antakya. The Turks call the Mediterranean "Akdeniz," the White Sea. The Turkish Mediterranean encompasses the eastern part of the province of Muğla and the entire coastal areas of provinces of Antalya, Mersin, Adana and Hatay. The western part of Turkey's Mediterranean Coast is well known, but the section east of Alanya is virtually unknown among tourists and rarely visited, despite its rich past, due to the lack of sufficient hotels and information.

The western part of the Mediterranean Coast is a mountainous region with a narrow coastal strip having many charming resorts, sunken cities and ruins of scores of fascinating ancient cities. This area was known in antiquity as Lycia, and the earliest people who inhabited it, the Lycians, were an independent-minded people noted for their bravery and their reverence for their dead. Their massive tombs, built right into the faces of the mountains, are architectural masterpieces that can't easily be copied by modern men. Towns like Fethiye, Kaş and Kemer have already become booming tourism centers, attracting travelers from all over the world. Travelers to this region go yachting, windsurfing, boating and exploring the hundreds of ancient sites which hug the coast. Saint Nichòlas, better known as Santa Claus, lived in Myra in the fourth century.

Five-star hotels: The Pamphylian Coast, with Antalya as the tourist hub of southwest Turkey, is a breadbasket region, a vast plain surrounded by the towering Taurus and Bey mountains. The region produces much cotton, citrus fruits and fresh vegetables. Antalya harbor and free trade zone is one of Turkey's leading export centers.

It was from Antalya (known as Attalia in antiquity) that St. Paul, with Barnabas, sailed on his last journey to Antioch (Antakya) to preach.

Many cities, including Perge and Aspendos, have flourished in Pamphylia in the past. Side and Alanya, built on ancient sites east of Antalya, today are booming resorts with each having a dozen five-star hotels and holiday villages crammed with wealthy European, Japanese and American vacationers. These two towns also have hundreds of pensions for the middle-class traveler and the budget-conscious visitor. The beaches of the Pamphylian Coast are among the best in Turkey with soft, golden sand, favored mainly by German tourists.

East of Alanya is the region that was known as Rough Cilicia, a place where the jagged Taurus Mountains tumble down to the sea abruptly. In the rugged Taurus Mountains, goats grow luxuriant coats. Their hair is woven into a rough fabric used in tent making. The main highway follows the ridges of the mountains and has stunning views of the Mediterranean. Anamur, the banana-growing capital of Turkey, is the most important resort in the area with its long sandy beaches and a magnificent Armenian-built castle. The mountains eventually give way to the vast Çukurova, a cotton-producing region, once known as Smooth Cilicia.

The first important town of note is Silifke – the name is a Turkish version for Cilicia. Silifke is a touristic region with beaches and many castles, including the fabled Kızkalesi, which stands on an island near the town. Silifke is located on the Göksu River delta, which is a rich breeding and wintering grounds for hundreds of species of birds, including pelicans.

Adana, Turkey's third largest city and a major industrial center, dominates the Çukurova. This region has produced two outstanding figures – literary giant Yaşar Kemal and Turkey's greatest industrialist, Haci Ömer Sabancı.

Other cities in the region include the ports of Mersin and Iskenderun and Antakya. This region is rich in history. A succession of empires ruled the area, from the Hittites, Greeks and Seleucids to the Romans, Byzantines and the Turks.

THE WESTERN MEDITERRANEAN

The western Mediterranean Coast extends from a line east of Marmaris to the resort town of Alanya and covers the ancient Roman provinces of Lycia and Pamphylia. The region has about 60 percent of Turkey's tourist accommodations, with huge hotels, holiday village complexes and thousands of pensions and campsites lining the coastline. Nearly half of the tourists who visit Turkey explore this 250-mile (400-km) stretch of territory.

Fire-breathing monster: The area has many well-known destinations such as Antalya, Side and Alanya, and also rarely-visited sites such as Yanartaş, whose eternal flames from the mountains led ancients to believe were the remains of the fire-breathing monster Chimera; the sunken cities around Kekova Island; Caunos where archaeologists have unearthed an important city; Dalyan, one of the last breeding grounds in the Mediterranean for gigantic marine turtles. The town is also famous for its boat rides among the reeds and its rejuvenating mud baths; and the high plateaus of Lycia where townsmen pitch up their tents during the sultry summers to escape the heat waves of the coast.

It was along the Lycian Coast that St. Paul led some of his early missionary activities to spread Christianity. In Patara, St. Paul embarked on his last voyage to Palestine. The rock tombs of Caunos, Fethiye and Myra are indeed incredible sites, built right into the faces of overhanging cliffs – a symbol of reverence for the dead.

One of the most important events that takes place in this region is the colorful Saint Nicholas Festival held every December 4 - 6 in the town of Demre to honor the original gift-bearing saint associated with the snowy winters of northern Europe. Saint Nicholas, a controversial Christian figure, was born in Patara, a city now covered by sand dunes, and became the first Bishop of

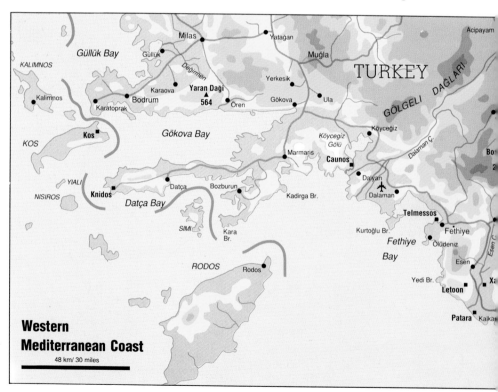

Western Mediterranean Coast

48 km/ 30 miles

Myra. His spirit continues to this day with the exchange of gifts during the Christmas season and on New Year's day.

A Blue Voyage into the wonderful 12 Islands of the Gulf of Fethiye from the town of Göcek, which is fast becoming an important yachting center because of its proximity to Dalaman International Airport, is strongly recommended for travelers who want to get away from the stress of modern urban living. Boat trips to the sunken cities of Kekova Sound, destroyed by earthquakes are also soothing. Travelers to these regions can go snorkeling among the baths which Cleopatra built, but which are now partly submerged.

Pirate's hideout: The region includes Olympus, a pirates' den that is now in complete ruins in a well-hidden gorge along the rocky Lycian coast. Visitors can also go to Uluburun, a barren cave near the small town of Kaş where underwater archaeologists are excavating the world's oldest known shipwreck, discovered by chance by a sponge diver in 1982. The shipwreck has shed light on the complex trade relations that existed some 3,600 years ago in the eastern Mediterranean.

Some of the most important events of early western history have taken place along the shores of the Turkish western Mediterranean. Alexander the Great's army thundered across Pamphylian Plain in a campaign to conquer the world and build an empire. Persian and Roman armies clashed with the recalcitrant Lycians. Cleopatra and Mark Antony frolicked in the many coves. Venetian Admiral Andrea Doria raided these shores in the 16th century in a vain effort to prevent the Turks from dominating the entire Mediterranean. From 1919-1921, the region was occupied by an Italian army as part of World War I spoils. But the Italians were forced to abandon the area when Turkish nationalists put up stiff resistance.

Today, this region is the pride of modern Turkey and the center for the nation's tourist development, waiting to be discovered and explored.

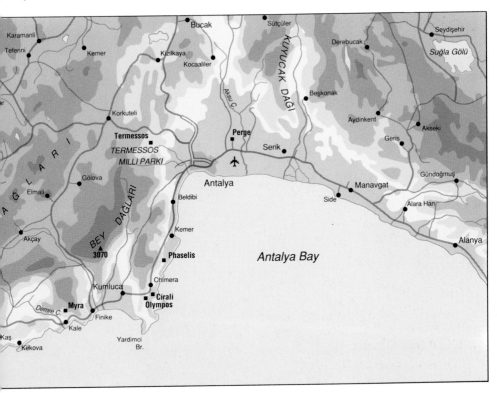

LYCIA

The Lycians, the earliest inhabitants of the rugged coast east of Marmaris known as Lycia, were a fierce sea-going people known for their exceptional bravery, pride, self-respect, and their determination to defend their independence at all costs. The Phoenicians and the Saracens of the old world dreaded encountering these warrior people. The Lycians, who inhabited this region 2,000 years ago, had their own 12-god Pantheon and dialect. More than anything else, the Lycians revered their dead. They carved their tombs, replicas of their homes, on the faces of mountains all over southwest Turkey. How they managed such engineering feats is a subject of much speculation even today.

Lycia can be reached from Marmaris by driving along route 400 past Köyceğiz, a town on the Köyceğiz Lake famous for its green houses, and taking the country road that forks to the right. This road leads to the charming village of Dalyan and to the ruins of Caunos, the first city of Lycia. Dalyan can also be reached by daily boating excursions from Marmaris, bypassing **Aksaz Limanı**, a bay where a big North Atlantic Treaty Organization (NATO) naval base is under construction. It takes about four hours to reach Dalyan by boat. The boats usually stop off at **Ekincik**, where passengers transfer to smaller boats that can navigate the shallow twisting Dalyan River, surrounded by reeds and marshes.

Dalyan, an unspoiled, cosy little resort on the Dalyan River, is one of the most relaxing sites of Turkey, facing the spooky rock tombs of Caunos. Its nights are lazy and calm and its riverside fish restaurants are superb. The best fish restaurant is the **Deniz Yıldızı** (Star Fish) just off the main square. Dalyan means fishery and it gets its name for the many fisheries along the river, which trap *kefal* (mullet) and *levrek* (seabass). These unusual breeds can live in both salt waters and fresh waters. They are caught returning to the sea after spawning at Köyceğiz Lake. Visitors who decide to spend some time in Dalyan should try *kefal*, a long gray fish, best served grilled. They should also try some tasty *pavurya* or *yengeç* (crabs) as an appetizer. The waiter usually brings a small hammer which is used to crack the shell of the animal to get at its delicious meat.

The most pleasant hotels and pensions in Dalyan are those along the river, but the Caretta Caretta Hotel, built by Nail Çakırhan, the recipient of 1982 Aga Khan Architecture Award, near the village square, may be the best.

A boat can be rented for a few hours to take tourists across the river to the ruins of **Caunos**, located on two separate levels. An ancient Carian and Lycian city, Caunos was once a thriving port. But like many ancient riverside cities along the Turkish Coast, its downfall came with the silting up of its harbor by the Dalyan River. In the fourth century B.C., the town was known as a

Left, the "Turtle Beach" at Dalyan. **Right**, enjoying a mud bath.

sickly malaria-ridden place with green-complexioned inhabitants. Among the ruins to be seen are an amphitheater, ancient walls, an acropolis hill, and of course the rock tombs, hewn right into the face of the cliff. Motorboats also travel upstream to special mud baths.

Marine turtles: Motorboats can be hired from Dalyan to Iztuzu Beach, popularly known as **Turtle Beach** at the mouth of the river. It takes about an hour to reach the six-mile (10-km) long beach, which resembles a long sand bar. Travelers can also reach the beach by car. A newly-built road from Dalyan to Iztuzu Beach winds along the marshes for nine miles (15 km). The water is shallow and safe, especially for children, and the beach is ideal for tossing frisbees, playing volleyball and building sand castles. Iztuzu Beach is one of the last remaining breeding grounds in the Mediterranean for the Loggerhead Marine Turtle *Caretta caretta*.

During the June-September turtle breeding season, the beach is closed to the public from 6 p.m. to 9 a.m. to pre-vent tourists from trampling on the turtles' nests. Resembling amphibious landing craft and each weighing 300 pounds (136 kilos), hundreds of female turtles, traveling there from as far as the West African Coast, invade the shore in June and July, almost always at night, and lay about 100 leathery eggs that resemble golf balls in the sand. The female turtle may lay eggs four times during the breeding season. Before lumbering back to the sea, the females cover their eggs with sand to protect them from predators. Nevertheless, predators such as foxes living in the hills come down to the beach at night and often find the nests by scent and feast on the turtle eggs.

Crawling seaward: It takes about six to eight weeks for the baby turtles to hatch. Breaking out of their shells, the baby turtles cling to one another like a double helix and claw their way up the sand for air and march to the sea. Hundreds of turtles are eaten alive by huge Ghost Crabs that lay traps for them in the sand. Hawks and other predatory birds catch

Rock cemeteries at Caunos.

the turtles which fail to reach the sea by daylight. In August and September, it is possible to see an army of little newly-hatched turtles crawl seaward on the beach.

Turkey's tiny environmentalist movement, assisted by West Germany's Greens Party, won its first major victory at Turtle Beach in 1987 when it successfully pressured the Turkish government to halt the building of a big Turkish-German hotel near the beach, asserting that the construction would endanger the newly-hatched turtles. The environmentalists argued that lights from the hotel would confuse the baby turtles, which would get lost and head inland instead of seeking the safety of the sea. The beach today is an environmentally protected zone. Guards keep watch over the beach area at night to prevent tourists and local farmers from trespassing – a measure to protect the turtles' nest.

From Dalyan another road leads through fertile farm lands of orange and tangerine groves to **Ortaca**, a cotton-producing town, and links up to the route 400. The town of **Dalaman**, just off the Muğla-Fethiye highway, has an international airport where hundreds of charter flights arrive daily, bringing tens of thousands of tourists daily from Europe, the United States and Japan. The only other thing Dalaman is famous, or notorious for, is a state paper mill, which is polluting the nearby Dalaman River, which empties into the Mediterranean south of the airport.

Göcek: From Dalaman the east-bound road soon climbs pine-covered mountains only to plunge to the town of **Göcek**, on the northwestern end of the Gulf of Fethiye. Göcek, only 19 miles (30 km) from Dalaman International Airport, is rapidly developing into an important yachting center. Many local as well as foreign chartering companies have already set up shop in the town, which has a population of only 2,122. Several five-star hotels will be built around Göcek in the early 1990s.

Despite its smallness, Göcek is indeed a town of true international char-

Bays of the Turquoise Coast.

acter. It is one of the few places in Turkey where newspapers and magazines from all over the world are sold. The town has a small pier with scores of yachts lining it. A number of seaside restaurants and coffeehouses face the bay. At the far end of the bay facing Göcek is an old Istanbul steam boat, *Halas*, docked by the shore. Owned by Haldun Simavi, a Turkish business tycoon and former newspaper publisher, the *Halas* is now being used as a luxurious floating hotel-restaurant. Nearby is a pier operated by SEKA, the state paper mills.

From Göcek it is possible to charter yachts to the 12 Islands of the **Gulf of Fethiye**, one of the most secluded and beautiful areas on the Turquoise Coast. Daily motorboat excursions to the **12 Islands** leave Göcek quay in the mornings. The day trip can also be made from Fethiye. Each passenger pays about $10 for the round trip. You can also charter a *caique*, inclusive of its captain, for about $100, if you want to be alone and have complete privacy.

As the boat heads away from Göcek, the first two islands you encounter are **Göcek Adası**, famous for its verdant pine forests, and **Zeytinli Adası**, a privately-owned estate with thousands of olive trees, both on the left.

Soon you reach **Yassıca Adaları**, an archipelago of small islands good for mooring and swimming, and the larger **Hacıhalil Adası**. The boat doesn't usually stop at any of these islands, but continues to the big island on the left, **Tersane Adası**, which has a protected cove suitable for anchorage. The boat will stop there for about half an hour, permitting passengers to swim ashore to explore the island. The ruins of several buildings, which were most likely inhabited by Greek families before the 1923 population exchanges, face the cove. Tersane means "shipyards" in Turkish, and the Greek families who once lived there built wooden-framed boats.

The Pig's Island: From Tersane, the boat crosses the narrow strait to **Domuz Adası** (the Pig's Island), an island that is

Selling watermelon in a horse-drawn carriage.

owned by Erol Simavi, the publisher of Turkey's biggest-selling newspaper, *Hürriyet*, and one of the most powerful men in the country. Simavi's villa stands amid what appears to be ancient ruins. Stopping at the island is forbidden. At the northwest corner of the island the remains of a nun's convent can be seen. Simavi has hosted many guests at his secret island retreat, including Prince Charles and Princess Margaret and other members of the British royal family, who have cruised along the 12 Islands in his private yacht.

The boat continues to **Hamam Cove**, which has several partially submerged ruins of buildings that some locals claim were the **Baths of Cleopatra**. The structures sank as a result of earth tremors. The skipper of the boat will stop for 90 minutes in the bay, allowing passengers to have lunch at one of the alfresco restaurants, open only in the summer. The break will also give visitors time to swim and explore the ruins using a mask and snorkel.

From Hamam Cove, the captain will take visitors to the westernmost point of the Gulf, **Bedri Rahmi Bay**. The bay gets its name from the cubist painting of a fish on a rock by the shore. It was painted in 1974 by the late Bedri Rahmi Eyuboğlu, a well-known painter who popularized the Blue Voyage with his great paintings and poetry. The region is also known as Taşyaka, or **Tombs Bay**, because of the many Lycian cemeteries and pigeonhole rock tombs along the jagged shoreline. The site was identified by the late George Bean as the ancient Lycian city of Crya. The boat will stop for about 30 minutes, enabling passengers to swim ashore and visit the rock tombs and admire Eyuboğlu's painting.

The next bay on the way back to Göcek is **Boynuzbükü**, a deep sheltered bay surrounded by pine trees where sail boats can anchor safely. A river, lined with reeds and oleander shrubs, empties into the bay. The government recently banned construction of several new hotels in this bay, including one by the former mayor of Istanbul,

Bedrettin Dalan, to protect its beauty. On day trips the motorboats return to Göcek on the same day.

Fethiye: A one-hour drive east from Göcek brings the traveler to the flourishing city of **Fethiye**. Once a minor market village, Fethiye has become a thriving tourism center in recent times. The town is immensely popular among French, German and British tourists and foreign yachtsmen. Fethiye is a yachting center for Blue Voyages into the Gulf of Fethiye, the 12 Islands, and the unforgettable region around Kekova Island, which has some of the most mysterious sunken cities in the world.

Fethiye has always been an important center for the export of chromium. Turkey is the world's biggest producer of this metal, which is mined all along the bulge of Lycia from the Gulf of Fethiye to Antalya.

In many ways, Fethiye resembles Bodrum. It has a rich nightlife with many pubs, discotheques and bars. Its downtown is lined with hundreds of gift shops, selling everything from carpets and leatherware to colorful T-shirts and blue glass beads to fend off the evil eye. The restaurants by the quay, the marina and the shopping district are lively during the evenings, visited by large crowds of tourists.

All this is strange for a town that had no road connections with any provincial centers as recently as 1950. At the time, all transportation was done by boat. The first organized tourist group to ever visit Fethiye came on a boat trip from Rhodes in 1963.

Telmessus: Fethiye dates back to the sixth century B.C. The town was once a grand Lycian city called **Telmessus**, and traces of the ancient settlement can be seen about the town, including the awesome rock tombs on the face of a cliff east of the city and several scattered heavy sarcophagi, including one next to the Town Hall (**Belediye Binası**). The town, however, is modern, having been reconstructed after the earthquakes of 1950 and 1957 leveled it

Situated at the eastern end of the big Gulf of Fethiye, the town is surrounded by tall mountains that are snowcapped in winter. A bulging headland and an island, popularly known as **Şovalyeler Adası** (The Knights' Island), protect the town, forming almost a big lake that is an ideal shelter for yachts.

Fethiye has many first-class hotels and holiday villages, the best of which is the spectacular holiday town **Club Letoonia**, operated by the French Club Méditerranée organization, and the **Club Hotel Aries** at Çali Beach.

Temple tomb: The rock tombs are just behind the city. Cars can be left on the base of the cliffs and the tombs can be reached by walking up a steep path. The most magnificent of these monuments to the dead is the **Temple Tomb of Amyntas**, who was a Lycian notable. A sarcophagus, weighing several tons, stands smack in the middle of the road, near the rock tombs. Neither the rock tombs nor the sarcophagus were damaged or even budged during the earthquakes that flattened Fethiye in 1950 and 1957. The local denizens have never considered pushing the sarcophagus off the middle of the road, claiming that if they were to move it even slightly "the whole world would shake." An acropolis hill at the back of the town is occupied by a castle, believed to have been constructed by the Knights of St. John.

Rafet Restaurant, indisputably the best restaurant in town, is located along Kordonboyu (the quay), just off Atatürk Caddesi, the main street that runs north-south through Fethiye. The restaurant is operated by Rafet Tuna, 55, a Turkish refugee from Bulgaria who settled in Fethiye in 1950. Tuna has run the restaurant for 35 years. Food at the restaurant, which specializes in grilled fish and delightful appetizers, is modestly priced. Guests buy the fish at daily prices written on a board next to the display refrigerator. All the guest needs to do is point to which fish he wants and the waiter weighs it and has it cooked for you. Rafet specializes in *orfoz* (dusky grouper) or *akya* (leer fish) and other seafood.

A night in town includes a visit to souvenir and carpet shops along Çarşı Caddesi, which is parallel to Atatürk Caddesi, followed by a visit to **Hotel Club Letoonia**, a sprawling holiday town across the bay on **Paçaraz Peninsula**, and a pub crawl in the town. Hotel Club Letoonia is only a six-mile (10-km) drive from Fethiye, following the coast past the marina. Automobiles are left at the entrance to the town's gate and visitors must walk through the sprawling complex along the middle promenade, to its discotheques and bars passing hundreds of fancy houses, which are part of the holiday complex but owned by Turkey's nouveaux rich, and luxury bungalows on different levels, where guests stay. From the holiday town, the flickering lights of Fethiye can been seen at night. The floodlit open air bar is at the farthest end of the peninsula, where young foreign men and women mingle with Turks.

The cosy **Entel Bar 1** on Türkocağì Sokak No. 6 in the center of town is a good place for a nightcap. The bar is operated by Gençağa Karafazlı, a friendly Turkish journalist, and his wife. The Karafazlıs also run **Entel Bar 2** behind the state hospital (Devlet Hastanesi) near Vizon Hotel. Other bars in Fethiye that stay open past midnight include the **Fisherman's Bar**, across the street from the quay, and **Cafe Bar** and **Bourbon Bar**, along Çarşı Caddesi. All provide live music.

Environs: Numerous excursions can be made to different resorts, towns and ancient Lycian cities from Fethiye. One of these excursions is to the ghost town of Kaya and the resort of Ölüdeniz. A dirt road, on which the massive sarcophagus stands, curves into the mountains behind the town for about six miles (10 km), passing dense pine and cedar forests, and winds down to a fertile plain. **Kaya**, formerly known as Kormylassos, stands on the side of a hill overlooking the plain. Kaya was once a wealthy Greek town of 5,000 people, the most populous in the region. The Greeks abandoned Kaya as part of the general population exchanges between Greece and Turkey at the end of the Greco-Turkish War of 1919-1922. (Nearly 1.5 million Greeks living in

Turkey switched places with 500,000 Turks living in Greece in 1923.) Kaya today is an eerie ghost town that is worth an early morning stroll. Hundreds of houses, with their roofs crumbled from the quakes that rocked the region, remain standing along rock paths. Two well-preserved churches, one built in 1888 and still having frescoes depicting biblical scenes, remain intact. Several chapels exist below the church on the hill.

The same road continues on to **Ölüdeniz**, the "Dead Sea," another six miles (10 km) from Kaya. (Ölüdeniz can also be reached directly from Fethiye. The turnoff to Ölüdeniz is on the Muğla-Antalya Highway.) Ölüdeniz is a misnomer. Although it resembles a perfectly calm lagoon, it has a small mouth opening to the sea through which boats could once enter. Ringed by mountains, pine trees and a long sandy beach, Ölüdeniz was an ideal shelter for yachts seeking protection from the stormy sea. But Ölüdeniz was closed to yachts in 1984 to prevent pollution of its crystal waters. The **Motel Meri**, a complex of private bungalows, has the best accommodations in the area.

The **Belcekız Beach**, along the lagoon, is one of the best sand beaches of Turkey. It becomes deep very fast, however, and is not suitable for toddlers or children learning to swim. The beach area is crowded and noisy in the summer. Scores of camp sites and motels have opened in the past six years along the beach, and more are being built in the mountains.

German paraglider: In addition to swimming at Belcekız Beach, visitors can parasail. There are several parasailing clubs available along the beach. They can also try paragliding from the top of Baba Dağı, a rocky peak of 6,520 feet (1,976 meters) dominating the coast. Paragliding resembles hang-gliding, except for the use of a parachute instead of a hang-glider. A former West German Air Force commando, Stefan Etler, leads paragliding expeditions daily during the summer months from

The ghost town of Kaya, near Fethiye.

Babadağ to Belcekız Beach, a 25-minute parachute glide. Etler works out of Deniz Camping, a privately-owned camping site with bungalows, and drives up five times a day to Babadağ to leap off the mountain with daring sportsmen.

Deniz Camping, which offers lunch and dinner and is open year round, is owned and operated by Hülya Gürkan, a British woman whose real name is Anthea, her son Osman and her husband, a former Turkish Air Force pilot. The Gürkans have been operating the campsite for 17 years and were the first people to open a campgrounds at the beach. The precedent-setting Gürkans have also recently restored 25 houses in an abandoned former Greek village in the mountains, operating them as a motel village complex, **Ocakköy**. The pleasant village, with its library, outdoor pool, bar and do-it-yourself craft shop, is located halfway between Ölüdeniz and Fethiye. Among the activities offered by the Gürkan family at Ocakköy is donkey riding along mountain trails.

Excursions can also be made from Fethiye to the ruins of five Lycian cities in the Xanthus valley, the main area of settlement in Lycia: Tlos, Pinara, Letoon, Xanthus and Patara. All six cities are on or near route 400, the highway linking Fethiye to Kaş.

Tlos is east of Fethiye, eight miles (12 km) to the town of Kemer reachable by taking a dirt road that forks left. Very little is known of the town. The site, discovered in 1838 by British explorer Sir Charles Fellows, dates back to as early as the 14th century B.C. In the Byzantine Period it was a bishopric that was under the spiritual jurisdiction of the Metropolitan Bishop of Myra. The ruins that can be seen are an acropolis hill, now occupied by a castle with some traces of the Lycian city walls, a stadium, an agora, a marketplace and Roman-built baths and a theater. Numerous rock tombs are cut into the side of the acropolis hill, of which the so-called **Tomb of Bellerophon** is the most famous. Bellerophon was a legendary Lycian hero who slew the Chimera

(a fire-breathing monster) flying over the Lycian mountains on his winged horse Pegasus. A frieze of Bellerophon riding Pegasus can be seen above the left door.

Pinara, southeast of Fethiye, located near the village of Minare, can be reached by a short dirt road that branches off the Fethiye-Kaş Highway south of Kemer. Once a great city, Pinara is believed to have existed since the Trojan War (1200 B.C.) and perhaps even earlier. The town is built on two acropolis hills. Only traces of the earliest city are visible, including several cisterns and rock-foundations of wood and mud-brick houses, built on a hill honeycombed with pigeonhole tombs. Many sarcophagi are scattered about the main acropolis hill, including one that is the largest in southwest Turkey. To the south are rock cut house tombs and remains of a Christian church, an odeon theater, a large house-type tomb dubbed the **Royal Tomb**, believed to be the funerary monument of a prince. Inside the Royal Tomb are various reliefs of different Lycian cities. Nearby are the agora, a temple and the main theater.

A 20-minute drive south from Pinara brings the motorist to **Letoon**, the ancient sanctuary of the Goddess Leto, mother of both Artemis and Apollo. The turnoff to Letoon is past the town of Esen and the village of Hazırlar. The shrine is about three miles (five km) off Fethiye-Kaş highway. Leto was the principal Goddess of the Lycians.

The ruins contain the foundations of three temples, the main one dedicated to Leto, and the others to Artemis and Apollo. They also contain a nymphaion, a kind of public bath, that is partially submerged in water. The site also contains a well-preserved amphitheater. In the middle of the **Temple of Apollo**, you can see a mosaic of a lye, the sun, a bow and arrow, the only known mosaic of the Lycian civilization.

Hera's wrath: According to popular Lycian myths, Leto was the mistress of Zeus. Leto incurred the wrath of Zeus' jealous wife, Hera, who hounded her and sent her into exile. In her peripatetic wanderings, Leto came upon a water fountain where she wanted to quench her thirst, but three nasty shepherds drove her away. After giving birth to Artemis and Apollo, according to the same myths, she returned to the site and turned the shepherds into frogs as a punishment.

The ancient city of **Xanthus** is just three miles (five km) away. Xanthus, the most impressive and important Lycian city, is off the Fethiye-Antalya highway, near the village of Kınık, along the Xanthus River (known today as Esen Çayı). A dirt road leads right into the ruins of the city, where cars can be parked.

On the left hand side is an outstanding amphitheater, and next to it two tombs. The so-called **Harpies Tomb**, an elevated funerary monument, gets its name from its reliefs showing the mythological harpies, half-birds, half-women monsters, carrying away dead children to the underworld. Next to it is the **Pillar Tomb**, a squat Lycian sarcophagus on top of a long, rectangular pillar. Facing the amphitheater is the agora on which stands the famous **Xanthian Steele**, a pillar tomb whose frame is covered with 250 lines of Lycian script, the longest ever discovered, and a Greek poem. On the other side of the road are ruins of two Byzantine basilicas and a monastery.

Mass suicides: The early history of Xanthus is obscure. It made its mark in history during Persian General Harpagus' invasion of the southwestern coast of Asia Minor around 540 B.C. The Persian army, conquering the coastal cities, swept into Lycia from Caria and was opposed by the Lycians. Defeated by Harpagus in battle, the Lycians retreated into their besieged city. Rather than surrender Xanthus, the Lycians gathered their wives and children into the acropolis which they set ablaze in a defiant act of mass suicide. They then marched out to fight the Persians and were killed to the last man.

The Lycians reenacted the tragedy 500 years later during the Roman Civil Wars. In 42 B.C., when Brutus arrived

Parasailing over the beach.

in Xanthus to raise money for his army for the coming showdown with Antony and Octavian, the Lycians withdrew into the city and slaughtered their families, built a big pyre in the center of the city and threw themselves into the flames.

The city was repopulated by descendants of the Lycians during the Byzantine period. But its end most likely came during the Arab invasions of Anatolia in the seventh century.

The great plunder: Xanthus was discovered by Sir Charles Fellows in 1838. Four years later, sailors from the British Navy, under Lieutenant Thomas Spratt's command, removed hundreds of statues and friezes from the site in what Turks today describe as a rape of the nation's archaeological wealth. All the statuary removed from Xanthus are now exhibited at the British Museum in London in the Xanthian Hall, including the sculptures of the magnificent **Neried Monument**, a beautiful tomb.

Six miles (10 km) south of Xanthus are the ruins of **Patara**, near one of Turkey's best beaches. A yellow sign points toward the ancient site of the Antalya-Kaş highway. Patara is the traditional birthplace of Saint Nicholas, the gift-bearing Santa Claus associated with the snowy winters of northern Europe. Patara was once a great commercial port, but today is partly covered by sand dunes and hidden by an almost impenetrable forest of thick bushes and trees, about 800 yards (728 meters) from the sea. The town waits to be systematically excavated.

Motorists pass an arch as they enter Patara. Vehicles can be parked in front of the restaurant behind the beach. The nearby amphitheater is half filled with sand. On the knoll between the beach and the theater stands an unusual structure believed to be some kind of water cistern. Next to it are ruins of what may be a lighthouse for guiding boats into the harbor, which is now silted up. Next to the harbor is the **Granary of Hadrian**, which is well preserved. An agora and a tomb are nearby. Patara was famous for its **Oracle of Apollo**, which vied with the Oracle of Delphi as the center of prophecy in the ancient world, but no trace of this building has ever come to light.

Patara's beach: Patara's 11-mile (18-km) long sandy beach is wonderful and worth bathing in. As it faces the open sea, however, Patara's waters are always turbulent. The strong undertow makes Patara's sea dangerous, especially for youngsters. There have been several reported drownings. The beach gets very hot in summer, requiring bathers to rent beach umbrellas.

The resort of **Kaş** is about 38 miles (60 km) east of Patara on the Fethiye-Antalya highway. The road to Kaş winds along the coast, passing **Kalkan**, a town popular with sunseekers, and many small beaches.

Like most towns on the Lycian coast, Kaş is wedged between mountains and the sea. In recent years, it has become a popular stopover for yachts on the Blue Voyage. Kaş faces the tiny island of Kastellorizon (Meis in Turkish), the farthest Greek island from mainland Greece. Meis, a resort island, gets all its supplies from Kaş, and all its hotel owners speak fluent Turkish. Each morning, several motorboats come to Kaş to carry food and other supplies to Meis.

There are several hotels and pensions in the town, but the Ekici Hotel overlooking the port and the Mimosa Hotel near the highway, are considered among the better and more comfortable ones. Several new hotels are being built on the far peninsula away from the crowded little town.

Kaş was the location for the ancient city **Antiphellus**, but little remains of the old settlement have survived to this day. There are several sarcophagi about the town, including one by the port and an elevated one on the square above Uzunçarşı Caddesi which features the heads of lions coming out of its sides. An ancient amphitheater is situated on Kaş' long peninsula, a walking distance from the town.

Hero carpet shop: Kaş has an extensive bazaar area, where there are numerous gift shops. The best carpet dealer in town, **Hero Carpet Shop** on Uzunçarşı

Caddesi, is owned by Ahmet Nesin, a book publisher and son of a prominent writer. Nesin, a Swiss-educated intellectual, spends his summers in Kaş.

Kaş has many fish restaurants by the port, lined with visiting yachts. Guests should try chicken or fish, which is caught fresh every day in this coastal area. Red meat should be avoided. The restaurants of this region are known to serve goat's meat, a local delicacy, instead of mutton or beef. Those unaccustomed to goat meat may experience painful diarrhea. Visitors should make certain that food prices are clearly listed at the front entrance of each restaurant. Compare prices with other restaurants. Several restaurants in Kaş have a reputation for overpricing food. The town also has several fine discotheques and late night bars.

Oldest known shipwreck: A short boat trip from Kaş brings one to Ulu Burun, where a team of Turkish and American underwater archaeologists have been excavating the oldest known shipwreck since 1984. The underwater archaeolo-gists are members of the Institute of Nautical Archaeology (INA), affiliated with Texas A&M University. The team is led by Professor George Bass, founder of INA, and Cemal Pulak, a Turkish marine archaeologist of international repute. The 14th-century B.C. vessel was discovered in 1982 at a depth of 150 feet (45 meters) by a sponge diver, who spotted what appeared to be "metal biscuits with ears," bringing the INA divers to the scene. The metal biscuits turned out to be huge copper ingots shaped like ox hides.

The discovery has shed considerable light on rather sophisticated Bronze Age Trade in the Eastern Mediterranean. The 50-foot (16-meter) vessel was carrying a hoard of goods from one port to another when it sank, possibly in a storm. Many of the relics that have been discovered are now in Bodrum's Underwater Archaeology Museum. Besides copper ingots, the scientists recovered Baltic amber beads, the first to be discovered outside Greece, a Mycenaean vase, Canaanite amphora,

A Gypsy with his dancing bear.

ebony from Nubia, unworked ivory, stone anchors, tins and glass.

Because the shipwreck is at such great depth, the recovery work has taken many years. Divers that go down are in constant danger of getting nitrogen narcosis or worse, the "bends." Those who go down can spend no more than 20 minutes under water.

In more than 1,700 dives, Bass has had a few mishaps. Once he ran out of air at 150 feet (45 meters) deep. "I was sure I was going to drown. But as I clawed my way to the surface, a Turkish friend grabbed me and gave me air," Bass once told a *National Geographic Magazine* interviewer.

Sunken cities: Kaş is also the center for boating trips to the nearby sunken cities around Kekova Island and the fishing village of Kale, famous for its necropolis of Lycian tombs. This is a full-day trip – boats leave for Kale from Kaş each morning at 8 a.m. and return around 6 p.m. This thoroughly enjoyable trip is advisable only for those who have time. With stopovers in numerous bays, it takes five hours to reach Kaleköy, the last destination. (Kekova Sound can also be reached by boat from Demre's port. A dirt road from highway 400 also goes to Kaleköy, but it isn't in very good condition.) The first site one comes to is **Aperlae**, east of Kaş, on the Sıçak Peninsula. Yachts can anchor in the bay and motorboats can tie up by the boat landing, known as **Sıçak Limanı**. The village of **Sıçak** is located in the hills about an hour's walk away. The boat landing is built along the ruins of Aperlae, an ancient Lycian city. The ruins include an acropolis, city walls, a necropolis of tombs and ruined houses. The most remarkable sights in Aperlae are the harbor, quay and many streets which are now under water by the boat landing. This was caused either by a rise in the sea level or by a major earthquake. Visitors are advised to snorkel with a mask to see the astounding sunken city.

East of Aperlae is **Kekova Sound** with several deep bays, protected by the elongated Kekova Island and several

The sandfilled theater at Patara.

258

smaller islands. Francis Beaufort, a British naval commander who surveyed the region in the early 19th century, recommended Kekova Sound as an anchorage for a naval fleet. "Its great extent, its bold shores and the facility for defense may hereafter point it out as an eligible place for a rendezvous of a fleet," he wrote in his book of surveys, *Karamania*.

Submerged houses: Numerous submerged houses and their foundations can be seen all along the northern shore of **Kekova Island**. At the western tip of the island, visitors can see the apse of a lone Byzantine church and remains of some houses. This was the Greek settlement of Tersane (shipyard), whose inhabitants are believed to have been boat builders.

A narrow channel across from Tersane leads to a wide hidden bay. On the shore stands the farming community **Uçağız**, with small, pleasant boat landings. Australian writer Rod Heikell who visited the hamlet in the late 1980s, reported seeing cattle wandering about the streets. East of Uçağız are the ruins of **Teimiussa**, a Lycian city, with numerous sarcophagi and rock tombs, and remains of a fortification.

The most charming village in Kekova Sound is **Kaleköy**, across the Kekova Island. A medieval crenellated castle stands dominating a craggy peninsula, surrounded by a necropolis of sarcophagi, overlooking the village. An ancient 300-seat theater is inside the castle. This was the site of ancient **Simena**. The villagers make their living from the sea catching fish and lobsters. The community has three jetties which double as restaurants during the tourism season. A lone Lycian sarcophagus standing in the water lures visitors to pose beside it for photographs. Nearby, in the middle of the bay is a rock with steps cut into it. This may have been a house or perhaps some kind of ancient light house.

Saint Nicholas Church: About 23 miles (50 km) east of Kaş is the farming community of **Demre**, famous for its many green houses. It was at Demre, known to the ancients as Myra, that

Sailboats in Kalkan.

Saint Nicholas, the original Santa Claus, worked in the fourth century. His church stands on a side street in the middle of the town next to a public park.

The ruins of **Myra** are north of the town. Myra's big amphitheater, the first structure one comes to, is of Roman style. In the west gallery are the inscriptions "Place of vendor Gelasius," and this was probably the stand where theater-goers could buy popcorn, nuts and other edibles to nibble on while watching a performance. Myra has the most impressive rock tombs on the entire Lycian Coast. The cliff facing Myra is honeycombed with rock graves, giving it a gloomy sepulchral atmosphere. Many of these tombs, to which one can climb following the trail up to the cliffs, have friezes of human figures or graffiti. The most striking cemetery is known as the **Painted Tomb** by which there are friezes of a man and members of his family, presumed to have been buried there.

Finike, Turkey's leading orange-producing community, is 25 miles (40 km) east of Demre. Finike is an unexciting market town by a river. In recent times, it has become a popular stopover for yachtsmen. Just before entering the town you come to a wide cove, known as **Andrea Doria Bay**, named after the 16th-century Venetian admiral who is said to have concealed his flagship there while fighting the Ottoman navy. There isn't much to see in the town, and its long sandy beach is unpleasant, cluttered with tons of soggy, rotting oranges thrown from nearby orange packaging plants.

The weather gets so sultry and humid in summer in this corner of Turkey that townsmen and villagers move to the cool mountain plateaus, where many have summer cottages, returning to the coast in September.

The best hotel in Finike is the clean **Baykal Motel Pension**, the only motel in Turkey where the owner personally provides a free taxi service for guests from the town to the pension.

Off beat site: For the next 32 miles (50

Afternoon in Kaş.

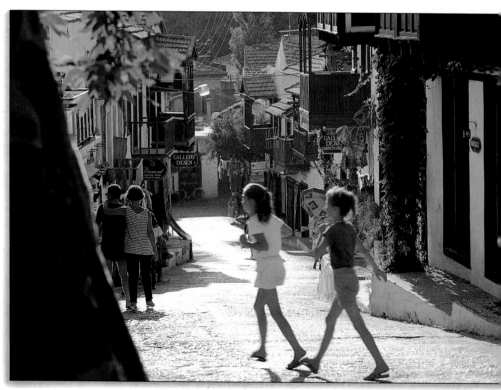

km), the road twists along the coast past the town of **Kumluca** and then winds up into the mountains blanketed by tall pine and cedar trees. To reach the ancient pirates' hideout of Olympus, motorists must turn right off the old Finike-Antalya highway followed by another right at a sign showing Çavuş and Olympus. After driving for about another mile turn left at the Olympus sign. A rough dirt road, full of potholes, leads to the ancient town. You must drive carefully if you don't have a four-wheel drive. The humps on the road damage the transmissions of low cars. It's best to visit the site in a jeep with a full tank of gas. No service station exists in this wilderness.

Olympus, a city in ruins, is located in a gorge between two steep mountains. A stream runs through the town, once a pirates' hideout, and the ruins are on both banks, covered by a jungle of bushes and trees. A Turkish guard sits near the entrance of the ancient site. Olympus, which probably means mountain in a pre-Greek language, is one of 20 sites and mountains in the eastern Mediterranean with that name. The town has never been excavated. Nearly 2,000 years ago, pirates controlled this settlement, raiding and plundering commercial ships plying the coast, but the Roman general Pompey finally stamped out piracy in the region after a military campaign.

Parts of a quay on the southern bank of the stream, and remains of a theater across the knee-deep water can be seen. On the northern bank was the main section of the city, and an acropolis on the hill by the beach is still visible. Several tiny sarcophagi, probably of children, stand with their lids partly open on the side of the hill. The walls of what were probably residential houses also stand on the northern bank along the river. The main necropolis is on the southern side of the river bank and has many ornate tombs.

The sea, with a pounding surf, is just 650 feet (200 meters) from the entrance of the settlement and the beach is a fabulous place to swim and have a picnic.

The Blue Voyage at Kaleköy.

The eternal flames of Yanartaş (the Burning Stone) are near the village of **Çıralı** on the face of a mountain. To get to Çıralı, motorists must backtrack to the Finike-Antalya highway and turn toward Antalya, soon reaching the new highway. They must turn right at the Çıralı sign. The dirt road goes downhill for about three miles (five km). A left turn at the small coffeehouse and a drive for another 1.3 miles (two km) will bring the visitor to another dirt road on the left that goes into the canyon. Motorists must leave the car at the end of the road and walk the rest of the way, following a trail into the mountain. The climb to Yanartaş takes about 45 minutes. **Yanartaş** is an outcrop of rocks surrounded by pine trees. Tiny flames shoot out of a dozen or more holes in these rocks.

The Chimera: The fires have been burning for thousands, perhaps millions, of years. The flames, according to myths, are the remains of the Chimera, the fire-snorting monster that once terrorized the coastal area. The Chimera, which had a lion's head, a goat's body and a serpent's tail, was slain by mythical Lycian hero Bellerophon who flew over the mountains with his winged horse Pegasus. (Mobil Oil Corp., the giant oil producing concern, uses Pegasus as its emblem.) But Turkish scientists say the fires are caused by a buildup of underground methane gas that can't be extinguished. If the flames are doused with water, they will come back alive in seconds. The area is volcanic by nature and may have considerable oil reserves. The state Turkish Petroleum Corp. has been searching for oil with some success over the past few years in the surrounding mountains. The fires of the Chimera can be seen at night from sea-going vessels sailing the coast.

Just below the Yanartaş are some unusual ruins believed to be a sanctuary for the fire God Hephaestus. One of the ruins, strangely, resembles a weird Byzantine chapel.

The Finike-Antalya road from the turnoff to Yanartaş swings through **Olympus National Park** over 44 miles

A sarcophagus stands in the water at Kaleköy.

(70 km) passing through verdant forests. To the left are the **Bey Dağları**, a mountain range with jagged peaks resembling the Rocky Mountains. The range is good for climbing, trekking and hunting.

Phaselis: Shortly after passing the village of Beycik a dirt road forks right leading to **Phaselis**, an ancient Greek city, situated on the tip of a peninsula. There is some confusion about the early history of the town. Some say the city was founded by Rhodian colonists in 690 B.C. Others claim it was founded much earlier by the seer Mopsus, who led Greek colonists to the southern coast in the wake of the Trojan War. Whatever its origins, the city today offers the visitor the chance to wander among Roman and Byzantine ruins of two harbors, a main avenue, aqueducts, baths, a theater, an agora and a temple. Pine tree-lined bays are the favorite haunt of those who seek to swim in the Mediterranean waters or to sunbathe and windsurf.

The resort of **Kemer** is the next stop on the road to Antalya. The town has many holiday villages, including Robinson Club Çamyuva, and Club Méditerranée, which operates the relaxing Kemer Holiday Village and the Palmiye Holiday Village. Several luxury hotels line the secluded beaches toward Antalya, including the Ramada Hotel and the Phaselis Princess Hotel. Benefiting from its spectacular natural surroundings and hefty World Bank loans, Kemer has developed into a booming tourism center.

The **Beldibi Caves**, where people of the Stone Age once lived, are located between Kemer and Antalya. In 1960, Turkish archaeologist Enver Bostancı discovered flint stones, bits of pottery, and a wall painting of a wild goat and other animal figures, indicating the inhabitants were hunters. The ancient findings are housed in the magnificent Antalya Museum.

The highway continues north and soon the black cliffs of Antalya come into view, beginning the wide plain of Pamphylia.

Sitting at the Chimera.

SAINT NICHOLAS

Each December 4-6, church scholars and amateur historians worldwide invade the farming community of Demre (ancient Myra), famed for its delicious red tomatoes and juicy oranges, to attend the world's only Santa Claus Symposium.

Saint Nicholas, the original Santa Claus, a legendary man of good deeds, worked and preached in Demre 1,700 years ago, and his reputation as a gift-bearer spread throughout the Christian world, many church scholars say.

Rattling bones: Although much controversy rages in church circles over the very existence of the Christian saint, the Church officially recognizes Saint Nicholas as an authentic historical figure, the first Bishop of Myra.

While skeptics still assert that Saint Nicholas never lived, others argue he was present at the Council of Nicaea of A.D. 325 where he slapped the heretic Arius with such force that the victim's bones rattled.

Born in the nearby city of Patara about A.D. 300, Saint Nicholas came to Myra as a young man. Not long after, he was elected the town's bishop.

Since Myra was a port as well as a farming town, Saint Nicholas first became the patron saint of sailors. The abandoned Saint Nicholas Church, where he purportedly delivered sermons, is located on one of the two main streets of Demre. The church is a Christian as well as a Moslem shrine. Saint Nicholas is known among Turks as Noel Baba, or Father Christmas. A statue of the saint, surrounded by children, stands in the courtyard.

Pirates remove remains: His marble sarcophagus lies inside the church, but his remains were stolen by pirates in the 11th century to Bari, a town on Italy's Adriatic Coast, and deposited in a church named after him. Thus he became associated with pirates, robbers and thieves. Turks, however, say that some of the saint's bones were pre-

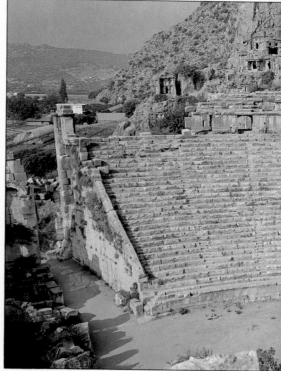

served and are those found in the Antalya Museum, a view that most church scholars say is farfetched.

When his fame reached northern Europe, his name was abbreviated to Claus, and Saint Nicholas became Santa Claus. The traditions of reindeer, elves, toys, sleigh and red, fur-lined attire were derived from the snowy winters of northern Europe. The gift-bearing associated with the Christmas season may have come from many tales of the original Santa. One story had him give a bag of gold each to the three daughters of a poor man as dowries to prevent them from becoming prostitutes. Another story deals with the so-called Pickled Boys: Three young famished lads came into Myra looking for work and a bite to eat. An evil, deranged butcher lured them into his shop and chopped them to pieces, intending to sell them as mincemeat. An angel, learning of the brutal killings, informed Saint Nicholas who immediately went to the butcher and restored the three young lads to life.

Divine nature: Tales have Nicholas saving shipwrecked sailors, resurrecting the dead, parting the waters of a wide river Moses-style, and recouping lost property. He is said to have saved Myra from famine, securing the arrival of corn-bearing ships to the port in time to prevent mass starvation. While inspecting a church under construction, the building collapsed on him, but the saint emerged unhurt.

During the three-day Saint Nicholas symposium and seminar, organized by the Orthodox Churches of the United States and Orion-Tur Turizm ve Seyahat Acentesı, an Istanbul-based Turkish Travel Agency, scholars and clergymen discuss the character and the life of the saint and trace his development as a Christian figure.

On December 6, the traditional date of Saint Nicholas' death, priests from the Orthodox Church Patriarchate hold two-hour liturgical services at the small Church of Saint Nicholas. The services and symposium coincide with the Saint Nicholas festival held in Demre.

ANTALYA AND ITS ENVIRONS

Antalya is the tourism center of southwest Turkey, often described as the "Honolulu of Turkey." Surrounded on three sides by snowcapped mountains, the Bey Dağları in the west and the Toros Dağları (Taurus Mountains) in the north and east, Antalya is situated on a vast fertile plain that was known in antiquity as Pamphylia. Antalya is also the region's agricultural and commercial hub. Antalya's farmers grow everything from cotton and citrus fruits to watermelons and fresh vegetables, which they supply to all corners of Turkey. (Antalya is the name of the city as well as the province.)

With its big port and its Free Trade Zone, the city is also a key Turkish exporting base. Cotton, chromium products and citrus fruits are shipped to the United States, Europe, Japan and the Middle East.

Its long, clean sandy beaches, unpolluted waters, ancient ruins, long summers and mild winters have made Antalya province appeal particularly to travelers from northern Europe. During March through May, it is possible to ski at the mountain resort **Saklıkent** (The Hidden City) and swim in the Mediterranean on the same day. The ski resort, which operates during the winter season, is in the Bey Dağları, only 30 miles (50 km) from the city.

Cave men: In addition to all forms of water sports, Antalya also offers travelers special tours for hunting, mountain climbing, trekking and cave exploration. The Beldibi and Karain caves, once inhabited by people from the Stone Age, are among the biggest in Turkey. The two caverns are within a few miles of the city.

Mountain climbing expeditions and trekking tours in the Taurus Mountains can be arranged through **Trek Travel**, an Istanbul-based travel agency.

Antalya International Airport, where hundreds of charter flights arrive daily in the summer, is only six miles (10 km) from the city center and within

two hours' driving distance to most of the resorts and historical sites of the region. A 100-mile (160-km) stretch of territory around Antalya has the greatest concentration of hotels in Turkey – these comprise nearly half of the country's bed capacity. Some 35 five-star hotels and holiday villages and thousands of smaller hotels and pensions have opened in the past five years to accommodate the tourism expansion, and 50 more big hotels are being built.

The city, which has a population of 275,000, is located on cliffs that suddenly drop into the Mediterranean. Antalya is a garden city with two parks, lined with palm trees. These are **Atatürk Park** and **Inönü Park** (sometimes referred to as the Karaalioğlu Park). Both offer stunning views of the Bey Dağları from these parks. Antalya's two beaches are outside the city: **Konyaaltı Plajı** and **Lara Plajı**.

The city's main streets, Orgeneral Kenan Evren Bulvarı, Cumhuriyet Bulvarı and Atatürk Caddesi run paral-

Left, Antalya's Fluted Minaret. Right, the **Konyaaltı Beach.**

lel to the sea and are lined with apartment buildings and clothing shops, selling the latest in European fashions.

The ancient city: The Old Quarter, known as Kaleiçi, is separated from the new city by a series of Roman walls, and faces the marina. Most of the buildings in this part of the town are splendid 18th- and 19th-century traditional wooden Turkish houses that have been restored to pensions or gift shops.

Antalya was founded by Attalus II, king of Pergamum (159-136 B.C), during the early days of his rule and was named Attaleia after him. The town was ruled successively by the Romans and the Byzantines. During the Crusades, the Crusaders used the port to carry out raids against Moslems in the eastern Mediterranean. The city was conquered by the Seljuk Turks in 1207 and ruled by their vassals, the Hamitoğlu tribe. But in 1361, Peter de Lusignan, King of Cyprus, captured the city. It finally fell to the Ottoman Turks in 1391. In 1919, the Italian army occupied the city after the Ottoman Empire's defeat in World War I but withdrew in 1921 when the Turkish nationalists, under Kemal Atatürk, put up armed resistance to the Allied occupation.

The most charming place to stay in town is the Kaleiçi Old Quarter where travelers have a choice of many delightful, modestly-priced pensions. This district can be reached by car taking the modern road downhill from Cumhuriyet Bulvarı. There is a public park just above the marina where cars must be left. Bed and breakfast at a Kaleiçi pension costs around $10. **Doğa Pansiyon,** a smartly-renovated house on the Iskele Caddesi, is highly recommended. The upmarket **Marina Hotel** on Mermerli Sokak and **Turban Adalya Hotel** near the marina are the best hotels in the Old Quarter.

The better hotels in town are the **Talya Hotel** (on Fevzi Çakmak Caddesi), which is favored by businessmen, the **Club Hotel Sera** (near Lara Plajı) which attracts wealthy German tourists, and the **Dedeman Hotel Antalya** (on the road to Lara Plajı), which has a

stupendous view of the Mediterranean and the Bey Dağları.

Antalya has a number of first-class restaurants. The **Hisar Restaurant** and **Kral Sofrası** and **Orkinos Restaurant** in the Old Quarter combine traditional Turkish dishes and seafood with an array of *meze* appetizers.

A compact city: Most of the city's historical sites can be seen in a two- or three-hour walk. A stroll of the town can start at Kaleiçi with a walk down to the marina, a former fisher-man's wharf, now a bustling port with many yachts, schooners and motorboats. Street vendors by the yachts sell juicy *ajur*, locally-produced long cucumbers, and *frenk yemişi*, a cactus fruit that tastes like a cross between watermelon and cantaloupe (said to help drop kidney stones).

A short walk uphill from Iskele Caddesi, a narrow winding street, brings you to the new town. Along this street are many souvenir shops. One shop with a courtyard sells colorful handmade *Döşemeatlı* carpets, and young girls show how they produce the carpets on looms. *Döşemealtı* carpets get their name from the village near Antalya where they are produced.

On one street corner a man sells local teas, spices and edibles, including aromatic *ada çayı* (island tea), *dağ çayı* (mountain tea) and *papatya çayı* (dandelion tea) and *tirmis*, which looks like corn but tastes like hazelnuts.

Fluted minaret: Soon the twisting street reaches one of the main squares of Antalya, the **Kaleiçi Square**, which is now used as the **Clock Tower**, once a part of the ancient city walls. To the left is the **Yivli Minare** (Fluted Minaret), a brick tower that today is the symbol of Antalya. The 122-foot (37-meter)-high tower was constructed in 1230 by Alaeddin Keykubat, a Seljuk Sultan. The original mosque to which it was attached was destroyed and replaced in 1373 by the **Alaeddin Mosque**.

Just south of the Fluted Minaret toward the marina at a lower level is the **Karatay Medresesi**, an Islamic religious school built in 1250 by a Seljuk

Antalya's Marina and Old Quarter.

notable. Near it, but on higher ground, are two tombs: **Zincirkıran Mehmed Paşa Türbe** built in 1378, and the **Nigar Hatun Türbe**, constructed in 1502. The two Islamic theological seminaries, **Atabey Armağan Medresesi** and the **Ulu Cami Medresesi** nearby are in ruins.

Immediately behind the Clock Tower is the 17th-century **Tekeli Mehmet Paşa Mosque**. The mosque is unique because the Son Cemahat Yeri (the last place of assembly) is inside the mosque, covered by domes, instead of being on the outside. Foreigners can enter mosques, but must take off their shoes at the entrance, like all Turks. Women have to cover their hair and arms with scarves. You cannot enter wearing shorts as it would be disrespectful toward worshippers and would sully the old prayer carpets inside.

Chic clothing shops: Cumhuriyet Bulvarı, which eventually becomes Orgeneral Kenan Evren Bulvarı, is the long street that runs on an east-west axis through the city. A left turn at the clock tower takes you to the main shopping district of the town with chic clothing stores and fancy seafood restaurants. To the left is the Mediterranean with the Bey Dağları in the horizon. As one walks up, one comes to **Cumhuriyet Meydanı** (The Republic Square) with the big equestrian **Statue of Kemal Atatürk**, founder and first President of the Turkish Republic.

About three miles (five km) down this street (on Orgeneral Kenan Evren Bulvarı) near the Konyaaltı Plajı is the **Antalya Museum**, which has a rich collection of prehistorical artifacts from the Beldibi and Karain caves, statuary from the Greek, Hellenistic and Roman periods and ethnographic displays of clothing and tents used by the nomadic Yörük Turks, who inhabit the surrounding mountains during the summer and the plain in the winter.

Two futuristic five-star hotels are under construction nearby: the Sheraton Voyager Hotel and the Steigenberger Falez Hotel, both overlooking the pebbly Konyaaltı Plajı.

Pickle juice: Right of the Clock Tower is Atatürk Caddesi, an avenue that cuts Cumhuriyet Bulvarı on a north-south axis. Several *lokantas* (poor men's restaurants) in the alleys near the intersection serve good *kebab* dishes. Shops nearby sell a variety of unusual jams, jellies and pickles. One of the most interesting jams available is eggplant marmalade. Ice cold pickle juice (*turşu suyu*) is an excellent thirst quencher.

A right turn along Atatürk Caddesi brings the traveler to **Hadrian's Gate** (Hadrianus Kapısı), a magnificent three-arch marble gate erected in A.D. 130 in honor of Roman Emperor Hadrian's visit to the city.

Further down the street is the **Belediye Binası** (The Municipality) and the entrance to İnönü Park, which is lined with palm trees. The park, named after Ismet İnönü, the second President of Turkey, has playgrounds for children, pleasant outdoor coffeehouses and benches to sit down and admire the stunning beauty of the sea and the distant mountains.

Roman tomb: A stroll to the eastern

Selling religious prayer beads and spoons.

end of the park brings you to the pleasant **Mermerli Coffee House** and the **Hıdırlık Kulesi**, a rotund tower that is believed to be a tomb of a Roman Senator from Antalya. The tower is a miniature version of Hadrian's Tomb in Rome. Walk up the street that intersects the tower and you approach the **Kesik Minare** (the Truncated Minaret). This odd structure stands next to the **Korkut** or **Cumanın Mosque**, now in complete ruins. Built originally in the fifth century as the **Panaghia Church**, it was converted into a mosque by Korkut, the son of Sultan Beyazıt II, who added the minaret. The mosque and the minaret were destroyed in a fire in the 19th century.

The marina, just 10 minutes away from the Kesik Minare, has many pubs and discotheques. **Club 29 Bar** is the most popular among the young for dancing and socializing.

Antalya festival: A good time to visit Antalya is during the annual Antalya Golden Orange Film Festival and Art Festival held in autumn, usually in late October or early November, when the leading Turkish motion pictures of the year are screened and the top films, directors, actors and actresses get the Gold Oranges awards. The Festival coincides with the *Akdeniz Akdeniz* (Oh Mediterranean Oh Mediterranean) *Song Contest*, when soloists from nearly 20 Mediterranean countries perform in an international song contest. The song contest is usually held at the ancient Roman theater in Aspendos, 25 miles (40 km) east of Antalya. The festivals are usually held in the first week of October; their dates are determined early in the year.

Antalya is a paradise for hunters. The surrounding Bey Dağları and Taurus Mountains are rich in game birds and wildlife. Travelers come from all over the world to Antalya to hunt for the European Ibex (*yaban dağ keçisi*), an agile mountain goat with upturned horns abundant in the mountains. Game birds such as quail, turtledoves, wild ducks, and woodcocks can be found. Wildlife open to hunting include foxes,

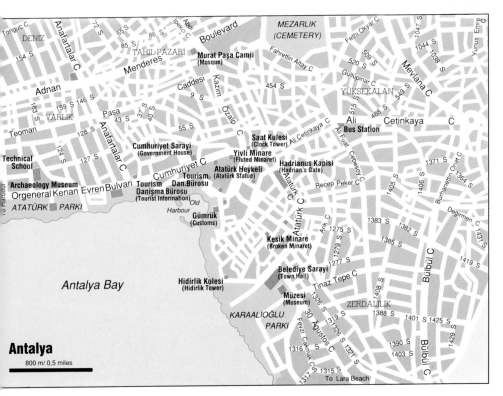

Antalya

800 m / 0,5 miles

rabbits and martens. Trout fishing is possible on the Manavgat, Akçayı, Karaçayı and Köprüçayı rivers in the province of Antalya. For information on hunting and trout fishing, contact the Antalya Hunters Association (Avcılar Derneği) in Kilit Hanı and the **Haydar Üstay Hunting Museum** in Arnavutköy, Istanbul.

Excursions from Antalya: Numerous ancient sites and resorts are reachable from Antalya. One enchanting site to visit near Antalya is the **Düden Şelalesi**, a stunning series of waterfalls set in a woodland park about six miles (10 km) outside the city near the village of Varsak. The waterfalls are situated on the **Düden River**, one of several rivers that nurture the Antalyan Plain, making it one of Turkey's most fertile regions. The best time to visit the site is in the morning or late afternoon when it is usually uncrowded. Several charming tea houses and outdoor restaurants, shaded by plane trees, are in the park. A Turkish version of *Snow White and the Seven Dwarfs* was once filmed in this setting.

The Düden River empties into the Mediterranean, plunging off Antalya's cliffs east of the city. A half-hour boat trip can be arranged from the marina to this site for a small fee. A smaller inland waterfalls east of the city is the **Kurşunlu Şelalesi**, which has a 17th-century water mill that was recently restored. The site is nine miles (15 km) from Antalya and can be reached by taking a road off highway E24/400 on the way to Alanya.

Nomadic carpets: The village of **Döşemealtı**, famous as a carpet-weaving center, is located north of Antalya on highway E24/650 to Burdur. The colorful pure wool Döşemealtı carpets are made by nomadic Yörük tribesmen who inhabit the Taurus Mountains. These carpets have geometric patterns and a color harmony of blues, dark greens and reds.

Nearby is a road that forks left to the **Karain Caves**, where men of the Stone Age lived from as early as 600,000 B.C. to the seventh century B.C. Turkish archaeologists who excavated at Karain

discovered the skull of a Neanderthal man and the fossil remains of an ancient elephant, hippopotamus and bear and tools dating back to the Paleolithic Period. Many of the findings are in the small **Karain Museum**, but some are also exhibited in the Antalya Museum. The cave is situated on the slope of the mountain above the museum. It covers a vast area consisting of several interconnected sections.

The **Kırkgöz Han**, a Seljuk inn with 40 rooms, is located on the Burdur Road, 15 miles (24 km) north of Antalya. Before reaching Döşemealtı highway 350, turn left toward **Korkuteli** off route E24 to Burdur. This road leads to **Evdir Han**, another Seljuk inn or caravansary. Evdir Han was built in 1219 and consists of a courtyard surrounded on four sides by porticoes. The southern entrance is magnificent with stalactites and geometric designs. Nearby are the ruins of the Byzantine settlement **Eudoxia**, with several water channels and scattered sarcophagi.

Hadrian's Gate.

272

Güver Uçurumu, a vast gorge forming a 705-foot (215-meter) drop down the cliffs, is located two miles (three km) north of Evdir Han. Formed millions of years ago, the gorge is indeed a stunning site.

The ruins of **Termessus**, one of the few cities in Asia that Alexander the Great could not conquer, are located in the mountains west of Güver Uçurumu. To get there take the road that forks left and has the sign reading Güllük Dağı Termessus Milli Parkı. The narrow, twisting road climbs into the mountains to the site. At one point all cars must be left in a car park and the rest of the way to Termessus (about one mile/2.2 km) must be ascended by foot. The region is considered a national park. Termessus, built on the slopes of several mountains, resembles an eagle's nest. During the Hellenistic and Roman periods it was a flourishing city with a population of 150,000 people. Now it is in complete ruins, abandoned in the fourth or fifth century.

Termessus was a Psidian city. The Psidians, who inhabited the mountainous region north of Antalya fought many wars against the invading Greeks. The site includes numerous city walls, the King Street, an observation tower, water cisterns, a necropolis, a gymnasium, bathhouses, a colonnaded street, an agora and an astounding theater overlooking the surrounding mountains. The **theater**, built during the Hellenistic Period, has a seating capacity of 4,200 people. The orchestra is covered with rubble, which tumbled most probably because of earthquakes. A smaller odeon or assembly hall on the upper reaches of the city could seat 600 people. The most important site in Termessus is the **Tomb of Alcetas**, a general of Alexander the Great who was defeated by Antigonas in 319 B.C. and sought refuge in the city. He committed suicide, preferring death to being returned to his enemies. The ruins of three temples are visible, including the **Temple of Zeus Solymeus**, the **Minor Temple to Artemis** and the **Major Temple of Artemis**. The **Soldier's Tomb**, which gets its name from the

shields, spears and helmet carved to the frieze on it, is in the necropolis. The **Founder's House**, west of the agora, is a Roman-type house in good condition.

Ancient cities: Scores of ancient ruins are east of Antalya, including Perge, Sillyum, Aspendos, Selge and Side, Seleucia in Pamphylia, Alarahan, on the road to the resort of Alanya, famous for its castle and golden beaches.

The E24/400 highway can be eventually reached by driving east-bound from Antalya on Cumhuriyet Bulvarı and Sudi Turel Caddesi, named after a former Energy Minister from Antalya.

The first major destination east of Antalya is **Perge**, which is in the hills on a dirt road off the Antalya-Alanya highway, 12 miles (20 km) from Antalya. Signposted in yellow, the ancient Roman site lies just after a turn on the left.

Vaulted stadium: As you enter Perge, the first building you drive past is a second-century Roman amphitheater with a seating capacity of 17,000 people. The main ruins are less than 900 yards (one km) off the amphitheater. Visitors can park their cars and walk past the stadium, one of the best preserved in all of the eastern Mediterranean. The 772 by 112 feet (234 by 34 meter) stadium could seat about 12,000 people. The vaulted sections at the sides were probably shops.

The main city, just off the stadium, was once encircled by walls, some of which are still standing. The walls once had 30 towers. The city was laid out in a grid pattern with two main intersecting streets. Entrance to the ruins is by the **Later Gateway**, which leads to the **City Gate Complex**, a horseshoe-shaped courtyard flanked by two towers. This area is the most fascinating part of the city. Niches built inside the complex walls contained statues of gods and local heroes, such as Mopsus and Clacas, the mythic founders of the city. This complex was turned into a kind of memorial by Plancia Magna, a wealthy Pergaean lady. Just behind this complex is the **Monumental Gateway**, a three-arched structure of two stories, which was also adorned with statues. To the right of the circular courtyard is the agora, the city's main shopping center.

The main thoroughfare of Perge is a colonnaded street with a water channel, running through the Later Gateway and the City Gate Complex. The water was brought to the city from a source at higher ground. About halfway up this avenue on the left is the **Church of Perge**, which was once a bishopric. At the end of the street, past the intersection, near the acropolis hill, is a **Nymphaion**. Turn left at the intersection to come first to a gymnasium, then a bath. A necropolis of several tombs are at the end of this street. Perge once boasted a famed temple dedicated to the Pergaean Artemis but its whereabouts today is unknown.

Nebulous early history: Perge's early history is nebulous. It is believed to have been founded by Greek migrants after the Trojan Wars. When Alexander the Great arrived in Pamphylia in the fourth century B.C., the Pergaeans submitted without a struggle. Alexander used Perge as a base for mopping up

operations on the coast of southwest Asia Minor. St. Paul stopped in the city during his missionary adventures. The city continued as a Greco-Roman city, and was a bishopric during the early Byzantine Period. But it was probably abandoned after the seventh-century Arab invasions.

The ruins of **Sillyum** are six miles (10 km) east of Perge. A dirt road forking left from the Antalya-Alanya highway leads to Sillyum, built on a high acropolis hill. Although it hasn't been excavated and isn't often visited, Sillyum is more impressive than many of its neighboring Pamphylian cities, according to the late George Bean. Greek settlers, possibly led by the seer Mopsus and his mixed multitudes, the same tribes that established Perge, founded the city after the fall of Troy around 1200 B.C. Alexander the Great during his sweeping campaign through southern Asia Minor in the fourth century B.C. besieged Sillyum, but abandoned his plan to conquer it, deciding it was not worth controlling the inland city.

Theater at Termessus in ruins.

274

Ramps: The first structure travelers encounter as they ascend the acropolis hill at Sillyum is the **Lower City Gate**, a horseshoe-shaped edifice consisting of two towers and a small courtyard. Further on are the ruins of a palace and a stadium. The most impressive ruins in Sillyum are the ramps that lead up to the acropolis. The lower one, constructed in Hellenistic times, is the best preserved.

Near the top of the acropolis hill is the **Upper City Gate**, from which one can see the necropolis below as well as the city tower. Several interesting buildings are located on the acropolis, including a well-preserved Byzantine structure, a public hall and a smaller building that has the most interesting feature in Sillyum, an inscription in the local Pamphylian-Greek dialect, dating from the third century B.C. Other buildings to be seen on the acropolis hill are an odeon, two theaters, a few houses, a 33-yard-long (30-meter) underground water cistern and several temples.

The Roman Theater: The next destination in the direction of Alanya worth visiting is **Aspendos**, located near the village of Belkız, about 30 miles (50 km) from Antalya. A dirt road with the sign Aspendos forks to the left. The road continues over the **Köprüçay** (the Eurymedon River) for about three miles (five km). The first ruins you come to are the remains of two public baths. Next is the great **Aspendos Amphitheater**, the most magnificent ancient theater in the world. As many as 20,000 people can be seated. The theater, which is used today to stage the *Akdeniz Akdeniz* Song Contest, has retained its fine acoustic qualities. Visitors should test the acoustics by walking up to the very top gallery of the theater, a steep climb, and sitting down. If someone on the stage below whispers or even drops a pin it can be clearly heard in the top gallery.

A grisly but unsubstantiated tale surrounds construction of this grand theater in the second century. There was once a king of Aspendos who had a lovely daughter, named Belkız. As the young woman had many suitors, the

The Gate Towers of Perge.

king announced he would wed his daughter to the man who would construct the greatest public structure in the city. The king could not decide between the two rival contractors who sought the marriage of Belkız. One of them built the spectacular theater. The other constructed important and equally impressive aqueducts to supply the city with water. In the end, the king cut his daughter in half, giving each man a part of her body.

A half hour is enough to explore the theater. The other buildings are not impressive and do not warrant more than a quick walk by. Near the theater, and on the same level, is a 710-foot (215-meter) long stadium. In the vicinity of the stadium are some sarcophagi and tombs, including one hewn out of the rocks.

An acropolis behind the amphitheater can be entered through three gates, of which the northernmost is best preserved though half-buried. The structures there include an agora, a market hall with several shops intact, a third-century basilica, a nymphaion, a council chamber and aqueducts. The aqueducts which carried water to the city from the mountains north, are the most impressive and best preserved water canals from the Roman period surviving in the eastern Mediterranean.

Visitors to Aspendos can return to the Alanya highway by crossing over the stone **Köprüçay Bridge**, built in the 13th century by the Seljuk Turks. The bridge is narrow but sturdy, and can accommodate one car at a time.

Selge: Soon another road forks left from the Antalya-Alanya Highway into the mountains through woods toward the towns of Taşağil and Beşkonak, leading to the ruinds of **Selge**. This road continues for the next 34 miles (55 km), passing Beşkonak. The road crosses a narrow Roman bridge, after which a side road to Karabuk must be taken. Selge is on the Zerk-Altınkay Road. Selge, built on the three hills, was a Psidian city. Psidia was the name of the mountainous lake district north of Pamphylia. Selge has numerous ruins,

The Roman theater at Aspendos.

including a theater, a stadium, a customs house, tombs and sarcophagi and temples to Zeus and Artemis. A two-mile (three-km) wall encircled the city, parts of which still stand today. In ancient times Selge was famous for its wines and olives.

To reach the resort village of **Side**, a captivating settlement, motorists must return to the Antalya-Alanya highway. Side is located next to the ruins of one of the oldest and most impressive ancient settlements in Turkey. The ruins are situated on a peninsula 50 miles (80-km) east of Antalya. A road forks right to Side near a service station before reaching the town of Manavgat.

Romantic setting: The presence of an inhabited village next to the ancient ruins makes the site romantic indeed. To get the full visual impact of the town, Side should be visited during the November-March off season. Only a few tourists will be seen in the village then. Therefore the deserted ruins amidst the empty streets of modern Side will overwhelm the visitor. Many tourists who

have visited Side have stayed on months, sometimes years, captivated by the charm of the village.

In summer, Side is crowded with tens of thousands of tourists and its hotels and pensions are fully booked. The village becomes commercialized. Loud music rising from scores of outdoor nightclubs, pubs and discotheques could easily drive anyone staying near the village berserk. Several five-star hotels have opened near Side, including Novotel Turquoise, Le Meridien Hotel, Asteria Hotel, Iberotel Side Palace and Robinson Club Pamfilya.

Side, which means "pomegranate," is a pre-Greek word that symbolized fertility. The city is believed to have been founded by migrants in the 13th or 14th centuries B.C. In the sixth century, the city was dominated by the Lydians and then the Persians. It was conquered by Alexander the Great in 334 B.C., and later controlled by the Ptolemites and the Seleucids. Between 188-78 B.C., the Kingdom of Pergamum gained hegemony over the city, transforming it

The Manavgat Waterfalls.

into an important commercial port, the remains of which can still be seen today. It became a Greco-Roman city, and an important Christian center. But it was abandoned in the 12th century. The present inhabitants of Side are the descendants of Turkish refugees who fled Crete during the uprising of 1898 and settled in this village.

Pulitzer prize winner: Side was made world famous by the late Alfred Friendly, former managing editor of the *Washington Post* and Pulitzer Prize winning American journalist who lived there many years. A foundation set up by Friendly's wife has helped finance the restoration of many sites in Side, including the temples by the harbor.

The first ruins to be seen are the aqueducts, the remains of city walls and a Nymphaion. Suddenly the **Side Amphitheater** looms up on the left, next to the agora. Across is the **Bathhouse Museum**. Visitors enter the city by driving past the Vespasian Monument and the Later City Gate, an arched structure. Cars aren't allowed in the town.

The best way to see the town is to walk down the main street to the harbor, once the commercial hub of Pamphylia, now a simple fisherman's cove. To the left are the **Temple of Apollo** and the **Temple of Athena**, both dating from the second century, and a ninth-century Byzantine basilica. The eastern shore of the town brings one to the **Temple of Men**, a moon Goddess. A crescent-shaped sandy beach extends east of the site for many miles. Soon one comes back to the amphitheater. The **State Agora** and **M-Building**, which resembles a palace, are just behind the well-preserved theater.

Stupendous view: Much of the walls around the city are either submerged in the sand or partly sunken in the sea. For a stupendous view of Side, visitors should climb to the top row of the amphitheater. The Museum is an ancient bath that has been restored and turned into a museum. It contains many fine Roman statues and sarcophagi, several of which are in the courtyard. The bathhouse, built during the Roman Period, is well preserved. It has an *Apo-*

dyterium or changing room, a *Catdarium* or hot room, a sweating room and a cooling room. The bathhouse was a place where men socialized and discussed local and political affairs.

The next town on the Antalya-Alanya highway is Manavgat, situated on the Manavgat River. Other than the pleasant riverside teahouses, there isn't much to see in the town itself, except for the bustle of the wholesale market from where trucks deliver the produce of the region, including giant melons, to other parts of Turkey. But a road forks to left before the entrance to the town toward Manavgat Şelalesi (Falls), the ancient town of Seleucia in Pamphylia and Oymapınar Barajı (Dam). This road goes 11 miles (17 km) to the Oymapınar Dam, one of the biggest hydroelectric dams in Turkey. A visit to the dam and its lake is worthwhile if permission to enter is granted by the guards. Three miles (five km) from the Antalya-Alanya road is the turnoff for **Manavgat Şelalesi**. A short walk leads to the falls. One of the best places in this

It's all in the family.

area to have lunch is by the picture postcard falls, along which there are several restaurants serving *alabalık* (trout) or *piliç şiş* (chicken on a skewer) or *piliç çevirme* (barbecue chicken) and tasty appetizers. The **Manavgat River** is one of Turkey's main sources for trout fishing. It is also only one of the few places in Turkey where river rafting has been tried by sports enthusiasts. Motorboat rides up the Manavgat River from Side and Manavgat are possible to a point further downstream.

Seleucia in Pamphylia is one of several cities in Anatolia named after the Seleucia kings of Syria. The most famous of these is Seleucia in Pieria, the ancient port of Antioch. Seleucia in Pamphylia is located about three miles (five km) north of Manavgat Falls and is reachable from the village Şıhlar. A turnoff points in the direction of Selevkiye (the Turkish for Seleucia). The ruins to see in Seleucia include an aqueduct, an ancient bridge, city walls, a bathhouse, an agora and an odeon.

Alanya is about 30 miles (50 km) from Manavgat along the E24/400 highway. The road follows the sea closely, passing many fine deserted beaches along the way to Alanya, including the **Incekum Beach**. About 19 miles (30 km) east of Manavgat a village road forks to the left and continues to the **Alarahan**, an inn constructed in 1232 by the Seljuk Turks, consisting of a courtyard surrounded by vaulted rooms and corridors. The inn also has a fountain and a *mescit* or small mosque. Nearby is fortress of **Alarakale**, built to protect the inn from marauders. Nearly halfway to Alanya is a 13th-century Turkish caravansary, **Serapsu Han** on the left.

Giant gastropod: Alanya (formerly Coracesium) is built around a rocky peninsula that resembles a gigantic gastropod from a distance. Jutting out to the sea like an immense mollusk, the red peninsula is crowned by a long crenellated fortress that was built by the Seljuk Turks in the 13th century to dominate the Mediterranean Coast. In ancient times, the peninsula served as

Aqueduct at Side.

the headquarters of Pamphylian pirates who raided passing commercial ships for booty and slaves.

Alanya has some of the finest beaches in Turkey. It's worthwhile spending some time swimming and tanning on the long beach that lies before Alanya. The first site in Alanya to be seen is the **Damlataş Cave**, on the edge of the peninsula before entering the city. The damp air in this claustrophobic cave with thousands of colorful stalactites is believed to be beneficial for those suffering from asthma and other respiratory diseases. But elder people with heart ailments should avoid it.

Alanya is a pleasant touristic town, located on the foot of the peninsula, with many seaside restaurants and hotels, of which the Club Alantur, Azak Hotel and Hotel Banana are highly recommended. The town has a broad Board Walk-like avenue and a fine harbor where big ships can dock. Alanya is known among Turks as "Little Germany" because of the tens of thousands of Germans who visit it an-

nually. The town's symbols are the 13th-century **Red Tower** (Kızıl Kule), a crenellated defensive building, and its ancient **shipyards**.

Alanya Castle, perched on top of the peninsula at a dizzying height of 800 feet (243 meters), dominates the coast, and overlooks the town and the majestic cliffs that plunge into the sea. The ancient walls around the old city wind four miles (seven km) uphill like the Great Wall of China, to **İçkale**, the citadel, capped by three towers. Inside is a courtyard with a Byzantine **Church of Saint George** (Aya Yorgi) and a pleasant outdoor coffeehouse.

A small outdoor shop in the courtyard sells baby dolls made from squashes, a particular art in this part of Turkey. At the northeast corner of the courtyard is the spot called the **Adam Atacağı**, (the place from where men are thrown). It was there that condemned men were hurled down the cliffs to their deaths. A condemned man would be pardoned, according to one legend, only if he could toss a pebble from that height into

A minaret spikes the sky in old Alanya.

the sea, an impossible task. Next to it is a deep open pit covered by railings that some people suggest was a dungeon where the prisoners were kept.

From the citadel, the **Cılvarda Burnu**, a rocky promontory on which there are the ruins of three buildings, including the town's mint (**Darphane**), a tower and a monastery complex, is visible. The only way to reach these buildings is to take a boat ride along the peninsula from Alanya to the promontory and walk up.

The Old Quarter: The inhabited **Old Quarter** of the city is in the middle section of the castle. A left road as you are about to leave the castle leads to the Old Quarter, passing the fortress known as the Ehmedek. In the Old Quarter, you can see the **Akçebe Sultan Mescidi** (small mosque) and **Türbe** (Tomb). These structures, built in 1230 by the Seljuk Sultan Alaeddin Keykubat I, consists of three sections, two of which contain tombs. Other buildings of note in this quarter are the **Mecdüddin Cistern**, which is still in use, a caravansary

(a kind of inn) that is comprised of a rectangular courtyard surrounded by rooms, a depot and the **Bedesten** (a shopping center). Nearby is the **Alaeddin Mosque**, a 13th-century structure that was reconstructed by Ottoman Sultan Süleyman the Magnificent in the 16th century.

Alanya is famous for its ice cream and **Bamyacı Ice Cream Parlor** in Güler Pınarı Mahalesi and **Keykubat Mevkii** in town makes the tastiest.

The **Kızıl Kule**, a five-story, 10-foot (33-meter)-high octagonal tower which now houses the **Ethnographical Museum** is a walking distance from downtown Alanya along the harbor. The museum exhibits Yörük tents, rugs and armor. Walk further down to the **Shipyards** (Tersane) nearby. Used by Seljuks to build their fleet, the dockyard is still used today to construct small boats. During the Ottoman Period, Alanya was one of the Turks' main naval bases. In the 16th century, Turkish navies turned the Mediterranean into a Turkish lake.

ΤΟ ΚΑΛΛΟΕ ΤΡΑ
ΥΠΟΤΕΚΡΥΠΤΟΜΕΝΗ
ΕΦΙΛΟΝ ΒΑΣΙΛΕΥΣΙΝΕΤ
ΖΑΜΕΝΟΝ ΚΑΘΑΡΩΣ

THE EASTERN MEDITERRANEAN

Turkey's eastern Mediterranean coast begins east of Alanya and ends along the Syrian frontier south of Antakya, stretching for 420 miles (672 km). The region was known to the Romans as the Cilician Coast. The area can be roughly divided into three distinct geographical zones: the rugged, mountainous terrain that stretches from Alanya to Silifke, which was known as Rough Cilicia; the vast fertile plains to the east, which was known as Smooth Cilicia, today's Çukurova; and the areas east of Adana, which extend into the Hatay, a province bordering Syria, with Antakya its capital.

Banana capital: In Rough Cilicia, the Taurus Mountains plunge into the Mediterranean over precipitous cliffs. Here and there are tiny valleys where bananas and olives are grown. The Alanya-Silifke highway winds along the ridges of the mountains. The banana capital of Turkey is Anamur, a town with a population of 30,000 halfway along Rough Cilicia. Anamur's banana growers are fond of saying their bananas taste better than the popular imported Cikita brand of South America. Anamur has miles of uncrowded golden beaches, dominated by a magnificent Armenian Castle. The ancient ruins of Anemurium are west of the town.

Rough Cilicia ends east of Taşucu and Silifke. The name Silifke is a Turkish version of Cilicia. Numerous sites of historic interest are near this coastal town, including the ghastly pits known as Heaven and Hell and the Kızkalesi (the Maiden's Castle), which stands on an island.

Neolithic settlement: Mersin, today Turkey's third biggest port after Istanbul and Izmir, started out as a neolithic settlement, rivaling in antiquity the oldest archaeological finds in Egypt and Mesopotamia.

The town of Tarsus, further east, was the birthplace of St. Paul the tentmaker,

Preceding pages, the mosaic of the Three Maidens in Silifke.

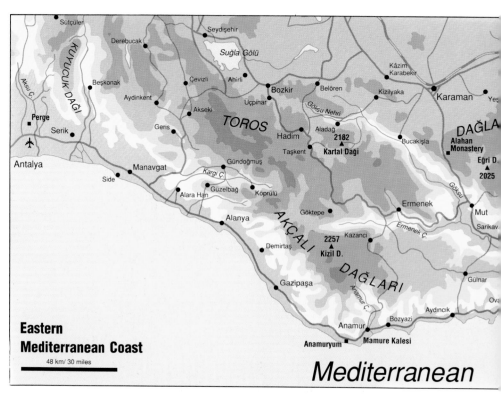

Eastern Mediterranean Coast
48 km/ 30 miles

Mediterranean

whose missionary journeys helped spread Christianity westward into Anatolia from Judea. Today it's a booming market town. It was also in Tarsus that Antony summoned Cleopatra for their first meeting that began their big romance and ended in their tragic deaths.

North of Tarsus, high up in the Taurus Mountains, engineers nearly 3,000 years ago built an East-West short cut through Asia Minor known as the Cilician Gates. The armies of Cyrus the Younger, Alexander the Great and the Crusaders marched through this mountain pass. A modern highway today crosses the Taurus Mountains at Ulukışla east of the Cilician Gates, connecting the Anatolian steppes with the Cilician Coast.

Industrial hub: Adana, Turkey's fourth largest city and cotton boom town, stands in the center of the vast Çukurova. Adana is a big industrial city, which produces cotton fabrics, tractors and harvesters and processed food, such as margarine. Numerous towns and cities can be reached from Adana, including Yumurtalık, which is the terminal of the 612-mile (980-km) Iraq-Turkey crude oil pipeline, which has a big port, usually lined with ocean-going oil tankers.

The port of Iskenderun, where a huge Soviet-built iron and steel complex operates, is east of Adana, surrounded by the Amanos Mountains.

From Iskenderun, the road climbs the mountains to Belen Pass, the ancient Syrian Gates, to Antakya (the former Antioch). This was the site of St. Paul's first ministry, the third largest city of the Roman Empire, outranked only by Rome and Alexandria. It was also in Antioch that the term Christians was first applied to the followers of Jesus. Today Iskenderun and Antakya (both of which belong to the province of Hatay) are the principal Arab-speaking cities of Turkey.

Antakya has an important museum which contains fine mosaics from the Hellenistic, Roman and early Christian periods.

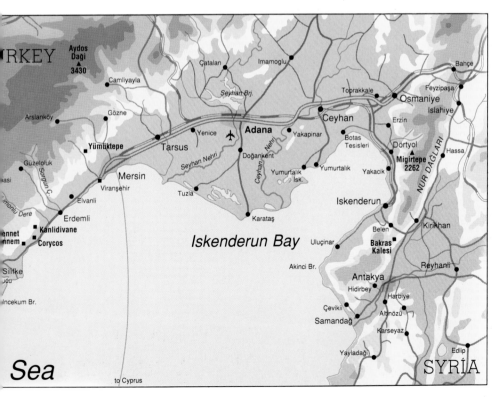

ROUGH CILICIA

Heading east beyond Alanya the highway takes to the sky on the arms of the Taurus Mountains as the first reaches of the **Cilician Coast** begin. For the next 420 miles (672 km), Cilicia's history unfolds like a colorful tapestry, its length textured with tales of conquests, corsairs and Cleopatra.

This stretch of the Mediterranean offers some of the country's most spectacular scenery and uncommon diversions. Where else can one end a day of castle-hopping with a sunset swim to a Crusader fortress, or drink from the Fountain of Knowledge after a sneak preview of Heaven and Hell?

Land of contrasts: Cilicia is a land of contrasting natural beauty that both beckons and repels. In ancient times the western region was known as "Cilicia Tracheia" (Rough Cilicia) as here, the Taurus Mountains crowd the coast, sending craggy slopes plunging into the Mediterranean. Cilicia Tracheia appeared so intimidating to the ancients that even Alexander the Great crossed it off his list after one look at its impenetrable terrain.

The eastern region, known as Cilicia Campestris (Smooth Cilicia), begins at the Lamus River, past Silifke, where the Taurus pull back from the coast, leaving a vast fertile delta that has long sustained civilization.

Cilicia was forever caught in the tug-of-war between rival kingdoms and aspiring powers and a succession of peoples ruled the land including the Phoenicians followed by the Greeks who fought in the Trojan War.

Pirates terrorize coast: The Roman Empire claimed Cilicia as one of its provinces and the Romans embarked upon a successful mission to wipe out Cilicia's most famous denizens: pirates. These buccaneers fed the Roman slave trade during the first centuries B.C., terrorizing the coastal cities and plundering Syrian ships as they passed on their way to Aegean trading ports. They ruled the waves unhindered until 67 B.C when General Pompey put an end to the motley lot and piracy disappeared until Arab ships pestered the Byzantines in the seventh century.

In the 12th century, the kingdom of Lesser Armenia flourished along the coast, allying itself during the next 300 years with the invading Crusaders, who left their Frankish touch in the string of medieval coastal castles. When Armenian rule faltered, the Lusignans arrived from Cyprus, only to be overwhelmed by the fierce Seljuk and Karamanid Turcomen tribes.

Prosperity and progress eluded Cilicia and the region succumbed to Ottoman rule in the 15th century, eventually receding into anonymity. It was only during the last half century that Cilicia reemerged, fueled by a drive to play a role in the country's economy.

Sustaining industry: The lowland of Cilicia Campestris is now called the Çukurova Plain and is the center of Turkey's cotton crop which amply sustains a burgeoning textile industry. Two commercial ports were built, in Mersin and Taşucu, opening trade lines with the outside world and helping establish the region as an industrial base.

A government agriculture project transformed the rugged slopes of Cilicia Tracheia into patchwork valleys, crisscrossed with banana plantations and olive, lemon and fig orchards. And best of all, centuries of obscurity have left most areas of Cilicia untouched. Cilicia Tracheia appears much the same as it did in Alexander's day: beautiful, unspoiled and treacherous.

Treacherous is just one way to describe the 136-mile (217-km) drive from Alanya to Silifke as the coast road twists its way above pine forest gorges and turquoise coves of Rough Cilicia.

Hairpin turns: If one is driving, travel must be limited to the daytime when the region's beauty can be appreciated and the hairpin turns seen!

Public bus companies serve the coast frequently and have terminals (*Oto Gar*) in Antalya, Side, Alanya, Anamur, Silifke, Mersin and Adana. Reservations need to be made a day in advance as the buses are always packed with locals, tourists and *asker* (soldiers) on their way to assignment.

Travelers should reserve a seat with a seaview, but they should prepare for the sun: none of the buses have smoked-glass windows.

Seleucid fortress: The first remains of ancient civilization in Cilicia lie in **Aydap**, ancient Iotepe, one of three fortress-cities established in the second century B.C. by Seleucid King Antiochus IV to protect Seleucid interests from invading pirates and mountain tribes. **Gazipaşa**, the next town, is the site of the king's second city (Selinus) now marked by meager ruins by the beach. Selinus made the social column in A.D. 117 when Roman Emperor Trajan died while passing through after the Parthian War. His death is considered by many to be the very point marking the beginning of the Roman Empire's decline.

The third and best preserved city is **Antiochia-ad-Cragum**, and it's exactly that – on a crag. Ruins run helter-skelter onto a rocky promontory which

once bore the brunt of continuous pirate attacks.

Leaving behind the ghost of Antiochus to fend for himself, the highway glides into a magnificent valley overgrown with terraced banana plantations which embroider the mountainside and run to the shores of a beautiful bay. This is **Kaledıran**, the ancient Calendiris, above which the skeleton of a Byzantine fortress keeps watch from a rocky ledge. The settlement is a good place to stop for a swim and sample the sweet *muz* (bananas).

Tasty carobs: Cilicia's forest is one of the most beautiful and well-tended in Turkey. Sleepy men sell *muz* under straw huts while young girls work the dangerous roads, balancing trays of nuts and fruit on top of their heads hoping to tempt tourists. The weird-looking brown pod stacked on a string is the carob (*keçiboynuzu*).

With Kaledıran in the distance, the road descends to a wide fertile delta, the Anamur Plain.

Straight ahead is **Anamur**, a town

with 28,000 residents, many of whom are unhappy that they have been ignored by travel books and tourists. Despite little historical significance, Anamur is a convenient base from which to visit surrounding sites. The town has an interesting Seljuk period mosque dating from the early 14th century, pleasant beachfront camping and a comfortable, sprawling three-star hotel, the Anahan.

Phoenician colony: Four miles (seven km) from the ancient city of Anemurium (Greek for windy place), sits **Anamur Burnu** (Cape Anamur). Originally a Phoenician colony, it later became a Hellenistic city and was incorporated into Roman Cilicia in A.D. 72. After continual harassment by pirates and mountain tribes, Anemurium was abandoned in the seventh century as the Arabs showed up.

A defense wall climbs to a citadel and two aqueducts run parallel to the main road through town. It's worth hiring a guide to uncover the many mosaics and frescoes which are hidden throughout the site of domed tombs and churches.

Cape Anamur is Turkey's closest point to Cyprus, only 40 miles (64 km) away. On a clear day one can easily distinguish the Beşparmak Dağları (the Pentadaktylos or Five Finger Mountains) that run along the northern coast of the Mediterranean island. Gigantic radars on Cape Anamur sweep the eastern Mediterranean for enemy aircraft and naval vessels.

Crusader fortress: The massive outline of **Mamure Castle** commands the coastline two miles (three km) east of Anemurium. One of the largest and best preserved Crusader fortresses in Asia Minor, it was first mentioned in the third century as a Roman stronghold before becoming a pirates' den. During the 12th century the castle was incorporated into Armenia's defense system, and later passed to the Lusignans of Cyprus, the Seljuks and the Karamanid Turcomens. The Ottomans moved in, added the mosque and other restorations and remained there until the sun set on their empire in 1923. The circular

stairway leads up the huge defense tower to a panoramic view of the castle's 36 towers and massive ramparts. Matches are needed to light its paths.

The **Köşebükü Mağarası**, one of Cilicia's famous wishing and asthma curing caves, is 11 miles (17 km) from Anamur in a lovely pine forest on the Taurus foothills. Locals believe the cave air cure asthma while others make pilgrimages to the cavern depths to throw money into a pit and ask for Allah's blessing.

Taxis are found at the bus station but meters seem out of fashion and price haggling is a necessary evil.

Softa Kalesi (Scholar's Castle) looms high on a ridge just eight miles (12 km) east of Anamur. A hardy hike is required to reach the massive defense walls of this 12th-century fortress. Before Softa Kalesi, the road winds through a beautiful forest and passes the government-run **Pullu Camping Grounds**, situated in a pine grove on its own private beach.

Aydıncık sits on a bay tucked between the arms of the Taurus Mountains 35 miles (57 km) from Anamur. Also known as Gilindere, it is the site of ancient Kelenderis, one of the oldest colonies in Rough Cilicia, founded in the fifth century B.C. by Greeks from Samos.

Further on, the village of **Boğsak** rings a turquoise bay punctuated by the ghostly **Provencal Island**, a perfect Halloween haunt as the island is blanketed with tombs, sarcophagi and medieval ruins. The Gothic arches of a Crusader chapel, built by the Knights of St. John, add to the general gloom.

On the western reaches of the bay sits **Liman Kalesi** (Harbor Castle), another medieval fortress built by the Armenians in the 14th century.

Taşucu, once a small village, is now a commercial port and one of two coastal departure points for the Turkish Republic of Northern Cyprus (the second is Mersin). Hotels and restaurants line the bay and on the edge of town a sprawling paper factory makes use of the abundant Cilician timber. Travelers who want to take the ferry to Northern Cyprus should stay here. Those traveling to Greece or to the Greek-controlled Southern Cyprus should not have their passports stamped for Northern Cyprus. (Officials will stamp a separate sheet of paper instead). A 14th-century Turkish fortress guards the beachhead.

Before Silifke, a sign points to **Aya Thekla** (Meryemelik in Turkish), a Christian pilgrimage site devoted to St. Thekla, St. Paul's first convert and Christianity's first female martyr. Thekla became one of Byzantium's most popular saints and her life story was the basis for the *Acts of Paul and Thekla*. According to the Acts, Thekla met Paul in Iconium (Konya) and was so moved by his preachings on the virtues of chastity that she cried out, "I shall cut my hair and follow thee whitersoever thou goest." With that pious promise, she ended her engagement and incurred the wrath of a jilted fiance who plotted revenge.

Divine intervention: Upon his orders, Thekla was stripped naked, set upon a pyre in a crowded amphitheater, and wild lions were sent in for the kill. Divine intervention prevailed, and as the Acts report, "there was about her a cloud, so that neither the beasts did touch her nor was she seen naked."

Thekla was released, became St. Paul's chief follower and founded a convent in a cave in Seleucia. One version has Thekla living to a ripe age, another claims she was murdered by thieves. Two basilicas were built in her honor. The first by Constantine after his conversion to Christianity and the second, located over the cave, was built in the fifth century by Emperor Zeno.

The underground chapel has frescoes and mosaics and has been turned into a small museum exhibiting locally-found sculpture.

One mile (1.6 km) inland is **Silifke**, the ancient Seleucia-ad Calcynum, founded in the third century B.C. by Seleucus I Nikator. Silifke is the largest town in Rough Cilicia and is divided by the **Göksu River**.

Silifke's **Archaeological Museum** is

190 yards (200 meters) from the bus station and opens daily. Numismatists will revel in the large collection of Hellenistic coins. Close by is the ruin of a Roman temple dedicated to Zeus.

Silifke is renowned for its folk dancers and each May hosts the international Music and Folklore festival.

The town's most visible site is a massive medieval fortress which looms atop a flat hill. This citadel was built by Byzantines in the seventh century as a bulwark against Arabs and passed to the Crusaders, Armenians and Seljuks before finally becoming Ottoman property in 1471.

Byzantine cistern: Below the hill lies **Tekir Ambarı**, an immense Byzantine cistern built from an ancient cave. Restaurants offering Silifke's famous creamy yogurt and a *"manzara"* (a view) have invaded the grounds.

One detour from Silifke must not be missed. The road winds through the **Göksu Valley** along one of the most scenic drives in Turkey and leads to the Alahan Monastery.

The Banana Man in Anamur.

Alahan Monastery is perched on a narrow mountain terrace nearly 7,000 feet (2,100 meters) above sea level and overlooks a fabulous view of the Göksu Valley.

Twenty-eight miles (45 km) out of Silifke the pine forests give way to olive orchards as life takes on a harsher edge and the first reaches of the Anatolian plateau begin. This is the domain of the nomad, whose straw huts line the roadside, their sides bulging with colorful *kilims (yastıks)* cushions.

Mut, the proverbial town-in-the-middle-of-nowhere appears on the horizon. The site of ancient Claudipolis, it was founded in 50 B.C. by Marcus Aurelius Polemo, who undertook the crazy task of uniting the wild mountain tribes under one kingdom.

After Mut, the Taurus range reappears and 15 minutes later a sign marks a 1.3 mile (two km) road to the fifth-century Alahan Monastery. A one-hour trek through the pine forest to the mountain ledge in the early morning is an exhilarating experience. Before the final bend, north toward Aloda, one can see early Christian cave churches carved into the cliff sides.

The Evangelist Church is the first part entered from the western terrace. The church's surviving portal has detailed friezes symbolizing the triumph of Christianity over paganism. A close examination shows saints Gabriel and Michael trouncing the likes of Cybele, the Anatolian mother goddess, as well as a bull and a priest of Isis.

The portal leads to a circular baptistery, which is next to the Eastern Church, a simple yet beautiful doomed basilica crafted by expert masons in the early-sixth century. Three interior arches, held by Corinthian columns, grace the central aisle.

Tempting trails offer short-cuts down the mountain, but a layer of pine needles make the going dangerous. Unless the traveler is a mountain goat or a sure-footed villager, he should stick to the beaten path. Buses passing from Konya to Silifke will stop to pick up travelers who wait by the road at Alahan's one and only cafe.

SMOOTH CILICIA

The second detour from Silifke is to **Uzuncaburç**, just 19 miles (30 km) to the north. This is the site of the former Olba/Diocaesarea, founded in the third century B.C. by Seleucis I Nikator. It is a peaceful and impressive site, displaying a medley of Hellenistic, Roman and Byzantine ruins.

It's business as usual in Uzuncaburç as villagers tend to vineyards, goats and apple orchards. Enterprising women have set up black wool nomad tents under which they sell their much-prized handiwork – ancient crafts at thoroughly modern prices.

Corinthian Order: After paying the attendant, you enter the city through the Roman parade gate. Head down the colonnaded street to the **Temple of Zeus Olbios** which was erected at the end of the third century B.C., making it the oldest known structure of the Corinthian Order in the world. Thirty of its columns still stand; four are topped with Corinthian capitals. In the grassy square to the side of the temple, sculpted friezes are lined up, displaying the exaggerated visages of lions, bulls and monsters.

To the west stands the **Temple of Tyche**, goddess of fortune. Five Corinthian columns, each reportedly cut from a single slab of Egyptian granite, tower above a massive foundation. To the north rises an original city gate with three well-preserved arches; one proclaims the town's name, Diocaesarea. Out by the entrance, the road leads north past a small cafe where the village men play perpetual games of *okey*, a simplified version of *mahjong*, between glasses of *çay* (tea).

The Long Tower: To the right stands a five-story, 73-feet (22-meter) Hellenistic tower which once served as a priest's tomb and later formed part of a defense and communication network with other towers throughout the region. The village took its name from the tower. Uzuncaburç means "long tower" in Turkish.

The road to Uzuncaburç winds through pine forests, passing through Demircili, the first-century Roman city of Imbrogin. Several unusual temple-like tombs can be seen, the most interesting is the double-decker **Çifte Anıt Mezarları** (Twin Monument Tombs), which is visible from the road.

Taxi anyone? *Dolmuş* depart for Uzuncaburç at 11 a.m. daily across from Silifke's Tourism Office. If you miss the *dolmuş*, share a cab. A private taxi costs as much as five times the shared amount.

Back on the coast road, stop at **Yapraklı Eşik** (The Cove with Leaves), a perfectly sculptured cove with enticing turquoise water. Its currents are of two different temperatures: the top layer is a chilly 8° Celsius, but the bottom layer is a soothing 23° Celsius.

Susanoğlu, the next village, has a wide bay and long beach. Local vacationers have turned this once pretty setting into an eyesore. Military-style barb wire fencing encloses the beach and the clutter of pensions, motels and cafes

Left, sunning before Kızkalesi. **Right**, an old costume displayed.

and the people crowding it.

In kinder days, Susanoğlu was known as Corasium, a major Byzantine port specializing in the salt trade. Traces of salt pans and catch basins are carved into the rocks on the east side of the bay.

Phallus of Priapus: A detour eight miles (12 km) north through Susanoğlu leads to the ancient city of **Paslı**, the best-preserved Roman site in the region and home of the famous **Mezgit Kalesi**, the **Temple Tomb of the Fearless Satrap** (Persian governor). From the monument's right side appears a remarkable relief – the outstanding **Phallus of Priapus**, the god of fertility and vitality, whose glorious presence bears testimony to the courage and fearlessness of the deceased. As the tale goes, Priape was the illegitimate son of Zeus and Aphrodite, and Hera, in a jealous fit, deformed the child, giving him a phallus equal to his height.

Priape, also known as God Bes, ranked high with the ancient Anatolians who erected temples and sacrificed donkeys in the deity's honor. Sacred wishing rocks, scattered throughout the countryside, were visited by young women who begged the God of Fertility for a good husband.

Rumor has it that village girls still make the pilgrimages to the monument in Paslı, and whisper, "Wake up oh my good fate, before my roses fade." Tiny bronze Priape statues and postcards are extremely popular with tourists who twitter at the prospect of shocking friends back home.

Narlıkuyu (Pomegranate Spring), is a sliver of bay lined with lively seafood restaurants and a small hotel, but it's the **Kızlar Hamamı** (the Bath of the Maidens) that lures visitors. This fourth-century Roman bath has a lovely floor mosaic depicting the **Three Graces**, Aglaia, Euphrosina and Thalis, the daughters Zeus had with Eurynome, daughter of the Ocean. The bath is housed in a small nondescript shed in the village and is open daily. A small fee is charged.

On the shore a spring sprouts fresh

The church in Heaven.

water into the sea – this is the **Fountain of Nus** (the Fountain of Knowledge). Its powers must be taste tested!

Across Narlıkuyu await the otherworldly sites of Cennet Deresi and Cehennem (Heaven's Stream and Hell), which form the **Corycian Cave Complex**. These massive sinkholes were created centuries ago when the ground collapsed from chemical erosion by an underground stream.

Cennet (Heaven) is an enormous pit, measuring 285 yards (250 meters) long and 77 yards (70 meters) at its deepest point. The stairway to heaven is lined not with "pearly gates" but with sagging trees, littered with paper talismans and petitions placed by superstitious visitors asking for cures and good luck. Obviously, anything will suffice, as snack bags and candy wrappers join hundreds of ribbons and shredded tissue paper strewn on the branches of the trees. It isn't a heavenly sight.

Descending the 452 rock steps into heaven's bowels may convince the visitor that he has accidentally landed in hell. The descent is foreboding as the air becomes stifling and the sun is blotted out by trees. A roaring sound, which grows louder with each step, does nothing to sooth the nerves.

At the grotto's end, the **Church of St. Mary** guards the entrance to the gloomy cavern, which according to mythology, was the Home of Typhon – the monster with 100 dragon heads and snakes for feet. The roaring sound comes from a river deep inside the cavern, which ancients believed was the River Styx, the river encircling Hades over which boatmen known as Charon ferried dead bodies.

Symbolic assurance: When the Byzantines arrived they were uneasy with the site's evil connotations and ascribed it heavenly powers, building a fifth-century basilica to honor the Virgin Mary at the cave's entrance, as symbolic assurance that Typhon was put to rest forever. The Church of St. Mary has well-preserved frescoes showing Christ with two saints.

Venture into the cave with the help of

_eft, the ;uardian to Iell. **Right**, a "ieze at "nlıdivane.

a guide and a lantern, but save your breath because the climb back to the real world is definitely hellish.

Cehennem (Hell) lives up to its reputation. The path to this chasm is lined with littered trees sporting paper petitions, this time asking to keep the hounds of hell at bay. The chasm resembles the open jaws of a monster, the perfect façade for the entrance to the underworld, as the ancients believed.

If the stairs of Heaven and sight of Hell leaves you gasping for breath, you should head to the **Wishing and Asthma Caves** (Dilek Astım Mağarası), also part of the Corycian Cave complex, and 330 yards (300 meters) west of Heaven.

The tiny resort village of **Kızkalesi** (Maiden's Castle) lies a few minutes east. Known as Corycus in ancient times, the Turks call it Kızkalesi after the Byzantine fortress of the same name which floats in a storybook setting 660 feet (200 meters) offshore. Its landlocked partner, the massive 12th-century Corycus rambles on the coast just east of the sea castle. At one time the fortresses were connected to each other by a sea wall which formed a secure port for Corycus.

Pirates' haunt: Corycus is believed to have been settled before the fourth century B.C. and during the second and third centuries B.C. it was a strategic harbor and a famous pirates' haunt. The region prospered under Roman and Byzantine rule but declined slowly over the following centuries and was eventually abandoned; only during the past 40 years have people returned. However, Kızkalesi of today, with its wild frontier town atmosphere, is far from its former days of splendor. The beach is crowded with hotels, motels and pensions – many only half-finished, and in the peak summer months the streets are filled with vacationers, mainly locals from Adana, with a sprinkling of curious foreigners. Club Barbarossa offers a decent escape from the maddening crowd and has a pleasant beach, nice pool and straight-on view of the Maiden's Castle.

A farmer drives his tractor through a colonnaded field.

Taxis are rare but *dolmuş* leave every 15 minutes from the main Mersin-Silifke road, leading in either direction. There are good places to swim all along the coast and they are best tested in late spring or early fall when the crowds are thinner. To explore the sea castle, you should either swim to it or rent a canoe from the public beach, or hire a guide and row a boat across.

Maiden's legend: Although built for military reasons, the fortress carries the standard medieval castle legend involving a maiden and the premise that neither love nor care can change the course of human fate.

The tale describes the King of Corycus, who upon learning that his daughter's fate was to die by a snake bite, shipped her off to the island castle, far away from the world's dangers. Naturally, a lowly reptile made its way to the princess (in a basket of figs sent by a well-intentioned suitor) and the princess met her fate.

Area police suggest young maidens remain sequestered in hotel rooms at night (to ignore this advice is to tempt fate), as Kızkalesi retains a rambunctious personality left over from its days as a pirate's hangout.

Bushes and snakes: The land castle of Corycus can be explored but it is not as exciting as its sea-girt partner. The interior is overgrown with bushes and oftentimes occupied by modern day, two-legged snakes of the village species.

Two miles (three km) from Kızkalesi is **Ayas**, ancient Elaeusa-Sebaste, founded partly on an islet, and known to the Romans as Elaeusa (Olives) and Sebaste (Augustus) to the Greeks. Three columns, a theater and necropolis remain.

The entrance to **Kanlıdivane**, the ancient settlement of Kanytelis, lies four miles (seven km) east in Kumkuyu. A two-mile (three-km) road leads to the city, which was founded around a huge sacred chasm. Houses, churches, cemeteries and cisterns remain. A Hellenistic tower, like that in Olba/Diocaesarea, stands at the hellish pit's southwest corner. Carved into the cliff underneath is a rock bas-relief showing a family of six. Of the five churches, the most impressive is the **Church of Papylos** at the northeast end of the hole.

Necropolis: Visitors must see the necropolis which lies in a small valley 330 yards (300 meters) away. Walk down the road that leads to **Çanakçı** and head left down the footpath to the south side of the gorge. There, nine reliefs glow from the red rock; one tomb shows a woman fashionably dressed in a tight gown; another is of a man reclining with a glass of wine.

The road to Mersin is dotted with aqueducts in almost every valley, which long ago tunneled water from the **Lamas Çayı** (the ancient Lamus River) to the ancient cities, before winding through the Cilician Plain and flowing into the Mediterranean. Although many ancient geographers placed Smooth Cilicia east of the Göksu River (the Calycadnus), Strabo, the most famous of Greek geographers, considered the Lamus River the boundary between Rough Cilicia and Smooth Cilicia, as here the Taurus disappears into the

Alahan Monastery, north of Silifke.

backdrop, leaving a wide fertile delta stretching to the foothills.

A right turn at Mezitli will take you to **Viranşehir**, less than one mile (1.6 kilometers) away. Viranşehir was founded in the seventh century B.C. by settlers from Rhodes who set up an important trading post. Shortly after, Attic colonizers took over, naming it Soli (sun in Greek). These people spoke a strange harsh dialect that both puzzled and amused their neighbors, giving birth to the word "solecism," which means an offense against grammar.

The Stoic School: Soli was also the birthplace of Chrysippus, a founder of the less-than-fun Stoic School of Philosophy, who in the third century B.C. wrote 750 books on stoicism, decreeing that "the wise man should be free from passion, unmoved by joy or grief and submissive to natural law." Stoicism, according to Dionysus of Halicarnassus, was a "monument of dullness."

In 91 B.C. the Armenian Tigranes chased the population out of Soli, and then pirates raised havoc until 67 B.C. when Pompey cleaned the coast of corsairs, burning 1,300 pirate ships and ending the buccaneering business in just three months. He repopulated Soli with his prisoners of war – demanding they behave – and renamed the city Pompeiopolis. The city originally was entered through a 500-foot (150-meter) long Via Sacra (Sacred Way), lined with 200 Corinthian columns which led to the harbor. Twenty columns remain,, standing firmly in a field of raspberry bushes.

Mersin is one of the oldest inhabited spots on earth and the capital of Içel Province. It has undergone positive changes in the past years – with a new harbor (third largest in Turkey) and oil refineries boosting its stature as a modern industrial city.

There isn't much history to see in Mersin unless you are a fanatic about excavation sites. Two miles (three km) away is the terraced mound of **Yümüktepe** – the original site of the city, which was excavated in the 1930s and 1940s. The oldest stratum dates back to the Stone Age.

Mersin has many quality hotels, like the five-star Atlıhan and the Mersin Hotel, many of which dot a lovely palm-lined boulevard. English is spoken at the Tourism Office, located on the east side of the harbor, and its personnel provide information about Northern Cyprus. There is a regular ferryboat service from Mersin to Gazimagosa (Turkish-controlled Famagusta) in Cyprus. *Dolmuş* buses run frequently through the city to Mersin Bus Station. From there, buses leave for all points east, west and north.

Soap opera: Sixteen miles (25 km) east of Mersin, **Tarsus** languishes on the banks of Tarsus Çayı, the ancient River Cydnus. The city commands a strategic position on the rich, fertile Cilician Plain and has a long history dating to the 14th century B.C. The area prospered under Hellenistic rule but like Soli, was brought to its knees by pirates and the Armenian Tigranes. Rome was impressed by Tarsus and proclaimed it the capital of its Cilician province in 64 B.C. And it was here that

Farmers pile cotton in sacks.

the world's first soap opera unfolded, as Mark Antony summoned Cleopatra to Tarsus with intentions of slapping her hand for supporting the rival Cassius. But poor Antony buckled under his surging male hormones as Cleopatra floated up the Cydnus in her gleaming golden barge under purple sail, and she was swathed to the teeth in flowing silks and reclining under the attentions of fawning slave boys.

Tarsus is best known as the birthplace of Paul the Apostle who worked as a tentmaker in the city until his preachings took him on the road. A well marks the site of his house.

A few ho-hum sites remain in Tarsus. There's **Cleopatra's Gate**, one of the city's original six entrances. Down from the gate is the "**Özgürlük Anıtı**," an inscription of independence carved into a stone which dates from the reign of Emperor Severus Alexander and proclaims that Roman Civil law will apply in Tarsus.

The local museum is worth a quick trip. Located in the **Kutupaşa Medre-** **sesi**, it contains numerous friezes, statuary and a Roman sarcophagus. The foreboding-looking mosque to the north was once a Gothic church.

Most noticeable in Tarsus are the endless carts, stands and markets overflowing with fruit and vegetables, adding the only splash of color against the gray town.

The **Cave of the Seven Sleepers** is nine miles (14 km) from Tarsus, and legend says early Christians hid here to avoid persecution by the Roman governor Dacianus. After awakening from a 100-year slumber they returned to town and attracted attention with their out-of-date fashions.

About 31 miles (50 km) north of Tarsus, after the town of Ulukişla, are the infamous **Cilician Gates** (Gülek Boğazı), actually a 4,160-foot (1,286-meter) narrow passage blasted through the Taurus range. It was one of the most important, and dreaded, mountain crossings in history and until recently was the only main connection between Tarsus and the Anatolian highlands.

Harvesting the crop in the Çukurova region.

ADANA AND THE EAST

In the middle of the Cilician Plain, now called Çukurova, lies **Adana**, Turkey's fourth largest city with about one million inhabitants. This fertile region 25 miles (40 km) east of the Taurus Mountains owes much of its wealth to the Ceyhan and Seyhan rivers, which for centuries have irrigated the vast fields.

But the area's wealth has only recently trickled down to the inhabitants, whose abject poverty as virtual serfs to greedy landowners is so aptly described by Adana's favorite scribe and Nobel Prize nominee, Yaşar Kemal. In fields near the city people continue to toil as they have for 100 years, backs bent and heads covered to protect against the harsh Adana sun. Yet here and there are signs of change: brightly painted clean houses, cars parked alongside the fields, the increasing number of schools and bustling markets.

Economic boom: In Adana, an economic boom is unmistakable. The city's strategic location as a major transport hub to Syria and Iraq, coupled with the growth of Turkey's textile industry and the nearby presence of a major U.S. Air Force base have all contributed to the growing economy. Construction is booming, particularly of five-star hotels and new apartment blocks – and the old village character of Adana has given way to a city feel.

Downtown Adana exudes a pleasant small/big city ambience with its spacious, tree-lined boulevards, elegant clothing shops and the 1950s Czechoslovakian-made Skoda cars.

Beyond the main avenues lies the real city, a settlement of shanties, substandard *gecekondu* housing and peasant farmers from the east who migrated to the city looking for work. City officials estimate that nearly nine out of 10 buildings of Adana are *gecekondu* dwellings that have been illegally built on private or public property by rural migrants. Vast *gecekondu* neighbor-

Left, emptying red peppers. Right, downtown Adana.

hoods built around downtown Adana lack proper drinking water, electricity and sewage treatment facilities. Nearly half of Turkey's malaria cases have been reported within the boundaries of the city.

Urban renewal: As part of an urban renewal project, a new city is being built on the outskirts of Adana that will provide housing for another one million people by the year 2000. Started by the former Mayor Aytaç Burak, a progressive contractor, the construction project will give Adana a new look. The new city is bisected by two avenues – **Orgeneral Kenan Evren Bulvarı**, named after the former President of Turkey, and **Turgut Özal Bulvarı**, named after the current head of state. The two men were responsible for sponsoring the construction of the new city.

The Cilician Plain is steeped in history from the Hittites onward, but in Adana itself there is a meager offering of ancient sites. The Roman Bridge **Taşköprü**, built by Hadrian in the second century, is still useful though it has little in the way of aesthetics.

The most impressive structure has to be the **Ulu Cami**, located in the historic district between an uninspiring bazaar and the auto repair and spare parts district. The exact date of the mosque's construction is debatable. Some say it was built in 1507 by Halit Bey, emir of the Ramazanoğlu Turks, and ruler of the region until the Ottomans conquered Adana in 1517. However, a plaque above the door puts the date of completion at 541, attributing it to both Halit Bey and his son, Mehmet Pasha.

Iznik tiles: The mosque has an interesting squat minaret and the tiles inside are said to come from the famed Iznik kilns. Adjacent to the mosque is a charming if a bit dilapidated park containing Halit Bey's Iznik-tiled mausoleum, a perfect place to sit and wait for an attendant to unlock the door and allow you into the mosque.

Across the street from Ulu Cami is a little teahouse, set in the midst of an old complex for religious studies. Despite its proximity to the mosque, the only

Adana during the Ottoman period.

thing being studied there now is backgammon and the fine art of conversation beneath shady trees.

Two other sites of interest are close by. The Ethnographic Museum, located on a small alley just off Inönü Caddesi and Ziya Paşa Bulvarı, houses a small but adequate collection of *kilims*, jewelry, weapons, musical instruments and clothing. The building may have been built by the Crusaders as one of their numerous churches, but an inscription above the entrance dates it in Greek letters to 1845.

Roman ruins: The **Adana Regional Museum** is an airy modern construction on Fuzuli Caddesi, the main road running along the Seyhan two blocks west of Inönü Caddesi. There is a generous collection of Roman ruins and a little garden filled with more ruins and old tombstones.

Apart from cotton, this region is best known for spicy *Adana kebab*. Although every restaurant menu sports this dish, the best ones are clustered on **Atatürk Bulvarı**, across the street from the Tourism Office. Those longing for an American-style snack can find comfort in the neighborhood around the U.S. Consulate, where restaurants offer hamburgers, french fries and lots of Coca-Cola memorabilia.

One other dish worth trying in Adana is *piliç şiş* (a *shish kebab* made from chicken instead of mutton). Visitors to the city should also try *şalgam suyu*, a salty, crimson drink made from the juices of turnips, beets and carrots, served in most Adana restaurants.

Adana is also famous for *bici*, a dessert of crushed ice, rice pudding, rose water and powdered sugar. Served in pretty glass bowls by men with pushcarts, *bici* is a nice change from the gallons of water you have to drink in the hot, hot weather.

Adana has several first class hotels, including the **Inci Oteli** on Kurtuluş Caddesi, and the **Büyük Sürmeli Hotel** on Özler Caddesi.

Marco Polo's town: Some 31 miles (50 km) south of Adana on the delta formed by the Ceyhan and Seyhan rivers lies **Karataş**, a sleepy port with little attraction save for its bathing beach. Another 25 miles (40 km) east of Karataş is the port of **Ayas**, noted by Marco Polo in the early-13th century as a bustling market spot for spices and fabrics. The contemporary visitor, however, must exercise his imagination to picture such a scene.

Much more splendid are the sites east of Adana off the E-5 highway on the way to Ceyhan. About 19 miles (30 km) past fields of cotton and more auto repair shops lies **Yılan Kalesi**, or Snake Castle. In an area where castles and fortresses are so numerous as to almost become mundane, this eerie structure high atop a hill that looks black from the road should not be missed. Reportedly built by the Armenians in the early-13th century, it was extended by the Crusaders. The origin of its name is unknown, although this area is rife with snake legends and possibly snakes.

Continuing on E-5, one turns inland towards Kadirli at the intersection for Ceyhan on the right to reach **Anavarza**, founded by the Romans in the first

Holding up the prizefighter.

century B.C. Driving on this narrow road you are thrust back decades, passing miles and miles of cotton fields broken up by the occasional splotch of color as women and men arduously pick the ripe cotton by hand, or a cluster of houses with sun-bleached clothing hanging out to dry.

Anavarza, which is off the road to the right (one should look for a yellow sign on the left-hand side of the road facing the opposite direction), is a picturesque village of 1,000 people living amidst Roman ruins.

Just across from the ancient walls, which are more or less intact, is a small sign saying "Museum." It looks more like a private house, which in fact it is, but the few Roman ruins and tombstones in the front garden are misleading on the quality of the exhibits inside. A small bath that has been excavated contains a fine mosaic in honor of ancient gods, and when water is thrown on it – as surely will be done by some of the people sitting around a table outside – it takes on an almost new character. A short hike through the family's backyard leads to another bath, this one slightly larger with a fish mosaic on the bottom.

A little further past the museum is the ancient city gate, still standing, beyond which lie seemingly indistinguishable rocks. Some of the young boys who hang around the arched gate will show the visitors where the amphitheater was and so on, but the area has never been properly excavated. In the distance looms a handful of castles atop a hill whose ascent is not easy, which is probably why the climb is used as an exercise course for soldiers at Adana's **Incirlik Base**.

Frustrating trip: In theory the road slicing between the two hills should lead straight to **Karatepe National Park** about 13 miles (20 km) southeast of Anavarza. In practice, driving along this road is likely to end in frustration and failure as the dirt roads, zig-zagging through the endless cotton fields, are unmarked. The various villages amidst the fields contain helpful residents, only

Placing bets at the cockfights.

CRUSADER CASTLES

Silhouettes of Crusader castles even in their ruined state beckon to explorers and hint of ancient glory and adventure. They bring up dreams of knights in shining armor, stirring battles, and colorful pageantry. The stone buildings which stand along the western coast of Turkey also give a real history. They witness to the skill, the energy and the artistry of their successive owners, in particular the Crusaders who invaded Anatolia from Europe in the 12th and 13th centuries.

Precision-made: The castles were precision-made instruments of military strategy. Generally they were composed of two concentric curtain walls interrupted with towers, a main gate and one of several postern gates in the outer wall. In the central area were living quarters for the lord, his accompanying knights and the farming community who would retreat behind the

walls during an attack, a chapel, cisterns, storage space and stables for the animals.

During the time of the Crusades, knights, because of their versatility, were often indispensable to any army . The armored knight on horseback wielding a sword, coupled with courage and resourcefulness, was capable of overwhelming opponents with more formidable weapons. Castles, in a way, were the knights' armor.

Battering rams: The varieties of forces employed against the men and their castles included catapults, archers' fire, battering rams, siege towers and sappers' tunnels. Under the protection of the archers' fire, men wielding a metal-pointed log could pick at the loose mortar in the wall, changing the point for a battering ram when the stones started to come apart.

Protected by towers: Entrances to castles posed special security problems. Often they were at the end of a sloping ramp to make the attackers work uphill. At Silifke (southwest of Mersin) the ramp was protected by a tower which exposed anyone approaching the gate to fire from behind. There might be several turns in the entrance to foil the rush of a battering ram, as at Bagras (south of Iskenderun). The confusion could be impounded by the entrance being dark, thus temporarily blinding those who had broken through.

Wooden siege towers higher than the ramparts of a castle that could be rolled up to its wall gave the attackers the advantage of firing down on the defenders. They, however, were subject to fire and being toppled by well-placed missiles from the castle.

More frightening in the long run to the defenders because they could not see them was the steady thud of sappers digging a tunnel below their walls. As the sappers proceeded, they shored up the tunnel with wooden struts which, when they reached their goal, they set fire to. The collapse of the tunnel brought down the walls above it. This was the method employed successively by the Arabs against Edessa (Urfa) in 1144.

Villagers and Anavarza Castle.

Maximizing control: Always the castle was sited to maximize the owner's control of his territory. It also was placed so that friends could communicate. From Yılan Kalesi which dominates the Cilician Plain above a curve in the Ceyhan River, one could see at least eight other castles in a 31-mile (50-km) radius, including Sis (Kozan), Anavarza and Toprakkale.

Castles were often on cliffs in mountain passes. **Güllek** stood above the Cilician Gates; the watchman there could spot the dust of an approaching horde two-days' away to the south, giving the defenders time to lay their supplies. Its rock base made it invulnerable to attack by sappers.

The surrounding rugged countryside was part of the defense of seaports such as **Corycus** (Kızkalesi). Corycus was linked by a sea wall to the offshore castle.

Blind spots: The height of the walls was improved by a moat, usually filled with water. The moat gave protection to the archers on the walls who, without it, were hampered by the blind spots at ground level.

Towers which jutted out from the curtain walls enabled the defenders to outflank the attackers. In Yılan Kalesi, the natural contours of the hill were incorporated into the angles of the walls to give the best advantage from several sides for defense.

The walls and entrance could be further protected by openings in the upper floors as at Silifke through which defenders dropped stones and boiling oil on the attackers.

Military architecture: The last-built of the Crusader castles in Turkey is that of the Knights of St. John at Bodrum. Dating from 1402 and built using stones from the Mausoleum of Halicarnassus, it survives as a magnificent example of 15th-century military architecture. Construction was stopped in the 16th century, for with the advent of gunpowder as a propellant, castles had become obsolete. Today a museum of underwater archaeology enhances its attraction.

Yılankale in Adana.

none of them have cars, so in each village conflicting directions are given. It's best to return to Anavarza and from there to Ceyhan.

Safely back on the E-5, the trip is straight to **Osmaniye**, where you turn left at the junction for Iskenderun south and Karatepe north. For here the road is well marked although a few miles up it turns to dirt and gravel but the scenery – lush green and rolling mountains – makes the pain worthwhile.

Karatepe, situated in a forest overlooking a breathtaking lake formed by a dam on the Ceyhan River, is a major site of Hittite remains dating approximately to the 12th century B.C. Knowledge of this culture is fairly scant for few records have been unearthed. In fact, the existence of this group of people – at the height of their power (from the 19th century B.C. to the 13th century B.C. they ruled Anatolia) they had clout and imperialistic appetite matching that of the Egyptians – was discovered only a century ago.

The open-air museum houses some two dozen sculptures and reliefs, all restored and exhibited one after the other under shady trees. The pieces seem in very good condition and some are extremely beautiful; there are animals, domestic scenes including a mother suckling an infant, and figures holding menacing-looking spears. For archaeologists, one of the more fascinating aspects of the discoveries here was the unearthing of tablets containing the first known examples of Hittite writing. Sadly, it is forbidden to take pictures, but at the entrance of the site it is possible to buy postcards and slides of what is displayed.

Another memorable site in the area is **Kadirli**, north of both Anavarza and Karatepe and situated on the banks of the Ceyhan River. Development has been slow in coming to this spot, which is perhaps why a wealth of ancient ruins remains. There are neolithic mounds, almost a dozen castles nearby and some Hittite reliefs. The road is rather torturous and given the number of ruins elsewhere and the almost surfeit of castles

The port of Iskenderun.

you can give this a pass. •

The Earth Castle: Leaving the national park and heading back to the E-5, you pass **Toprakkale**, or Earth Castle, built in the 10th century by Byzantine Emperor Nicephorus II Phocas. This castle was bitterly fought over by the Armenians, the Crusaders and the Arabs as it was a vital outpost guarding the route leading from the Cilician Plain to the Hatay region, the same route travelers must still follow to reach Iskenderun and beyond.

Toprakkale also signals the beginning of the Plain of Issus, where Alexander the Great defeated the Persian armies under Darius III in 333 B.C. Darius is said to have fled the field, leaving behind even his harem. The victory thus gave Alexander room to begin his sweep of Syria and finally ancient Palestine. Turning south at the intersection at Osmaniye and Toprakkale, the E-5 road enters the Hatay, Turkey's southernmost province.

The **Hatay** was given to Syria under a French mandate after the collapse of the Ottoman Empire, but was returned to Turkey in 1939. For many years Syria has wistfully claimed the Hatay as part of its territory, saying that Turkey's sovereignty over the province is illegal. Contrary to international realities, Syrian maps still show the Hatay as part of its national boundaries. Turkish authorities find Syrian claims absurd. But because of its proximity to Syria and its historic importance as a major port and trading center, the Hatay attracted numerous minorities and nationalities, leaving to the region a rich heritage of languages, cultures and religions.

Cheap accommodations: In general, this region tends to be very inexpensive for the traveler. The price of food can run as low as half of what one would pay in Istanbul, while the best hotels (so far nothing available higher than four-stars) often cost $60 for a double. Partly because the Hatay draws few tourists, and partly because it is a region noted historically for a mix of peoples, the locals are friendly solely because they are pleasantly surprised to see a stranger. While there is little in terms of local crafts to buy (unless one counts boxes of laundry detergent and cigarettes smuggled from Syria), in Antakya particularly it is possible to find interesting pieces of carved wood.

The northern part of the Hatay is now dominated by oil refineries and steel plants, which fill the sky with evil-smelling smoke. The first town is **Dörtyol**, the end of the line for the oil pipeline traveling from the Kirkuk oil fields in Iraq.

Dörtyol is followed by the ancient port of **Payas**, now alternatively referred to as Yakacık on most maps but Payas on road signs. The harbor has long since been filled up, but is still worth visiting because Payas is the site of an extremely well-kept 16th-century Ottoman mosque complex reportedly built by Yavuz Pasha under advise from the most celebrated of all Ottoman architects, Mimar Sinan.

Truck route: It is easy to drive right past Payas town, as you will probably be boxed in between precariously balanced trucks journeying to the Syrian

Walking by Elvis Presley rugs.

YAŞAR KEMAL

Yaşar Kemal, Turkey's most eminent novelist and a perennial candidate for the Nobel Prize, likes to emphasize his rural roots. "I am a peasant," says the burly, six-foot (1.8-meter) tall author. "I was born in a village."

Best known for his novels of social protest that take place in the rural settings of his native Çukurova (Cilician Plain), Kemal has been compared to William Faulkner and Nikos Kazantzakis for his depth and keen observations, and penetrating factual accounts of changing village life in Turkey and of his rich use of the Turkish language. His use of colloquial language, dialect and curses, straight from the villages of the Çukurova Plain, is extraordinary and natural.

The transformation of the Çukurova from an underdeveloped rural farm belt to an industrial region, where feudal ownership of land still prevails, is a theme widely used in Kemal's novels. His chief characters are the common people: cotton farmers, peasant villagers, seasonal migrant workers, and brigands, fighting against an oppressive class of feudal landlords, who own entire villages.

Kemal was also the first writer in Turkey to describe in detail rural blood feuds between rival family clans, instigated by conflicting claims over women and property.

The Financial Times once described Kemal as "a man who tells, like no other, the tale of Turkey under change."

His best known novel, *Memed, my Hawk*, has been translated into many languages. The four-book epic tells the story of Memed, a young Çukurova lad who escapes his village, controlled by a tyrannical, exploitative feudal landlord, to become a Robin Hood-like bandit. From his hideout in the Taurus Mountains, Memed leads a pack of *eşkiya* (brigands) to steal from the rich and give to the poor and plots his revenge against the landlord who killed his loved one, a young village girl he tried to elope with. About the protagonist Memed, Kemal says: "I can't kill the son of a bitch. He has taken me over. When I started writing *Memed, my Hawk*, I was 24 years old and he was 21. When I completed the fourth book on him, I was 65 and the bastard was still 24."

Yaşar Kemal is a pen name he started using in the 1950s. He was born Kemal Sadık Gökçeli in the village of Gökçeli near Adana in 1922. His father came from a line of feudal landlords and his mother from bandits. He was five years old when he witnessed the stunning murder of his father in a mosque, a shocking event that was to propel him toward a career as a writer.

As a young lad, he worked as an apprentice to the *aşıks*, the traveling bards of Anatolia who roamed the countryside with their *saz*, a banjo-like instrument, singing songs about love and heroism and religion. From these traditional minstrels, Kemal learned the art of story-telling.

Kemal dropped out of high school to take an odd assortment of jobs, including working as a cotton picker, factory worker, and as a petition writer. He worked three years as a night watchman in a public library in Adana, where he read every book on the shelves during the long, lonely nights and memorized some of the great Greek classics, including Homer's *Iliad* and the *Odyssey*. In 1950, he migrated to Istanbul to start a journalism career with the newspaper *Cumhuriyet*, where he quickly became a star feature writer.

His first novel, *Memed, my Hawk*, brought him national recognition and international acclaim. In the early 1980s Peter Ustinov made a motion picture based on the book, filmed in Yugoslavia.

In his book *Iron Earth, Copper Sky*, Kemal describes the sufferings and hardships of the seasonal migrant workers arriving in Çukurova from nearby impoverished mountain villages to pick cotton.

In *A Murder in the Iron Workers Market*, written in 1974, and *Yusufcuk*

Yusuf, published a year later, Kemal tells of an emergence of a new type of feudal landownership system, influenced by the arrival of industrial development in the region. The new landowners, cunning as ever but not as effective as in the past, fear that the workers will one day unite to undermine them. These landowners attempt to dominate the workers by fomenting squabbles and clashes among them.

More than 112 editions of his books have been published overseas, and his works have been translated into English, French, German, Russian, Spanish and other languages.

In 1982, the French Critics Association awarded him the *Del Duca Prize*, a $30,000 award whose earlier recipients included Jean Anouilh of France, Argentinean poet Jorge Luis Borges, Italian novelist Ignazio Silone and Senegal's former President, the poet Leopold Sedar Senghor.

Two years later, French President François Mitterand presented him with the *Legion of Honor*, an honor he shared with Italian film director Federico Fellini, the late Dutch documentary film maker Joris Ivens and Elie Wiesel, a Nobel Prize-winning American novelist who achieved fame through his writings about the Jewish holocaust in Europe during World War II.

Many of his novels have been translated into English by his wife Thilda, a woman Kemal describes as "my most important and trustworthy friend in the whole world."

He despises many of the inevitable changes taking place in Çukurova where mechanized agriculture has replaced the horse and plough.

In an interview with the *International Herald Tribune*, he described how these changes are altering the environment for the worse: "In the 1920s there were 10 large marshes in Çukurova, filled with all kinds of birds – there were even flamingos. There were gazelles. Then in the 50s the tractor arrived and nature changed immediately – no more marshes, no more gazelles."

Novelist
Yaşar Kemal.

border. From the road, the town looks uninteresting, filled with car repair shops, dirty teahouses and down-at-the-heels hotels.

There are no signs off the main road pointing to the complex, so it is best to turn right after the first block of shops, and then simply head towards the sea and the castle, slightly visible in the distance. For all the dirt and traffic of the main road, the back of Payas is remarkably clean and quiet. Sheep and cows graze idly by the walls of the caravansary, while olive tree groves, wandering bushes and flowers give the area a sleepy character.

As you enter the caravansary, immediately on the right are the old baths, now boarded up and guarded by wayward cows. Beyond the squat roof of the *hamam* is a 13th-century Crusader Castle, later repaired by the Ottomans and used as a sort of housing complex centuries ago. In surprisingly good condition, the huge iron door will be opened by the elderly watchman, who can usually be found sitting by the

crumbling stairs. It is best to ascend to the top of the castle walls, from which you have a spectacular view out to the Mediterranean and across the town. Little remains within the castle grounds save for a few ruins of old houses now partly obscured by overgrown grass.

Islamic schooling: As you leave the castle, you will see, almost straight ahead, a courtyard framed by a mosque and a students' quarters. Whether official or not, the mosque is back in use, and visitors are likely to see a group of young children – girls on one side and boys on the other – busy studying the Koran. The students' quarters have been transformed into latter-day apartments, with laundry drying from trees and women squatting by the courtyard's walls chopping vegetables and playing with babies.

Coming out of the courtyard you turn right to enter the covered bazaar, a narrow hallway with a vaulted ceiling. Perhaps there are plans to reopen the bazaar for the shops are all newly numbered and framed by plate-glass

Planting crops in the Çukurova.

windows. If you exit the bazaar from the entrance, you will see on the right buildings that were probably used to house the soup kitchen and more apartments.

Travelers must return to the E-5 to drive to Iskenderun. Driving at night is perhaps one of the best times to make the one-hour trip. By sunset, the road clears a bit of cars, and what during the day is a horribly crowded, polluted site is transformed after dusk: puffs of smoke from steel plants disappear gently into the night against a backdrop of blinking factory lights and bright red, yellow and white flames.

Iskenderun: At first sight **Iskenderun** is not very exciting. The streets are narrow and crowded with cars, pedestrians and fruit sellers pushing wooden carts. The city is bordered on one side by a busy port – whose position is slowly being usurped by Mersin – and on the other side by the Amanos Mountains rolling into Syria.

Iskenderun was known as Alexander-atta after its founder Alexander the Great, and Iskender is the Turkish equivalent for Alexander. The 175,000 people in the city are a mix of the multi-nationals who populate the Hatay.

Now Turkey's southernmost port, it was originally founded as a port town by Alexander the Great to celebrate his victory over Darius III, but its importance dwindled after the founding of a Seleucid port near Antioch a few years later.

Tasty prawns: There isn't much to see or do in Iskenderun, although there is a wide promenade along the Mediterranean which offers a pleasant walk and numerous beer and teahouses. Across the street from the promenade are large, outdoor restaurants serving traditional Turkish *meze* dishes with fresh fish and giant-sizes prawns. One *meze* dish that must be tried in Iskenderun is *humus*, an appetizer made from crushed chick peas, flavored with lemon and parsley. This and other Arabic dishes found in Iskenderun have been influenced by the city's proximity to Syria. The only hotel of note in Iskenderun is the **Hataylı Hotel** on Osmangazi Caddesi.

The Hittite Lions in Antakya Museum.

HACI ÖMER SABANCI

If Yaşar Kemal is the man who introduced central Anatolian life to the world through his vivid portrayals of a young peasant boy struggling against an exploitative landowner in *Memed, my Hawk*, then Hacı Ömer Sabancı is the man who showed that it is possible to overcome these harsh conditions.

For Hacı Ömer started as a peasant boy toiling in the region called Çukurova, a fertile plain whose vast spreads of cotton turned into great wealth in the late 1800s as American and European demands for cotton could no longer be met by their own farmers. But unlike Memed and other peasants who fill Kemal's novels, Hacı Ömer's fight against poverty ended not in gunshots and mountain pursuits, but in the creation of the world-renowned Hacı Ömer Sabancı Holding Company.

In the New York-based *Fortune Magazine*'s list of 500 top overseas corporations for 1988, Sabancı Holding ranked number 186, one of two Turkish groups to make the list. With assets of $3.9 billion, 31,372 employees, 600 bank branches and holdings in education, health and cultural institutions in addition to 100 factories in textiles, food, plastics, tires, automobile parts, cement, paper, electronics, pharmaceuticals and agribusiness, Sabancı Holding is a testament to one man's ability to conquer the greatest odds.

In many ways, Hacı Ömer's life mirrored that of the dissolution of the Ottoman Empire and the founding of the Turkish Republic. Born in Akçakaya village in Kayseri province in 1906 or 1903 (there is some dispute over the exact date), he left to seek his fortune in Adana in the early 1920s, just after Turkey's eventual founder, Mustafa Kemal (Atatürk), delivered the region from its three-year occupation by the French following the Ottoman Empire's defeat in World War I.

The whole country was reeling from shock of defeat and the threats to its ever-diminishing borders. Hundreds of thousands of Turkish men were wounded or died in the war, and the economy lay in tatters. Hacı Ömer's father had been killed in the war too, fighting the enemy in some distant battlefield. But in the Çukurova region, there was great hope for the world still wanted cotton and the fields were still blooming. So like many other young men who trooped off to Adana in search of a livelihood, Hacı Ömer started off in a cotton factory, washing cotton for 85 piasters a day. But this young man, who not only had the desire to make money but had the will as well, slowly became well-known in Adana for his thriftiness and, more important, his commercial drive and sense. Soon, he was acting as an employment agency, matching workers with job openings. After the founding of the Republic in 1923, Hacı Ömer was picked to restart factories abandoned in Adana by Armenian and Greeks during the intercommunal strife both before and immediately following the end of the French occupation.

When it was legislated in 1934 that all

Industrialist Haci Ömer Sabancı.

people must take a surname, Hacı Ömer, by then a wealthy factory owner, took the name Sabancı – meaning ploughmaker – so as never to forget his roots.

By the end of World War II, the country embarked on a modernization program through the help of the Marshall Plan, and businessmen were at the forefront of the changes. Hacı Ömer, already a millionaire, was never a man to pass up a business opportunity and he quickly realized that if he wanted to expand his holdings even further, he would need a bank. With a bank, he could easily obtain money for his new enterprises and still practice his renowned thriftiness by encouraging others to save their money which in turn could finance his new operations.

At the time, banking was still a profession mainly left to the foreign minorities, and the general public was usually too poor to worry about savings or kept their savings in the form of gold hidden under their beds or stashed somewhere else. But Hacı Ömer, with an appetite for risk and the insight that made him such a successful businessman, realized that a stronger economy would support and need banks, and so he became a founding partner of Akbank in 1948. Akbank today ranks among the 200 largest banks in the world in assets and profits.

By the mid-1950s, he had moved into apartment construction and textiles, establishing in Adana the giant Bossa factory, one of the world's largest textile mills. A few years later he acquired majority shareholding in the bank and started up an insurance company.

In his personal life, he was just as demanding, teaching his six sons the value of thrift, insisting they take advantage of the formal education he had to pass up. His wife, Sadıka, whom he married in 1928, stood by him as he dreamt and built his family fortune. In 1949, Hacı Ömer acquired a mansion along the Bosphorus in Istanbul, which continues to serve as the family home.

Hacı Ömer never forgot his Anatolian roots, but he also remembered that modern Turkey grew out of the splendors of the Ottoman Empire, and this fanned his love for fine antiques and furniture. Each piece to him symbolized more than sheer economic or utilitarian value, but it represented a story much like his own: creation, use and appreciation for fine craftsmanship. If he had one spendthrift side to him – and tales of him avoiding taxes to save money even when he was a wealthy man are legendary – then it was in the pursuit of collecting pieces of the past. His love of art was best exemplified at the Sabancı Villa on the Bosphorus, where many objects of master painters and sculptors can still be seen today. His only other pastime was chatting with friends about business or smoking a *nargile*, or hookah, in Emirgân, a town on the Bosphorus near his home.

An earthy man who spoke with an atrocious rural accent, Hacı Ömer always dressed like an Anatolian peasant and never wore a tie in his life, even when meeting the President of the Republic. He hung up on the wall of his house a harness he had used while working as a young *hamal* – a beast of burden – to carry huge bales of cotton on his back, as a reminder to himself and his family of his humble origins as a cotton worker.

Hacı Ömer died in 1966, but the fortune he so carefully amassed and the friendships he maintained with people from peasants in Adana up to high government officials did not disappear. Thousands mourned his passing and Adana today has countless signs of his love for Turkey, from his factories and banks to a cultural center and educational institutions established by Sabancı Holding.

His eldest son died in 1979, but the other five sons continue to work in the company now headed by Sakıp Sabancı, the second oldest son.

It is virtually impossible to travel anywhere in Turkey today without seeing the SA initials in front of a factory or company name, a symbol now not only of one man's ability to amass great wealth, but of Turkey's growing economic power.

Iskenderun is also an important naval base. A boot camp for Turkish naval infantry, with a live-sized concrete destroyer in its midst, can be found on the road to Antakya.

After leaving Iskenderun, a right turn off the E-5 will take the motorist along the Gulf of Iskenderun to **Arsuz**, a little resort village thought to be the site of the Seleucid town of Rhosus, built in 300 B.C. The hamlet, which has a pleasant beach, contains the remains of several ancient buildings and city walls. Many of the old mansions in Arsuz were built by the French when they ruled the area under a League of Nations mandate from 1919-1939. A Crusader castle stands further south near the promontory known as **Hınzır Burnu** (the Cape of Pigs), which is the western side of the peak known as **Musa Dağı** (The Mountain of Moses). The mountain was the scene of intense fighting in 1915 between insurgent Armenians and the Turkish army. The stand of the Armenian rebels was made famous by Franz Werfel in his acclaimed novel, *Forty Days in Musa Dagh.*

Returning to the E-5, the road turns away from the sea and into the **Amanos Mountains**. A road forks to the right to **Soğukoluk**, a breezy plateau town where many of Iskenderun's wealthy families have summer villas. Numerous hotels in the town serve visiting Arab businessmen. Before the 1980 military coup, Soğukoluk was an infamous, naughty brothel city, where young Turkish girls trapped into prostitution were literally sold as concubines to visiting Arab sheiks. Despite official disclaimers, rumors persist that prostitution and white women slave trade continues there.

The Syrian Gates: Back on the E-5, the road narrowly winds its way around the Amanos Mountains, from which you have a terrific view of the **Orontes Valley** – part of the **Amik Ovası** – whose flowing fields and generous greenery attest to the area's fertility and source of the region's wealth. This section of the road is called the **Belen Pass**, formerly known as the Syrian Gates for its strate-

A mosaic of the sea god Poseidon at the Antakya Museum.

gic location between the sea and Antioch. **Belen** itself is a small village whose fame rests upon the belief that its waters hold curative powers. For those who dare, open water fountains in the city center offer the traveler a cool drink.

As you drive towards Antakya (Antioch), you will notice that the sides of the road are dotted with ancient Roman walls and mounds, all unexcavated sites of earlier life. After the pass there is a turnoff for **Bagras Castle**, a medieval fortress reportedly built by the Byzantines in the 10th century. This fortress passed through the hands of the numerous empires that stormed the region, finally falling to the Crusaders in 1097. After the Ottomans conquered the region in the 16th century the fortress was abandoned.

The road continues its slow dip into Antakya – set on the banks of the **Asi Nehiri** (the Orontes River) – through the fertile Amik Plain. Virtually every hill along the way contains stone outcroppings from previous civilizations, but most are unmarked and barely visible, so it is best to wait until Antakya for your exploration.

Antakya, better known by its ancient name of Antioch, was founded in 300 B.C. by Seleucus Nikator, a lesser general in Alexander's army. Following Alexander's death, Seleucus added Syria and Mesopotamia to his empire that started in Babylonia. Antioch became the capital city of the Seleucid Empire and made a name for itself as a busy commercial center.

Antioch passed to the Romans in 81 B.C., and in 64 B.C. it was made capital of the Roman province of Syria. Antioch's splendor became known throughout the Hellenistic world and the population grew to almost half a million. Numerous Roman rulers, including King Herod of Judea, gave public buildings to the city, and spacious villas and temples cropped up in the area. Many of the beautifully detailed mosaics that were so popular with the Romans – used as bath floors and as decorations in salons and gardens – are now on display in the **Antakya Ar-**

chaeological Museum.

Antioch was the scene for St. Paul's first ministry. It was here that the term "Christian" was first used to describe the followers of Jesus.

But the city suffered from devastating earthquakes and, as the Roman Empire began to disintegrate, Antioch came under attack. It was sacked numerous times by the Persians and the Arabs, the latter of whom captured the city in A.D. 638. The Byzantines took it back in 969, only to lose it again – this time to the Crusaders. Once again made the capital, its glorious history ended in tragedy in 1268, when the Mamelukes of Egypt sacked the city and drove out the remaining inhabitants.

Virtual decay: For centuries Antioch lay in virtual decay. Old engravings made by 19th-century travelers show Antioch as a scattering of ruined buildings along the Orontes, with sheepherders the only sign of life in the once-bustling city.

Since the founding of the Republic and the development of this region as an

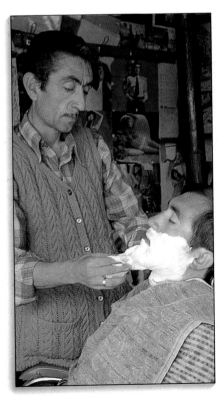

Having a close shave.

important farming and once again commercial center, Antioch's population has grown to over 200,000 and the city is full of new apartment blocks and streets crowded with boutiques such as **Benetton** and **Levi's**.

Excavations conducted in the 1930s discovered numerous ancient sites within and around the city, most famous of which are the many mosaics dating from early Roman times, now on display in the Archaeological Museum. For a sight of these mosaics alone it is worth traveling to Antakya. The majority of these mosaics date to the second and third centuries. The collection is the world's most extensive gatherings of Roman mosaics. Many were found virtually complete and the colors are almost as brilliant as they once were. The museum also includes a nice collection of Roman coins, along with pottery and jewelry.

Otherwise Antakya is filled with various sites of Christian and Roman significance. Within the city itself is a Roman bridge (circa A.D. 200) crossing the Asi River, a very small but charming bazaar in the center of town, and numerous beautiful mosques. The outline of the ancient city walls, about 19 miles (30 km) in length, gives some idea of the city's former fame.

Daily tours: Primarily because of the amazing mosaics found in the museum, and because of the city's location on the road to Syria, Antakya has built itself up as a tourist center, and almost daily tour buses disgorge their French and German passengers outside the Büyük Antakya Hotel, located across the street from the museum. The people who work at the Tourist Information Office off **Atatürk Caddesi** at the first roundabout into the city are very helpful and will often offer to personally accompany the visitor if he has trouble locating a specific site.

The food tends toward *humus, shish kebab* and *meze* dishes, served in the best restaurants found along **Hürriyet Caddesi**, which runs from the left bank of the Asi River south. On the streets, vendors sell fresh fruit drinks and *bici*.

Village girls skip rope during a Sunday outing.

Letter from the Publisher

Old friends in many parts of Asia greet each other with the salutation 'Apa Khabar' (ah-pah car-bar). They are saying, 'How are you?' and 'What's news?'. In the Malay-Indonesian tongue, 'Apa' is a word that denotes a question. That is why we are called APA Publications. Our books are designed for a traveller with an enquiring mind, who wants to get beneath the skin of a place and find out what goes on beneath the surface.

The first Insight guide – Insight Bali – was published in 1970. The team of young writers, designers and photographers who contributed to that guide had never produced a book before. Their ambition was to capture the essence of that fascinating island, its people and its vital culture. The result was hailed as a totally new type of guide, praised for its evocative photography and perceptive writing and above all for presenting an honest and penetrating portrait of the real Bali.

Twenty years on, we are still winning awards and critical acclaim for our guides. We have grown from a small, Asia-oriented firm into an internationally renowned company which operates worldwide. We have over 100 titles in print in a variety of languages, distributed by our co-publishers and distributers in more than 40 countries. Many more titles are in preparation.

Yet our essential philosophy has not changed: each guide is produced by a team of creative photographers and journalists – some are seasoned professionals, others are talented young people at the start of their career. All have an intimate knowledge of their subject and are motivated by the challenge of capturing the spirit of a place: not only to produce a thoroughly practical guide but also to convey a sense of what it is like to be one of the people who live there.

That is why, when you turn the pages of an Insight guide, you will find pictures full of people – not posing for the camera but going about their everyday life and work. That is why you will read articles on subjects as diverse as pub culture in Dublin, the art of political compromise in Brazil or the movie industry in India – each one providing a real insight into what makes each place and its people unique.

You will not find such material in other guide books and – with sales of over a million and a half Insight guides a year – it is clear that many readers share our philosophy. We view our readers as true explorers, people who travel in order to learn. They know that the experience of travel is much more rewarding when based on a broad understanding of all the vital aspects of a place and its people.

As a logical extension of that philosophy, we also want to build a closer relationship with our readers. We want your feedback – tell us how you use the guides – before, during or after a journey, what you like and dislike about them; tell us about any error or omission that you find, either using the enclosed reply card, or by letter. Let's keep the communication lines open!

Selamat jalan; Happy travelling

Hans Höfer
APA Publications

"I was first drawn to the Insight Guides by the excellent "Nepal" volume. I can think of no book which so effectively captures the essence of a country. Out of these pages leaped the Nepal I know — the captivating charm of a people and their culture. I've since discovered and enjoyed the entire Insight Guide Series. Each volume deals with a country or city in the same sensitive depth, which is nowhere more evident than in the superb photography."

Sir Edmund Hillary

The refreshing and eye-catching *bicis* are best eaten with lots of ice.

The best hotel in town is the four-star **Büyük Antakya** Hotel on Atatürk Caddesi.

Like the whole of the Hatay, Antakya's population is mixed, and Arabic vies with Turkish as a first language. A majority of the Arabs of Antakya are Alevis, members of Turkey's Shiite community. There is a small Jewish population here, numbering about 150 people, and an equally tiny Christian population.

Jewish community: The **synagogue** is located on the eastern bank of the Asi River, right behind the **Old Market District** on Kurtuluş Caddesi. It is only open on Saturday mornings and Jewish holidays. Disguised as a government building with a picture of Atatürk above the doorway, it is not easy to locate. Walk to the Habib Naccar Camii and then ask directions of one of the small tradesmen sitting outside their shops drinking tea. The **Habib Naccar Camii**, constructed in the 17th century,

is one of the finer mosques in the city and is well worth a visit.

Kurtuluş Caddesi itself is the new version of ancient Antioch's famed main street. The ancient street, constructed around 30 B.C. with colonnades running on either side of the street that was supposedly over 30 feet wide and two miles long, has been replaced by modern buildings and *hans* (commercial centers) and pavements with automobiles and trucks.

The first Christian community: Antakya is famous for the grotto **Church of St. Peter**, just outside the city on the road to Halep (Aleppo). This is allegedly the oldest working church in existence, and it is here that St. Peter together with St. Paul and Barnabas reportedly preached from a cave around A.D. 47 and the world's first Christian community was founded. The grotto church is said to have a secret tunnel through which believers could flee when under persecution.

During Antioch's heyday, it was renowned for its **Shrine of Daphne**,

A young woman carries her baby on her back.

now located in Harbiye, a cool verdant plateau eight miles (13 km) south of Antakya on the road to Samandağ.

According to myth, this is the spot where Apollo pursued Daphne and she was changed into a laurel. There is some contention over whether this was really the setting, but its beauty – cascading waterfalls set among small ledges of pine trees above the Asi River – makes it an appropriate setting. The conqueror of the region, Emperor Seleucus, built a temple and oracle complex to the god Apollo here, and later Roman rulers added even more temples and palaces. It was allegedly here that Cleopatra and Antony married and where the Antioch Games – precursors of the Olympics – took place. But Daphne fell along with Antioch, and although it remains a favorite holiday spot for locals and visiting Arabs, one's imagination must be put into full force to see its former beauty and charm.

The grove itself is filled with little open air *kebab* restaurants whose patrons sit around tables balanced precariously on rocks along the bubbling streams. Garbage is everywhere and the waterfalls are obscured by the hordes of people who tramp around looking for an empty picnic table. Above Daphne is a street of hotels and fish restaurants, except that fish is rarely on the menu and the ones available look like they swam too long near the oil terminal of Dörtyol.

The area was also made famous during the Roman-Byzantine reign by the activities of St. Simeon the Elder, who around A.D. 420, having decided that the way of faith was to avoid the world, took to a mountain top east of Antioch, and perched himself on a pillar. He kept moving to higher and higher pillars before finally settling on a point falling across the Syrian border near Yayladaği.

But his style of faith proved popular, and his most faithful disciple, St. Simeon the Younger, ascended **Samandağ** (the Mountain of St. Simeon) reportedly at the age of seven, to preach and pray around A.D. 520. The two churches dedicated to him atop the mountain remain in a state of disrepair due to tremendous earthquakes, but reaching them is not easy.

Samandağ (also the name for the city), about 12 miles (19 km) from Antakya, is Turkey's southernmost city where the Asi River feeds into the Mediterranean. This city is the modern town of Antioch's ancient port, **Seleucia ad Peiria**. Seleucia was the original capital of the Seleucid Empire until 281 B.C., when Seleucus was assassinated and his son Antiochus took the throne and moved the capital to Antioch. It was originally one of four cities founded by Seleucus.

Ruined harbor walls still dot the beach front, while nearby is the **Tunnel of Vespasian**, a huge series of water sluices carved out of rock near the sea and dated to A.D. 79. You can hike around in the water tunnels, enjoying the solitude of the spot, which makes for a refreshingly pleasant change from the noisy beach below.

As a resort area, Samandağ is less than attractive. Garbage tossed in the sea by passing ships is regularly washed ashore, the sea looks dirty and the undertow is treacherous. Many people have drowned off the shore.

From the center of the town itself there is an interesting albeit rough road that leads to **Hıdırbey**, a tiny village which boasts **Hıdır's Tree**, reportedly sprouted from the staff of a Moslem Prophet Hıdır. Legend has it that the Old Testament Prophet Moses met with Hıdır for instruction near this spot. In Turkish, Hıdır – or Hızır – refers to an extraordinary being who wanders the earth performing miracles.

Facing Musa Dağ, Hıdırbey is set in a sort of valley through which runs a pretty creek. The tree is definitely there, although it is not quite as big as some say it is. After the long, hot drive, it is best just to buy a cold drink from the little shop nearby and like all locals sit and stare at the tree and the creek. Unless you are very adventuresome and have a full tank of gas, it is better to return on the same road you have come in, for it is unclear where the road goes after Hıdırbey.

Right, old men with watermelons

TRAVEL TIPS

GETTING THERE

BY AIR

There are many daily flights from major European, American, Middle Eastern and Far Eastern cities to Istanbul's Atatürk International Airport, from where you can get regular **Turkish Airlines** connecting flights to Izmir, Antalya, Dalaman and Adana. Many charter flights operate from Europe to Antalya, Dalaman and Izmir, making it easy to get to the Turkish Coast.

Imsık Airlines provides direct flights from Istanbul to Izmir and Bodrum daily on 18-person passenger planes. Airfare is slightly more expensive than other domestic airlines but provides quick access to the Bodrum area.

Istanbul, Ankara, Izmir, and Antalya all have international airports. Adana airport can be reached by domestic transfer.

A British-Turkish joint venture is constructing an international airport at Güllük, north of Bodrum, which will go into operation in the early 1990s.

Duty free shops in the arrival lounges provide liquor, cigarettes, perfume and something quite expensive in Turkey: instant coffee.

BY SEA

Regular boat services operate during the summer from various Greek islands to Turkish resort towns on the Aegean, including Ayvalık, Izmir, Kuşadası, Bodrum and Marmaris. **Turkish Maritime Lines (Deniz Yolları)** also has a regular passenger boat service along the Turkish Coast from Istanbul.

BY RAIL

There are regular train services from Istanbul and Ankara to Izmir, Aydın, Denizli, Tarsus, Mersin and Adana. Izmir can also be reached from Bandırma.

There are also regular train services operating between Istanbul and Venice, Munich and Vienna, stopping off in many major cities in between.

The train is the cheapest form of transportation in Turkey. Breakfast, lunch and dinner are served aboard the train, but are not included in the price. It is a good idea to book a private compartment if you are traveling on an overnight train.

BY ROAD

Frequent bus services operate between major Turkish cities and any of the popular spots on the Turkish Aegean and Mediterranean. Those journeying long distances in summer often travel at night, when it is cooler. Bus travel is inexpensive and varying in comfort, depending on the company. Most of the buses are Mercedes 302, but not all have air conditioning. Deluxe Varan buses are almost always air conditioned. Bus companies having the most routes in the southern coast are **Pamukkale** and **Kaş Turizm**. Bus travel is not recommended for the visitor who dislikes cigarette smoke. The northern Turkish Aegean can easily be reached from Bulgaria and Greece. Motorists can also drive to the eastern Turkish Mediterranean from Aleppo, Syria.

TRAVEL ESSENTIALS

PASSPORTS AND VISAS

For visits up to three months, nationals of the following countries may enter Turkey with current passports without a visa: Australia, Austria, Bahamas, Bahrain, Barbados, Belgium, Canada, Denmark, Djibouti, Fiji Islands, Finland, France, Gambia, Federal Republic of Germany, Gibraltar, Greece, Grenada, Hong Kong, Iran, Ireland,

Iceland, Italy, Jamaica, Japan, Kenya, Kuwait, Liechtenstein, Luxembourg, Mauritius, Malta, Monaco, Norway, Netherlands, New Zealand, Oman, Qatar, St. Lucia, Saudi Arabia, San Marino, Seychelles, Singapore, Spain, Switzerland, Trinidad, Tobago, Tunisia, Turkish Republic of Northern Cyprus, Uganda, United Arab Emirates, U.S.A. and the Vatican.

Nationals of Portugal, Rumania and Yugoslavia require a valid passport (visas not required) for stays up to two months. Malaysian citizens may stay up to 15 days with valid passports (visas not required).

Nationals of all other countries must obtain a visa from the nearest Turkish Embassy or Consulate.

MONEY MATTERS

The Turkish Lira (TL) is the currency used in Turkey. Denominations in coins are 50 TL, 100 TL, 500 TL, and in banknotes 1,000 TL, 5,000 TL, 10,000 TL, 20,000 TL and 50,000 TL. Foreign exchange rates are published daily in Turkish newspapers and posted in the banks.

There is no limit on the foreign currency that can be brought into or taken out of Turkey.

Money transfers can be withdrawn as TL with no problems. If a transfer is withdrawn as a foreign currency, a commission of up to three percent is usually charged.

FOREIGN EXCHANGE

Money can be changed almost anytime at the airports. Banks have 24-hour operations at Istanbul Atatürk Airport.

HEALTH

No vaccinations are required, but it is a good idea to have cholera shots if you are planning to travel in the countryside. The change in bacteria content in food may cause diarrhea.

Fruits and vegetables should be washed well. Tap water is generally safe, but may have a disagreeable taste. Bottled water is recommended in more rural areas.

Be cautious with local animals, such as dogs and cats, since many do not have rabies shots.

QUARANTINE

A rabies vaccination certificate for domestic animals and hunting dogs is required. It must be issued 48 hours before departure for Turkey and translated into Turkish by a Turkish Embassy or Consulate.

WHAT TO WEAR

Dress differs from region to region. In the cities, shorts are not very common, but in coastal towns and resorts on the Aegean and Mediterranean, colorful Hugo Boss beach shorts and La Coste T-shirts are popular. Beachwear and light cotton clothing are recommended.

During the hot, sultry summer months, it is a good idea to wear a hat or cap, and use plenty of sunscreen. Rubber sandals and slippers can also be worn on the beaches of southern Turkey.

Most Turkish women adopt western dress. Women wearing çarşafs, black veils covering the body from head to toes, are usually peasant villagers or Saudi tourists. As a sign of respect for Islam, women must wear head scarves and cover their arms and legs when visiting mosques. Miniskirts and shorts should not be worn in mosques. Women should dress conservatively in rural areas and small towns away from coastal resorts.

CUSTOMS

Visitors to Turkey may bring in the following duty free: 400 cigarettes, 50 cigars, 2.2 pounds (one kilogram) of tobacco, 2.2 pounds (one kilogram) of coffee, 3.3 pounds (1.5 kilograms) of instant coffee, up to seven bottles of spirits of which no more than three shall be of the same brand.

Valuable items such as fur coats, electronics, antiques, sports and camping equipment, and video cameras brought into the country will be registered into the owners' passports. Travelers leaving without these imported items would have to pay duties. Entry of firearms and diving equipment are subject to authorization.

Sharp instruments such as harpoons or knives cannot be transported in hand luggage in transit to Turkey. They should be placed in check-in baggage.

Gifts not exceeding $185 may be brought into the country duty free. Gifts up to $111 may be sent by mail up to one month before and 15 days after the *Ramazan* (Sacrificial) *Bayramı* and New Year.

Taking antiques (100 years or older) out of Turkey is illegal and considered an act of smuggling. Proof of purchase is needed for items such as handmade carpets. A certificate from a directorate of a museum is required for old objects.

ENTRY BY YACHT

Upon docking the yacht at a Turkish port, the captain must meet with authorities and make necessary declarations. Entry into Turkish waters will be recorded in the captain's passports and canceled upon departure. Ports acceptable for entry are: Trabzon and Samsun (on the Black Sea), Tekirdağ and Bandırma (on the Sea of Marmara), Istanbul (on the Bosphorus), Çanakkale (on the Dardanelles), Akçay, Ayvalık, Dikili, Izmir, Çeşme, Kuşadası, Güllük, Bodrum, Datça and Marmaris (on the Aegean); Fethiye, Kaş, Kemer, Antalya, Alanya, Anamur, Taşucu, Mersin and Iskenderun (on the Mediterranean).

Registration must be renewed if yachts depart from Turkey. Yachts are to be moored for winter lay-up, replacement of person registering, or completion of the specified sailing route. Registration of log is valid for three months.

Yachtsmen must adhere to their registered sailing routes. Health certificates issued for foreign yachts are valid for three months under condition that no foreign port has been entered. In the case of death or contagious disease, port authorities must be notified.

Foreigners entering Turkey may leave their vessel at a licensed marina up to two years for winter lay-up, repair and maintenance services and can leave the country by other means. Yachts over 30 NRT must pay a lighthouse fee.

GETTING ACQUAINTED

GOVERNMENT AND ECONOMY

Turkey is a secular republic with an elected parliament. Organized into 71 provinces, Turkey is bordered by Bulgaria, Greece, the Soviet Union, Iran, Iraq and Syria. It is a member of the North Atlantic Treaty Organization (NATO), the Organization of Economic Cooperation and Development and the Council of Europe. The nation is also an associate member of the European Community. With 800,000 men under arms, it has the second largest army in NATO after the U.S. Its capital is Ankara.

Turkey's main crops are wheat, cotton, tea, tobacco, hazelnuts, fruit and vegetables. Major exports include textiles, steel, chromium, bauxite, manganese and hazelnuts.

Turkey is one of the world's leading producers of textiles. Its production is so vast that Turkish textiles are often imported by countries with quota limitations under labels of other foreign manufacturers.

GEOGRAPHY AND POPULATION

Turkey has a population of 55 million. Six out of ten Turks live in cities while the rest inhabit villages. The nation is one of the largest in Europe and is about the size of Britain and France combined. It is surrounded by the Mediterranean, the Aegean and the Black Sea. The country has 300,000 square miles (780,000 square km) of territory. Three percent of Turkey lies in Europe, and this region is known as Trakya, or Thrace. Ninety-seven percent of the country lies in Asia and is called Anatolia, a rugged region covered by mountainous terrain surrounding vast fertile plains and steppes, nurtured by several winding rivers, including the Euphrates and Tigris rivers. The European and Asian parts of the country are separated by the Dardanelles in the southwest, and the Sea of Marmara and the Bosphorus in the northeast. Most of the population lives in the west along the verdant coastal plains.

TIME ZONES

Turkish Standard Time is seven hours ahead of Eastern Standard Time and two hours ahead of Greenwich Mean Time.

CLIMATE

The Aegean and Mediterranean shores of Turkey have hot and dry summers and mild winters. Average temperatures in Celsius are:

	Jan.	April	July	Oct.
Izmir	9	20	30	21
Antalya	11	22	32	23

CULTURE AND CUSTOMS

Emphasis is placed on the family in Turkey. Children are very important and are expected from every couple. They are the future of each family. Although the economics of supporting a family in Turkey are strained, the average family has two or three children. In rural areas, where big families are emphasized, couples may have eight to nine children, but how they manage to survive is uncertain.

Women are still expected to marry by the time they reach 25. The role of the woman is changing. In larger cities there are plenty of women in the work force, serving in all the professions. Many women are teachers, doctors, lawyers, scientists, administrators and business managers. But in many Turkish families the tradition of male bread-winner and female housewife lives on.

Because Turks are so family-oriented, the Turkish language has provided for the specific naming of each family (gender is always evident) member. An older brother is an *ağabey*. An older sister is an *abla*. An aunt from the mother's side is a *teyze*, while an aunt from the father's side is a *yenge*.

An uncle from the mother's side is called *dayı* while an uncle from the father's side is known as an *amca*. The bride's sister-in-law is called *görümce* while the groom's sister-in-law is a *baldız*.

Some words clarify age. An older person

as *siz* – the formal you or thy. A younger person or close relative is *sen*.

The family structure is still very tight. Retirement homes don't exist in Turkey. Often three generations live together under one roof, partly because it is more economical but also because the displacement of an older member is seriously frowned upon by society.

ELECTRICITY

Electricity in Turkey is 220 volts. The speed for electronics is fifty cycles. Two-round prongs are the standard plugs for normal appliances.

BUSINESS HOURS

Government offices are open from 8:30 a.m. to noon and 1:30 p.m. to 5:30 p.m. Commercial banks are open from 8:30 a.m. to noon and 1:30 p.m. to 5 p.m. The main post offices in cities and resorts, from where you can make phone calls, are open 24 hours, even during public and religious holidays. In resorts, some banks have exchange offices which open till late in the evening.

HOLIDAYS

IN 1990

Jan. 1	New Year's Day
April 23	National Sovereignty and Children's Day
April 26-29	Şeker Bayramı (The Sweet Holiday. This Moslem holiday, which follows the Ramazan fasting period, comes 10 days earlier each year.)
May 19	Youth and Sports Day
July 3-8	Kuban Bayramı (The Sacrificial Holiday. This Moslem holiday is observed after the pilgrimage to the Islamic holy lands and comes ten days earlier each year.
August 30	Victory Day
October 29	Republic Day

January 15-16	Selçuk Camel Wrestling Festival
March 18	Çanakkale Naval Victory Festival
March 21-24	Manisa Mesir Macunu Festival
May 6-13	Ephesus Arts and Culture Festival
May 20-26	Silifke Music and Folklore Festival
May 25-27	Denizli Pamukkale Festival
May 30-June 3	International Bergama Festival
June 24-27	Foça Music, Folklore and Watersports Festival
July 1-7	Edirne Kırkpınar Grease Wrestling Tournament
July 3-8	Çeşme Sea Festival
July 5-10	Iskenderun Culture and Tourism Festival
July 16-21	Kuşadası Gold Pigeon Song Contest
August 10-14	Çanakkale-Troy Festival
August 24-28	Alanya Folk Dance Festival
September 1-21	Izmir International Trade Fair
September 22-October 12	Mersin International Festival
October 1-9	Antalya International Arts Festival
December 3-7	Antalya/Demre St Nicholas Symposium and Festival

RELIGION

Turkey is 99 percent Moslem, but small pockets of Christians and Jews live in the big cities and in the rural areas of eastern Turkey. Turks are predominantly Sunni, but one out of every six Turks is *Alevi* (Shiite). Pious Turks pray in mosques which conduct services five times a day. The call to prayer, known as the *ezan*, is sung by muezzins, and sometimes even played on tape, from minaret tops. Izmir, Adana, Iskenderun and Antakya have churches serving different Christian denominations and synagogues for the Jewish community.

COMMUNICATIONS

MEDIA

Newspapers: *Cumhuriyet* is considered the most serious national newspaper with special emphasis on the arts, national and local politics, economy and foreign news. Other major newspapers are *Hürriyet, Güneş, Milliyet, Sabah* and *Tercüman*. More gossip-oriented papers are *Günaydın, Tan* and *Sabah*.

Two English language newspapers are published in Turkey: the *Turkish Daily News*, a daily published in Ankara, and *Dateline*, a weekly that comes out in Istanbul. Both provide concise coverage of Turkish political and economic issues and contain a variety of helpful facts for English-speaking foreigners in Turkey.

RADIO

The *BBC, VOA, Voice of Germany, Radio Moscow* and other broadcasts can be picked up on shortwave radio. On local FM radio, the third program of *TRT* (*Turkish State Radio and Television Company*) has newscasts in English, German and French at 9 a.m., 12 p.m. and 10 p.m.

TELEVISION

Three television channels operate in Turkey, all state owned. Some films broadcast in English and can be picked up on FM Radio Four in English. Channel Two broadcasts the news in English at 9:30 p.m.

POSTAL SERVICES

Turkish postal services, strangely, are among the most reliable in the world. A post office is called a **PTT**. In addition to mailing letters and sending telegrams from a PTT, you can make local, long distance and foreign phone calls. Most PTTs now also have fax and telex services.

TELEPHONES

Public telephones operate with tokens (*jeton*) sold in three sizes. Small tokens are for one-minute calls, medium and large tokens for long distance and overseas calls. Telephone cards are sold and are more practical, but only special telephones can be found at the PTT and large hotels and marinas. Phone booths, oddly, don't always work. It's best to book a call from your hotel or pension. When making a long distance call in Turkey, dial 9 first, then the city code, and then the number. When making an overseas call, dial 9, wait for the beep, dial 9 again, and then dial the country code, city code and then the number.

TELEPHONE CODES

The following are the telephone code numbers of Turkey's major cities and resorts on the Aegean and Mediterranean:

City Name	Telephone Codes
Adana	71
Alanya	3231
Anamur	7571
Ankara	4
Antakya	891
Antalya	31
Aydın	631
Ayvalık	663
Balıkesir	661
Bergama	541
Bodrum	6141
Bursa	24
Çanakkale	1961
Çeşme	5492
Çeşme-Ilıca	5493
Dalaman	6119
Dalyan(in Muğla province)	6116
Datça	6145
Denizli	621
Diyarbakır	831
Eceabat	1964
Edirne	181
Enez	1848
Erzurum	011
Eskişehir	221
Fethiye	6151
Finike	3225
Foça	5431
Gelibolu	1891
Giresun	051
Ipsala	1846
Iskenderun	881
Istanbul	1
Izmir	51
Kalkan	3215
Kaş	3226
Kayseri	351
Kemer	3214
Konya	33
Köyceğiz	6114
Kuşadası	636
Malatya	821
Manisa	551
Marmaris	612
Mersin	741
Muğla	6111
Pamukkale	6218
Samsun	361
Selçuk	5451
Silifke	7591
Sivas	477
Şanlıurfa	8711
Trabzon	031

INTERNATIONAL CODES

Australia	61
Austria	43
Belgium	32
Canada	1
Denmark	45
Egypt	20
Fed. Rep. of Germany	49
Finland	358
France	33
Great Britain	44
Greece	30
Holland	31
Hong Kong	852
India	91
Iran	98
Iraq	964
Ireland	353
Italy	39
Japan	81
Norway	47
Saudi Arabia	966
Spain	34
Sweden	46
Switzerland	41
Syria	963
United States	1

OTHER USEFUL NUMBERS

Directory Assistance: 011
Intercity Operator: 031
International Operator: 032
Telegrams by Phone: 091

EMERGENCIES

SECURITY AND CRIME

Violent crime is rare in Turkey. Theft by pickpockets is on the rise in crowded urban settings. Cars with cassette players and radios are also a popular target. In larger cities, parking in well-lit places is a good safeguard.

POSSESSION OF DRUGS

It is hoped the visitor to Turkey hasn't been introduced to the country through the film *Midnight Express*. Penalties are heavy for possession of drugs (which includes hashish), but being Hollywood, there was much exaggeration in this film. Drugs are produced for medical purposes, and drug abuse and alcoholism are low.

MEDICAL SERVICES

Unless it is an emergency, wait until you've returned home for medical treatment. English, German or French speaking doctors who have been trained abroad, can be found in the cosmopolitan areas.

Local pharmacies (*Eczane*) can provide antidotes for minor ailments, bruises and cuts. Antibiotics can be purchased without a prescription. A list of hospitals follows.

ANTALYA

Ak Deniz Üniversitesi Tıp Fakültesi Hastanesi
(Mediterranean University Medical School Hospital)
Kepezbaşı
Tel: (31) 112056, 119200

Devlet Hastanesi (State Hospital)
100 Yıl Stadı Karşısı
Tel: (31) 112010

Sosyal Sigortalar Kurumu Hastanesi
Anafartalar Caddesi
Tel: (31) 111555/112846

BODRUM

Devlet Hastanesi (State Hospital)
Turgutreis Caddesi
Tel: (6141) 1068

Bodrum Klinik (Clinic)
Sağlık Ocağı
Turgutreis Caddesi
Tel: (6141) 1353

IZMIR

American Hospital
9 Eylül Üniversitesi Yanı,
Alsancak
Tel: (51) 132046

DOCTORS

ENGLISH-SPEAKING

Dr. Oktay Ergine
(General Practitioner)
Özel Idare Iş Hanı Kat 8
Tel: (31) 119206

Dr. Hüseyin Sipahioğlu
(Internist)
Anafartalar Caddesi 15/8
Tel: (31) 124400

Dr. Günseli Akaydın
(Internist)
Anafartalar Caddesi 15/2
Tel: (31) 120567

Dr. Tuncay Saatçi
(Ophthalmologist)
Özel Idare Iş Hanı Kat 8
Tel: (31) 119206

Dr. Çiçek Akbaş
(Obstetrician)
Kenan Evren Bulvarı Ekim Apt.
Tel: (31) 115426

Dr. Numan Sandal
(Dentist)
Özel Idare Iş Hanı Kat 8
Tel: (31) 120581

GERMAN-SPEAKING

Dr. Fuat Kurnaz
(Gynecologist)
Anafartalar Caddesi 52/1
Tel: (31) 129849

Dr. Murat Akalın
(Pediatrician)
Akalın Apt. Kat 1
Tel: (31) 124918

Dr. Cemil Cabir
(Eye, Ear and Nose Specialist)
Ali Çetinkaya Caddesi 485 Sokak
Tel: (31) 120619

FRENCH-SPEAKING

Dr. Halil Akkoyun
(Obstetrician)
Doğu Garajı Karşısı
Tel: (31) 124442

Dr. Erhan Ildız
(Obstetrician)
Akdeniz Caddesi
Tel: (31) 113306 /115976

GETTING AROUND

MAPS

General maps of Turkey can be obtained free of charge from the various Tourism Information Bureaus along the Turkish Coast. Detailed regional, provincial and city maps are available at most booksellers.

FROM THE AIRPORT

Taxis are readily available at all airports 24 hours during the summers. Most car rental services have offices at the major airports along the coast and in Istanbul. Regular shuttle buses also operate at Istanbul Atatürk Airport, Izmir Adnan Menderes Airport, Antalya and Adana Airports to the main Turkish Airlines ticket offices in the cities which are usually not more than a half hour's drive away. They also carry passengers for a small fee. A regular service bus operates from Dalaman Airport to Marmaris, two hours away.

WATER TRANSPORT

The **Turkish Maritime Lines (Türkiye Deniz Yolları)** operates a regular passenger line service to the Turkish Aegean and Mediterranean from Istanbul with stops at major ports and resorts. They provide first-class accommodations and service and excellent opportunities for sightseeing. All boats depart from Sirkeci, Eminönü or Karaköy, and it is advisable to make early reservations for touristic cruises.

One of the best and cheapest ways to reach Izmir from Istanbul is a combination boat and train trip: Passenger boats leave from Sirkeci daily to Bandırma, a pleasant town on the Asian shores of the Sea of Marmara, and train departs from there to Basmane Station in Izmir. The trip takes about 10 hours and costs less than $10.

ÇANAKKALE CAR FERRY SERVICE

Regular passenger and car ferryboats operate on the Dardanelles every hour between Çanakkale on the Asian side separately to Eceabat, and Kilitbahir on the European side. Ferryboats on the Gelibolu-Lapseki line operate every two hours. Daily ferryboats also operate to the Turkish Aegean island of Gökçeada (Imroz) from Çanakkale and Kabatepe on the Gallipoli Peninsula. The Turkish Aegean island of Bozcaada (Tenedos) can be reached by daily ferryboats from Odun Iskelesi south west of Çanakkale. As both Gökçeada and Bozcaada are in military zones, foreign nationals need to get permission from the provincial authorities in Çanakkale (Vilayet Binası) to go to the islands.

IZMIR FERRY

Istanbul-Izmir: Departing Fridays 3 p.m. all year round. Summer time only on Mondays and Wednesdays at 2 p.m.

MEDITERRANEAN AND AEGEAN CRUISE

A 10-day to two-week cruise with stops in Dikili, Izmir, Kuşadası, Bodrum, Marmaris, Fethiye, Antalya, Alanya, Mersin and Iskenderun departs Wednesdays from Istanbul at 2 p.m. May 27-September 16.

PASSENGER FERRIES

Apart from the numerous cruises by Turkish Maritime Lines in the Mediterranean, several foreign shipping companies have regular boat services to the ports of Istanbul, Izmir, Kuşadası and Bodrum.

CAR FERRIES

Turkish Maritime Lines sails the Venice-Izmir-Istanbul route every 15 days April 4-June 13; a weekly service operates June 20-September 30. Venice-Izmir leaves Saturdays at 9:30 p.m. Ferryboats operate between Mersin and Magosa (Famagusta in the Turkish Republic of Northern Cyprus) three times a week year round. A private company operates ferryboats regularly between Taşucu and Girne (Kyrenia) in Northern Cyprus.

FERRY LINES BETWEEN TURKEY AND GREECE

Ayvalık-Lesbos: April through October daily boat service except Sundays. Price $15 adult one-way; $25 two-ways on same day; $15 motorcycles; $120 caravans. Crossing: two hours.

Bodrum-Cos: Daily service in summer. Price $10 adult one way; $15 return same day; $25 return open date; $15 motorcycles; vehicles $40 up to 1,650 pounds (750 kg); $60 up to 2,200 pounds (1,000 kg); $80 up to 2,750 pounds (1,250 kg); and $100 for caravans. Crossing: one and a half hours.

Marmaris-Rhodes: Daily service in the summer. Price: $20 adult one way; $50 motorcycles; $65 cars; $100 minibus; $150 caravan. Crossing: three and a half hours.

TURKISH MARITIME LINES OFFICES

Ankara:
Sakarya Caddesi
Inkilap Sokak 4, Kızılay
Tel: (4) 1331273
Telex: 423323

Istanbul:
Rıhtım Caddesi, Karaköy
Tel: (1) 1440427/1499222
Telex: 22339

Izmir:
Yeniliman, Alsancak
Tel: (51) 210094/210077
Telex: 52247

AIR TRANSPORT

TURKISH AIRLINES RESERVATION OFFICES

Adana
Stadyum Caddesi 1
Tel: (71) 143143

Ankara
Hipodrom Caddesi Gar Yanı
Tel: (4) 3124900/3124943

Antalya
Hastane Caddesi. Özel Idare Iş Hanı
Tel: 112830/123432

Dalaman
Hava Limanı
Tel: (6119) 1899

Istanbul
Şişhane Terminal
Tel: (1) 1454208

Izmir
Büyük Efes Oteli Altı
Tel: (51) 141220/135121

Marmaris
Atatürk Caddesi 6 30/B
Tel: (612) 13751/13752

Mersin
Belediye Uluçarşı 22
Tel: (741) 152232

OTHER DOMESTIC AIRLINES RESERVATION OFFICES

ISTANBUL AIRLINES
Istanbul
Incirli Caddesi 50 Daire 4
Bakırköy
Tel: (1) 5831641 (8 lines)
Atatürk Airport,
Domestic Flights Terminal,
Tel: (1) 5734093/5732920 Ext. 734

IMSIK AIRLINES
Istanbul
Atatürk Airport
Domestic Flights Terminal
Tel: (1) 5745818

Izmir
Adnan Menderes Airport
Tel: (51) 513363

Bodrum
Imsık Airport
Tel: (6141) 2189/1763

PRIVATE TRANSPORT

Driving within Turkey requires the utmost alertness of the driver at all times. Winding coastal roads, while breathtakingly scenic, can be dangerous.

Numerous car rental agencies, such as Avis, Hertz, Europcar, Budget and Airtour have offices in major cities and resort towns on the Turkish Coast. Renting a car costs about twice as much in Turkey than it does in Europe and the U.S. Jeeps as well as chauffeur-driven cars and limousines can also be rented.

CAR RENTAL SERVICES

AVIS OFFICES

Adana
Ziya Paşa Bulvarı 11/B
Tel: (71) 133045/134824/150476
Telex: 62854
Adana Airport
Tel: (71) 157830 Ext. 302
(71) 157850 Ext. 302
Telex: 62854

Alanya
Hükümet Caddesi 135
Tel: (323) 13513/14990
Telex: 56590

Ankara
Tunus Caddesi 68/2
Kavaklıdere
Tel: (4) 1672313
Telex: 46080
Esenboğa Airport
Tel: (4) 3121633
Domestic Flights Terminal
Tel: (4) 3122820 Ext. 570
International Flights Terminal
Tel: (4) 3122820 Ext. 670
Hilton Hotel
Tel: (4) 1260403
Telex: 46080

Antalya
Fevzi Çakmak Cad. Talya Apt. Altı 2B
Tel: (31) 116693/119483
Telex: 56056
Antalya Airport
Tel: (31) 217780 Ext. 364

Ayvalık
Sarımsaklı,
Kahramanlar Mahalesi
Meydan Sitesi 6
Tel: (663) 41273
Telex: 53588

Bodrum
Neyzen Tevfik Caddesi 80
Tel: (6141) 2333/1996
Telex: 50209

Çeşme
Kervansaray Motel
Tel: (549) 27029
Telex: 51903

Dalaman Airport
Tel: (6119) 1588
Telex: 51201

Denizli
Atatürk Bulvarı, Gazi Ilkokulu Arkası
Tel: (621) 44059
Telex: 53588
Pamukkale
Durak Souvenir
Tel: (6218) 1169.

Fethiye
Atatürk Caddesi 18/B
Kordon
Tel: (6151) 6076
Telex: 50802
Hotel Club Letoonia
Tel: (6151) 4967/3331.

Iskenderun
Hemden Seyahat Acentesi
Ziya Gökalp Caddesi
Divan Han 3/3
Tel: (881) 30344

Istanbul
Atatürk Airport
Tel (1) 5731452, 5734660, 5736445/
5744403
Telex: 28561
Cihangir
Avis Otoparkı
Tel: (1) 1454272, 1513911/1511313
Telex: 38144
Divan Hotel
Tel: (1) 1465256
Telex: 38144

Hilton Hotel
Tel: (1) 1487752
Telex: 38144
Kadıköy
Bağdat Caddesi
Alageyik Sokak 196/4
Selamiçeşme
Tel: (1) 3553665/3504878
Sultanahmet
Seventour Alemdar Caddesi 2/C
Tel: (1) 5126953
Telex: 38144
Taksim
Yedikuyular Caddesi 4/A
Elmadağ
Tel: (1) 1417896/1412917

Izmir
Şehit Nevresbey Bulvarı 19/A
Alsancak
Tel: (51) 211226/216139
Telex: 53588
Adnan Menderes Airport
Tel: (51) 511211/511839
Telex: 51195

Kaş
Andifli Seyahat Acentesi
Tel: (3226) 1978
Telex: 56586

Kemer
Liman Caddesi Park Yeri Karşısı
Tel: (3214) 1372
Telex: 56056
Iberotel Art
Tel: (3214) 2611
Telex: 56056
Ramada Resort
Tel: (3214) 3257
Telex: 56056
Robinson Cub Çamyuva
Tel: (3214) 1510
Telex: 56056

Kuşadası
Atatürk Bulvarı 26/B
Tel: (636) 11475/14600
Telex: 58567

Marmaris
Atatürk Caddesi 30
Tel: (612) 14607/12638
Telex: 50599

Mersin
Sahil Yolu
Nail Göksu Iş Hanı 75
Tel: (741) 23450/24813

Side
Yalı Mahalesi
Cağdaş Pansiyon Yanı
Tel: (3213) 1348
Telex: 56471
Otel Asteria
Tel: (3213) 1830
Telex: 56471
Novotel Turquoise
Tel: (3211) 4721
Telex: 56471
Robinson Club Pamfilya
Tel: (3211) 4702
Telex: 56471
Termessos Turizm
Tel: (3213) 1633
Telex: 56471

BUDGET RENT A CAR OFFICES

Head Office
Tepebaşı Katlı Otoparkı
Beyoğlu 80050 Istanbul
Tel: (1)1450766/1495714/1491308/
1519884
Fax: (1) 1491514
Telex: 25908

Other Istanbul Offices
Taksim
Inönü Caddesi Kunt Apt. 33/1
Gümüşsuyu
Tel: (1) 1523444/1526749
Atatürk Airport, Int. Arrivals Terminal
Tel: (1) 5741635/5746010/5732920
Ext. 3459

Adana
Gazipaşa Bulvarı 40
Tel: (71) 170754 /175462
Telex: 62906

Alanya
Keykubat Caddesi 63/B
Tel: (3231) 17382/19088, Telex: 56512

Ankara
Esenboğa Airport
Domestic Arrivals Terminal
Tel: (4) 3245028/3122820 Ext. 730

Antalya
Orgeneral Kenan Evren Bulvarı
Içli Apt. 70
Tel: (31) 126220/176235/126372
Fax: (31) 125046
Telex: 56085
Fevzi Çakmak Caddesi 57
Tel: (31) 113845, 113629
Telex: 56195 or 56007
Antalya Airport
Tel: (31) 217780 Ext. 368

Bodrum
Tepecik Mahalesi
Neyzen Tevfik Caddesi 86/A
Tel: (6141) 3078
Telex: 50185

Dalaman Airport
Tel: (6119) 1961/1291
Telex: 51285

Izmir
Gaziosmanpaşa Bulvarı 1/1E
Tel: (51) 258012/258013
Fax: (51) 252674
Telex: 53741
Adnan Menderes Airport
Arrivals Terminal
Tel: (51) 513086/512626 Ext. 1015
Telex: 53764

Kemer
Yat Limanı Inişi Hakkı Saygan Sitesi
Tel: (3214) 2809/2129
Telex: 56475
Club Salima Kemer
Kızıltepe Mevkii
Tel: (3214) 1521 and 1524 Ext. Budget
Club Salima Beldibi
Kemer Beldibi Mevkii
Tel: (3184) 8361

Kuşadası
Inönü Bulvarı
Üyücü Apt. 5
Tel: (636) 14956/14962
Telex: 58635

Marmaris
Atatürk Caddesi
Taşarkası Sokak 12
Tel: (612) 14144, 15774/15024
Telex: 50535

WHERE TO STAY

HOTELS AND RESORTS IN NORTHERN AEGEAN

The following is a list of hotels and resorts rated in terms of their excellence to a star rating (indicated by the number of asterisks) which the prospective lodger might find helpful. Hotels without asterisks are operated under a municipal licence. The Turkish Coast is broken down to regions and cities, and hotels are listed alphabetically.

AYVACIK

Behram Oteli
Behram Kale Köyü
Tel. (1969) 12753

ÇANAKKALE

Anafartalar Oteli **
Kayserili A. Paşa Caddesi
Tel: (1961) 4455

Emre Family Pension
Güzelyalı Köyü
Tel: (1961) 28017

Grand Truva Hotel **
Yalıboyu Caddesi
Tel: (1961) 1024
Fax: (1961) 1886
Telex: 58280

Tusan Oteli Intepe **
P.K. 8 Intepe
Tel: (1961) 1461
Telex: 58280

EDIRNE

Balta Hotel **
Talatpaşa Caddesi 97
Tel: (181) 15210
Fax: (187) 13529
Telex: 37187

Kervan Oteli *
Talatpaşa Caddesi 134
Tel: (181) 11382

Park Oteli **
Maarif Caddesi
Tel: (181) 14610

Sultan Oteli *
Talatpaşa Caddesi
Tel: (181) 11372

GELIBOLU

Abide Oteli
Morto Körfezi, Seddülbahir
Tel: (1891) 1429 Ext. Abide Hotel

Boncuk Otel **
Sütlüce Kale Köyü
Tel: (1891) 1461. Ask operator for
Boncuk Hotel

KEŞAN

Yener Hotel ***
Demirciler Caddesi 18
Tel: (184) 13660

HOTELS AND RESORTS IN SOUTHERN AEGEAN

AYVALIK

Çam Motel **
Orta Çamlık 12
Tel: (663) 11515

Group Hotels ***
Sarımsaklı Mevkii
Tel: (663) 12311/41045/41046
Fax: (663) 41194
Telex: 52817

Küçük Başkent Motel
Sarımsaklı Plajı
Tel: (663) 41116

Murat Reis Oteli **
Altın Kum Mevkii
Küçükköy
Tel: (663) 41456
Telex: 53939

Sevo Motel *
Sarımsaklı
Tel: (663) 41166
Telex: 52817

BERGAMA

Tusan Bergama Moteli
Bergama-Izmir Yolu
Çatı Mevkii
Tel: (541) 1173

BODRUM

Aksu Oteli ***
Cumhuriyet Caddesi 155
Tel: (6141) 4418/4419
Fax: (6141) 1833
Telex: 50254

Artemis Pansiyon
Cumhuriyet Caddesi 117
Tel: (6141) 2530

Atrium Otel ***
Fabrika Sokak 21
Tel: (6141) 2181

Ayaz Hotel
Gümbet Mevkii
Tel: (6141) 1174/3504

Bodrum Hotel
Neyzen Tevfik Caddesi 2/1
Tel: (6141) 2269/2270/2347.
Telex: 50125

Club Kadıkale
Kadıkalesi, Turgutreis
Tel: (6142) 1271/1821/1891
Fax: (6142) 1272

Club M Holiday
Village and Hotel *****
Değirmendere Mevkii
Tel: (6141) 2581

Manastır Hotel ***
Barış Sitesi
Kumlubahçe Mahalesi
Tel: (6141) 2854/2858/2775/2776
Fax: (6141) 2772
Telex: 50143

Park Palas Oteli
Gümbet Mevkii
Tel: (6141) 1504 and 2294

Sami Beach Hotel ***
Gümbet Mevkii
Tel: (6141) 1048/1848/1662/2837
Fax: 2838
Telex: 53757, 50100, 50140

TMT Holiday Village
Akçabük Mevkii
Tel: (6141) 1222/3004/, 1207/8 and 1232
Telex: 52504

Milta Torba Holiday Village
Torba
Tel: (6141) 2343
Fax: (6141) 2351
Telex: 52585

BURHANIYE

Urut Hotel **
Hürriyet Meydanı 14
Tel: (6731) 1105
Telex: 58336

ÇEŞME

Altınyunus Holiday Village
Boyalık Mevkii
Tel: (549) 31250
Telex: 53868

Boyalık Beach Hotel ****
Boyalık Mevkii
Tel: (549) 27081, 27341/27352
Fax: (549) 27331

Inkim Oteli ***
Yaykın Mevkii
PTT Karşısı
Tel: (549) 33900
Telex: 51922

Kanuni Kervansaray Oteli
Tel: (549) 26490
Telex: 53868

Turban Çeşme Oteli ****
Ilıca Mevkii
Tel: (549) 31240
Fax: (549) 31388
Telex: 51901

Turban Ilıca Oteli **
Dereboyu Mevkii Boyalık
Tel: (549) 32128

DATÇA

Perili Köşk
Tel: (6145) 44027

Hotel Club Dorya ***
Esenada
Tel: (6145) 1614/1593/1303

DENIZLI

Altuntur Ticaret Odası Oteli **
Oğuzhan Caddesi 1
Tel: (621) 16176/16693
Fax: (621) 36713
Telex: 59560

DIKILI

Perla Hotel
Şehit Sami Akbulut Caddesi 97
Tel: (5419) 1145

DIDIM

Didima Hotel *****
Akbük
Yenihisar Kasabası
Tel: (6351) 3290

Hergül Otel **
Altın Kum
Tel: 1175

May Hotel *****
Akbük
Yenihisar Kasabası
Tel: (6351) 4077
Telex: 46616

FOÇA

Club Méditerranée Foça Holiday Village
Tel: (5431) 1607/2176/1147

Fax: (5431) 2175
Telex: 53909

Hanedan Oteli **
Büyükdeniz Sahil Caddesi
Tel: (5431) 1515

IZMIR

Anba Hotel ***
Cumhuriyet Bulvarı 124
Tel: (51) 144380
Telex: 53711

Balçova Termal Motel
Ilıca Mevkii
Tel: (51) 159442

Billur Hotel ***
Anafartalar Caddesi 783
Tel: (51) 136250/139732
Telex: 53252

Büyük Efes Oteli *****
Gaziosmanpaşa Bulvarı 1
Tel: (51) 144300
Fax: (51) 258695
Telex: 52341

Hisar Hotel ***
Fevzipaşa Bulvarı
Tel: (51) 145400
Fax: (51) 258830
Telex: 51102

Izmirim Hotel ***
Gaziler Caddesi 284
Yenişehir
Tel: (51) 330207/336751
Telex: 53765

Izmir Palas Oteli ***
Vasıf Çınar Bulvarı 2
Tel: (51) 215583
Telex: 53041

Karaca Oteli ***
1379 Sokak 55
Tel: (51) 144445, 144426/191940
Fax: 131498
Telex: 53093

Kilim Oteli ***
Atatürk Bulvarı
Tel: (51) 145340
Telex: 53041

KUŞADASI	MARMARIS

KUŞADASI

Akdeniz Oteli ***
Karaova Mevkii
Tel: (636) 16971
Telex: 58552

Efe Oteli ***
Güvercin Ada Caddesi
Tel: (636) 13660
Telex: 13660

Fantasia Hotel *****
P.O. Box 134
Tel: (636) 18600, 18550
Fax: (636) 12765
Telex: 58610

Imbat Oteli ****
Kadınlar Plajı
Tel: (636) 12000
Fax: (636) 14960
Telex: 58582

Kısmet Oteli ***
Akyarlar Mevkii
Tel: (636) 12005
Telex: 58556 and 58459

Martı Hotel ***
Kadınlar Plajı
Tel: (636) 13650
Fax: (636) 14700
Telex: 58548

Onur Hotel *****
Yavansu Mevkii
Tel: (636) 13727/12213
Fax: (636) 13727
Telex: 58644

Özçelik Hotel ***
Atatürk Bulvarı, Yat Limanı Karşısı
Tel: (636) 14490
Fax: (636) 14505
Telex: 58569

Tusan Hotel Kuşadası ***
31'ler Plajı Mevkii
Tel: (636) 14495
Fax: (636) 14498
Telex: 58540

MARMARIS

Altın Yunus Hotel *****
Pamucak Mevkii
Tel: (612) 13617
Fax: (612) 11214
Telex: 50601

Hawaii Oteli ***
Çıldır Mevkii
Tel: (612) 14003

Iber Oteli ***
Içmeler,
Pamucak
Tel: (612) 16377
Telex: 50541

Lidya Oteli ***
Siteler Mahalesi 130
Tel: (612) 12940
Telex: 53896/52540

Marbas Oteli ***
Içmeler Köyü
Tel: (6125) 1058/1043/1069
Telex: 50503

Martı Holiday Village
Içmeler
Tel: (6125) 1440
Fax: (6125) 1448
Telex: 50553

Munamar Hotel ****
Içmeler
Tel: (6125) 1360
Fax: (6125) 1359
Telex: 50607

Turban Marmaris Holiday Village
Tel: (612) 11843
Telex: 52529

Turunç Hotel ****
Turunç Köyü
Tel: (612) 14913
Fax: (612) 14917

Yavuz Oteli ***
Atatürk Caddesi 10
Tel: (612) 12937
Telex: 50500

MUĞLA

Petek Oteli
Marmaris Bulvarı
Tel: (6111) 3135

ÖREN

Efrem Motel
Tel: (5484) 1299

WESTERN MEDITERRANEAN

ALANYA

Alara Oteli ***
Yeşil Köyü
Tel: (3237) 1146/1153
Telex: 56613

Azak Hotel ***
Atatürk Caddesi
Tel: (323) 11759
Telex: 56444

Banana Oteli ***
Gazipaşa Caddesi
Tel: (323) 13595/11548/14394
Telex: 56629

Club Alantur
Dimçayı Mevkii, Çamyuva Köyü
Tel: (323) 14416
Fax: (323) 14419
Telex: 56645

Kaptan Oteli ***
Iskele Caddesi 62
Tel: (323) 14900
Fax: (323) 12000
Telex: 56675

Serapsu Hotel *****
Konaklı Köyü
Tel: (3235) 1476
Fax: (3235) 1072
Telex: 56447

Sunshine Hotel ****
Çamyolu Köyü
Tel: (3231)1241/1112

ANTALYA

Antalya Motel
Lara Yolu 84
Tel: (31) 114609
Telex: 56231

Club Hotel Sera *****
Lara Mevkii
Tel: (31) 123170
Fax: (31) 131279
Telex: 56070

Dedeman Hotel Antalya *****
Lara Yolu
Tel: (31) 217910
Fax: (31) 124500
Telex: 56047

Doğa Pansiyon
Selçuk Mahalesi
Iskele Caddesi 15
Kaleiçi
Tel: (31) 113946

Hotel Marina
Kaleiçi
Mermerli Sokak 15
Tel: (31) 175490
Fax: (31) 111765

Lara Oteli ***
Lara Yolu, P.O. Box 404
Tel: (31) 190142
Telex: 56231/56048

Sheraton Voyager Hotel *****
Konyaaltı Mevkii
Tel: (31) 182182
Fax: (31) 318995
Telex: 56288

Start Oteli
Aliçetin Kaya Caddesi 19
Tel: (31) 211200
Fax: (31) 211211
Telex: 56062

Steigenberger Falez Hotel *****
Konyaaltı Plajı Mevkii
P.K. 808 Antalya
Tel: (31) 185000
Fax: (31) 1311181
Telex: 56081

Talya Oteli *****
Fevzi Çakmak Caddesi
Tel: (31) 115600
Telex: 56111

Turban Adalya Oteli ****
Kaleiçi Yat Limanı
Tel: (31) 118066

DEMRE

Club Datça Holiday
Iskele Mahalesi
Tel: 1170

FETHIYE

Club Hotel Aries
Çalış Plajı
Tel: (615) 16850
Fax: (615) 14059

Club Méditerranée Hotel Club Letoonia
Paçaraz Burnu
Tel: (615) 14966
Tel: (615) 14222
Telex: 50832

Hotel Likya *
Yat Limanı Karşısı
Tel: (615) 11169/11690
Telex: 53948

Hotel Pırlanta
Birinci Karagözler Mahalesi
Tel: (615) 14959
Fax: (615) 11686

Meri Hotel **
Ölüdeniz
Tel: (615) 14444/16060
Fax: (615) 11482
Telex: 53948

FINIKE

Baykal Motel Pension
Tel: (3225) 1774

KALKAN

Pirat Hotel ***
Tel: (3215) 1178
Telex: 56527

KAŞ

Ekici Hotel ***
Tel: (3226) 1417, 1823
Fax: (3226) 1823
Telex: 56529

Mimosa Hotel **
Tel: (3226) 1272/1472/1990
Fax: (3226) 1368
Telex: 56530

KEMER

Alda Club Holiday Village
Beldibi
Tel: (3184) 3214/8151
Fax: (3184) 8159

Aldiana Holiday Village
Kızıltepe Mevkii
Tel: (3214) 2230

Art World Hotel *****
Kızıltepe Mevkii
Tel: (3214) 2611
Telex: 56570

Club Méditerranée Kemer Holiday Village
Tel: (3214) 1510/1009
Fax: (3214) 1018
Telex: 56689

Club Méditerranée Palmiye Holiday Village
Tel: (3214) 2890
Fax: (3214) 1296
Telex: 56615

Club Robinson Çamyuva
Tel: (3214) 1510
Fax: (3214) 1518
Telex: 56698

Eldorado Holiday Village
Tel: (3214) 2993/2997
Telex: 56623

Kiriş World Hotel *****
Tel: (3214) 1896

Otem Hotel ****
Yat Limanı Karşısı
Tel: (3214) 3181
Telex: 56543

Phaselis Princes Hotel *****
Tel: (3214) 2079
Fax: (3214) 2079
Telex: 56460

Ramada Resort Hotel *****
P.O. Box 654
Beldibi Mevkii
Tel: (3214) 3254
Telex: 53643

KÖYCEGIZ

Kaunos Hotel
Cengiz Topel Caddesi 37
Tel: (6114) 1288/1835

Özay Hotel
Tel: (6114) 1300/1361
Telex: 50024

SIDE

Asteria Hotel *****
Tel: (3213) 1830
Fax: (3211) 1830
Telex: 56584

Iberotel Side Palace *****
Sorgun, Manavgat
Tel: (3211) 4715
Fax: (3211) 4714
Telex: 56495

Le Meridien Hotel ****
P.O. Box 25
Tel: (3211) 4830
Fax: (3211) 1967
Telex: 56515

Novotel Turquoise Side *****
Manavgat, Sorgun Acusu Mevkii
Tel: (3211) 4722
Fax: (3211) 4721
Telex: 56515

Robinson Club Pamfilya
Sorgun
Tel: (3211) 4700
Fax: (3211) 4708
Telex: 56586

Turtel Side Holiday Village
Selimiye Köyü
Tel: (3213) 1002/1093

Fax: (3211) 2226
Telex: 56596/56683

EASTERN MEDITERRANEAN

ANAMUR

Anahan Oteli **
Tahsin Soylu Caddesi 109
Tel: (7571) 3511/1045

ANTAKYA

Büyük Antakya Hotel ****
Atatürk Caddesi 8
Tel: (891) 13426
Telex: 66632

ISKENDERUN

Hataylı Hotel ***
Osmangazi Caddesi 2
Tel: (881) 11551
Telex: 68138

Arsuz Hotel
Arsuz
Tel: (881) 21782
Telex: 68676

KIZKALESI

Club Barbarossa
Tel: (7584) 1089/1090/1364/1366
Fax: (7584) 1090
Telex: 67752

MERSIN

Atlıhan Hotel ****
Istiklal Caddesi 168
Tel: (741) 24153
Fax: (741) 17618
Telex: 67374

Mersin Hotel ****
Gümrük Meydanı, P.O. Box 264
Tel: (741) 21640
Fax: (741) 12625
Telex: 67180

CAMPSITES

ADANA

Raşit Ener Kampı
Iskenderun Yolu Üzeri
Girne Bulvarı
Tel: (71) 212758

ALANYA

Alanya Kamping
Avsallar Köyü
Alanya
Tel: (3231) 1488

Kervansaray Mokamp
Alanya 110 Km
Tel: (3231) 5259

BODRUM

Ayaz Kampı
Gümbet
Tel: (6141) 1174/2956

DATÇA

Aktur Kamping Tatil Sitesi
Emecik Köyü
Tel: (6146) 1164

EDIRNE

**Kervansaray Ayşe
Kadın Mokamp**
Tel: (181) 11290

Fifi Mokamp
Demirkapı Mevkii
E-5 Highway
Tel: (181) 11554
Telex: 37217

FETHIYE

Deniz Kamping
Ölüdeniz
Tel: (6156) 6012/6008
Fax: (615) 12921
Telex: 52820

GÜMÜLDÜR

Denizatı Kamping
Tel: (5463) 19366

IZMIR

Kervansaray Inciralti Mokamp
Balçova
Tel: (51) 154760

KEMER

Turban Kızıltepe Kamping
Tel: (3214) 1113

KIZKALESI

Kervansaray Kızkalesi Mokamp
P.O. Box 7
Erdemli
Tel: (7585) 1221

KUŞADASI

Kervansaray Mokamp
Izmir-Kuşadası Yolu
Tel: (636) 11106
Telex: 58551

MARMARIS

Amazon Kamp
Tel: (612) 11682

ÖREN

Altın Kamp
Tel: (54841) 2432

URLA

U Kampı
Çeşme altı
Tel: (5444) 21

FOOD DIGEST

WHERE TO EAT

ANTALYA

Hisar Restaurant
Kaleiçi
Tel: (31) 115281

Kral Sofrası
Liman
Tel: (31) 126736

Orkinos Restaurant
Liman
Tel: (31) 111641

Yedi Mehmet Restaurant
Konyaaltı Beach
Tel: (31) 111641

Yörükoğlu Restaurant
İnönü Parkı
Tel: (31) 111641

BODRUM

Ahtapot Restaurant
Uslu Çıkmazı
Tel: (6141) 3143

Amphora Restaurant
Neyzen Tevfik Caddesi 14
Tel: (6141) 2368

Balık Restaurant
Yeni Çarşı No 28

Çavuş'un Yeri Restaurant
Geriş Yalısı
Yalıkavak

Chinese Restaurant
Neyzen Tevfik Caddesi 220
Tel: (6141) 3136

Dolphin Restaurant
Hilmi Hisan Meydanı
Uslu Pasajı
Tel: (6141) 3143

Gemibaşı Restaurant
Neyzen Tevfik Caddesi 168

Gözegir Indian Food Restaurant
Cumhuriyet Caddesi
Tel: (6141) 2541/3737

Han Restoran
Kale Sokak

Italian Restaurant
Neyzen Tevfik Caddesi
Yalı Çıkmazı
Tel: (6141) 3241

Meryemana Restaurant
Neyzen Tevfik Caddesi

Mausolos Restaurant
Neyzen Tevfik Caddesi 10
Tel: (6141) 4176

Mindos Restaurant
(Cumhur'un Yeri)
Gümüşlük

Teras Restaurant
Gümüşlük

ÇEŞME

Körfez Restaurant
Tel: (5492) 66718

Liman Restaurant
Tel: (5492) 67011

FETHIYE

Chinese Restaurant
Yat Limanı Karşısı

Pizza 74
Atatürk Caddesi

Rafet Restaurant
Kordonboyu
Tel: (615) 11106/111721/12676

Yacht Restaurant
Yat Limanı Karşısı

MARMARIS

Birtat Restaurant
Yat Limanı
Tel: (612) 11076

Chez-Amos Restaurant
Musayeri Sokak
Kaptanoğlu Sitesi
1st Floor
İçmeler
Tel: (6125) 1021

Chez Zühal
Barbaros Caddesi 23/A
Tel: (612) 16720

Papila
Barbaros Caddesi 35

Pronto Pizza
Kemeraltı Mahalesi
Kemal Ilgaz Sokak 22/23
Tel: (612) 16920

Yakamoz
Barbaros Caddesi 47
Tel: (612) 15160

Yellow Rose Restaurant Bar
İçmeler
Tel: (6125) 1383

Yüksel Restaurant
Atatürk Caddesi 26
Tel: (612) 14395

THINGS TO DO

YACHTING

Arranging a Blue Voyage: Many European and some American travel agencies specializing in trips to Turkey organize yachting holidays to the Turquoise Coast – the area from Bodrum to Antalya. However, chartering through a local agency in Bodrum, Marmaris, Fethiye and Antalya not only cuts down costs but also enables a wider selection of yachts and fares. These agencies also arrange transfers from airport to hotels in Turkey. Any travel agent in Bodrum or Marmaris can make reservations for a Blue Voyage, a cruise along the Turquoise Coast. As a rule, one third to half of the boat's charge is taken in advance, at the time of reservation. If you are already on the Turquoise Coast, you can bypass the agency and rent a yacht yourself. This is even cheaper, but you must be sure of what you are choosing.

BODRUM CUP

If you wish to cruise in a *gulet*, you must consider participating in the Bodrum Cup, a regatta held at the Gulf of Gökova. In 1990, the Cup will be held October 20-27. This is not only a race in which you can crew, but it is also a chance to get acquainted with Turkish wooden-framed yachts and Turkey's magnificent sailing grounds. The program for 1990 includes stops in Gökova, Knidos, Datça, Bencik, Serçe and Ekincik; a sampling of anchorages as good as any express tour allows. For reservations, contact Era Yachting in Bodrum.

Major bareboat agencies are usually connected with foreign agencies and are mostly sold out in the summer. So, do not leave it to chance, and reserve early.

RENTAL PRICES

Bareboat prices change according to the size of the yacht and the season. In March or November, a 47-foot (14-meter) *Sun Kiss 47* is priced at $1,200 to $1,500 per week. The highest price is in July or August, when a one-week rental of the same nine-berth yacht is $2,400-$2,700. A small, 26-foot (eight-meter), four-passenger *Gib Sea 27* in March or November costs $400-450 per week and in July and August the same boat costs $1,000.

Bodrum-built *gulets* (the name derives from the French *goelette*, meaning schooner) are priced on a per diem basis. A 39-48 foot (12-15 meter) boat with two or three cabins sells for around $225-275 a day in May and October. In July, prices soar to $300 and in August climb to $400. A more luxurious 63-66 foot (19-20 meter) *gulet* can be rented for $600-800 a day in August or as low as $300 in October. Maximum-size luxury yachts over 66 feet (20 meters) go for as high as $1,250-$1,300 in August and $600-800 in the lower season.

QUAYSIDE BARGAINING

Just call any travel agency in Bodrum or Marmaris to find out about prices. During the low season quayside bargaining can lower prices by as much as half. Certain agencies market the Blue Voyage on a per cabin basis as well. That means if you can't find enough friends to share a boat, you can join a number of strangers on the same boat. You will have your own cabin, most probably with a bathroom. The passengers eat together and conform to the program of the boat. Depending on which season one takes the one-week Blue Voyage, it would cost $275 to $400 per person.

FLOTILLA CRUISE

Though it somewhat dampens the sense of adventure and individuality that is the essence of being at sea, a middle-of-the-road solution for those who want to steer their own ship but lack the skill and/or the courage to go it alone is chartering a bareboat in a "flotilla cruise." In a flotilla cruise, three to 12 yachts will form a group, headed by a guide who leads the way and attempts to solve problems, ranging from broken transmission gear to bee stings, as they come up. Turkish bareboat operators favor French-made yachts. The majority of the fleet consists of Jeanneaus and Benettaux with occasional Moodys and a few German and Scandinavian models. The yachts are fairly new and kept in above average condition. The better known companies change the bulk of their yachts every five years or so.

BAREBOAT CRUISE

For all practical purposes, a bareboat is the charterer's own yacht, a vehicle of freedom. The boat is easy to sail shorthanded. Inside, it is apt to be cozy and comfortable. One does not have to contend with a crew, who, no matter how friendly, is a stranger. A bareboat leaves the charterer free to explore and experiment, and match skills against the elements.

ALL ABOUT GULETS

Yachts are classified according to their rigs in the tradition of seamanship: schooners, sloops, ketches and others. A *gulet* was actually a schooner with a rounded stern. Turkish yachting agencies applied the term to any boat whose rounded rump resembled a *gulet*. In the last few years, owners began building yachts with transom sterns, *aynakıç* (mirror ass), which gave them more room below decks to squeeze more cabins into. The term *gulet* then expanded to describe yachts of any shape, except the smaller, double-ended triandils. A *gulet* in the strict sense is considered superior to the *aynakıç* because it has to have more overall length per cabin. Secondly – and perhaps this is the most important – in the farthest astern of the deck, there is a small aftcastle embellished with soft mattresses and cushions in the shade of the awnings, known as a "pigeon nest." To many connoisseurs, the essence of a Blue Voyage is enjoying the journey lying on the pigeon's nest. Since almost all meals are taken in the open air, too, a *gulet's* wide deckspace is a welcome comfort.

CHARTERING WITH CREW

Wooden charter yachts with crew vary in size from 33 feet (10 meters) to 83 feet (25 meters). They have from a single to eight, even ten, double cabins, sometimes with upper bunks. The interiors are generally decorated with massive wood and make a pleasant bedroom. Lockers and drawers solve the problem of storage in the cabins. Lighting is usually natural with sunlight flowing in from the portholes. A proper wooden yacht carries no less than 2.5 tons of freshwater, at least five times more than a bareboat.That means the voyagers can often have two showers a day – a blessing in hot weather and salty seas – virtually impossible to have on a bareboat. Heated pressurized water is almost a standard item on *gulets*.

Crews, according to the size of the boat, vary from two to four. They do all the work, including preparing the meals. However, many captains are willing to allow an eager guest to play with the ropes and lines, steer the boat or enter the galley and mess it up in the name of cooking a "special."

Pastimes in an anchored *gulet* include skin diving, fishing, windsurfing, rowing, or motoring in a dinghy; at additional cost possibly water skiing or waterbiking – though the agency should be well forewarned to provide these. A *tavla* (backgammon) tournament is a must on a *gulet*. Consumption of food and beverages increases by half during a Blue Voyage, but with hardly any effect on dieting ladies.

Blue Voyagers must hike. Taking to the densely vegetated hilltops to discover invariably some ruin in every anchorage is a joy. The backdrop of an embroidered coastline, the azure sea, the clear blue sky, make it a perfect setting for photography. Afterwards, it is possible to lie in the back of the *gulet*, eating sandwiches and drinking tea from tulip-shaped glasses. The Blue Voyage is the ultimate experience in relaxation that the visitor to the Turkish Coast should take at least once.

YACHT CHARTERING

The following travel agencies specialize in yacht chartering on the Turkish Coast. The single asterisk denotes that the company is a major bareboat agency:

ANTALYA

Akay Turizm Seyahat Acentesi
Cumhuriyet Caddesi 52
Tel: (31) 112747/119847/125990
Telex: 56033

**AK-HA Turizm
ve Seyahat Acentesi**
Orgeneral Kenan Evren Bulvarı
Sıtkı Göksoy Apt. No. 40 Kat 1
Tel: (31) 111120/117770
Telex: 56011

Pamfilya Tourism Seyahat Acentesi
30 Ağustos Caddesi
Işıklar Göksoy Apt. 577B
Tel: (31) 121401
Telex: 56133

Turban Seyahat Acentesi
Kaleiçi
Tel: (31) 123678

BODRUM

Ada Yacht
Neyzen Tevfik Caddesi 124
Tel: (6141) 2460

Admiral Tour
Neyzen Tevfik Caddesi 68
Tel: (6141) 3276

Ağantour
Dr. Alimbey Caddesi 32/2
Tel: (6141) 2962/3276

Anba Tour
Neyzen Tevfik Caddesi 212/6
Tel: (6141) 2659/6273

Bitez Yachting Ltd.
Yargı Çıkmazı 4
Tel: (6141) 2454/4588

Bodrum Tour
Neyzen Tevfik Caddesi 216
Tel: (6141) 3376

British Tour
Cevat Şakir Caddesi 19
Tel: (6141) 3140/5344

Camel Tour
Cevat Şakir Caddesi 13
Tel: (6141) 2070

Crusader Cruising
Neyzen Tevfik Caddesi 216/1
Tel: (6141) 2619

Data
Kasaphane Caddesi 30
Tel: (6141) 6642/6643

Deniz Yacht Tourism
Çarşı Mahalesi Gerence Sokak 7/1
Tel: (6141) 6001

Duru Koş Turizm
Karantina Sokak 47
Tel: (6141) 1868/2624

Duru Turizm
Atatürk Caddesi 22
Tel: (6141) 1413/6756

Ege Yacht Service *
Neyzen Tevfik Caddesi 202/B
Tel: (6141) 1517/1734

Era Turizm
Neyzen Tevfik Caddesi 4
Tel: (6141) 2310/2054

Flama Tour
Neyzen Tevfik Caddesi 154
Tel: (6141) 1842/1894

Gino Tours
Dr. Alimbey Caddesi 200/9
Tel: (6141) 2962/3276

Group Tours
Dr. Alimbey Caddesi 30/2
Tel: (6141) 2962/3276

Halikarnas Travel Agency
Yeni Çarşı 32
Tel: (6141) 2397/2035

Ibrahim Şakir "Tuyika"
Iskele Meydanı 8
Tel: (6141) 2578/1808

Karya Tour
Dr. Alimbey Caddesi 6
Tel: (6141) 5843/5844

Kültür
Neyzen Tevfik Caddesi 210
Tel: 1266/4664

Merhaba Turizm
Iskele Turizm 67
Tel: (6141) 2749/1086

Motif Turizm *
Neyzen Tevfik Caddesi
Tel: (6141) 1536/2309

Penguen Yachting
Cevat Şakir Caddesi
Kardeşler Pasajı 1/A
Tel: (6141) 1968/5060

Pupa Yachting *
Firkateyn Sokak 19
Tel: (6141) 2398/5857

Sun Yacht
Neyzen Tevfik Caddesi 186
Tel: (6141) 2445

Turquoise Tours
Atatürk Caddesi 204
Tel: (6141) 2236

Uncle Sun Yachting and Travel
Atatürk Caddesi 61/B
Tel: (6141) 2659/5501

Yacht Tours
Neyzen Tevfik Caddesi
Tepecik Mahalesi 98

Yeşil Marmaris *
Atatürk Caddesi 81
Tel: (6141) 3091/2375

FETHIYE

**ALESTA Yachting
and Travel Agency**
Across from Marina
P.O. Box 88
Tel: (6151) 1861/1610
Fax: (6151) 2571

Borina Yachting
Tel: (6151) 2550

**Likyatur Tourism
and Boat Agency**
Atatürk Caddesi 34
Tel: (6151) 1690/1749/1220
Telex: 50803

Yes Yachting
Karagökler Mahalesi
Tel: (6151) 12258

KUSADASI

UMAY Tours Travel Agency
Atatürk Bulvarı
Konuk Işhanı 38/9
Tel: (636) 17145/13611/16005
Telex: 58578

MARMARIS

Alp Turizm ve Yatçılık
Barbaros Caddesi 68
Yat Limanı
Tel: (612) 16671/14268
Fax: (612) 14592
Telex: 50587

ATC Charter Group
P.O. Box 166
Tel: (612) 13835
Fax: (612) 16550
Telex: 50536

Es-Er Yachting
Kısayalı 120
Tel: 16994
Telex: 50554

Euro-Tour Yachting Agency
Yat Limanı
Denizkıyı Sokak 25
P.K. 96
Tel: (612) 14388/16121
Telex: 52121

Gino Yatçılık
Yat Limanı
Tel: (612) 16380
Telex: (612) 16380

Med Yat
Amos Oteli
Tel: (612) 12698

Mengi Yachting
Hacı Sabri Sokak No. 7/a
Pk. 104 Marmaris
Tel: (612) 14841
Fax: (612) 14841
Telex: 50565

Setur Yatçılık*
Kordon Caddesi
Tel: (612) 12638

Tura Turizm
Atatürk Caddesi 30/c
Tel: (612) 11923/13043
Fax: (612) 14643
Telex: 50514

**Yeşil Marmaris Tourism and Yacht
Management**
Barbaros Caddesi 11
Tel. (612) 11033/12290/12291
Fax: (612) 14470
Telex: 50548

YACHT MAINTENANCE

BODRUM

Bodrum Yacht Marine
Dr. Alimbey Caddesi 58

Canel Ticaret
Uğur Canel
Cevat Caddesi 102

**Dr. Yusuf Civelekoğlu Durukos
Yacht Agents**
Karantina Caddesi
Tel: (6141) 1868/2624

**Ortoper Ihtiyaç Maddeleri Turizm ve
Yatırım Şti.**
Dr. Alimbey Caddesi 19

Ekrem Özdamar
Yeni Çarşı 24
Tel: (6141) 1766

Onan Genset Service
Mehmet Turgay
Cevat Şakir Caddesi 102
Tel: (6141) 1650

Promarine
Opposite the Marina
Tel: (6141) 2610

Tuğrul Acar
İçmeler
Tel: (6141) 1184/1754

MARMARIS

Bay Marina
Marina
Tel: (612) 11818

Escapade
Tel: (612) 13165

WATER SPORTS

In addition to yachting and sailing, windsurfing, scuba diving, sea biking, parasailing, banana boat riding are becoming extremely popular all along the Turkish Coast from Ayvalık to Silifke. Bodrum's Gümbet Beach is already renowned as one of the world's leading windsurf centers, competing with places like Maui of the Hawaiian Islands. Below is a list of Turkish companies involved in water sports along the Bodrum-Fethiye region:

BODRUM

Alpha Surf Center
Hotel Baba
Gümbet
Tel: (6141) 2307/2103

Dost Surfing School
Hotel Sami
Gümbet

Gülev Su Sporları Merkezi Ltd.
Gümbet

Windsurfing Bodrum
Dr. Alimbey Caddesi 31
Tel: (6141) 2913

MOPED RENTALS

Gümbet Market
Gümbet
Tel: (6141) 2040/6779

Mylasa Hotel
Cumhuriyet Caddesi 34
Tel: (6141) 1846/1254

Turquoise Tours
Atatürk Caddesi
No. 59
Tel: (6141)1507/3078

SCUBA DIVING

Scuba diving is becoming popular all along the Turkish Coast, where numerous sunken cities and marine life abound. But Bodrum has always been the center of Turkey's scuba diving because of its sponge divers and underwater archaeologists. Scuba diving schools exist in Bodrum, Marmaris, Fethiye and Çeşme. An authorized local diving guide must accompany foreign divers at all times. Diving is permitted in only certain areas. It is strictly forbidden to dive where there are ancient shipwrecks, which are protected by the state as national treasures. Anyone diving in these areas without a permit may land himself in jail. Local diving guides must be either **PADI** or **CMAS** certified and have a Turkish diving licence (*Balık Adamı Belgesi*). Folowing is a list of scuba diving centers.

BODRUM

Data Travel Services
Belediye Meydanı
Neyzen Tevfik Caddesi 26
Tel: (6141) 2970

Sea Co. Ltd.
Yangı Çıkmazı
Tel: (6141) 2454

Gettur
Neyzen Tevfik Caddesi 72
Tel: (6141) 2309/1535/3522

FETHIYE

Medusa Sub-Diving Center
Fevzi Çakmak Caddesi 19-B
Opposite the Marina
Tel: (6151) 2824

MARMARIS

Professional Diving Center
Tel: (612) 13512

Octopus Diving Center
Rıhtım Sokak
Akyıldız Pasajı 3
Tel: (612) 13612/15786

HUNTING

Between August and March one can hunt ibex, bear, roe deer, wolf, coyote and wild boar on the Turkish Coast.

The ibex, an agile, wild mountain goat with stupendous upturned horns, is found in Antalya in the Cevizli Gidengelmez Mountains, in the Pozantı-Karafil and Demirkazık Mountains in Adana, in Cehenemderesi around Mersin and Tarsus, and in the Mut-Mersin Kestel Mountains.

Ibex and roe deer are also found in Arsuz, in the Hatay area.

All animals must be hunted in designated hunting areas determined by the Forestry Management Department (Orman İşletme Müdürlüğü). Wild boar, wolf and coyote may be hunted all year round in specific areas.

Obtain a hunting permit (Özel Avlandırma Izin Belgesi) from a travel agency before coming to Turkey.

A fee of $50 is charged for each day of hunting. It is illegal to kill animals that one can't carry. It is also illegal to hunt by means of traps, lights or poisons.

The hunting season for henna partridges, sand partridges, sand grouses and rabbits is between October 7 and December 31.

In order to guarantee a standard level of hunting, hunters are required to be members of internationally-recognized hunting organizations.

Pamfilya Travel Agency organizes hunting tours throughout the Turkish Coast. Its offices are:

ISTANBUL

Pamfilya Inc.
Cumhuriyet Caddesi 111/3
Elmadağ
Tel: (1) 1488520/1478735

OVERSEAS OFFICES

125 Avenue Jupiter
Bte. 5, 1190
Brussels, Belgium
Tel: (02) 3475415

Osdorfer Land Str.
2000 Hamburg 55,
West Germany
Tel: (49) 040-8701485

CULTURE PLUS

The Turkish Coast is an open-air museum with the ruins of several hundred ancient Hittite, Carian, Lycian, Greek and Roman cities. And there are scores of museums, operated by the Ministry of Culture, where excavated artifacts from ancient sites are on display. Here is a series of museums, grouped by province.

NORTHERN AEGEAN

EDIRNE

The Edirne Museum
The Museum of Turkish
and Islamic Arts

ÇANAKKALE

The Morto Bay 1915 Dardanelles Campaign Museum- (under the Mehemetçik War Memorial).
Archaeological Museum
Sultaniye Castle War Museum
Kabatepe War Museum
Alçıtepe War Museum (Private)
Museum of Troy
Ruins of Troy
Ruins of Alexandria Troas
Ruins of Assos

SOUTHERN AEGEAN

IZMIR

Ruins of Pergamum (Bergama)
Pergamum Museum (Bergama)
Archaeological Museum (Izmir)
Atatürk Museum (Izmir)
Agora Sites
Ethnographical Museum
Çeşme Museum
Ephesus Museum
Ruins of Ephesus
Church of St. John Monument
House of Virgin Mary
Ödemiş Museum

AYDIN

Ruins of Priene
Ruins of Miletus
Miletus Museum
Ruins of Didyma
Aydın Museum
Ruins of Nysa
Ruins of Alinda
Aphrodisias Museum
Ruins of Aphrodisias

DENIZLI

Ruins of Pamukkale/Hieropolis
Laodiceia

MUGLA

Ruins of Heracleia Under Latmus
Ruins of Euromos
Ruins of Iassus
Ruins of Labraynda
Milas Museum
Beçin Kale
Bodrum Museum of Underwater
Archaeology
Mausoleum of Halicarnassus
Ruins of Cedrae
Ruins of Ceramus
Ruins of Datça
Ruins of Loryma
Marmaris Museum
Ruins of Caunos
Fethiye Museum
Ruins of Letton
Ruins of Pinara
Ruins of Tilos

ANTALYA

Ruins of Xanthus
Ruins of Patara
Ruins of Kekova Island
Ruins of Kaleköy
Ruins of Myra
St. Nicholas Church
Ruins of Olympus
Ruins of Phaselis
Antalya Museum
Ruins of Termessos
Karain Caves
Ruins of Perge
Ruins of Aspendos
Ruins of Sillyum
Ruins of Side
Castle of Alanya
Red Tower (Alanya)
House of Atatürk

IÇEL

Heaven and Hell
Alahan Monastery
Kanlıdivane
Pompeiopolis
Kızkalesi

ADANA

Archaeological Museum
Atatürk Museum
Ethnographical Museum
Karatepe Museum
Misis Mosaic Museum
Ruins of Anavarza
Ruins of Castabala
Ruins of Şar

HATAY

Antakya Archaeological Museum
Grove of Daphne

LANGUAGE

SURVIVAL TURKISH

Travelers to the Turkish Coast will find many English, German and French speakers. Nevertheless some basics of the Turkish language may be needed.

Turkish is a phonetic language. All words and letters are pronounced as they are written. There are several vowels and consonants in Turkish, such as c, that are pronounced differently than in English. These are given in a list below, as well as their pronounciations.

c is pronounced like j as in jam.

ç (c cedilla) is pronounced like ch as in chicken.

ğ (soft g) is silent and lengthens the preceeding vowel.

ı (undotted i) is pronounced like a short e as in open. i is pronounced like a long e as the first e in evening or i in ink.

ö (o umlaut) is pronounced like o umlaut in Köln in german or oeu in French as in boeuf.

ş (s cedilla) is pronounced like Sh as in shell.

u is pronounced like a double o (oo) as in book or rook.

ü (u umlaut) is pronounced like a round u as in the French word unite or für in German.

USEFUL PHRASES

hello	*merhaba*
help	*imdat*
thank you	*sağol*
cheap	*ucuz*
expensive	*pahalı*
good night	*iyi geceler*
just a minute	*bir dakika*
good morning	*merhaba*
far	*uzak*
near	*yakın*
please	*lütfen*

NUMBERS

one	*bir*
two	*iki*
three	*üç*
four	*dört*
five	*beş*
six	*altı*
seven	*yedi*
eight	*sekiz*
nine	*dokuz*
10	*on*
11	*on bir*
12	*on iki*
13	*on üç*
14	*on dört*
15	*on beş*
16	*on altı*
17	*on yedi*
18	*on sekiz*
19	*on dokuz*
20	*yirmi*
21	*yirmi bir*
30	*otuz*
40	*kırk*
50	*elli*
60	*altmış*
70	*yetmiş*
80	*seksen*
90	*doksan*
100	*yüz*
101	*yüz bir*
200	*iki yüz*
1,000	*bin*
1,000,000	*milyon*

HOTEL TERMS

hotel	*otel*
room	*oda*
room price	*oda fiyatı*
bed	*yatak*
single bed	*tek yatak*
double bed	*çift yataklı*
bathroom	*tuvalet*
shower	*duş*
breakfast	*kahvaltı*
lunch	*öğle yemeği*
dinner	*akşam yemeği*

FURTHER READING

ANTIQUITIES SMUGGLING

Pearson, Kenneth, and Connor Patrica. *The Dorak Affair*, Michael Joseph, London, 1967.

ARCHAEOLOGY

Akurgal, Ekrem. *Ancient Civilizations and Ruins of Turkey*, Haşet Kitabevi, Istanbul, 1985.

Alkım, U. Bahadır. *Anatolia I*, Nagel Publishers, Geneva, 1968.

Aşkın, Mustafa. *Guide Book of Troy*, Galeri Troya, Çanakkale, 1981.

Bayhan, Suzan. *Priene, Miletus and Didyma*, trans. Anita Gillett, Keskin Color, Istanbul, 1989.

Bean, George E. *Aegean Turkey*, Ernest Benn Limited, London, 1979.

——————*Lycian Turkey*, John Murray, London, 1989.

——————*Turkey Beyond the Maeander*, Ernest Benn, London, 1980.

——————*Turkey's Southern Shore*, Ernest Benn, London, 1979.

Danışman, H.H. Günhan. *Archaeological Perspectives: Anatolian Archaeology in 1980's*, Redhouse Press, Istanbul, 1983.

Garsting, John. *Prehistoric Mersin: Yümüktepe in Southern Turkey*, Oxford, 1953.

Lloyd, Seton. *Early Highland Peoples of Anatolia*, Thames and Hudson, London, 1967.

Mellaart, James. *Earliest Civilizations of the Near East*, Thames and Hudson, London, 1965.

Metzger, Henri. *Anatolia II*, Nagel Publishers, Geneva, 1969.

Muller, Herbert. *The Uses of the Past*, Oxford University Press, Oxford, 1952.

Pamukkale (Hierapolis), Net Turistik Yayınları A.Ş, 1986.

Schliemann, Heinrich. *Ilios, The City and Country of the Trojans*, Harper & Brothers, New York, 1881.

Seyfert, Oskar. *Dictionary of Classical Antiquities*, Meridian Library, New York, 1956.

Toksöz, Cemil. *Ancient Cities of Lycia*, Toksöz Publications, Istanbul, 1988.

Umar, Bilge. *Trakya*, Akbank Kültür Yayını, Istanbul, 1978.

BIOGRAPHY

Kinross, Lord. *Atatürk: The Rebirth of a Nation*, K. Rustem & Brother, Nicosia, Northern Cyprus, 1981.

Tanju, Sadun. *Hacı Ömer Sabancı: The Turkish Village Boy who Built an Industrial Empire*, trans. Geoffrey Lewis, World of Information, Saffron, Walden, 1988.

THE CRUSADES

Atiya, Aziz Suryal. *The Crusades in the Later Middle Ages*, Methuen & Co. Ltd., London, 1938.

Fedden, Robin and John Thomson. *Crusader Castles*, John Murray, London, 1957.

Gibbon, Edward. *History of the Decline and Fall of the Roman Empire*, Vol. 6; Phillips, Sampson and Co., Boston, 1851.

Krey, August C. *The First Crusade*, Princeton University Press, 1921.

Lamb, Harold. *The Crusades: Iron Men and Saints*, Thornton Butterworth Limited, London, 1931.

——————*The Crusades: The Flame of Islam*, Thornton Butterworth Limited, London, 1931.

Müller-Wiener, Wolfgang. *Castles of the Crusaders*, McGraw-Hill Book Company, New York, 1966.

GENERAL GUIDEBOOKS

Anderson, Brian and Eileen Anderson. *Landscapes of Turkey around Antalya*, Sunflower Books, London, 1989.

Aydıngün, Haldun. *Aladağlar: An Introduction*, Redhouse Press, Istanbul, 1988.

Boulanger, Robert. *Hachette World Guides, Turkey*, trans. Margaret Case, Hachette, Paris, 1960.

Brosnahan, Tom. *Turkey: A Survival Kit,*

Lonely Planet, South Yarra, 1987.

Darke, Diana. *Guide to Aegean and Mediterranean Turkey*, Michael Haag, London, 1987.

Demirsar, Metin. *Short Stay on the Turquoise Coast*, Apa Publications, Hong Kong, 1990.

Dörtlük, Kayhan. *Guide of Museums: Antalya*, trans. Anita Gillett, Keskin Color, Istanbul, 1989.

Dubin, Marc and Enver Lucas. *Trekking in Turkey*, South Yarra, 1989.

Fodor's Turkey 1983, Fodor's Modern Guides, New York, 1982.

Freely, John. *The Western Shores of Turkey*, John Murray, London. 1988.

Goltz, Thomas. *Insight Guide: Turkey*, ed. updated and revised by Metin Demirsar, Apa Publications, Hong Kong, 1990.

Kinross, Lord. *Europa Minor: Journeys in Coastal Turkey*, John Murray, London, 1956.

Harrel, Betsy. *Mini Tours Near Istanbul Book Two*, Redhouse Press, Istanbul, 1978.

Kalças, Evelyn Lyle. *Bodrum and its Castle*, Bilgehan Basımevi, Izmir, 1989.

——————*Izmir Roundabout*, Bilgehan Basımevi, 1989.

Mehling, Marianne, ed. *Turkey: A Phaedon Cultural Guide*, Phaidon, West Germany, 1989.

Sewell, Brian. *South from Ephesus: Travels in Aegean Turkey*, Arrow Press, Tiptree, Essex, 1989.

Stark, Freya. *Alexander's Path*, Century Hutchinson Ltd., London, 1986.

——————*Ionia A Quest*, Century Hutchinson Ltd., London, 1988.

——————*The Lycian Shore*, Century Hutchinson Ltd., London, 1989.

Tonguç, Leyla, ed. *Antalya and its Surroundings*, Dünya Süper Veb Ofset A.Ş, Istanbul, 1989.

Tourist's Guide Turkey, Ministry of Press, Broadcasting and Tourism, Ankara, 1963.

Turkey, Hachette World Guides, Paris, 1960.

Turkey, Nagel's Encyclopedia-Guide, Geneva, 1968.

Williams, Gwyn. *Turkey: A Traveler's Guide and History*, Faber and Faber, London, 1967.

HOMER, CLASSICAL LITERATURE AND MYTHOLOGY

Aeschylus. "Agamemnon" in *The Complete Drama*, vol. 1, trans. Morshead, Random House, New York, 1938.

Bulfinch's Mythology, The Modern Library, New York, 1971.

Butcher, S.H. and A.Lang, *The Odyssey of Homer*, The Macmillan Company, London, 1911.

Euripides. "The Trojan Women" in *The Complete Greek Drama Vol. 1*, trans. Gilbert Murray, Random House, New York, 1938.

Hamilton, Edith. *Mythology*, Little Brown and Co., Boston, 1940.

Homer. *The Odyssey*, trans. E.V. Rieu, Penguin Books, Baltimore, 1946.

Kitto, H.D.F. *The Greeks*, Penguin Books, Harmondsworth, 1967.

Lang, Andrew. *The Iliad of Homer*, The Macmillan Company, London, 1911.

Lattimore, Richmond. *The Iliad of Homer*, University of Chicago Press, 1971.

Reinhold, Meyer. *Essentials of Greek and Roman Classics*, Barrons Educational Series Inc., 1946.

Virgils Works, trans. J.W. Mackail, Modern Library, New York, 1934.

SAILING AND YACHTING

Heikell, Rod. *The Turquoise Coast of Turkey*, Net Turistik Yayınları A.Ş, Istanbul, 1988.

Reis, Piri. *Kitab-ı Bahriye: Volume I*, The Historical Research Foundation, Istanbul Research Center, Istanbul, 1988.

TRAVELS OF ST. PAUL

Blake, E.C. and A.G. Edmonds, *Biblical Sites in Turkey*, Redhouse Press, Istanbul, 1986.

Ramsay, W.M. *The Cities of St. Paul*, Baker Book House, Grand Rapdis, 1963.

Schillebeeckx, Edward. *Paul the Apostle*, Crossroad, New York, 1983.

The New English Bible, Oxford, 1970.

TURKISH CARPETS

Ayıldız, Uğur. *Contemporary Handmade Turkish Carpets*, Net Turizm Ticaret ve Sanayi A.Ş., Istanbul, 1982.

Yetkin, Şerare. *Historical Turkish Carpets*, Türkiye Iş Bankası Cultural Publications, 1981.

TURKISH HISTORY

Cook, M.A., ed. *A History of the Ottoman Empire to 1730*, Cambridge University Press, Cambridge, 1976.

Davison, Roderic H. *Turkey*, Prentice Hall, Englewood Cliffs, 1968.

Moorehead, Alan. *Gallipoli*, Harper and Brothers Publishers, New York, 1956.

Price, M. Phillips. *A History of Turkey from Empire to Republic*, George Allen and Unwin Ltd., London, 1968.

Shaw, Stanford J. *History of the Ottoman Empire*, Volume I, Cambridge University Press, Cambridge, 1987.

Shaw, Stanford J. and Ezel Kural Shaw. *History of the Ottoman Empire and Modern Turkey, Volume II*, Cambridge University Press. Cambridge, 1987.

YAŞAR KEMAL'S NOVELS

Anatolian Tales, trans. Thilda Kemal, Collins and Harvill Press, London.

Iron Earth, Copper Sky, Trans. Thilda Kemal, Collins and Harvill Press, London. 1989.

Memed, my Hawk, trans. Thilda Kemal, New York, 1961.

The Legend of the Thousand Bulls, trans. Thilda Kemal, Collins and Harvill Press, London 1976.

They Burn the Thistles, trans. Margaret E. Platon, Collins and Harvill Press, London.

USEFUL ADDRESSES

TOURIST INFORMATION

The following is a list of the overseas bureaus of the Turkish Tourist Information Department.

AUSTRIA
Singer Str. 2/8, 1010 Vienna
Tel: (0222) 5122128/5122129

BELGIUM
Rue Montoyer 4, 1040 Bruxelles
Tel: (02) 5138230/5138239

DENMARK
Vesterbrogagde 11A 1620
Copenhagen V
Tel: (01) 223100

FEDERAL REPUBLIC OF GERMANY
Baseler Str. 37, 6   Frankfurt MI
Tel: (0611) 233081/233082.
Karlplatz 3/1, 8000 Munich 2
Tel: (089) 594902/594317

FRANCE
02, Champs-Elysées, 75008 Paris
Tel: 145627868

ITALY
Piazza della Republica,
56-00185   Roma
Tel: (6) 462957/4741697

JAPAN
Turkish Embassy 33-6
2 Chome Jingumae Shibuya-ku-Tokyo
Tel: (03) 4706380/4705131

NETHERLANDS
Herengracht 451
1017 BS Amsterdam
Tel: (020) 266810

SAUDI ARABIA
Turkish Embassy
Medina Road Kilometer 6
Al Arafat Street, Jeddah
Tel: 6654578

SPAIN
Plaza de Espana, Torre de Madrid
Planta: 13 Of: 3 Madrid 28008
Tel: 248014/2487114

SWEDEN
Kungsgalen 3, S-111 43 Stockholm
Tel: (08) 218620/218630

SWITZERLAND
Talstrasse 74, 8001 Zurich
Tel: (01) 221080

UNITED KINGDOM
170-173 Piccadilly First Floor
London IV 9 DD
Tel: 7348681/7348682

UNITED STATES
821 United Nations Plaza
New York, N.Y. 10017
Tel: (212) 6872194
2010 Massachusetts Avenue N.W.
Washington D.C. 20036
Tel: (2002) 8338411/4299844

LOCAL TOURISM INFORMATION OFFICES

ADANA
Atatürk Caddesì 13
Tel: (71) 111323/118857

ALANYA
Çarşı Mahalesi
Kalearkası Caddesi
Tel: (3231) 1240

ANKARA
Gazi Mustafa Kemal Bulvarı 33
Tel: (4) 2301911/2317380

ANTALYA
Cumhuriyet Caddesi 91
Tel: (31) 111747/115271

BERGAMA
Zafer Mahalesi
Izmir Yolu Üzeri 54, Tel (541) 1862

BODRUM
12 Eylül Meydanı
Tel: (6141) 1091

ÇANAKKALE
Iskele Meydanı 67
Tel: (1961) 1187

ÇESME
Iskele Meydanı 6
Tel: (5492) 6653

DATÇA
Belediye Binası
Iskele Mahalesi
Tel: (6145) 1163

EDIRNE
Talatpaşa Asfaltı 76/A
Tel: (181) 15260/21490

FETHIYE
Iskele Meydanı 1
Tel: (6151) 11527

FOÇA
Atatürk Mahalesi
Koca Girişi
Tel: (5431) 1222

IPSALA
Ipsala Hudut Kapısı
Tel: (1846) 1577

ISKENDERUN
Atatürk Bulvarı 49/b
Tel: (881) 11620

ISTANBUL
Karaköy Maritime Station
Tel: (1) 1495776
Hilton Hotel
Tel: (1) 1330592
Atatürk Airport
Tel: (1) 5737399
Sultanahmet
Divan Yolu Caddesi
Tel: (1) 5133428

IZMIR
Gaziosmanpaşa Bulvarı
Büyük Efes Otelı Altı
Tel: (51) 199278

KAŞ
Cumhuriyet Meydanı 6
Tel: (3226) 1238

KEMER
Belediye Binası
Tel: (3214) 1536/1537

KOYCEĞIZ
Kordon Göl Park 1
Tel: (6114) 1703

KUŞADASI
Iskele Meydanı
Tel: (636) 11103

MARMARIS
Iskele Meydanı 39
Tel: (612) 11035

MERSIN
Inönü Bulvarı
Liman Giriş Sahası
Tel: (741) 16358

MUĞLA
Belediye Atapark Sitesi
Tel: (6111) 3127

SELÇUK
Atatürk Caddesi 1/2
Tel: (5451) 1228/1845

SILIFKE
Atatürk Caddesi 1/2
Tel: (7591) 1151

EMBASSIES AND CONSULATES

Listed below are the foreign embassies and consulates located in Ankara, Istanbul, Adana and Izmir.

AUSTRIA
Atatürk Bulvarı 189
Kavaklıdere, Ankara
Tel: (4) 1342172

BELGIUM
Nenehatun Caddesi 75
Gaziosmanpaşa, Ankara
Tel: (4) 136163

CANADA
Nenehatun Caddesi 75
Gaziosmanpaşa, Ankara
Tel: (4) 1361275

DENMARK
Kırlangiç Sokak 42
Gaziosmanpaşa, Ankara
Tel: (4) 1127558
Consulate: Istanbul
Silahhane Caddesi
Izmir Palas Ap. 31/1
Teşvikiye, Şişli
Tel: (1) 1404217

EGYPT
Atatürk Bulvarı 126
Kavaklıdere, Ankara
Tel: (4) 1266478

FEDERAL REPUBLIC OF GERMANY
Atatürk Bulvarı 114
Kavaklıdere, Ankara
Tel: (4) 1265465
Consulate: Istanbul
Inönü Caddesi
Ayazpaşa, Taksim
Tel: (1) 1437220/1450705

FINLAND
Farabi Caddesi
Galip Dede Sokak 1/20
Kavaklıdere, Ankara
Tel: (4) 1265921

FRANCE
Paris Caddesi 70
Kavaklıdere, Ankara
Tel: (4) 1261480
Consulate: Istanbul
Istiklal Caddesi 8
Taksim
Tel: (1) 1434387/1431852

GREECE
Ziya-ül Rahman Caddesi 9/11
Gaziosmanpaşa, Ankara
Tel: (4) 1368861

INDIA
Cinnah Caddesi 77/A
Çankaya, Ankara
Tel: (4) 1382195

IRAQ
Turan Emeksiz Sokak 11
Gaziosmanpaşa, Ankara
Tel: (4) 1266118/1263907

ITALY
Atatürk Bulvarı 118
Kavaklıdere, Ankara
Tel: (4) 1265460

JAPAN
Reşit Galip Caddesi 81
Gaziosmanpaşa, Ankara
Tel: (4) 1361290

NETHERLANDS
Köroğlu Sokak 16
Gaziosmanpaşa, Ankara
Tel: (4) 1361074
Consulate: Istanbul
Istiklal Caddesi 393
Beyoğlu
Tel: (1) 1495310

NORWAY
Kelebek Sokak 20
Gaziosmanpaşa, Ankara
Tel: (4) 1379950

PORTUGAL
Cinnah Caddesi 28/3
Çankaya, Ankara
Tel: (4) 1275055

SAUDI ARABIA
Abdullah Cevdet Sokak 18
Çankaya, Ankara
Tel: (4) 1366921

SPAIN
Abdullah Cevdet Sokak 18
Çankaya, Ankara
Tel: (4) 1380392

SWEDEN
Katip Çelebi Sokak 7
Kavaklıdere, Ankara
Tel: (4) 1286735.
Consulate: Istanbul
Istiklal Caddesi 4971
Beyoğlu
Tel: (1) 1435770

SWITZERLAND
Atatürk Bulvarı 247
Çankaya, Ankara
Tel: (4) 1274316
Consulate: Istanbul
Hüsrev Gerede Caddesi
Teşvikiye, Nişantaşı
Tel: (1) 1486070

SYRIA
Abdullah Cevdet Sokak 7
Çankaya, Ankara
Tel: (4) 1394588

UNITED KINGDOM
Şehit Ersan Caddesi 46/4
Çankaya, Ankara
Tel: (4) 1274310
Consulate: Istanbul
Meşrutiyet Caddesi 26
Galatasaray
Tel: (1) 1447540

CREDITS

INDEX

C

J

K

L

M

N

U & Ü

V

W - X